DATE DUE

MY 2 2 08			

DEMCO 38-296

Melville's City argues that Melville's relationship to the city was considerably more complex than has generally been believed. By placing him in the historical and cultural context of nineteenth-century New York, Kelley presents a Melville who borrowed from the colorful cultural variety of the city while at the same time investigating its darker and more dangerous social aspects. She shows that images both from Melville and from popular sources of the time represented New York variously as Capital, Labyrinth, City of Man, and City of God, and she goes on to demonstrate that he resisted a generalizing or totalizing representation of the city by revealing its hybrid identity and giving voice to the poor, the displaced, and the racially excluded. Through close examination of works spanning Melville's career, Kelley forges a new analysis of the connections between urban and literary form.

CAMBRIDGE STUDIES IN AMERICAN LITERATURE AND CULTURE

Melville's City

Continued on pages following the Index

MELVILLE'S CITY

Literary and Urban Form in Nineteenth-Century New York

WYN KELLEY

Massachusetts Institute of Technology

CAMBRIDGE
UNIVERSITY PRESS

:e of the University of Cambridge
ton Street, Cambridge CB2 1RP
York, NY 10011-4211, USA
gh, Melbourne 3166, Australia

© Cambridge University Press 1996

First published 1996

Printed in the United States of America

Library of Congress Cataloging-in-Publication Data
Kelley, Wyn.
Melville's city : literary and urban form in nineteenth-century
New York / Wyn Kelley.
p. cm.
Includes bibliographical references (p.   ) and index.
ISBN 0-521-56054-3 (hc)
1. Melville, Herman, 1819–1891 – Knowledge – City and town life.
2. Melville, Herman, 1819–1891 – Knowledge – New York (N.Y.)   3. New
York (N.Y.) – Intellectual life – 19th century.   4. City and town life
in literature.   5. Cities and towns in literature.   6. New York
(N.Y.) – In literature.   7. Literary form.   I. Title.
PS2388.C52K45   1996

813'.3 – dc20   95-41195
                                                                           CIP

A catalog record for this book is available from the British Library.

ISBN 0-521-56054-3 Hardback

To
Millicent Clarke Kelley

and in memory of
Bayne Kelley

Contents

═══════════

Illustrations

Acknowledgments

═══════

Mindful of Melville's warm dedications to the friends and family who supported his writing, I wish to thank the many people who have helped make this book possible.

I have been especially fortunate in teachers: Richard Brodhead at Yale University and George Dekker, Jay Fliegelman, and Albert Gelpi at Stanford University all inspired and nurtured my abiding interest in Melville from its deep roots. I have also been lucky in my colleagues at MIT; all have been wonderful to work with, but I am especially grateful to Peter Donaldson, Mary Fuller, John Hildebidle, Ruth Perry, Harriet Ritvo, Stephen Tapscott, David Thorburn, Rosalind Williams, and Reed Woodhouse for their advice and support along the way. Briony Keith and Janet Salzman have freely contributed their help and humor to all my projects.

There were many times when someone's offer to read or discuss the manuscript got me over tremendous hurdles. I thank John Bryant, Gail Coffler, Wai-chee Dimock, Anne Janowitz, Tia Lombardi, Leo Marx, and Merton M. Sealts, Jr., for their well-timed encouragement.

I could not have finished the book without the valuable readings, advice, and support of Robert S. Levine, Sheila Post-Lauria, and Laurie Robertson-Lorant. Their kindness and generosity never failed me, nor failed to inspire my efforts.

I feel especially grateful to my editors at Cambridge University Press, Eric Sundquist and T. Susan Chang. I thank Eric Newman and Barbara Folsom for their skill and care in editing the manuscript.

Two people who supported my work from the beginning but did not live to see its completion deserve my warmest thanks: my uncle William Kienbusch and family friend Robert Wallace. I have continually relied on the boundless friendship of Sally Dey and Sandra Grindlay. The members of the JE Collective have cheered me on many times and will be relieved to see the book finally done.

My family have lived with me and this project for many years. To Bayne and Millicent Kelley I owe the deepest gratitude for their unstinting love and care. Fiona Kelley, Liza Little, and George Morgan sustained my work

xi

in countless ways. Britt and Bayne Peterson came into being along with the manuscript and have given its growth the wonder of their own lives. And Dale Peterson generously supplied the abundant grant of time and love that enabled me to finish this book.

Abbreviations

T   *Typee: A Peep at Polynesian Life*, ed. Harrison Hayford, Hershel Parker, and G. Thomas Tanselle (Evanston and Chicago: Northwestern UP and the Newberry Library, 1968)

O   *Omoo: A Narrative of Adventures in the South Seas*, ed. Harrison Hayford, Hershel Parker, and G. Thomas Tanselle (Evanston and Chicago: Northwestern UP and the Newberry Library, 1968)

M   *Mardi: And a Voyage Thither*, ed. Harrison Hayford, Hershel Parker, and G. Thomas Tanselle (Evanston and Chicago: Northwestern UP and the Newberry Library, 1970)

R   *Redburn: His First Voyage, Being the Sailor-Boy Confessions and Reminiscences of the Son-of-a-Gentleman, in the Merchant Service*, ed. Harrison Hayford, Hershel Parker, and G. Thomas Tanselle (Evanston and Chicago: Northwestern UP and the Newberry Library, 1969)

WJ   *White-Jacket, or, The World in a Man-of-War*, ed. Harrison Hayford, Hershel Parker, and G. Thomas Tanselle (Evanston and Chicago: Northwestern UP and the Newberry Library, 1970)

MD   *Moby-Dick, or, The Whale*, ed. Harrison Hayford, Hershel Parker, and G. Thomas Tanselle (Evanston and Chicago: Northwestern UP and the Newberry Library, 1988)

P   *Pierre, or, The Ambiguities*, ed. Harrison Hayford, Hershel Parker, and G. Thomas Tanselle (Evanston and Chicago: Northwestern UP and the Newberry Library, 1971)

IP   *Israel Potter: His Fifty Years of Exile*, ed. Harrison Hayford, Hershel Parker, and G. Thomas Tanselle (Evanston and Chicago: Northwestern UP and the Newberry Library, 1982)

PT   *The Piazza Tales and Other Prose Pieces, 1839–1860*, ed. Harrison Hayford, Alma A. MacDougall, Hershel Parker, and G. Thomas

Tanselle (Evanston and Chicago: Northwestern UP and the Newberry Library, 1987)

"RMC"   "Rich Man's Crumbs"

CM   *The Confidence-Man: His Masquerade*, ed. Harrison Hayford, Hershel Parker, and G. Thomas Tanselle (Evanston and Chicago: Northwestern UP and the Newberry Library, 1984)

C   *Clarel: A Poem and Pilgrimage in the Holy Land*, ed. Harrison Hayford, Alma A. MacDougall, Hershel Parker, and G. Thomas Tanselle (Evanston and Chicago: Northwestern UP and the Newberry Library, 1991)

Corr   *Correspondence*, ed. Harrison Hayford, Hershel Parker, and G. Thomas Tanselle (Evanston and Chicago: Northwestern UP and the Newberry Library, 1993)

Journal   *Journals*, ed. Harrison Hayford and G. Thomas Tanselle (Evanston and Chicago: Northwestern UP and the Newberry Library, 1989)

BP   *The Battle Pieces of Herman Melville*, ed. Hennig Cohen (New York: T. Yoseloff, 1963)

BB   *Billy Budd, Sailor*, ed. Harrison Hayford and Merton M. Sealts, Jr. (Chicago: Chicago UP, 1962)

Log   *The Melville Log: A Documentary Life of Herman Melville, 1819–1891* (New York: Gordian Press, 1951)

Introduction:
Proud City, Proudest Town

Is this the proud City? *Battle-Pieces* (106)

Some leading thoroughfares of man
In wood-path, track, or trail began;
Though threading heart of proudest town,
They follow in controlling grade
A hint or dictate, nature's own,
By man, as by the brute, obeyed.

Clarel (496)

This book is about Melville and nineteenth-century New York, a culturally self-conscious place, which during his life grew from an important market town into a cosmopolitan center that to many epitomized the great city. For twentieth-century readers the words "town" and "city" have attained distinct, agreed-upon meanings, but the above quotations from Melville's works suggest that for a nineteenth-century writer these terms may not have fallen into their present modern classifications. The "proud City" of *Battle-Pieces* (Charleston) and the "proudest town" of *Clarel* (Jerusalem) seem, if anything, to reverse the expected terms, especially when placed side by side as they are here; for Jerusalem, one of the world's most ancient and significant cities, seems to deserve the title of "proud City," whereas Charleston might more rightly claim that of "proudest town," one of many such proud towns in nineteenth-century America.[1] For twentieth-century urbanized Western culture, the city is an accomplished fact, a familiar entity. Certain places, because of their size, history, social density, political and economic power, and structural grandeur, have even come to define "city": Jerusalem, Rome, Cairo, New York. Others just don't measure up. We see the terms as relative to each other – a city is a large town – but also, at a certain point, distinct – a town is not a small city. Melville's puzzling use of the words here and elsewhere raises questions about how they were viewed in an earlier time, when perceptions

1

and definitions of the city in America were growing and changing along with the cities themselves.

I look at the city as a site of contested meanings and social conflict, not only in American culture at large, but also more specifically in the culture of New York during its period of unprecedented growth, the years roughly corresponding to those of Melville's life, 1819–91. It is less a history of social attitudes toward the city than of the literary forms by which members of the culture sought to define and contain that disturbing growth within manageable limits. This contest and effort at containment, of course, reflect a political struggle that lies beyond the scope of this book but has received full treatment elsewhere.[2] My aim in viewing the culture through its literary forms is to stress a continuity between two kinds of cultural productions: the form of the city itself – its plan, its parks, promenades, and wharves, its political wards and social districts, its monuments and its streets – and the literary forms in which it finds representation – books, periodicals, guidebooks, and the visual arts. Both urban form and its popular literary representations enter into Melville's work, shaping his plots, coloring his language, and signaling his dialogic relation with the city and its culture.

In the development of self-consciousness that produced debate over the meaning of the words "town" and "city," New York middle-class culture revealed its deepest fissures and anxieties, anxieties that Melville shared in and also criticized. When we begin to understand these words as keys to a cultural contest over the meaning of urban form and the uses of urban space, then Melville's engagement in this contest becomes crucial, not only for what it tells us about Melville's art, but also for what it reveals about the development of urban culture in a vital city at a critical time. By placing the words "town" and "city" in their historical context and removing the obstacles of what they mean only to us, I intend to recover Melville's dialogue with New York – the town, the city, and the culture of letters and arts that celebrated it.

"Town" and "City"

Melville complicates the problem of locating these terms precisely by using the terms "town" and "city" seemingly interchangeably. For example, although in the opening pages of *Moby-Dick* he describes New York specifically as a city – naming it "your insular city of the Manhattoes" (3) – his landlubbers are "[p]osted like silent sentinels all around the town"(4). As I will show, however, although Melville often seems to use the two words loosely, applying "town" to cities and using both to refer to ships, his looseness is not casual. The fact that the two words seem to be mixed up with each other reveals, first, an underlying cultural debate over the meaning and value of "town" and "city" and, second, Melville's knowledge that the terms enclose a significant dialectic.

We can approach that dialectic through etymology.

In linguistic, historical, and political terms, the connection between the words "town" and "city" is complex. Simply put, they enact a relationship between a native and an imperial power, enclosure and incorporation, ground and culture. "Town" is an Anglo-Saxon word meaning, in its first, now obsolete, sense, simply "an enclosed place or piece of ground, an enclosure: a field, garden, yard, court" (*OED*). Its cognates in German and the Scandinavian languages have the meaning of "hedge" or "fence." "City," deriving from the Latin *civitas*, owes its primary meaning to the root *civis* or citizen; hence it first signified the people who make up a community, only later acquiring the meaning of *urbs*, the "place occupied by the community." "Town," then, is first enclosed ground; "city" is at first people, or community.

Civitas also implies a political history of its imposition on subject populations: it is the name Romans used for the principal political and religious centers of Gaul. In England, however, the word entered less easily into the culture: "though there were *civitates* in Britain also in Roman times, the word was not adopted by the Angles and Saxons, who applied the name *burh* to all towns alike." This linguistic act of resistance persisted into the thirteenth century, when *cité* "applied, both to foreign, and particularly ancient cities" and to "places mentioned in the Bible, which were really mere villages, *e.g.* Nazareth, Nain, Bethlehem." In Roman and early Britain, then, "city" was "[n]ot a native designation, but . . . at first a somewhat grandiose title, used instead of the OE *burh*." This linguistic history thus suggests that "city" was at first a word and concept alien to English-speaking peoples. It signified a foreign culture, not just of Rome but of the distinctive Bible sites, and for some time remained alien or superfluous to the native English *burh*. Well before the time the word had an American usage, however, it had developed its modern meaning of size, political organization, and centrality.

The linguistic relationship between the words "town" and "city," it seems clear, does not imply linear historical progress, towns developing inevitably into cities as they increase in size and complexity. Rather, this etymology indicates a political and social conflict over the meaning of organized communities. But reconstructing that debate as an opposition between "city" and "town" challenges the whole pastoral tradition based on a distinction, not between "city" and "town," but between "city" and "country." This ancient and classic opposition has fixed both terms as essential categories, defining the aesthetic and pleasurable, it would seem, in the terms of one basic comparison. As Raymond Williams has shown, even though "the real history [of city and country and their different formations] . . . has been astonishingly varied," the pastoral tradition has remained remarkably consistent: "[i]n and through these differences, all the same, certain [conventional] images and associations persist."[3] The act of enclosure, specifically the English Acts of Enclosure, signaled the death of the old agrarian communities, the "country," and the rise of the capitalist system that urbanized the remaining landscape. Williams, who writes movingly of growing up in a small mining town, indicates that the pastoral mode, by essentializing "city" and "country," has erased "town."

In a sense, various twentieth-century disciplines have simply deepened the old country–city opposition by deepening its roots. Through anthropology, psychology, urban sociology, structuralism, and cultural studies, the city appears not just as its modern metropolitan end product but as implied, and in a sense already accomplished, in earlier or substructural forms of social organization, technological development, and even psychological tendencies. The anthropologist Clifford Geertz, for example, has argued that humanness does not exist outside of culture: "Without men, no culture, certainly; but equally, and more significantly, without culture, no men."[4] In a different discipline, the urban planner, historian, and Melville biographer Lewis Mumford sees the city as grounded in the earliest social constructions of human beings:

> To come close to the origins of the city we must, I submit, supplement the work of the archaeologist who seeks to find the deepest layer in which he can recognize a shadowy ground plan that indicates urban order.... Before the city there was the hamlet and the shrine and the village: before the village, the camp, the cache, the cave, the cairn; and before all these there was a disposition to social life that man plainly shares with many other animal species.[5]

For Mumford, the same deep structures that produce language and social life, ritual and symbolic action, create urban form as well. To some degree he appropriates Freud's extraordinary image, in *Civilization and Its Discontents* (1930), of the mind as a city, a psychological Rome. For the mind, Freud argues, may maintain different stages of its evolution at the same time in one place. Unlike the physical Rome, where archaeologists search for relics of the past among its present ruins, the mind can keep all the layers of its history intact and simultaneous. Freud embarks on an elaborate "phantasy" of what such an imaginary Rome would be like:

> Now let us, by a flight of imagination, suppose that Rome is not a human habitation but a psychical entity with a similarly long and copious past – an entity, that is to say, in which nothing that has once come into existence will have passed away and all the earlier phases of development continue to exist alongside the latest one. This would mean that in Rome the palaces of the Caesars and the Septizonium of Septimius Severus would still be rising to their old height on the Palatine and that the

castle of S. Angelo would still be carrying on its battlements the beautiful statues which graced it until the siege by the Goths, and so on.[6]

Freud suggests a "phantasy" city where "town" may continue to live on the same site as "city," but his Rome is still, even in an imaginative reconstruction, an imperial city, not a town. In this reading, "city" can exist in opposition only to "country" because "town" has already been absorbed into "city." Ironically, the disciplines that have sought to chart the modern development of the city, seeing it in newly complex and various ways, have also served to anchor more firmly than ever its cultural meaning in opposition to "country."

When placed in historical relation to "town," and in the history of urban form and growth, "city" loses its essential meaning and assumes a more relative character. Etymologically the two words reveal a political struggle between two urban forms, one native and one alien. But the etymology also reveals a difference between "town" as ground, or enclosed space, and "city" not as ground but primarily as citizenship, the body of people who give meaning to the place where they live: a distinction, in other words, between *space* and *place*.[7] "Country" in this formulation becomes a third term, not for villages and other preurban formations but for something closer to "nature" or even "wilderness." If we turn specifically to "town" and "city" in history, we see that they can exist not only in distinction from each other but also on the same site in a political and dialectical relation – the relation Melville implies when he calls New York both a city and a town. New York is both because it is contested ground, a place in the process of becoming, rather than a finished work, the city that is defined by its difference from "country." Our modern concept of "city" has, like Romans overrunning Britain, swallowed up and incorporated the older notion of "town." Restoring "town" allows us to recover the historical context for this dialectical, changing, and contested relationship.

If "town" is first and primarily "enclosure," it implies the building of walls to mark and protect space. Although we assume from the common meaning of "town" that this space is shared and communal, citizenship, or the idea of a body of people devoted to some communal identity, ideology, or mission, is not necessary to "town" as it is to "city," derived from *civitas*. Before space can become place, before topography can become culture, or physical construction become social construction, a notion of political dominance or superiority must emerge. For a city to know itself as such, that superiority may be measured against other peoples and races or against other towns. "City" is a *relative* term as well as a distinct social and political organization. A city defines itself in relation to towns by virtue of its size, its economic, religious, or political importance, its acts of incorporation and other forms of political organization. These acts of definition, in turn, produce *civitas*, a sense of particular cultural identity, loyalty to the community, distinctive rituals and practices, the "rites of assent" that Sacvan Bercovitch has shown to be at the heart of a unifying ideology.[8] This is not to say that towns cannot have distinctive identity and culture, but that the *meaning* of that place and its culture comes from its position relative to the city and the dominant culture. That meaning is the product of a particular history of urban form.

Town and City in New York

The history of cities and towns in America shows that European settlers brought with them the cultural meanings of "town" and "city," though these urban forms took some time to emerge in the new continent as the early settlements battled for status. Colonial America, like Roman Britain, was a collection of towns, even for some time after England lost political control over the colonies. These towns competed with each other, at first economically and then politically and culturally, for dominance. An early indication of this competition appears in the contest over where the national capital should be. In selecting a new site, Washington, over the established ports of Philadelphia and New York, the new American government was not only declaring its independence from the old colonies and states but also asserting the meaning of Washington as a *city*. Washington, D.C., may be thought of, and by its founders was thought of, as a significant departure from European capitals that evolved from towns. By establishing itself first and foremost as *civitas*, with its national meaning already defined, Washington was planned and perceived from the beginning as a city, even when it also clearly appeared for a long time to be a mosquito-infested swamp.[9]

New York, on the other hand, was a town for some time before it became a city. Although Dutch settlers quickly recognized the natural advantages that made it an ideal port and fort, advantages that the English exploited as well, and although it held a certain political significance in the early national period, when New York served briefly as capital both of the new United States and of the State of New York, commercially it suffered in the economic rivalry with other dominant ports such as Boston, Philadelphia, and Charleston.[10] Nevertheless, when with the completion of the Erie Canal in 1825 its superior location in relation both to Europe and the American interior became manifest, New York began to grow in population, land mass, economic importance, and eventually cultural richness with what seemed to many observers both exhilarating and alarming speed. It is easy to see why its early history as "town" diminished in significance as its meaning as "city" evolved.

But there is another reason why New York's history as town, as space before it became place, came to seem inconsequential to antebellum

America. For just as American history escaped or seemed to erase its European antecedents, starting history over again in a "special, self-enclosed *American* form" (Bercovitch, 38), so urbanization in America condensed into a few short decades, or in some cases practically obliterated, the long centuries of European preparation. As Raymond Williams has shown, London was known as "The City" by the time America became itself. And just as Rome served as the model for urban London, so London served as an instructive guide for New York. New York, then, was in some ways already a city even when it was a town, for Americans could read New York's destiny in London and, before long, in Liverpool, Manchester, Glasgow, and Dublin as well. As I will show in Chapter 1, New York early experienced itself in relation to English and European capitals, early fashioned itself as a city like London and saw itself through the eyes of foreign urban visitors. Even as "town," then, New York aspired to "city." Once having achieved "city," New York may be said to have repressed "town," except in nostalgic reminiscences of a more innocent, organic, manageable community.

In the case of nineteenth-century New York, urban ideology clearly shaped history. New York saw itself as a city even before it became a city by European standards. And space soon had to give way to place, geography to culture, as the city shaped its landscape to suit its needs. The problem with any landscape is that physically it can resist the imposition of culture. New York presented a particularly unpromising physical terrain for urban settlement, one that challenged early planners, graders, and developers. That physical resistance, the narrowness and insularity of its space, engendered social resistance too. New York, because of its increasing social diversity within rigid geographical constraints, provided an enclosed ground for contest over the meaning of culture and *civitas*. The making of "city" in New York did not evolve without struggle. And, taking place within a short period of time, the physical and social development of the city evidenced the conflict between "town" and "city" even as the culture tried to erase the "town."

Urban Form in Literary New York

This book will show how the culture of New York – as seen in books, magazines, pamphlets, tracts, graphic arts, dioramas and panoramas, urban plans, and parks – tried to impose its own form on a changing and contested landscape. In the ways New York cultural artifacts, from the printed word to the built environment, conceived of the city, we can see how *civitas* established and perpetuated itself in a turbulent period of development. Looking outward to Europe and inward to other American towns, New York culture tried to make space into place by giving it the cultural meanings of certain urban forms, forms that had worked in the past to give meaning to cities like London, Paris, Rome, or Jerusalem. Among these forms appear the oldest symbolic constructions of the city in Western culture: as Capital, as Labyrinth, as City of Man, and as City of God. Along with other conventional constructions such as City on the Hill or Vanity Fair, Babel and Babylon, Anthill and Beehive, Sodom and Gomorrah, they are familiar relics of the pastoral tradition. Applied to a city rapidly constructing itself, however, and constructing itself, too, during a revolution in industry and capitalism, these labels take on a newly complex meaning. They do not seek merely to describe the emerging metropolis but to manage it, to shape it according to a changing social reality. The dominant ideology that emerged from many contending urban ideologies tried to control the resistance of "town" to "city" through a literature celebrating urban growth at the same time that it implicitly imposed urban form.

For "town" had a particular place and meaning in the New York landscape. It encompassed the original settlement located at the tip of Manhattan, bounded on the west and east by mighty rivers and on the south by the old fort, the Battery, and the sea. The only open boundary was its northern limit, which over time marched ever northward. When Grant Thorburn in his 1845 memoir described laborers on Wall Street digging up an old post from the original wall, he marked one of those Ur-moments in the city's recognition of its past history as town, a time when Wall Street meant the old town walls that enclosed its original boundaries rather than the site of business and commerce that it had become.[11] At other times, City Hall and the Park, Union Square and Fourteenth Street, or even the upper reaches of Fifth Avenue came to mean the outer edges of the "town." But generally it centered on the old "Walking City," the heart of New York, containing the waterfront, the Bowery, lower Broadway, Wall Street, and Five Points, New York's most impoverished district. As New York expanded and became more noticeably a city, the old town remained as a reminder of the city's heart.

It also served as a pocket of resistance to New York's growth, as a visible reminder of what becoming a city had cost the old town. As lower Manhattan became more socially dense, politically corrupt, and spatially constricted, it challenged the popular ideology of urban expansion, opportunity, and prosperity for all. And seemingly the more urgent that challenge became, the more visibly the older sections of New York entered into the popular culture as sites of interest and anxiety. The city began to have a cultural as well as a geographical map, with Five Points, the Bowery, Wall Street, Trinity Church, Astor Place, the elite Fifteenth Ward, and the waterfront defining its social and moral regions.[12] In the literature and arts of New York, "town" acted out its resistance to "city" even as the culture generated forms of containment in a never-ending flood.

As I plan to show in selecting four of these cultural representations of urban form – namely, the Capital, the Labyrinth, the City of Man, and the City of God – literature promised to defuse middle-class anxiety over urban growth by imaging it in manageable ways. In the urban literature of New York, a variety of literary forms confronted the problem of urban growth, and the social struggle over who would define and control that growth, by offering certain rewards to the middle-class reader. I will be considering four of these literary forms and the way they manage the problem of urban form.[13]

The first is the spectator sketch, deriving from the essay form popularized by Addison and Steele in the *Spectator* papers and their imitators in England and America. As Terry Eagleton has shown for English and Dana Brand for American writers, the usually white, male spectator, by the way he moves about a great capital, observing and recording his impressions, reveals certain class attitudes, privileges, and constraints.[14] He has the freedom of a middle-class gentleman-writer negotiating an open, accessible "walking city." But his freedom also distances him from his subject, limiting the scope of his insights and framing them through wit, which removes him from feeling. For him the city is to some extent the Bakhtinian carnival, a market fair in which he can stroll and shop for experiences.[15] But unlike the working-class or peasant crowd that Bakhtin celebrates, urban London crowds do not offer the spectator festive redemption. He does have a community, but it is the community of his middle-class domestic and coffeehouse readers, not that of the carnival. As someone who has the freedom to travel through the city, however, and to collect its sights for the reader's consumption and pleasure, the spectator mediates between reader and city, offering a witty, enlightened, and above all safe way to negotiate a new terrain.[16]

The world that the spectator traverses so confidently, though a cultural capital, is in many respects a large town only beginning to emerge as a city. In American literature, such practitioners of the spectator essay as N. P. Willis, George Curtis, and Ik Marvell seem to have confined their wanderings to the parts of old New York where one could still see most of the town in a day's walk. As the city expanded, its size literally exhausted the capacity of middle-class spectators to cover it. And the flight of the middle class from a downtown becoming more obviously the domain of immigrants from Europe and rural America changed the nature of that old New York so that it began to seem unrecognizable, menacing, and impenetrable – a place that writers like George Foster, Ned Buntline, and George Lippard described as a labyrinth.[17] This part of New York seemed to be full of misery and mystery, sunshine and shadow, as the contrasts between old town and new city became more visible and painful to spectators' eyes. The literature of the labyrinth – the sensational urban novels based on works by Sue and Reynolds, the urban reform literature and tracts, and the journalistic "plunges" into an urban underworld – allowed

the middle-class spectator or innocent provincial youth to enter a dangerous urban terrain but also to travel through it safely in the hands of
the experienced guide, the writer. These works challenge the ideology of
urban growth and expansion by showing the poverty, vice, and desperate
danger the city's victims suffer; but they also promise to extricate the
reader, through various strategies of reform, classification, and flight.

Both of these literary forms, the spectator sketch and the labyrinth
literature, offer a model of *engagement* in the conflict over urban space.
In each a protagonist enters New York, travels its terrain, and observes,
even participates in, the social struggle for representation in the urban
culture. In a sense, both of these models accept the presence of an older
town occupying the same space as a newer city and making its demands
heard. The protagonist's efforts to enter and travel through that space, to
claim it for literature, are seen as heroic endeavors. Other literary forms,
however, manage the conflict by offering a model of *escape* from an urban
world that has become altogether too challenging to the human spirit.
This pattern, in some ways similar to the old pastoral narrative, takes its
most radical form in the romantic novels that have been considered the
classics of American literature: for example, *The Pioneers, Moby-Dick,* or *The
Adventures of Huckleberry Finn.*[18] Just as important to New York culture, however, if not more so, were the works that offered escape from the pressures
of shrinking urban space without enforcing a departure from the city.
Among these, some of the most significant were the domestic and sentimental novels that configure the home as a redemptive domain apart
from the city. Alexander Welsh has shown how Dickens conceived of London as the City of Man, the home as a City of God.[19] Feminist criticism
has further shown how the separate spheres of gender give new meaning
to a concept of a City of Man as separate from – and indeed antagonistic
to – the City of Woman, the home. In this analysis, the literature that
celebrated the home as an alternative to the wicked or unjust city, assign-
ing moral power to women, managed the challenges of urban life, not by
entering the city, but by withdrawing from it to another sphere.[20] One
question raised by domestic literature is whether one can find a home in
the city, not only a physical space in which to live but also an ideological
realm in which to find salvation and autonomy.[21]

Another strategy, closely related to that of domestic literature though
seemingly at an opposite pole, offers withdrawal from urban space without
leaving urban culture. One might call this the masculine version of the
feminine, domestic quest for freedom from an overwhelming urban environment: the narrative of Old World travel. Unlike the pastoral pattern,
which signals a complete break from the city, a flight into the wilderness,
the narrative of travel to Europe or the Holy Lands allows the protagonist
to encounter the city in a less threatening guise, even in some sense to
seek it out, as in a pilgrimage to an ideal city – Rome, Jerusalem, Mecca.

As writers like Hawthorne and James found the American city increasingly hostile to their notions of urban culture, they turned to older cities, for which they had not only Murray's guides and Cook's tours but also classical literary traditions as aids in negotiating an urban landscape.[22] Whereas domestic literature imaged the City of God as the home, pilgrimage literature imaged it as the ancient city. Both offered models of successful engagement with an urban environment, not by entering the contested urban space but by creating and moving within an alternative urban culture.

New York, then, as a subject for literary representation, took on a variety of forms during the period when Melville inhabited the city.[23] Although we are accustomed to the dark, modern, monolithic view of New York as Big City presented in films like Fritz Lang's *Metropolis* or Tim Burton's *Batman*, in urban novels like Fitzgerald's *The Great Gatsby* or Tom Wolfe's *The Bonfire of the Vanities*, in urban studies drawing from Georg Simmel's "The Metropolis and Modern Life," Max Weber's *The City*, or Lewis Mumford's *The City in History*, New York in the nineteenth century was not yet finished, and its cultural forms show a city very much in the making.[24] The literary forms I have selected are only some of the many venues where this making took place, and they did not proceed logically or chronologically in the order I have described as a convenience for this book. They do, however, provide a rich context within which to understand the cultural debate over the meaning of urban space and urban form in nineteenth-century New York.

Melville and the City: Problems in Criticism

The idea that Herman Melville participated in this debate may come as a surprise to some readers. When Melville complained that he would be remembered as the "man who lived among cannibals,"[25] he accurately predicted his canonization as a writer in the pastoral mode. Of course, it should be clear that the pastoral tradition was itself an urban phenomenon, formed in response to the growth of great cities in the ancient world, but it is predicated on the notion of the city as radically distinct from the country. Because America offered European urban refugees a New World in which to plant their cities, the American errand has appeared, most notably in the writings of American critics of what Donald Pease has called the Cold War school,[26] as a pastoral enterprise. Melville's *Moby-Dick*, along with Cooper's *The Last of the Mohicans*, Irving's "Rip Van Winkle" and "The Legend of Sleepy Hollow," Emerson's *Nature*, Thoreau's *Walden*, Hawthorne's *The Scarlet Letter*, Twain's *The Adventures of Huckleberry Finn*, and the nature poems of Bryant and Dickinson, have been seen as outstanding examples of a literature that affirms the possibility of escape from the wicked city and a redemptive immersion in the ideal world of nature.

Melville has seemed to embody that tradition, with *Moby-Dick* defined as classic in its terms. In fact, in the self-enclosed rituals of canon formation, *Moby-Dick* has created the conventions according to which it has assumed classic status.[27]

Having in a sense produced the criteria according to which one may define a great work, *Moby-Dick* also, for many early-twentieth-century critics, effaced Melville's other works, especially those which more directly confronted the problem of the city, and particularly the one to do so most openly, *Pierre* (1852). The main problem in talking about Melville and the city is that the subject has traditionally been invisible. Indeed, many of Melville's early critics saw him simply as anti-urban because his "greatest" books concerned the sea and not the city. In one of the first works to address the urban attitudes of Melville's period, Morton and Lucia White declare that "enthusiasm for the American city has not been typical or pre-dominant in our intellectual history"; Melville is part of the "anti-urban roar."[28] Newton Arvin probably felt he had defined Melville's genius by contrasting him unfavorably with "his great contemporaries Balzac and Stendhal, Dickens and Thackeray," and in claiming that "his imagination shared no common ground with these observers of the social, the contemporary scene, of business, the church, the great world, the modern city." Although Melville wrote about all these things, Arvin sees him as cut off from "the novel of 'real life,' " as finding no common ground with other great writers of the city. Yet Arvin himself remarks of *Redburn* that the descriptions of Liverpool have "a power quite comparable to that with which Balzac's Parisian Inferno is rendered, or Baudelaire's *fourmillante cité*, the London of *Bleak House* and *Our Mutual Friend*, or the Dublin of *Ulysses*. Melville's Liverpool, too, like his Lima, is a City of the Plain." Although recognizing the power of Melville's urban scenes in *Redburn*, Arvin still in effect subordinates *Pierre*, "Bartleby, the Scrivener," *Israel Potter*, and *The Confidence-Man* and any notion of Melville as a writer of the city: "from the point of view of poetic value, almost nothing Melville later did is comparable to his one very great book."[29] Richard Chase compounds this basic distinction – sea/city, good/bad – with critical psychosexual elements when he claims, in an argument that appears in decades of Melville scholarship: "The author of *Moby-Dick* was a successful artist, a man of power, intelligence, and authority. By comparison the author of *Pierre* was a weak, regressive, dark-souled, and earth-minded man."[30] Melville's decision after *Moby-Dick* to write of the locale he knew best seemed to his biographer Leon Howard to plunge him into a period of "Misdirections."[31]

If the post–World War II generation saw Melville as anti-urban, the Vietnam generation has worked to establish Melville as a social writer embedded in his national culture. This body of criticism, though not always addressing city and town in Melville's fiction, has nevertheless made it possible to speak of Melville's responses to nineteenth-century politics and culture. Leo Marx paved the way by demonstrating that *Moby-Dick*, even if it casts itself off from land, takes with it the industrial processes and hierarchical structures that mark emerging industrial capitalism. Michael Rogin has fully demonstrated that Melville knew about and actively participated in the political debates of his day,[32] and Wai-chee Dimock has argued that Melville engaged complicitly in American politics by adopting Manifest Destiny practices in his own writing.[33] Although some critics have retaliated against male-dominated literary canons by excluding Melville from theirs – Jane Tompkins does so most directly in *Sensational Designs* – others have considered Melville as part of a culture expanding its female audience. Ann Douglas concluded that the "feminization of American culture" emasculated writers like Melville, and other critics have claimed that Melville's reactions to female readers ran the gamut from ignorance to misogyny,[34] but recently critics have attempted to place Melville in a more flexible and dialogic relationship with women's writing and female readers. For example, Hershel Parker and Laurie Robertson-Lorant have written about Melville's domestic life, and Charlene Avallone, Sheila Post-Lauria, and David S. Reynolds have placed Melville's work in the context of popular fiction in ways that have done much to replace the older notion of Melville as tragic, isolated male genius.[35] As Robert K. Martin, James Creech, and Caleb Crain have shown, gay studies open up the possibilities for reading Melville's sexuality in new contexts.[36] Recent considerations of Melville in relation to race, beginning with Carolyn Karcher, have further worked to connect him to his contemporary culture. Writers like Henry Louis Gates, Jr., Toni Morrison, Sterling Stuckey, and Eric Sundquist have all made it clear that the American canon is inconceivable without reference to the minority cultures within or near its borders. Melville studies have reflected this redrawing of cultural boundaries through attention to texts like "Benito Cereno" and *Moby-Dick*, which, as Paul Lauter has shown, until recently evoked color-blind readings.[37] Finally, studies by Michael Gilmore, Nicholas Bromell, and Cindy Weinstein have shown Melville's relation to the class issues that formed constructions of labor and the market in the antebellum period.[38] As this only partial list of recent developments in Melville studies shows, strenuous efforts have moved Melville from the wilderness into his contemporary cultural context.

Despite the wealth of approaches to Melville in his culture, there is surprising silence on his profound consideration of New York as town and city.[39] Some recent books suggest an increased interest in urban culture, if not in urban form.[40] Recent work on the city, however, has generally not addressed the old suspicion that Melville is somehow an anti-urban writer, one who either removes himself from the city in distaste, as in his nautical fiction, or aims subversively to undermine it from within, as in his urban tales like "Bartleby, the Scrivener: A Story of Wall-Street."[41] Regarding the first point, Melville's distaste for the city, critics have focused on his representation of the city in his short fiction, *Pierre,* and *Israel Potter,* as a dark, dismal place. So, in Melville's work, "Cities are invariably Evil, heartless, remorseless, indifferent"; "Melville's record of Pierre in the city is a description of disappointment, frustration, and pain"; Bartleby's New York is "the closed world"; "New York is blank, heartless, and cruelly indifferent"; "*Israel Potter* is characterized by failure, frustration, and bleakness as the author's imagination turns insistently to a landscape of desolation"; "The black, demonic aspects of the City are uppermost in Melville's mind when he draws upon urban imagery in the short works between *Pierre* and *Clarel.*"[42] The issue for many critics has traditionally been to identify the presence of the city as a motif in Melville's writing, not, in general, to analyze it.[43] Their conclusions, drawing on the pastoral opposition between country and city, support the mid-twentieth-century view of Melville as longing to escape from the city, which he can represent only in dark allegorical terms as a City of Dis.

The charge that Melville cannot write about the city except in allegorical terms as a dismal place, and that therefore his urban writings evade realistic representation, reflects an ahistorical tendency to view mid-nineteenth-century urban literature through the lens of late-nineteenth-century realism and naturalism. As Leo Marx argues, urban realism cannot be a standard for fiction that makes "a commitment to an essentially non-representational and often expressly *anti*-realistic method of composition."[44] A cursory glance at Melville's contemporaries shows that even the most conscientious mid-century attempts at realism were suffused with the period's extravagant rhetorical styles: religious harangue, sensational description, and sentimental excess. By looking at Melville's urban fiction in the context of popular contemporary genres, we can see that he enthusiastically employed, even as he sometimes parodied, the current conventions of representing the city. As for the assumption that he described the city as a gloomy place because he himself was depressed, this ignores the fact that even in his most cheerful books Melville used urban references, strategies, and forms. Melville did not limit his consideration of the city to those works which represent it most directly or seem most gloomy about its meaning.

The second, more fully explored avenue of criticism sees Melville's urban narratives as subversive of a culture David Reynolds has called Conventional. In turning to the short story, a form alien to the epic novels that he supposedly favored, and in adapting his style to urban audiences, Melville purportedly signaled his despair over having to abandon writing "[w]hat I feel most moved to write."[45] Through irony, however, he used his urban fiction to undermine his reader's expectations and subvert the conventions of mainstream culture.

The idea that Melville used urban subjects and conventions subversively is nevertheless problematic. I do not want to remove the subversion model entirely but to adapt it according to two principles. One is that of Bercovitch's analysis, which suggests that subversion is necessarily a compromising endeavor in American culture, which, because of its exceedingly flexible ideology, has absorbed dissent into a remarkably homogeneous consensus. Certainly the recent cultural criticism of Melville supports this conclusion when it shows Melville's embrace of popular forms and publishing venues. As both Bercovitch and Clifford Geertz argue, ideology can engender as well as constrict individual expression. A close study of Melville's writing strategies shows him finding rich resources in all kinds of cultural productions. To see him as subverting them all suggests a particularly rigid and negative reading of his creative habits.[46] But I would also adapt Fishkin's argument that a study of language and where it comes from can subvert the subversive. She presents Twain in a position of cultural ambivalence, torn between his love for the rich language and resources of a cultural and racial minority and his desire to fit in with the Victorian social milieu where he aspired to live and publish. Although Twain's work has been seen as subverting that Victorian culture through humor and by an escape to the wilderness, Fishkin's analysis shows a deeper level of subversion, on the level of the African American language he used, which works to subvert Twain's aims by challenging his racial and cultural centrality to the narrative. In adopting the literary forms native to his own urban culture, literary forms that did not subvert the dominant urban ideology so much as enact the tensions within it, Melville gave his own cultural ambivalence full play. Melville did feel distaste for the city, but he also embraced it and returned to it again and again. How are we to explain this paradoxical attitude? How can he work both to subvert and to engage in the city and its cultural practices at the same time?

These questions, though, proceed from a prevailing twentieth-century assumption that literary greatness depends on a modernist aesthetic of complexity, subversion, and irony. As Paul Lauter argues, Melville has been admired for his attacks on culture and for his cleverness in sneaking in those attacks under the guise of engaging travel narratives. More recently, he has been judged for not conducting the quarrel more openly, but even that critique depends on the almost universal perception that Melville, even when he uses popular conventions, continually subverts them. In studying Melville's relation to urban culture and forms, however, I have seen subversion as an inadequate model for a practice that, like the city itself, is elastic and dialogic.[47] Melville clearly did work to subvert urban forms that he found oppressive, inadequate, or unjust. But he also drew upon the rich resources of New York culture for ideas, language, plots, and narrative strategies as they suited his needs. His literary practices, then, borrow their distinctive coloring from the urban culture he lived in and represented in his fiction and poetry. Even though he left New York for significant periods, he remained a New Yorker and kept up his dialogue with the culture throughout his whole life.

Proud City, Proudest Town

So far I have been making an argument for New York as a singular case in cultural studies. Because of the unique demands of and for space in New York, the culture generated a particular ideology of place. This ideology offered various constructions of urban form that created the illusion of space within a terrain that threatened to constrict or eliminate it for many city dwellers. Through evocations of a walking city, a penetrable labyrinth, a domestic refuge, or an Old World cosmopolis, middle-class popular urban literature created fictional space where characters might move and breathe with the freedom that the national democratic ideology promised the individual. The fictional construction of urban form worked to solve the problem of class struggle over space in New York.

One might say that Melville was only one of many New York writers who tested that cultural solution in his writing. Edgar Allan Poe, Fanny Fern, George Foster, Lydia Maria Child, Walt Whitman, Emma Southworth, George Lippard, Frederick Law Olmsted, all come to mind as writers who engaged in New York's cultural dialogue over city and town. Melville has not received attention for his part in the debate. Yet the depth of his response to New York, growing out of complex biographical as well as intellectual and professional experiences, left marked traces in his fiction. If his trenchant criticism of the city's development did not perform its cultural work for his period, as the writings of his contemporaries did, it certainly has the potential to do so now.

The quotations that head this chapter begin to define Melville's particular contribution to the debate over the meaning of New York in the nineteenth century. New York, as Melville's writings and as countless magazine articles and works of fiction proclaimed, was proud of its growth as a commercial giant. It was seen as the epitome of American capitalism, its triumphs and its discontents. Within Melville's immediate family, men sought their fortunes in New York, confident in the opportunities promised by business (Allan Melvill, the father), politics (Melville's brother Gansevoort), and the law (brother Allan). Both Herman and his brother Thomas, who became a sea captain, participated in shipping, one of New York's most booming enterprises. Melville's question, "Is this the proud City?" challenges his New York readers' pride, a pride he knew intimately and criticized vigorously.

If the quotation from *Battle-Pieces* succinctly frames Melville's challenge to New York as city, his lines from *Clarel* reconstruct New York as town, a

place with "heart," where the "controlling grade" of the original landscape still exerts its influence over man and beast. Melville's portrayal of
Jerusalem in *Clarel* does not suggest that he sees it as an urban ideal, a
true City of God. His Jerusalem is every bit as noisy, contentious, stratified,
and bewildering as Gilded Age New York. But it still contains "a hint or
dictate, nature's own" of its history as space.[48] Melville's granddaughter,
Eleanor Melville Metcalf, describes her grandfather walking every day
through the city's streets: "Setting forth on a bright spring afternoon for
a trip to Central Park, the Mecca of most of our pilgrimages, he made a
brave and striking figure as he walked erect, head thrown back, cane in
hand, inconspicuously dressed in a dark blue suit and a soft black felt
hat."[49] As long as Melville lived in New York, he made that daily pilgrimage into the Mecca of New York, into the "heart of proudest town." Daily
he experienced, even bumped into, its conflicts between town and city,
landscape and culture. In balancing as he did the richly ambivalent nuances of "proud City" and "proudest town" throughout a long career,
Melville sustained his culture's profound shock with uncommon resilience
and creative perseverance.

* * * * * *

For purposes of analysis, I have divided this book into two parts. The first,
"Traveling the Town," takes up the strategies of engagement that I see
attempted in the spectator and labyrinth literature. Chapter 1 introduces
these literary forms by looking at the implications of encountering contested urban space, both as a biographical issue in the Melville family and
as a cultural problem in popular literature. Chapters 2 and 3 read Melville's early novels, ending with *Pierre*, in the context of such popular literary forms. Part II, "Escaping the City," begins in Chapter 4 by exploring
the strategies of withdrawal from contested urban space implied in *Moby-
Dick*. Chapter 5 then returns to *Pierre* and the literature concerning the
home in Melville's work of the 1850s, and Chapter 6 looks at the pilgrimage to an ancient city as it appears in *The Confidence-Man* and *Clarel*. The
Conclusion considers Melville's late poetry and *Billy Budd*.

Although I am working with large cultural constructions, my main concern is with the way Melville responds to and uses these in his own fiction.
I see Melville as a somewhat marginal figure who, because of his lack of
a secure place in the city, found it difficult and indeed wrong to impose
such confident social and literary forms on a diverse urban environment.
The New Critics of the 1950s and 1960s saw Melville's social and intellectual ambivalence as a well-developed position, a profound and ultimately tragic irony. I question whether Melville had as much literary
self-consciousness and control as their notions would suggest. I see him
instead as moving fluidly but not with ease through a complex urban

landscape, receiving the impact of its social concussions without the long habit of denial and distancing that many modern urban-dwellers have cultivated. I see him as considering many urban attitudes, from exuberant celebration of the city's energy, diversity, and excitement, to despair over its emptiness and heartlessness, from wonder to revulsion; and his work contains many cities as well: ancient and modern, European and American, earthly and utopian. Rather than imagining a totalizing city, a single vision of urban form and significance, Melville entertains a multiplicity of urban forms and perspectives. In that fact resides his main difference from a culture eager to contain the city's miseries and mysteries in a single, easily assimilated urban form.

Thus, although I have offered certain clearly defined forms of my own – chapters that seek to organize and contain the urban models in Melville's work – I use them mainly as a convenience and always with a sense of Melville's habit of recombining handy materials into new, shifting, and plastic variations. My goal has been to recover Melville's rich urban cultural context but at the same time to show how he evaded and protested against rigid cultural forms, maintaining an uncomfortable position both inside and outside of their boundaries. I find his discomfort with sweeping cultural representations of urban realities and his urgent challenges to those who exploited them among his most valuable legacies to our own time.

PART ONE

Traveling the Town

1

Urban Space

Soon, the spires of stone on the land, blent with the masts of wood on the water; the crotch of the twin-rivers pressed the great wedged city almost out of sight. They swept by two little islets distant from the shore; they wholly curved away from the domes of free-stone and marble, and gained the great sublime dome of the bay's wide-open waters.

Pierre (354)

Before we can begin to talk about urban form in New York culture, we need to see how social and physical constructions of urban form grew out of the debate over how to use urban space. When New York saw itself as a compact though growing town, its inhabitants felt they had ample room, not only for themselves, but for their anticipated future needs. New York in the early years of the nineteenth century appeared, to many, a sweeping vista of opportunity stretching along a richly promising waterfront, north through farmland and countryside, to the barely perceptible or conceivable horizon of Harlem Heights. As New Yorkers began to experience anxiety about that space, however, at a point that I see exhibited most graphically in the furor over the gridiron plan of 1811, attempts by different interests to manage and exploit urban space emerged in the print and graphic culture in different images of urban form. New York began to be seen not as the town it was but as the city it was destined to be. And different descriptive and narrative strategies developed to give that desired city an imaginable shape.

This chapter looks at the problem of urban space as it manifested itself in three characteristic cases: first, in the urban plans of 1811 and 1857; next, in the experience of the Melville family as it struggled, like many other middle-class families in New York, to find space to live and work in a town that was developing rapidly into a gigantic city; and finally in the popular culture, which tried to represent strategies for moving through this challenging urban space. In all three areas – urban planning, the life

21

experience of a single family, and the print culture – early-nineteenth-century inhabitants of New York seem to have tried out or responded most fully to two opposite strategies for encountering the city: the mode of mastery and that of surrender. That is, in many cultural productions New Yorkers seemed to oscillate between a confident sense of being able to take in the whole town in one view, one day, or one masterful stroke, and a more subdued, sometimes romantic sense of submission to the city's rhythms and ways. Ishmael, with characteristic enthusiasm, announces and embraces both attitudes in the opening pages of *Moby-Dick*. At one moment he proclaims a panoramic view of the whole city seen with a spectator's eye: "There is now your insular city of the Manhattoes, belted round with wharves as Indian isles by coral reefs" (3). At the next he slips into a meditative surrender to the city's multiple experiences: "Circumambulate the city of a dreamy Sabbath afternoon. Go from Corlears Hook to Coenties Slip, and from thence, by Whitehall, northward. What do you see?" (4). In one instance, Ishmael inserts himself aggressively into urban space, claiming that "it requires a strong moral principle to prevent me from deliberately stepping into the street, and methodically knocking people's hats off" (3). But at the same time he describes the streets as sweeping crowds of unresisting landsmen to the docks: "Right and left, the streets take you waterward"; New Yorkers flood into them, "pacing straight for the water, and seemingly bound for a dive" (4). One can step into the street, knocking people's hats off, dominating and mastering urban space, or one can melt into an urban crowd. Both strategies, as this chapter will show, offered different problems and opportunities to people living in early-nineteenth-century New York.

Urban Planning in New York

Between the New York Commissioners' Plan of 1811 (the survey that established New York streets on the gridiron plan) and Frederick Law Olmsted and Calvert Vaux's 1858 proposal for Central Park (the "Greensward Plan") emerged the New York of Melville's early experience and fiction. These two documents mark the beginning of, and then an important turn in, the story of New York's antebellum development. For by imposing and later modifying the city's gridiron plan, the city government revealed its ideology of urban space. The gridiron was to have an incalculable effect on the lives of New Yorkers and on Melville's urban experience. It was implicated, as a model of urban structure and ideology, in other plans, maps, visual arts, and literature of the period. And in spite of the improvements that Central Park promised and provided, it remains today an essential fact of urban culture in New York. The story of these two plans tells a story of the politics of urban space that was critical to Melville's period.

We can see the 1811 plan (Figure 1) as the city government's attempt to regulate, expand, and prepare for the future spatial needs of the town. The New York commissioners, Gouverneur Morris, Simeon DeWitt, and John Rutherford, who adopted the plan, and John Randel, Jr., who drew the map, envisioned a city neatly laid out in rectangles. In fact, two earlier surveys (1785 and 1795) had organized the city on a precise grid about as far north as Greenwich Village, with the strong diagonals of Broadway and the Bowery varying the shape of the island's southern tip. The commissioners decided to lay out the new streets extending north to Harlem according to an even more rigid plan, and in so doing, they rejected the more baroque designs of planners like Pierre L'Enfant. L'Enfant's plan for Washington varied its rectangular grid with diagonals, circles, and malls intended to produce European elegance and pleasing vistas. The New York commissioners gave some thought to these considerations but decided in favor of a few simple, practical principles. The first of these was housing and real-estate speculation. In considering "whether they should confine themselves to rectilinear and rectangular streets, or whether they should adopt some of those supposed improvements, by circles, ovals, and stars, which certainly embellish a plan, whatever may be their effects as to convenience and utility," the commissioners felt overwhelmingly the force of convenience and utility: as they explained in their remarks appended to the plan, "they could not but bear in mind that a city is to be composed principally of the habitations of men, and that strait sided, and right angled houses are the most cheap to build, and the most convenient to live in."[1]

Aware that the plan left little room for open space and parks, the commissioners went on to justify it in further, explicitly nationalistic terms:

> It may to many, be matter of surprise, that so few vacant spaces have been left, and those so small, for the benefit of fresh air, and consequent preservation of health. Certainly, if the City of New-York were destined to stand on the side of a small stream, such as the Seine or the Thames, a great number of ample places might be needful; but those large arms of the sea which embrace Manhattan Island, render its situation, in regard to health and pleasure, as well as to convenience of commerce, peculiarly felicitous. (Stokes, 1: 472)

Such urban pride may seem quaint to us now, but it did little to accommodate city dwellers' real need for fresh air and healthy open space. New York already had a history of epidemics that argued forcefully against the commissioners' claims.[2] And although the city's exposure to the rivers did indeed make for open space on the waterfront, the shoreline quickly filled up with wharves for the ocean shipping on the East River and the inland transport on the Hudson. The Battery, Castle Island, Governors Island,

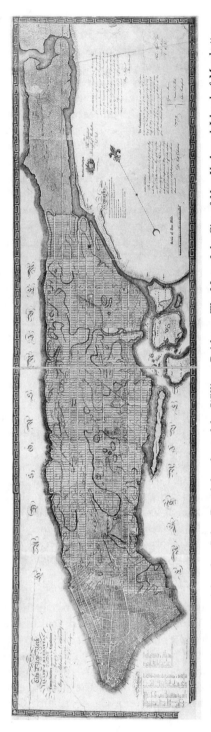

Figure 1. Peter Maverick, after John Randel, adapted by William Bridges, *The Map of the City of New York and Island of Manhattan*, engraving, 1811. (Courtesy Eno Collection, Miriam and Ira D. Wallach Division of Art, Prints and Photographs, The New York Public Library: Astor, Lenox and Tilden Foundations)

Hoboken, and Brooklyn provided room for "pleasure," but Brooklyn was not a park, nor were sufficient areas set aside to the north or inland. (The interior area that eventually became Central Park remained open for many years because it was too hilly and rocky to pave over, but it was seen as a squatters' domain rather than as providing valuable municipal space.)[3] The commissioners' remarks about health were further undermined by the city's poor water supply. The Collect Pond, which had offered fresh water, fishing, and recreation in the early years of the city, had become foul through overuse and because of the tanneries along its shore. In 1802 the city proposed to fill in the pond, and by 1812 the new area was covered with streets. It would not be long before further epidemics and massive downtown fires would forcefully demonstrate the dangers of crowding, inadequate water, and lack of open space in the older parts of the town.

The commissioners, then, had plenty of reasons to be defensive about a plan that offered little help in these areas. But, in fact, issues of health, pleasure, and the city's potential superiority over Paris and London concerned the commissioners less than the economic realities of real-estate speculation in New York: "the price of land is so uncommonly great, it seemed proper to admit the principles of economy to greater influence than might, under circumstances of a different kind, have consisted with the dictates of prudence and the sense of duty" (Stokes, I: 472). But this farsighted concern for future speculators brought the commissioners into direct conflict with other users of urban space. In surveying the land, the commissioners found themselves battling with local landowners who objected to having their land divided by the proposed streets and with speculators who had laid out the land according to the plan most profitable to themselves. After some attempts to accommodate property owners, the commissioners imposed their own plan with an eye, not to the convenience of city dwellers, but to the future disposition of the land. They may have thought that they had made a more "egalitarian" system by eliminating the old allotments that favored the wealthy; perhaps they hoped to create a "republican landscape that would preserve access to proprietorship by facilitating the subdivision and circulation of land."[4] They ended up pleasing no one. Randel, who later wrote plainly that the plan served mostly the "buying, selling and improving of real estate," bore the brunt of numerous lawsuits brought by individuals angry at the surveyors' disregard of property; the Common Council had to pass a special act to allow the surveyors to trespass and cut down trees during the course of their work. In their quest for regularity, the commissioners paid little attention to any topographical feature except the heights of Harlem. Recognizing that Harlem might come to be settled before the low-lying areas to the south, they jocularly explained that "they have in this respect been governed by the shape of the ground." In all other respects, however, they considered the shape of the ground not at all and hence encountered strong hostility. In "A Plain Statement addressed to the Proprietors of Real Estate in the City and County of New York," the author complained that the "changes wrought in the face of this island by the present mode of levelling and filling, and thus reducing it to a flat surface" were "lamented by persons of taste as destructive to the greatest beauties of which our city is susceptible." The commissioners were accused of being the kind of men, "who would have cut down the seven hills of Rome, on which are erected her triumphant monuments of beauty and magnificence and have thrown them into the Tyber or the Pomptine marshes." In spite of their provisions for a parade ground, a few small parks, a reservoir, and a market, amounting to about 500 acres of open land, the commissioners were seen to have fallen prey to the very "pernicious spirit of speculation" they claimed to be trying to regulate.[5]

Especially in comparison with the majestic plans of Philadelphia and Washington, the commissioners' plan seems excessively utilitarian and unimaginative. Nevertheless, they did recognize one essential fact – namely, New York's destiny as a great commercial city. New York lost its opportunity to be the national capital in 1790, when the Congress moved to Philadelphia, and by 1797 it had ceased to be the state capital as well. Yet while Boston, Philadelphia, and the still underpopulated Washington conceived of themselves as the nation's cultural and political capitals, New York was swiftly surpassing them in population and commercial dominance. Plans for the construction of the Erie Canal began as early as 1810, Fulton's *Clermont* had made its first trip to Albany, and New York had eclipsed its rivals in Atlantic trade by the time the commissioners wrote their defense. A foreign visitor, John Lambert, in 1807 called New York "the first city of the United States for wealth, commerce, and population," taking particular note of the prosperous display of stores and fashion on Broadway, the intense speculative activity on Wall Street, and the "forest of masts" along the wharves. "Every thought, word, look, and action of the multitude seemed to be absorbed by commerce. The welkin rang with its busy hum, and all were eager in the pursuit of its riches."[6] In many ways, then, the Commissioners' Plan was ideally suited to a city that placed a high value on rapid growth, level and easy access in all directions, and public walking, not in scenes of natural beauty but in shopping and commercial districts. The map clearly inscribed its urban ideology on the Manhattan landscape and determined that landscape's new shape forever.

If we move ahead almost fifty years to the debate over Central Park, however, it seems clear that the commissioners' response to the issues of access, growth, and speculation in the developing city had not served its inhabitants well. Especially in the decades between 1840 and 1860 the population soared, from 312,710 in 1840 to 515,547 in 1850 to 813,669 in 1860.[7] To any observer, the changing social composition of the city's lower wards made the demands and needs for urban space obvious. As the old town became dominated by commerce and manufacturing, the wealthy moved uptown, leaving older residences to new immigrant populations. It seemed clear, beyond their requirements for adequate housing, that the laboring classes needed space for recreation and fresh air, as the Battery and City Hall Park proved increasingly insufficient to contain Sunday crowds. And as Broadway and other fashionable avenues became more congested and socially heterogeneous, the middle and upper classes sought space where they could walk, ride, and promenade in genteel surroundings.[8]

One might assume, then, that the Olmsted-Vaux plan for Central Park (Figure 2) somehow "solves" the problem of the 1811 Commissioners' Plan, that by creating a large natural landscape within the city the planners were reversing – or at least countering – the process of uncontrolled speculation, growth, and congestion that threatened to make the city intolerable. The Central Park plan did indeed aim to undo the bad effects of the Commissioners' Plan, but it could not and did not challenge the basic profit motives behind it. Nor did the park movement alter the political structure that kept the control of urban space in the hands of an elite. In fact, the Central Park plan subscribes to many of the same economic concerns that engendered the Commissioners' Plan. The land had lain open for years, being considered a social and natural wasteland by the wealthy inhabitants on its fringe. Because of its topographical unevenness and rocks, it had resisted the relentless grading that leveled most of the rest of New York. Clearly the land was not generating tax revenues or raising property values in the way the New York gentry would have liked, but they expressed their need for urban space as a lament over the lack of handsome parks like those found in London. "The *Parks, Squares,* and *Public Gardens* of London beat us clean out of sight," said Horace Greeley. Instead of the grand open spaces of London, "[d]eluded New-York has, until lately, contented itself with the little door-yards of space – mere grass-plots of verdure, which form the squares of the city, in the mistaken idea that they are parks," as the great landscape and home designer Andrew Jackson Downing put it. Frederick Law Olmsted himself, contemplating the area that would eventually stand as the monument of the parks movement, called it "filthy, squalid and disgusting," full of "heaps of cinders, brick-bats, potsherds, and other rubbish." Putting the land to use would serve a number of practical as well as aesthetic aims. William Cullen Bryant, in 1844, stressed the need to "rescue any part of it for health and recreation," Henry Tappan endorsed bringing "the beauty and freshness of the country" into the city, and Downing foresaw that "a large public park would not only pay in money, but largely civilize and refine the national character."[9]

As these statements show, the plans and hopes for the park revealed

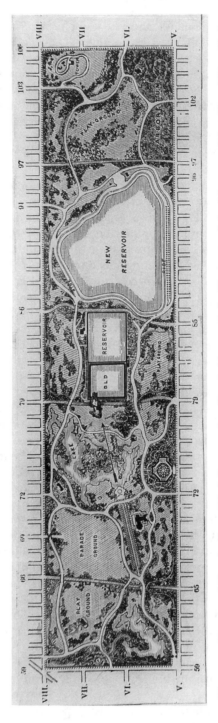

Figure 2. *Greensward Plan for Central Park*, Presentation Sketch No. 4, 1858. (Courtesy of the Museum of the City of New York, on long-term loan from the Department of Parks)

the intense political conflicts surrounding the idea. The coalition behind the selection of a central site, rather than the Jones Wood on the shore-line, included property owners and gentlemen aiming to improve the district and the city's attractions, merchants hoping to open up public space without raising taxes, Democrats trying to outwit the Whig Jones Wood scheme, and the Democratic mayor, Fernando Wood, who, among many political motives, saw the necessity of employing those devastated by the bad winter and worse economy of 1855.[10] For the planners themselves, Olmsted and Vaux, the park was designed to settle class conflict in a divided city by celebrating a democratic American spirit, making space in the city for all classes to meet. Olmsted, for example, struggled to prevent the city from accepting Richard Morris Hunt's designs for elaborate imperial arches at the entrances to the park, arguing that they belonged to the world of European monarchy, not to an American republic: as Vaux put it, "the park typifies what we have been fighting for, and the gates typify what we have been fighting against – it is Nap[oleon] III in disguise all over." At the same time, Olmsted recognized that democratic mingling could not take place freely in the park without some restraining influence: visitors "will need to be trained in the proper use of it, to be restrained in the abuse of it," and to that end he created a park patrol modeled on the new metropolitan police, to reinforce the harmonizing power of nature. In a similar political irony, Olmsted, presenting himself as one opposed to the city in all its aspects, worked tirelessly to eliminate visible signs of the city inside the park by sinking the transverse streets below the level of the paths, masking the boundaries with thick foliage, and building numerous remote areas like the Rambles, intended as quiet retreats. Yet he himself owed his appointment as supervisor of the park to complex political bargaining by which it was decided that since the original chief engineer, Egbert L. Viele, was a Democrat, the new planner must be a Republican. Work on the park was considerably hastened when discontented laborers, unemployed during the Panic of 1857, marched on Olmsted's office, demanding jobs. Thus, along with the aesthetic principles that promoted natural beauty, the patriotic hopes for American democracy, the desire to rival Europe, and the longing for a more human, fresher urban environment, went the vexed economic and political issues of the late 1850s.[11]

As well as defining a historical debate over the developing shape of New York, the Commissioners' Plan and the Greensward Plan bring into focus a cluster of ideas about the city: what Leo Marx has called an "American ideology of space." Marx has shown the contradictions in a pastoral myth that on the one hand celebrates the agency of nature in purifying Americans of bad European habits and influences, and on the other celebrates the American imperative to conquer the wilderness, eliminate its inhabitants, and convert it into a garden. Both strains – the "primitivist" urge to escape from civilization into a healing natural domain and the "utilitarian" model of subduing the wilderness – operate in the creation of cities. Both march under the banner of progress and improvement. Taken together, each justifies the other: the guilt that accompanies the exploitation of nature may be assuaged through a pastoral retreat, and the anxiety that comes from escaping the city may be assuaged by seeing oneself as a pioneer, in the vanguard of civilization. The myth is complex precisely because it tries to do so much, to yoke such contraries.[12]

The planners of New York tried to satisfy these conflicting urges too. Both the Commissioners' and the Greensward Plans tried to meet primitivist and utilitarian needs. The commissioners genuinely believed in the healthful influence of two rivers embracing an island city; then, satisfied that New Yorkers had easy access to the water – in part *because* of the gridiron plan – they concentrated on the utilitarian considerations of straight-sided rectangular housing and land prices. Olmsted and Vaux responded to the primitivist urge for a garden within the city; but they also operated from utilitarian impulses to "improve" the land, to create a garden where only a wasteland had existed before, and thus to raise the value of property in the vicinity as well as the quality of life for city dwellers. The commissioners seem to have been more utilitarian than Olmsted, Olmsted more primitivist than the commissioners, but in fact both existed along an ideological continuum. Illogical as the American fusion of primitivist and utilitarian motives may seem, it worked in New York because the pastoral myth essentially served the purposes of capitalist growth.

The Melville Family and Urban Space

The Commissioners' and the Greensward Plans offer examples, not only of how an American ideology of space worked in a city that saw space as a valuable premium, but also of how two different strategies managed the social challenges of a growing city. The Commissioners' Plan clearly sought to master urban space, as the commissioners confidently carved up the landscape and set to work surveying, grading, and paving it regardless of the terrain and the people dwelling on it. The Greensward Plan, though clearly taking as masterful control of the land, bowed to the pressures of an increasingly diverse population, shrinking public and private space, and shifting political alliances, as the working classes found voice and power. Without actually surrendering to the landscape or its people, the Greensward Plan offered an aesthetic of surrender, as it created a natural environment where the stroller might lose himself or herself in reverie. Recognizing that the city had practically obliterated the natural landscape, Olmsted and Vaux recommended that the park "interfere with its easy, undulating outlines, and picturesque, rocky scenery as little as possible."[13] As far as it could, then, the Greensward Plan aimed to surrender to the city's natural terrain rather than impose its own form – although, indeed, the landscaping required to bring about the park's scenic effects demanded enormous labor.[14]

Central Park, applauded as a masterpiece of park design, makes an aesthetic and practical virtue of its surrender to the politics of urban space. One can find similar compromises going on in individual lives, as city dwellers struggled to achieve a place in an increasingly contentious city. The Melville family is surprisingly representative of the problems faced by middle-class New Yorkers during an especially turbulent period of development.[15] Herman Melville's father, Allan, provides a spectacular example of the failure to master urban space and urban stress. His sons, made wise by his instructive model, opted for more devious methods.

The story of the Melville family in New York shows that they participated in characteristic patterns of settlement, movement, and flight as they sought to master urban space. Like many city dwellers, they more often rented than owned their living space. But that basic insecurity was compounded by constant upheavals in the economy and just as disturbing plagues and epidemics that seemed to turn the town upside down. Their attempts to keep the family intact, to find adequate and healthful living quarters, and to integrate their domestic and working spaces mirror similar problems in the culture at large. In the end, Allan Melvill's efforts to master the city, to read its codes – so alien to what he had learned growing up in the town of Boston and traveling through the older cities of Europe – produced shattering results for his family.

Allan Melvill would seem to have been well prepared for his entrepreneurial ventures in the new city. When he moved to New York in 1818 with his wife and two children, he had been conducting a successful imports business in Boston for years. A tireless traveler, he made long trips every one or two years to the textile and fashion centers of Europe – Paris, Brussels, London, and numerous other towns – to buy fabrics, laces, ribbons, and hose. These he distributed all over New England, not unlike the early Yankee peddlers. On one of his frequent trips to Albany, he met Maria Gansevoort and married her, but marriage and the births of Gansevoort (1815) and Helen Maria (1817) did not stop his travels. Maria and the children stayed in Albany while Melvill, though missing them acutely, continued to fulfill his business obligations all over the New England seaboard. A trip to Paris in 1818, however, convinced him that New York was "destined to become the commercial emporium of our Country, it is daily rising in wealth and splendour."[16] As the American port most accessible to Europe, it provided a better market for French goods than the more provincial Boston could. He moved his family to the city and noted proudly in his diary, on May 12, 1818: "Commenced Housekeeping at No 6 Pearl Street, Mrs. M. & the children who had been on a visit to her mother in Albany since the 6th April, having rejoined me on this day, to my great joy.''[7] On August 1, 1819, Melville was born in that house, which was just a short walk from his father's office and warehouse in Pearl Street, the center of the fabrics trade and itself just a few steps from the docks and slips along the East River. At this point, although the family could not know it, they had achieved a kind of urban ideal: a home in the thriving, relatively stable, close-knit town that lower Manhattan still remained.

A number of factors, however, combined to disrupt the family's early stability. One was the precariousness of Allan Melvill's business, a misfortune only partly his fault. When the port of New York reopened in 1815 after the War of 1812, European merchants dumped their goods on the unprotected American market. What they could not sell to American merchants, they sold directly at auction, thereby depressing the local market. The Tariff Act of 1816 did a good deal to protect American manufactures, and New York recovered well from the war, as its Atlantic and coastal shipping increased, and the Erie Canal was completed in 1825 and brought western trade to New York. But these very developments brought financial instability to the city, as great numbers of banks were established, real-estate prices skyrocketed, and speculation in businesses and western land strained Wall Street and the lending institutions. Eventually, in the 1830s, President Jackson took measures to restrain irresponsible banking practices and curb speculation, but by then the banks, in debt to their European lenders, had run out of specie, and the pressure on them produced the Panic of 1837. In antebellum New York, fortunes rose and fell as spectacularly as buildings and neighborhoods did.[18]

Allan Melvill was dead by 1832 but by then had already undergone years of reverses that, in their swift cycles, closely followed the patterns of speculation, complicated by disease, in the city. Panic over fever imitated and alternated with business panics, bringing sudden changes in the family's living habits and spaces. The first in Melville's life, a yellow fever epidemic in 1819, turned the commercial waterfront area into a wasteland: "the alarm has so much increased, that most of the Merchants in Water, Front & South Streets, & many in my immediate Neighborhood in Pearl Street, between old Slip & Wall Street, *the proscribed District*, have removed" (*Log*, 4). As a result, Allan Melvill's business collapsed. But by June 1820, "my prospects brighten," and although August was "proverbially dull," he was able to move his family away from Pearl Street to a more spacious location at 55 Courtlandt Street and to relocate his revived business to 134 Pearl Street, a location "des plus frequentées dans la Rue et les affaires vont assez bien" (*Log*, 6, 7, 8).

The improvement in Allan Melvill's fortunes convinced him that he was now a true man of the city, that he had mastered its ways. In 1822 he wrote importantly, though not without traces of anxiety, to Lemuel Shaw, claiming that he had no time for his old leisurely pursuits:

I have become in spite of myself exclusively a Man of Business, & given up Books & every thing disconnected with Trade, which in this most industrious of all busy Cities requires unremitted personal attendance, the competition being much greater than you can imagine from your experience among our commercial acquaintance at Boston; – as a place of Business New York stands unrivalled, & in this respect I prefer it to any other, thus far I have succeeded beyond my expectations. (*Log*, 10–11)

Rather than reading books, Allan congratulated himself on his success in reading the market of New York. Another epidemic sent the family to Albany in the summer of 1822, however, and Allan reported that "New York is in a most deplorable condition, the Inhabitants south of Courtlandt St & Maiden Lane are flying in all directions, & no one can anticipate the consequences of such a calamity" (*Log*, 11). His fortunes remained stable in the climate of anxiety about both disease and business, but the two were linked in his imagination: "I trust our City may escape the Fever this season . . . the mere apprehension of its recurrence suspends the regular operations of business & checks speculative enterprises" (*Log*, 14).

To protect his family from the ravages of both fever and speculation, Allan sought ever more living space, in a pattern that in the end contributed to his ruin. In spring of 1824, the Melvills moved to 33 Bleecker Street, which both Allan and Maria described as giving the family more space but also new kinds of space. Maria liked the wide hall, the "handsome & convenient Basement room for a Nursery," the "lofty ceilings" of the second floor, and even the attic: "The Stair case continues to the Garret without interruption where you enter a large space on either side of which you enter two Pretty bed chambers with large dormer windows comfortable for any Person & the Prospect extensive & pleasing" (*Log*, 17). That "Prospect" seemed to her a pleasant vista of her own social prospects as well, for it included "[t]hose elegant white Marble Houses in Bond Street – & also in Broadway [which] present themselves to the View from the back windows" (*Log*, 17). For Allan Melvill, too, the house represented a spatial ideal, especially as the whole family had been sick that winter, and "our House has resembled a private Hospital" (*Log*, 17). The new house, with "a vacant lot of equal size attached to it, which will be invaluable as play ground for the Children," offered a healthy situation – "an open, dry & elevated location" – that succeeded in "almost uniting the advantages of town & country," although because Allan now had to commute to his new store at 162 Pearl Street, he would not be able to lunch at home (*Log*, 17). He consoled himself, however, that "we shall be amply compensated by a residence, which will obviate the necessity of their [Maria and the children] leaving town every summer" (*Log*, 18).

Temporarily, at least, Allan succeeded in uniting his family and his business interests, and both remained healthy for some time. But in removing his family space so completely from his work space, Melvill had brought about the division of his life into separate spheres that was to alienate many men from both throughout the nineteenth century. Believing that he was binding all the parts of his life more securely together, Melvill had actually suburbanized his private life.

As a sign of this process of alienation, Allan's letters reflect his sense of bewilderment and dismay at the progress of his business. Like the fever, Allan's troubles seemed to rear up with no warning, and he appears to have been mystified by the workings of the market. In quite a different vein from the confidence with which he announced himself as a man of business to Lemuel Shaw, in 1826 he expressed to Peter Gansevoort his frustration over his inability to read the business world aright:

> Business is . . . dull & unprofitable, . . . & it requires a keener vision than mine, to discern among the signs of the times, any real symptoms of future improvement, there is a kind of Equality of Commerce at home & abroad, the result of labour saving power & modern inventions, which however beautiful it may appear in theory, in reducing all to a common level, or a kind of universal joint stock company, has in my humble opinion, already impaired the public welfare. (*Log,* 27)

Melvill, an aristocratic Boston provincial, found the new democratic workings of New York commerce threatening and bewildering. His solution to the problem of reading the signs of the times was to attempt to make himself an invisible agent in the workings of commerce, to gain control of the market by entering into a *"confidential Connexion"* (*Log,* 29), a speculation of his own.[19] Borrowing heavily from his family and friends, he concocted a scheme in which his own financial involvement was to remain secret. Again, he hoped by this fraudulent arrangement to unite family and business interests, to ensure their health. When the lease on 33 Bleecker Street expired in February 1828, Melvill again took a spacious house – there were now seven children – on the most fashionable street in New York, Broadway, between Bond and Great Jones Streets. Maria rejoiced in the move – "I have at last gained my point which has always been a House in Broadway – My Spirits are better & I am a more agreeable companion than I have been for some time past" (*Log,* 33) – but Allan seems to have recognized the unreality of his situation. The prosperous show of genteel stability masked an increasingly "fearful & protracted struggle" (*Log,* 33) with debt, and Maria's mother and Allan's father wrote codicils to their wills to protect their estates from Allan's depredations upon them. In 1830 Allan went bankrupt and, facing lawsuits, moved his family to Albany. Still borrowing frantically from one family member to pay off another and making frequent trips to New York to salvage his business, Allan hurtled toward his final illness and death in January 1832.[20]

To the end, Allan saw himself as the victim of the spirit and human agents of commerce in New York. Before he died, he marked verses 4 and 5 of Psalm 55 in his Bible:

> My heart is sore pained within me: and the terrors of death are fallen upon me.
> Fearfulness and trembling are come upon me and horror hath overwhelmed me. (*Log*, 51)

Although these lines seem a logical choice for one facing a painful and ignominious death, later verses suggest even more forcefully the hidden sources of Allan's distress in the city, in horrors more immediate, social, and urban than eternal:

> Destroy, O Lord, and divide their tongues: for I have seen violence and strife in the city.
> Day and night they go about it upon the walls thereof: mischief also and sorrow are in the midst of it.
> Wickedness is in the midst thereof: deceit and guile depart not from her streets.
> For it was not an enemy that reproached me; then I could have borne it: neither was it he that hated me that did magnify himself against me; then I would have hid myself from him:
> But it was thou, a man mine equal, my guide, and mine acquaintance.
> We took sweet counsel together, and walked unto the house of God in company.

These lines contain many of the themes central not only to Allan Melvill's life but also to Herman Melville's fiction. The lines stress urban deceit and division, a division that begins on the tongues of men and extends to the walls and streets, the Wall Streets, themselves. Deceit and guile, wickedness and sorrow, violence, strife, and mischief are embedded in the very stones of the city, as well as in the words and hearts of men. But deeper and more horrifying than the open violence and strife is the urbane treachery of friends, men of the same class and company, who walk together to the house of God and hold sweet counsel. That sweet counsel, the confidential language of equals, is the discourse and currency of the city, where commerce brings men into confidential connections only to ruin them. Allan Melvill felt that that sweet counsel, so treacherous, had brought him to the terrors of death. He died in an anti-urban frame of mind indeed.

For Herman Melville and his brothers, however, in the aftermath of their family disaster, New York did not represent violence and strife, sorrow and mischief. All went to New York to seek their fortunes. Gansevoort gladly gave up his father's failing fur and cap business, which finally collapsed in April 1837 during the Panic, and headed for New York, where he began studying law. Maria relocated the rest of the family to the village of Lansingburgh in 1838 – a move that represented her desperate financial situation, not a longing for the countryside – and Herman lampooned the village mercilessly in his "Fragments from a Writing Desk." He and his brothers, nevertheless, felt deeply the pressure of their family's need, and by a combination of circumstances – Gansevoort recovered from a fifteen-month illness and returned to New York, Herman decided to embark for Liverpool, and Allan visited Gansevoort's friend A. W. Bradford to escape his job as an Albany law clerk – all reunited in New York in May 1839. Herman and Allan later returned to Lansingburgh, but Gansevoort made a base for them in the city. After some fruitless schoolteaching, and travels as far west as the Mississippi in search of employment, Melville went to New York and, after a few weeks of dinners at Gansevoort's expense, shipped on a whaler, the *Acushnet*. During the years Herman was at sea, Gansevoort practiced law – first, in 1842, at 51 William Street, and then, by 1845, at 10 Wall Street. Allan went to work for Bradford and then at 10 Wall Street, but avoided the path Gansevoort took into Tammany politics and Polk's presidential campaign.

The patterns of Melville's lifelong relationship with New York City suggest that he always saw it as his home, though unlike his father he did not dream of mastering its inner commercial workings. After his travels he returned to Albany, but early in 1845 he went to stay with Gansevoort, where he worked on *Typee*. Gansevoort went to London that summer to take up his post in the American legation, while Herman awaited news of the manuscript in New York and Lansingburgh. *Typee* came out in 1846 to considerable acclaim, and Melville began to make numerous trips to New York, cultivating editors and making literary acquaintances like Evert Duyckinck, while Allan handled his brother's literary affairs from the city. In November 1846, Melville went to New York with the manuscript of *Omoo* and stayed there to begin *Mardi*. Preparations for his marriage to Elizabeth Shaw took him out of New York that summer, but after the wedding in August 1847, Herman and Elizabeth, Allan and his new wife, Sophia Thurston, Maria, and the Melville sisters all moved together to 103 Fourth Avenue. For the first time since the house on Broadway, the Melville family expressed its confidence in its prospects by making a significant real-estate commitment. For Herman, at least, domestic and work space were united in a way the family had not achieved since when they lived on Pearl Street, a short walk from Allan's shop.

Melville lived in New York for the next three years, traveling to London and Paris in 1849, and writing *Redburn*, *White-Jacket*, and the first sections of *Moby-Dick* before moving his family to Arrowhead in Pittsfield, Massachusetts. Ironically, although he lived away from the city for the next thirteen years (1850–63), he also traveled more widely and restlessly during this period and to more cities than at any other time in his life except for his years at sea. Besides the frequent trips to New York to visit his friends and publishers and to finish *Moby-Dick* and *Pierre*, Melville also made his second journey to Europe, followed by a lengthy tour of the Mediterranean and the Near East in 1856–7. In the three succeeding winters, he traveled through the United States on lecture tours; in 1860 he journeyed to San Francisco with his brother Tom; in 1861 he took a job-seeking trip to Washington followed by a winter in New York; and by spring of 1862 he was making plans to move the family back to New York, a move that finally took place in October 1863, when he settled the family at 104 East 26th Street.

Although Melville undoubtedly loved the Pittsfield farm, he had been working in one way or another to leave it since 1852, when the strain of publishing seven novels in six years caused him to consider seeking a consular post elsewhere. As his writing career produced less income, as his mental and physical health failed, even with the therapeutic trips abroad, as the lecture circuit sapped his strength, as the Civil War drained his spirits, Melville worked even harder to obtain a government appointment of some kind. A road accident prevented him from moving to New York earlier than he did. It seems clear, then, that in the Melville family's mind, the Pittsfield years, though productive for Herman's writing, also contained stresses and illnesses which, unlike the choleras and fevers that drove his family away from New York in his youth, necessitated a return to the city in his middle age.

Once back in New York, Melville stayed in one house, worked at one job (at the Customs House, for nineteen years), and made few significant excursions for the remaining twenty-eight years of his life. Like many New Yorkers, he progressed northward with the island but came to rest far south of the upper-class mansions rising up along Fifth Avenue. He missed the Panic of 1857, the movement for Central Park, the Civil War mobilization, and the rise of Boss Tweed, but got back in time for the end of the war, Lincoln's funeral cortege, Tweed's fall, the completion of Central Park (in 1876, the year of the centennial and *Clarel*), the building of Grand Central Terminal (1871) and the Brooklyn Bridge (1883) and the first elevated railways. Although he worked hard at his job throughout those years, he also wrote steadily, publishing *Battle-Pieces* in 1866, *Clarel* in 1876, and private editions of *John Marr and Other Sailors* (1888) and *Timoleon* (1891). *Billy Budd* remained on his desk when he died.

Melville's quiet return to his native city seemed to his friends, family, and practically nonexistent public a surrender of the sense of spatial mastery he had experienced at sea and at Arrowhead. Those who knew Melville was living in New York at all, those who, like Julian Hawthorne, sought him out on his "quiet side-street in New York" (*Log*, 782), considered him buried alive, a wraith and a hermit. Julian Hawthorne described him as melancholy: "he made no intelligible response. His words were vague and indeterminate; and again and again he would get up from his chair and open or close a window with a stick having a hook at the end, which he kept by him seemingly for that purpose" (*Log*, 783). To the young Hawthorne, Melville seemed like one gasping for air, dying for lack of space. In his last years, writers for the newspapers remarked on the phenomenon of Melville's still remaining alive in New York, long after his fame had died. Melville himself signaled his alienation in various ways: by refusing to talk to visitors about his writing, by checking gloomy passages in Schopenhauer's *Studies in Pessimism*, by scoring these lines in Balzac: "New-York, – a place where speculation and individualism are carried to the highest pitch, where the brutality of self-interest attains to cynicism, where man, essentially isolated, is compelled to push his way for himself or by himself" (*Log*, 830). These lines, a secular version of the psalm Allan Melvill had marked in 1832, fit as closely the New York of his father's life as the Gilded Age city Melville inhabited. In one sense, New York may have seemed a constant in Melville's life, a landscape of deceit and sorrow such as his father witnessed.

But Melville's books suggest that his early hopes for the city as a place where he could move and thrive were not disappointed. Although the spirit of commerce did not in the end enrich Melville any more than it had his father, the city nevertheless provided the largest market of readers he had, and for some time he enjoyed there the experience of being in an urban literary circle. Most of all, however, Melville made his works of fiction and poetry models of space where his characters might live and move. Just as Central Park created space within a city that was fast becoming a wasteland – a space where Melville went for long walks every day of his last years – Melville's fiction, too, opened up space where he might issue his challenge to the city's masters. In abdicating his father's failed ethic of mastery, Melville found new opportunities in surrendering to the city's unique structures and energies.

Panorama and Labyrinth

The two examples I have been discussing, one political and one personal, suggest that the problem of mastering urban space proved a crisis for groups and individuals contending for a place in the city. In cultural representations of the city, however, the strategies of both mastery and surrender appeared as valid and aesthetically empowering ways of encountering it. Maps and pictures, books and articles in antebellum New York show the strong appeal of two different ways of viewing the urban

Figure 3. Carolus Allardt, *The Restitutio-Allardt Map and View,* copper engraving, 1673. (Courtesy of the Museum of the City of New York)

landscape: one from the air, in a panoramic view, and one from the ground, where the city more and more over time resembled a labyrinth. Certainly these ancient and conventional tropes were not new to New York. But as different cultural forms show, images of the city as either panorama or labyrinth resolved the political tensions over contested urban space by delivering an aesthetic and moral charge, by allowing the reader or viewer to experience urban space in a pleasurable way.

The habit of viewing the city panoramically begins with the earliest prints of Dutch New Amsterdam and British New York, when the city represented a growing colonial power.[21] The early maps often include a panoramic view taken from Brooklyn or the river, in which the tiny houses and even tinier people, if there are any, appear against an enormous sky and river filled with ships, presumably from Europe. The "Restitutio Map and View" (1673) (Figure 3) is typical in the way it subordinates the view of the town to an ornate allegorical tableau and encloses it in a tidy frame.

In "A South Prospect of the Flourishing City" (1717) (Figure 4), a six-foot panorama drawn by the English artist William Burgis, who took his view from Brooklyn Heights, the city appears densely settled and populated, but still assimilable from a single point of view, still graced with reclining allegorical goddesses and heraldic devices, and still open to a large, beneficent sky. The numerous pictorial and narrative details show working people engaged in their livelihoods, while genteel "spectators" point out the delights of the town to their visitors and women friends. A careful reading of the picture gives the viewer an experience of traveling through the town, from south to north, along the picturesque waterfront; the interior remains hidden but imaginable. The density of shipping tells its own story of trade, fishing, ferrying, and pleasure that rivals the city itself in importance. Until the Revolution, views of New York consistently reflected the European colonizers' confidence in themselves, in their own power to enclose the city in a pictorial frame.[22]

Postcolonial American views of New York, especially during its years as the national capital, reflect the same kind of pride. In the surge of development that followed the Revolution, many new buildings appeared and became the subjects of paintings and prints. Although these pictures bring the viewer down to the ground, they still take a lofty view, showing few people and little if any urban life. Some views contrasted the growing city with a pastoral foreground – Brooklyn or Harlem Village or Collect Pond – in compositions that emphasize the harmony rather than the tensions of the contrast. It was not until New York lost its status as capital and began its period of commercial expansion in the nineteenth century that pictures of the city began to include ordinary people and scenes of urban life. For some time, however, the artist's point of view remained genteel and detached, observing urban change from a spectatorial distance.

One element in this detachment was foreignness. Early-nineteenth-century views of New York appeared in books and prints by artists like Pierre Lacour, Charles-Balthazar-Julien Fevret de Saint-Memin, the Baroness Hyde de Neuville, J. Milbert, and Anthony Imbert from France, August Köllner from Germany, Archibald and Alexander Robertson and George Harvey from England, Edward Burkhardt from Switzerland, and Baron Axel Leonhard Klinckowstrom from Sweden. In imitation of European artists, American artists often went to Europe before coming back to paint their own city. John Vanderlyn, after years of studying art in Paris and Rome, had his earliest success with an exhibition of panoramas of Versailles in a rotunda that he built for that purpose. More than Europeanness, however, an elite bias selected the busiest, most fashionable, and most picturesque elements of the city as suitable for representation. Even where the subject was working-class, as in William J. Bennett's view of "South Street from Maiden Lane" (1828) (Figure 5), a waterfront

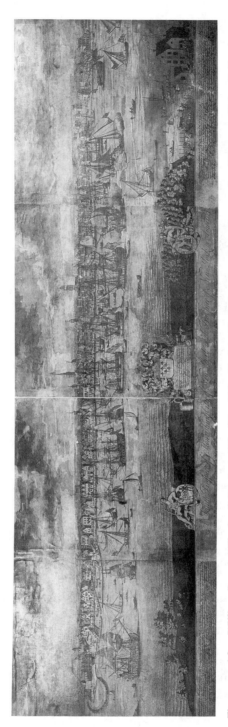

Figure 4. After William Burgis, *The South Prospect of the City of New York in North America*, engraving, 1761. (Courtesy Print Collection, Miriam and Ira D. Wallach Division of Art, Prints and Photographs, The New York Public Library: Astor, Lenox and Tilden Foundations)

Figure 5. William James Bennett, *View of South Street from Maiden Lane, New York City*, ink and watercolor, 1828. (Courtesy of the Metropolitan Museum of Art, Bequest of Edward W. C. Arnold, 1954. The Edward W. C. Arnold Collection of New York Prints, Maps and Pictures)

scene that would have been completely familiar to Melville, the narrative point of view remains panoramic. In this view, the dockside loungers appear as agreeable participants in a lively scene where even the dense lines of shipping to one side and buildings on the other leave plenty of space for horses and pedestrians to pass and sunshine and light to fill the sky. Later comic or reformist views of the wharves would emphasize the crowded buildings blocking the sun, the degenerate idlers filling the street, and the grocery store that was almost certainly a gin shop spewing out drunks. But little of that street culture enters into views before 1840.[23]

The rise of a new middle- and working-class Democratic party in New York, along with the development of cheap lithographs and mass journalism, produced a native, professional class of artists committed to local subjects, reportorial accuracy, and reform. The tremendous vogue for panoramas continued, but now the density and complexity of New York strained panoramic conventions. Burkhardt's panorama (1842–5) (Figure 6) in eight sections resembles earlier panoramas in taking in the whole city in one confident view, but now that view originates from *within* the city, from the steeple of the North Dutch Church, rather than from Brooklyn or some other distant point. Now one gets a sense of the city's extent,

Figure 6. *Burkhardt's Panorama of New York*, 1842–5. (Courtesy of the New York Historical Society)

Figure 7. J. W. Hill, *New York – The Papprill View from St. Paul's Chapel*, aquatint, 1848. (Courtesy of the Museum of the City of New York, the J. Clarence Davies Collection)

its vast expanse of rooftops that obscure the streets or make them visible only as deep cuts in the surface. In an even more ambitious project, E. Porter Belden in 1845–6 built a scale model of the city twenty by twenty-four feet that, according to an advertisement, was a "perfect piece of mechanism, representing every building and other object in the city." In detailing the astounding number of these objects – 200,000 buildings, 30,000 trees, 5,000 ships – Belden emphasized the daunting labor of accurately representing such a great city. Only a few years later, J. W. Hill's view of "New York from the steeple of St. Paul's Church, looking East, South, and West" (1849) (Figure 7) shows the city's size and density as faintly ominous, as he contrasts sunwashed storefronts with darker, hidden streets. People and omnibuses seem dwarfed by the tall buildings on each side, and the distant river suggests little relief, such as the commissioners hoped for, from urban surroundings. Although people have never stopped taking panoramic views of New York – the development of Central Park gave a new impetus to uptown panoramic views in the 1860s and 1870s, as did the construction of Brooklyn Bridge in 1883 and the first skyscrapers and elevated railroads after that – nevertheless, the difficulty of taking in the whole city at a glance already seems evident in mid-century urban art.[24]

In coming down to the ground, mid-century artists did not always surrender their spectatorial views of the city. Many prints and paintings of the period enshrine New York's institutions – prisons, hospitals, churches, and charities – the private residences of the wealthy, and the centers of commerce, fashion, and trade. Others celebrate an urban unity of spirit in representations of Louis Kossuth's or Jenny Lind's appearances in New York, or the fireworks and fountains at the opening of the Croton Reservoir in 1842. Increasingly, however, artists turned their attention to the "other" New York of immigrants, taverns, prostitutes, the poor and working classes. As Tammany Hall became more powerful in city and to some degree national politics, drawing votes from newly naturalized immigrants and workers rather than property owners, those classes became a political force as well. Efforts at reform brought many middle-class observers, especially women, into the homes of the poor, and neglected areas like the Five Points became tourist curiosities to middle-class visitors. Dickens made a point of visiting the Five Points shortly after strolling down Broadway, and his visit reflects the desire, shared by Europeans and anxious Americans alike, to test American democratic ideology against its cities and their slums. Much mid-century urban art focused on people in the street, rather than buildings, as a political act of representation.[25]

The artist's descent to the street, to the people, creates a quite different notion of space from that found in the panoramic view. One can still get broad vistas and open sky, gracious buildings and people in harmony with them, but more often the urban environment closes in on the viewer, cutting off the spectator's freedom of movement and breadth of vision. In a view of Wall Street from Trinity Church drawn by E. Purcell, "New York in 1849" (Figure 8), the buildings loom over tiny people, making the street a deep ravine full of shadows. In James H. Cafferty and Charles G. Rosenberg's painting, "Wall Street, half past 2 o'clock, Oct. 13, 1857" (Figure 9), the date of the onset of the Panic of 1857, the men crowded together in the foreground, a sea of suits and top hats, stand against a backdrop of buildings jammed together in an equally uncomfortable way. The distant spire of Trinity Church, often used in earlier views of Wall Street as a kind of spiritual counterpoint to the houses of commerce and exchange, has been squeezed in by buildings that appear nearly as high as, and much more substantial than, the church. And although early views of Wall Street often show the street itself as a spacious avenue, the Cafferty-Rosenberg painting makes the street disappear beneath the volume of people and buildings.[26]

A series of articles published in *Putnam's Monthly Magazine* in spring of 1853, Clarence Cook's "New York Daguerreotyped," offers a similar sense of the ambivalent representations of the city at mid-century. The articles joyfully celebrate New York's many beautiful buildings, its churches, universities, benevolent institutions, and private homes – all grand in scale and meticulously illustrated. The few street scenes, however, as opposed to pictures of free-standing buildings, show streets in disrepair or under construction, with ponderous rows of buildings blocking the sky and cre-

NEW - YORK, IN 1849.

PUBLISHED AND SOLD BY ROBERT SEARS, 128 NASSAU STREET, N.Y.

Figure 8. Steven Weekes, after Edward B. Purcell, *New York in 1849*, colored wood engraving, c. 1849. (Courtesy of I. N. Phelps Stokes Collection, Miriam and Ira D. Wallach Division of Art, Prints and Photographs, The New York Public Library: Astor, Lenox and Tilden Foundations)

Figure 9. James H. Cafferty and Charles G. Rosenberg, *Wall Street, half past two o'clock, October 13, 1857,* oil on canvas, 1857. (Courtesy of the Museum of the City of New York, gift of the Hon. Irwin Untermeyer)

ating a cavernous effect. Alongside the other illustrations of urban prosperity and growth, these suggest ruin and decay. The view of Dey Street (Figure 10), for example, shows a dark avenue, sparsely peopled, stretching indefinitely into a dreary distance. "Dey-street, which, but a short time since, was exclusively occupied by private dwellings and boarding-houses, has been entirely torn down and rebuilt for the accommodation of dry-goods dealers." In the same paragraph that pays tribute to "our merchants, who constitute a calico aristocracy," the author observes that "[i]t

Figure 11. Matthew Hale Smith, *Sunshine and Shadow in New York*, frontispiece, 1868. (Courtesy of the Museum of the City of New York, gift of Grace M. Mayer)

disturbing sociohistorical developments, developments that challenge the dominant political ideology of democracy and liberty for all. In literature too, the same motifs occur, not as literary embellishments but as fundamental and often powerful structures of meaning. I want to look closely at two authors who described New York in the 1840s: Charles Dickens, in *American Notes* (1842), and Lydia Maria Child, in *Letters from New York*

Figure 12. C. M. Jenkes, *Astor Place Riot*, painting, 1849. (Courtesy of the Metropolitan Museum of Art, the Edward C. Arnold Collection of New York Prints, Maps and Pictures, bequest of Edward C. Arnold, 1954)

(started in 1841). Both were visitors to New York, to some extent genteel spectators writing for distant friends and thus panoramic in their movements and points of view. But both were also drawn into the city's depths and wrote of them as moralists and compassionate witnesses. Their striking similarities in choice of subjects and point of view show how certain ways of seeing New York had already become conventional. Their differences, partly gender-related, point to further nuances in the ideology of urban space. Both, however, show the power and effectiveness of certain traditional modes of viewing the city.

Dickens's *American Notes* reveals the variety and ingenuity of some of these urban conventions, which, in spite of their outrage over the book, many Americans admired and imitated. He begins, like the early maps of New York, with a sweeping panoramic view from the river which, in its careful use of detail, imitates the full impact of the city on the senses:

> I awoke from my nap in time to hurry up, and see Hell Gate, the Hog's Back, the Frying Pan, and other notorious localities, attractive to all readers of famous Diedrich Knickerbocker's History. We were now in a narrow channel, with sloping banks on either side, besprinkled with pleasant villas, and made refreshing to the sight by turf and trees. Soon

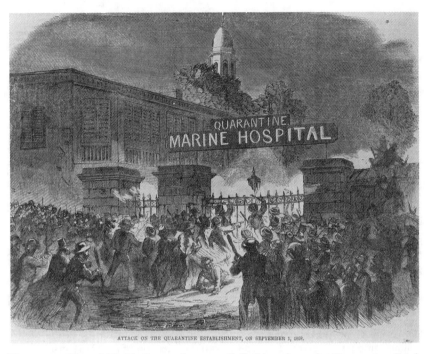

ATTACK ON THE QUARANTINE ESTABLISHMENT, ON SEPTEMBER 1, 1858.

Figure 13. *Harper's Weekly*, September 11, 1858, "Attack on the Quarantine Establishment on September 1, 1858." (Courtesy of General Research Division, The New York Public Library: Astor, Lenox and Tilden Foundations)

we shot in quick succession, past a lighthouse; a madhouse (how the lunatics flung up their caps, and roared in sympathy with the headlong engine and the driving tide!); a jail; and other buildings: and so emerged into a noble bay, whose waters sparkled in the now cloudless sunshine like Nature's eyes turned up to Heaven. (67–8)

This is urban picturesque at its most self-conscious. Nature appears in complete harmony with the city, and the city, even its howling lunatics, with it. All the noise and busyness of the port is embraced by a sympathetic spirit that harmonizes everything. And beyond nature, the whole scene is embraced by Washington Irving, the eminent American spectator whose *History of New-York* encloses Dickens's perception of the scene.

Dickens's survey of the city itself falls into three sections: a stroll down Broadway ending at the Tombs prison, a "plunge" into Five Points, and a fatigued account of the charitable institutions he visited. In this rather brief chronicle of his travels around New York – a good deal briefer, at any rate, than his description of Boston – Dickens falls into a number of the standard essayistic modes that Melville and many writers of his gen-

Police repulsing an attack by a mob on the offices of the New York Tribune during the draft riots of 1863. The Tribune's editor, Horace Greeley, recognizing the need for additional men if the North was to win, had come out for the Administration bill, which allowed the wealthy to buy substitutes if drafted. These views are from contemporary sketches in Harper's Weekly

Figure 14. *Harper's Weekly*, August 1, 1863, "The Draft Riots, 1863." (Courtesy of the Museum of the City of New York, gift of the Police Department of New York City)

eration adopted. One is that of the chatty guide: "Shall we sit down in an upper floor of the Carlton House Hotel (situated in the best part of this main artery [Broadway] of New York), and when we are tired of looking down upon the life below, sally forth arm-in-arm and mingle with the stream?" (69). Another is the satirist of the world of fashion: "Heaven save the ladies, how they dress! We have seen more colours in these ten minutes, than we should have seen elsewhere, in as many days. What various parasols! what rainbow silks and satins!" (69). Then there is the mournful jeremiad against capitalists: "Many a rapid fortune has been made in this street [Wall Street], and many a no less rapid ruin. Some of these very merchants whom you see hanging about here now, have locked up money in their strong-boxes, like the man in the Arabian Nights, and opening them again, have found but withered leaves" (70). And turning to sentimental anecdote, he takes a condescending look at two Irish immigrants who have difficulty reading a letter but have labored to bring a large family over from Ireland and maintain them in a "strange land" (70). This panorama of observations comes in the genteel and urbane diction so successful in both American and English journalism.

In his visit to the Tombs, however, Dickens announces his turn toward

another genre: "What is this dismal-fronted pile of bastard Egyptian, like
an enchanter's palace in a melodrama! – a famous prison, called The
Tombs. Shall we go in?" (71). We are entering the world of sensational
urban melodrama indeed, as Dickens describes a dark, airless prison
where the inmates sit gloomily in cells, unable even to exercise in the yard
and condemned to a life of hopeless anguish. A cheerfully callous guard
explains that the name of the prison derives from the suicides that took
place there when it was first built; and the prisoners lack clothes-hooks
because, "When they had hooks they *would* hang themselves, so they're
taken out of every cell" (73). Dickens views the execution yard, which he
calls a place of "frightful mystery," and then describes the prisoner's notion of his own space: "Between the criminal and them [the community],
the prison-wall is interposed as a thick gloomy veil. It is the curtain to his
bed of death, his winding-sheet, and grave. From him it shuts out life. . . .
All beyond the pitiless stone wall, is unknown space" (74). Like Bartleby's
lawyer, Dickens here walks a fine line between melodrama and philosophy. He moves adroitly from a sentimental account of chastened murderers to a terrifying image of the vast open space beyond the prisoner's –
or anyone's – wall.

Moving back into Broadway, Dickens then shifts to urbane humor on
the subject of pigs. Here he uses a popular and successful device, the
mocking evocation of genteel society:

> Here is a solitary swine, lounging homeward by himself. . . . He . . . leads
> a roving, gentlemanly, vagabond kind of life, somewhat answering to that
> of our club-men at home. He leaves his lodgings every morning at a
> certain hour, throws himself upon the town, gets through his day in
> some manner quite satisfactory to himself, and regularly appears at the
> door of his own house again at night, like the mysterious master of Gil
> Blas. (74)

The urbane diction – "lounging," "rambles," "gentlemanly, vagabond,"
"club-men" – points backward to the world of the Addisonian spectator
and forward to Melville's Ishmael and the paradise of bachelors. And the
mention of Gil Blas introduces another favorite theme, that of Le Sage's
Diable Boîteux, who raises the roofs of houses and reveals all within, in a
combination of the panoramic and labyrinthine views. Dickens's continuing remarks, that the pig is "in every respect a republican pig," "a great
philosopher," and "a prodigal son" (74–5), embellish the humor with
manifold allusions in ways that Ishmael often delights in.

As night comes on, the "bright jets of gas" (75) give the city a new
light and allow Dickens to make the ironic contrast so familiar to readers
in the 1840s, as, leaving the world of restaurants and amusements behind,
"[we] plunge into the Five Points" (76). Here all illusions of open space
and free travel disappear as he enters "these narrow ways, diverging to

the right and left, and reeking everywhere with dirt and filth" (76). Here too, with the exception of his visit to the Tombs, Dickens makes his first entry *into* anything, the "low" taverns of the sailors ("these haunts"), the "leprous houses" where people are dying of fever, the "cramped hutches full of sleeping negroes" (77–8). Characteristically, Dickens does not linger long over such dismal scenes. He manages to amuse himself even in Five Points by attending a "break-down" and enjoying the exuberant dancing of the "Five Point fashionables" (78).

Dickens ends his description of the evening with a moralistic refrain on the Tombs: "Look at them, man – you, who see them every night, and keep the keys. Do you see what they are? Do you know how drains are made below the streets, and wherein these human sewers differ, except in being always stagnant?" (79). Although the language is conventional, Dickens implicitly raises the level of his moral critique to a social and political one, involving every citizen. He continues in the political vein by concluding with his reflections on the great number of fires in New York: "It was more than hinted, in an official report, not long ago, that some of these conflagrations were not wholly accidental, and that speculation and enterprise found a field of exertion, even in flames" (80). Brief as these remarks are, they point directly to "the pernicious spirit of speculation" at the heart of New York's social and political life. Then, after a dutiful visit to the asylums and jails of Long Island, Dickens leaves New York.

Many nineteenth-century authors writing about the city owed a great debt to Dickens, as certainly Lydia Maria Child and Herman Melville did, and to the style of humorous-genteel-sentimental-melodramatic-ironic urban observation that he made successful. Lydia Maria Child's *Letters from New York* indicate that she adopted many of Dickens's techniques, but she also shows significant differences in the way she views urban space and the spectator's travels through it.[30] Like Dickens, Child is a visitor in New York, staying there only temporarily. But whereas Dickens sees himself as on his way to Philadelphia, Child is traveling toward what she calls the Infinite. Dickens moves about New York to record his impressions – or, one suspects, to confirm his prejudices – according to a predetermined itinerary. He knows exactly what he wants to see. Child wanders. She visits many of the same places Dickens did, but her main object is not the places themselves. Rather, she views them typologically, as embodiments of spiritual meaning. This moral and spiritual view of the city deepens the spectator's observations, so that even in her panoramic moments she looks labyrinthically beneath the surfaces of things.

Calling New York "the great Babylon," Child begins by announcing a change in her way of seeing phenomena:

There *was* a time when all these things would have passed by me like the flitting figures of the magic lantern, or the changing scenery of a

theatre, sufficient for the amusement of an hour. But now, I have lost
the power of looking merely on the surface. Every thing seems to me to
come from the Infinite, to be filled with the Infinite, to be tending
toward the Infinite. Do I see crowds of men hastening to extinguish a
fire? I see not merely uncouth garbs, and fantastic flickering lights of
lurid hue, like a tramping troop of gnomes, – but straightway my mind
is filled with thoughts about mutual helpfulness, human sympathy, the
common bond of brotherhood, and the mysteriously deep foundations
on which society rests; or rather, on which it now reels and totters.

But I am cutting the lines deep, when I meant only to give you an
airy, unfinished sketch. (14)

The last sentence exhibits some wavering, as she has just been proclaiming
her new power to cut deep, to look beneath the surface. The rest of the
statement, however, demonstrates clearly how she means her sketches to
differ from those of other urban spectators. The urban fire, which seemed
to Dickens an example of corrupt city politics and capitalist connivings,
seems to her an emblem of brotherhood and sympathy. Dickens, too,
talked about sympathy in his panoramic description of New York, describing it as the power that harmonizes nature and commerce. Child, however, sees it more labyrinthically, as the "mysteriously deep foundations
on which society rests." Then she qualifies that view, saying that perhaps
society "reels and totters," like a drunkard, on its base. Like Dickens, she
exhibits confidence in the power of sympathy, but she also fears false
appearances and knows that the foundations of society may not hold firm.

Whether Child adopts a panoramic strategy, sweeping across a variety
of subjects in one letter, or descends to a single, compelling, mysterious, or frightful point, she tends to look for an eternal truth behind the
mask of appearances that flicker before her like the images in a magic
lantern or theater. When she visits Five Points and the Tombs, for example, she looks beyond the scene rather than within it, as Dickens would:

It is said a spacious pond of sweet, soft water, once occupied the place
where Five Points stands. It might have furnished half the city with the
purifying element; but it was filled up at incredible expense – a million
loads of earth being thrown in, before perceivable progress was made.
Now, they have to supply the city with water from a distance, by the
prodigious expense of the Croton Water Works.

This is a good illustration of the policy of society towards crime. Thus
does it choke up nature, and then seek to protect itself from the result,
by the incalculable expense of bolts, bars, the gallows, watch-houses,
police courts, constables, and "Egyptian tombs," as they call one of the
principal prisons here. (27)

Child sees the filling in of Collect Pond as a kind of original crime that
has polluted the earth in a fundamental way. It is regrettable but appro-

priate, then, that the Five Points and prison now stand on that spot. Furthermore, although she sees that pollution as a great moral wrong, she also connects it with political wrongdoing. The filling in of the pond shows the same spirit that oppresses the poor and then punishes them, at great expense, for the crime of being poor. Dickens makes a similar point when he accuses society in his tirade at the Tombs: "you, who see them every night, and keep the keys." But by making the remarkable link between the Tombs and the vanished Collect Pond, Child deepens the crime, taking it to the "deep foundations on which society rests." In that sense, she sees the city not only as a physical labyrinth, but as a labyrinth in time and a political labyrinth as well.

Child extends the labyrinth metaphor throughout the *Letters* in a variety of ways. In a romantic mood, she rambles through Greenwood Cemetery, where "it is exceedingly easy for the traveller to lose his way in labyrinthian mazes" (50). Here, as in the many excursions she makes to suburbs and parks, she longs to lose herself in a natural labyrinth. In another moment, however, she yearns to save a four-year-old newsboy from "the deep and tangled labyrinth, where false echoes and winding paths conspired to make him lose his way" (95–6), a labyrinth both spiritual and social. She also sees the large urban crowds as a kind of labyrinth that threatens to swallow her up in its anonymous mass: "amid these magnificent masses of sparkling marble, hewn *in prison*, I am alone" (94). Her sense of loneliness and alienation is specifically urban: "It is sad walking in the city. . . . The loneliness of the soul is deeper, and far more restless, than the solitude of the mighty forest" (94). Like Dickens, Child is no stranger to cities – she speaks frequently of the beauty of Boston – but in New York she is "weary" and distressed by the pervasive poverty: "Hungry eyes, that look as if they had pleaded long for sympathy, and at last gone mute in still despair. Through what woful, what frightful masks, does the human soul look forth, leering, peeping, and defying, in this thoroughfare of nations" (94).

The oppressive sense of confinement leads Child to find relief in, of all things, a fire that decimates her neighborhood. By clearing the street, the fire opens up space: "This great fire, like all calamities, public or private, has its bright side. A portion of New-York, and that not a small one, is for once thoroughly cleaned; a wide space is opened for our vision, and the free passage of air" (114). But space continues to be a problem for Child, as she begins to feel increasingly hemmed in: "I am tempted to say of the Nineteenth Century, as the exile from New Zealand did of the huge scramble in London streets, 'Me no like London. Shove me about'" (129). She frequently compares the city to a prison and escapes by strolling along the Battery at night, where the ocean air and peaceful solitude give her some consolation. But even as the city oppresses her, her sense of "the Infinite" makes her see the labyrinthine streets and walls as permeable appearances, and she frequently arrives at a hopeful conclusion. After the fire has cleaned the street and opened it up, it leaves ruins: "Piles of stone and rubbish, left by the desolating fire, looked more hot and dreary than ever; they were building brick houses between me and the sunset" (162). The sight of a beggar child picking a clover blossom, however, changes her mind: "Then I saw plainly that walls of brick and mortar did not, and could not, hem me in" (163–4). Child sees that the city's structures embody social and political structures which the intellect can penetrate. The city is an illusion.

Both Dickens and Child, finding the city psychologically challenging, adopt a style suitable to the challenge. Dickens represents the vitality and variety of urban life through the many different styles and narrative modes he favors. He uses the pose of the friendly guide as a way of mitigating urban alienation and fear. He steps boldly into the urban underworld, taking his reader on a tour of the city's worst sights, but then steps just as boldly out, using the quick cut, the abrupt shift in tone from pathos to humor, as his escape. Through his impressive command of the city's terrain, his stylistic virtuosity, he remains firmly in control of the urban experience. Child, on the other hand, surrenders to the city's moods and ways, letting its terrain guide her footsteps as she wanders intuitively about the town. She makes a virtue of her rambling style, asserting that her digressions show "What a strange thing is the mind! How marvellously is the infinite embodied in the smallest fragment of the finite!" (25). Because she claims to be writing letters to an intimate friend, her writing serves the purpose of relief and therapy, as well as of conveying impressions and opinions. Stylistically and psychologically, then, Dickens remains on a panoramic plane whereas Child descends into a personal labyrinth. Although they agree on everything from temperance to slavery to prison reform to the evils of money and the basic goodness of children, these nuances of style reflect their subtle differences in point of view.

Of course, the two models of urban encounter offered by Dickens and Child suggest a gender dichotomy as well. Dickens's mastery of the city seems undeniably masculine, Child's surrender feminine. Elizabeth Wilson's analysis of an urban aesthetic makes it possible to discriminate between gendered modes of urban experience:

> In these [nineteenth-century European and American] cities the intelligentsia divided. Some immersed themselves in the new element of urban life – the *flâneurs* we have already encountered; others aimed to impose order, planning and control; yet others railed against the city altogether, and sentimentalised a lost rural idyll. The first two of these contrasting approaches might be said to correspond to a feminine and a masculine approach: surrender and mastery.[31]

Wilson's terms permit a reading of urban literature according to gendered modes of thought rather than to gender alone, especially as she associates the generally male flaneur with the "feminine" approach of surrender. They suggest, too, a way of placing Melville within this general scheme. For Melville seems, at different times in his career, to have adopted for his characters both patterns of mastery of and surrender to urban form. Indeed, Melville's adept use of the different urban styles and modes available to him may also help to explain the reluctance of early critics like Weaver, the Whites, Chase, and Arvin to consider his urban writing comparable with *Moby-Dick* in sophistication. Is it possible that, acknowledging in some part, as all these writers did, the place of the city in Melville's writing, it did not consort with their view of his "best" work as being his most masculine; that in his sea fiction they felt that Melville adopted an aesthetic of mastery, confident, spectatorial, and in control, like that of Dickens, whereas in his more obviously urban pieces, his characters surrender to the difficulties of the city in what seems a more feminine mode, doubting, wandering, and labyrinthine, like Child's? Have readers been made uncomfortable by a representation of the city that is less "successful" than his representation of the sea?

If such a reading influenced earlier twentieth-century critics, it need not hinder us now. In his representations of urban space, Melville borrowed from but avoided confining himself to cultural paradigms. Succeeding chapters will show that, even in his nautical fiction, he included various urban styles and structures, that he moved between "masculine" and "feminine" modes of encountering them, and that he developed these well before he took up the subject of the city more directly. In his urban fiction, his typical stance as narrator is neither that of the urban insider, the master of the city, nor that of the urban poet, the flaneur who surrenders to its moods. Rather, he adopts for his own purposes the urban structures and styles of his period, drawing from the characteristic narrative poses of the spectator in a large capital city, the provincial entering a labyrinth, and later, the sojourner in a wasteland City of Man, and the pilgrim in the cosmopolis or City of God. We shall see how these strategies allowed Melville to create fictional space within the constricted terrain of a town rapidly becoming a city.

2

Spectator in the Capital

═══════════

I come but to roam and see. "Rich Man's Crumbs" (298)

In Chapter 1, I discussed urban space as a political and social issue in Manhattan as it began to outgrow its original limits. Although by the time Melville began writing New York had by no means filled up its available space, it was already perceived as a great city competing with European capitals for commercial and cultural supremacy, yet also as a densely crowded place with insufficient public and private room for its newly expanding population.[1] The debates over urban plans that sought to control urban space show strong opposing sides: middle-class residents against speculators, working-class and poor tenants against landlords, immigrants competing with industry for the use of downtown space, unpropertied masses versus propertied elites. But the experience of the Melville family as it struggled to live, work, and move freely in New York suggests the attractions of an urban ideology that promised something for everyone. In spite of its shrinking and controlled space, as well as the opinion of many city dwellers that "great cities are not, to the mass of their inhabitants, favorable to the growth of virtue,"[2] New York appeared to many, as it had to Allan Melvill, as the great "commercial Emporium of our Country." The richness and variety of cultural responses to the city indicate that, even where there was ambivalence, as in the accounts of Dickens and Child, artists and writers eagerly made their own claims to urban space, traveling determinedly through its congested terrain. The political and social conflict over its uses, then, while creating anxiety and stress for many urban inhabitants, also produced an outpouring of popular literary forms.

Many of these popular works contribute to the cultural debate over urban space and growth by imaging the city in certain ways. More than mere metaphors, images of the city as Capital, Labyrinth, City of Man, City of God, and others like them, imply different underlying conceptions of urban form even when they describe the same city. The Capital, for example, growing out of the walled town, has a compact, centralized structure into which people and goods may flow freely, where money and ideas may circulate with ease. As a national showplace, it contains the institutions, universities, theaters, and markets that declare its distinctive culture and ideology. The Labyrinth, on the other hand, suggests an environment where such freedom of movement, such circulation of bodies, goods, and ideas, is blocked or deflected. This city resembles, not the ambitious urban designs of L'Enfant or Haussmann, with broad boulevards for walking and display, but the dense structure of old London or old New York. Many writers have described images of the city in literature, and certainly these images bring compelling symbolic resonances to urban writing.[3] In focusing on the implications of urban *form* in these images, however, I am drawing attention to the connection between urban form and literary form – that is, between the ways in which both display and contain conflicts over the uses of urban space.

It should be clear that when I talk about "urban space," either as physical space experienced by city dwellers or as it is represented in literary works, I am using a somewhat paradoxical term. "Space" implies limitless, free, open expanse. A town, however, as I defined it in the Introduction, encloses space and gives it form. By circumscribing space, by making it familiar and removing the terrors of limitlessness, a town soon makes space into place – that is, a landscape of known objects and landmarks.[4] Urban space, then, is domesticated, made intimate, like the houses, nests, and shells that Gaston Bachelard describes in *The Poetics of Space*.[5] In a town one could say that space is not a threatening issue, because there is neither too much of it, as there is on the ocean or the prairie, nor too little, as in a crowded city. A large city, however, which during its growth has managed to swallow up and control much more space than the town, has real spatial problems. On the one hand there is too much of it, as the city has grown beyond the size that inhabitants could domesticate and make familiar; and on the other there is too little, for residents must share the available space with more and more people, businesses, vehicles, and systems. Urban space, then, is by its nature peculiar space – space that is not space.

Add to that peculiarity the local features of a specific town or city, its history and social composition, and the notion of space becomes even more complex. As an abstract idea, urban space almost defies representation. Given a particular *form*, however, whatever that may be – plaza, forum, street, cellar – within a certain kind of city – colonial outpost, religious shrine, sin city – and urban space becomes imaginable. And when urban space is enclosed in literary representation, it becomes place in a fictional realm, a familiar landscape of urban images, modes of discourse, and signs.

When I talk about the Capital, then, as an urban form, I am not describing it solely as an image of urban life but as a social and literary construction of the city that gives form and meaning to otherwise bewildering urban space. Although urban capitals may have a certain structural form – the radial or grid plan or whatever – the important fact to the people who live there and generate its culture is how they experience its space. How do people move in this environment? How easy or difficult is it to traverse the city? Can one find space in which to live and work? How do people talk? What styles and codes do they use? We can ask these questions about a historical city, but they also apply to literary works.

In this chapter, I will be looking at the way New York appeared in certain literary productions as a bustling capital similar to eighteenth-century London in its preindustrial stage of development. This urban form calls up a particular urban protagonist – the middle-class, usually male, spectator based on Addison and Steele's creation but enhanced by the Knickerbocker nuances of Washington Irving, Nathaniel Parker Willis, and Lewis Gaylord Clark. The spectator's heroism is in part defined by his mastery of urban space, by the ease with which he travels through the town, reads its people and signs, and interprets them for urban readers. In drawing on this popular literary figure, Melville was, in part, as Perry Miller has so forcefully demonstrated, using the conventions that he thought would gain him acceptance in genteel literary circles.[6] But Melville made one important innovation: he transported the spectator, with his characteristic forms of discourse and modes of urban travel, into the Pacific. That in itself was not new: Washington Irving had done something similar for the American prairies and the European countryside. But Melville's Pacific space is social and contested ground. The spectator goes there not only to lose himself in nature but also to experience culture – the native culture of the islanders and his own urban culture as it collides with theirs.[7] Melville would later use many spectators in his urban fictions, from the man-about-town Harry Bolton of *Redburn* to the suave Glendinning Stanly of *Pierre*, from the New Yorkers of his magazine sketches to the cosmopolitans of *Israel Potter*, *The Confidence-Man*, and *Clarel*. In his earliest novels, *Typee, Omoo,* and *Mardi,* they may seem out of place. Spectators, after all, belong in cities; one cannot imagine the Addisonian spectator or the Parisian *flâneur* wandering through the Pacific. But by grafting a local urban form onto an exotic landscape, Melville challenges the genteel urban culture from which the spectator comes. Rather than using the convention to signal his being part of that culture himself, although indeed he was, Melville uses various subtle and some violent methods of discrediting the spectator. In *Typee* he lames him, in *Omoo* he imprisons him, and in *Mardi* he makes him into a murderer. This is not to say that Melville's sole purpose in transplanting the spectator to the Pacific is destructive; the spectator is far too useful and in some instances sympathetic a character for Melville to dispose of him. But as a figurehead for Melville's early efforts at cultural criticism, the spectator works both to lead the way and to reveal his own position as work of artifice.

The Spectator in New York

New York was political capital of the nation for only a few short years, but by the time Melville returned from his voyages in 1844, it had become America's commercial capital and was working hard to establish itself as a cultural capital as well. Although the Panic of 1837, which had contributed to the Melvill family decline and Melville's launching himself on the seas, left a legacy of economic turbulence throughout the antebellum period, the increased volume of trade from abroad and the interior boosted investors' and merchants' confidence, and with a steady rise in immigration and population, the city soon surpassed its rivals, Boston, Philadelphia, and Washington. Although, as the next chapter will show, this was also the period of growing consciousness of urban problems, producing a wide variety of reform movements and a literature of urban exposé, metropolitan pride also flourished, exhibiting itself in booster journalism, panoramas, architecture, and the arts. That urban confidence helps to explain the popularity of Melville's first novels; for he was able to capture the adventurous, entrepreneurial spirit of the capital even in his narratives of the sea, and to speak with the urbane accent many readers admired. Although he eventually came to distrust the class assumptions on which the spectator rested, Melville also found him a tremendously useful source for his own writing.

The literary figure of the spectator arose in England at the intersection of two historical phenomena: global exploration and urban growth. To some extent Addison and Steele adapted to the urban scene the methods of explorers like Cook, Byron, Bering, Bruce, and Wallis, who, pushing into previously unknown areas of Polynesia, Asia, and Africa, began to make the world seem to Londoners a knowable place. The names of England's most durable eighteenth-century works suggest the influence of travel on the arts: Swift's *Gulliver's Travels*, Sterne's *A Sentimental Journey*, Goldsmith's *A Citizen of the World*. Many others rely on travel as an essential element of the plot: Smollett's *Roderick Random*, Fielding's *Tom Jones*, Defoe's *The Adventures of Robinson Crusoe*, and Johnson's *Rasselas*. Even more striking is the number of London periodicals with names like *The Adventurer, The World, The Observer, The Lounger, The Rambler, The Idler, The Mirror, The Looker-On*, most of them outgrowths and imitations of *The Tatler* and *The Spectator*. These suggest the fertile ground that popular urban periodical writing found in travel literature and the implied promise of the journals – namely, that one did not have to leave the city in order to find the benefits and delights of travel. One had simply to ramble, lounge, hold up the mirror, and see; or read an author who did the same.[8]

But Addison's spectator inhabits an expanding city where the impact of foreign exploration is being felt in new commercial ventures, a larger and more cosmopolitan population, and an increasingly powerful middle class challenging the dominance of older elites. The spectator, by traveling through the city, maps and negotiates its terrain for his readers, educates them in the city's challenges, and, by attempting to establish a universal urban language and decorum, works to mediate those challenges. With moral purpose – to educate and unify a diverse population – a firm commitment to middle-class values and virtues, and a mission to establish new critical standards of taste, *The Spectator* aims to create an ideal city out of an urban crowd.[9]

That literary task requires and produces a particular kind of urban protagonist. The city's large size, its crowds and traffic, the vitality of its commerce, and the busy use citizens make of its public spaces impose certain demands on the spectator's character. In order to receive as many impressions as possible, he must remain detached, free to move everywhere, and relatively inconspicuous; and in order to absorb them all, he must maintain a posture of intellectual tolerance and self-restraint. He has offered himself up to a public life of unceasing activity, traveling through "most publick Places" where he cultivates men of every class: sometimes "thrusting my Head into a Round of Politicians at *Will's*," sometimes joining "the little Committee of Politicks in the Inner-Room [at St. James's Coffee-House] as one who comes there to hear and improve," and frequently attending the haunts of scholars, journalists, Tories, theatergoers, or "the Assembly of Stock-Jobbers at *Jonathan's*" where he may "sometimes pass for a Jew."[10] The spectator's extraordinary flexibility gains him access to the worlds of fashion, commerce, theater, family, government, and even the suburbs, yet only because he defines himself, though ironically, as an observer rather than a participant in these worlds:

> I never open my Lips but in my own Club. Thus I live in the World, rather as a Spectator of Mankind, than as one of the Species; by which means I have made my self a Speculative Statesman, Soldier, Merchant and Artizan, without ever medling with any Practical Part in Life. I am very well versed [though a bachelor] in the Theory of an Husband, or a Father, and can discern the Errors in the Oeconomy, Business, and Diversion of others, better than those who are engaged in them. . . . In short, I have acted in all the parts of my Life as a Looker-on. (4–5)

The spectator has complete confidence in his ability to play these parts and, more importantly, in the moral and social benefits his readers will derive from his efforts.

A vision of an ideal city, a great capital, sustains the Addisonian spectator's enterprise. He has prepared himself for his task by acquiring a genteel education at the university, followed by extensive travels throughout Europe and Egypt. Instead of returning to the small village where he was born, which has not changed since William the Conqueror's era, he settles in London, where he can make his discoveries available "for the benefit of my Contemporaries" (5). Here, as in Athenian Greece, he hopes to contribute to a lively intellectual culture. For "It was said of *Socrates,* that he brought Philosophy down from Heaven, to inhabit among Men; and I shall be ambitious to have it said of me, that I have brought Philosophy out of Closets and Libraries, Schools and Colleges, to dwell in Clubs and Assemblies, at Tea-Tables, and in Coffee-Houses" (44). This public urban culture attracts his ideal readers, an audience of "Brothers and Allies, I mean the Fraternity of Spectators who live in the World without having any thing to do in it; and either by the Affluence of their Fortunes, or Laziness of their Dispositions, have no other Business with the rest of Mankind but to look upon them. . . . In short, every one that considers the World as a Theatre, and desires to form a right Judgment of those who are the Actors on it" (45–6). Although Addison and Steele, along with their contemporaries Defoe, Richardson, Johnson, and Fielding, considered themselves as writing for a private domestic audience that included women – "there are none to whom this Paper will be more useful, than to the female World" (46) – they placed the spectator predominantly in a coffeehouse and theater culture of male fraternity.[11]

Melville, of course, would have absorbed this urban culture through his own education, which reflected the tastes of well-born Anglophile gentlemen like his father. As Redburn nostalgically recalls of his father's books, "there was a fine library edition of the Spectator, in six large volumes with gilded backs; and many a time I gazed at the word '*London*' on the title-page" (7). Himself a traveler, Allan Melvill had much firsthand knowledge of the spectator's native city, and also owned guidebooks like *The Picture of London for 1818.* Besides *The Spectator,* Melville might have read his father's volumes of *The Tatler* and *The World* or been amused by *The Celebrated Mrs. Pilkington's Jests; or The Cabinet of Wit and Humour. To Which Is Now First Added, a Great Variety of Bon Mots, Witticisms, and Anecdotes of the Inimitable Dr. Swift.* . . . He would also have encountered the didactic texts that shared the moral world of Addison's spectator. Allan Melvill owned Chesterfield's *Principles of Politeness and Knowing the World* and Gregory's *A Father's Legacy to his Daughters,* as well as Fenelon's *Treatise on the Education of Daughters.*[12] These and other moral works he recommended to Melville's cousin Guert Gansevoort in 1824: "Guide to Men & Manners – comprising Chesterfield's principles of Politeness, Burleigh's precepts, *Mothers advice to a Son* &c –" (*Log,* 19). In school Melville read Lindley Murray's *English Reader,* which consisted of moral essays by Blair, Johnson,

Addison, Goldsmith, Young, Fenelon, and Doddridge, as well as poems by Cowper, Milton, Thomson, Pope, Gay, and Gray.[13] These models of ethics, according to Murray, also provided models of style: "Purity, propriety, perspicuity, and, in many instances, elegance of diction, distinguish them. They are extracted from the works of the most correct and elegant writers."[14] Donald Davie calls this combination of moral and stylistic urbanity "chaste": "A chaste diction is 'central,' in Arnold's sense; it expresses the feeling of the capital, not the provinces. . . . The effect is a valuable urbanity, a civilized moderation and elegance; and this is the effect attainable, as I think by Goldsmith, and not by Shakespeare."[15] Goldsmith's urbanity held its sway over Allan Melvill's mind and directed the progress of his sons' education far more powerfully than did Shakespeare, who was to seize Melville's imagination only later.[16]

Although Donald Mitchell, one of New York's most popular spectators, might say that *The Spectator* "could and would never succeed now" in America,[17] the spectator prototype spread throughout the literary culture of New York. The advent of a "Silent Man" who produces "a Sheet-full of Thoughts every Morning" (Addison, 5) may have occurred as early as 1722 with Benjamin Franklin's Mrs. Silence Dogood (written by a man who educated himself by imitating *Spectator* essays). But it reached a pinnacle in Washington Irving's works, beginning with the *Letters of Jonathan Oldstyle, Gent.* in 1802 and the *Salmagundi* papers of 1807. Like those of the English spectator, Irving's essays combined travel with urban observation and an urbane style. Many of his early essays and stories in *The Sketch Book, Bracebridge Hall,* and *Tales of a Traveller* mingle his travels abroad with other forms – the urban sketch, folk or Gothic tale, or romantic landscape description. In works like *A Tour of the Prairies,* Irving successfully combined the graceful style of the urban spectator with the magnificent subject of the American landscape. And in his histories of New York and Spain, Irving traveled as effortlessly through time as he had done in cities and over plains. He created the Knickerbocker spectator, faithfully reproduced in Lewis Gaylord Clark's periodical, *The Knickerbocker Magazine,* which Melville's Uncle Peter Gansevoort carefully preserved.[18] It is certainly appropriate that, through Gansevoort Melville, Washington Irving was *Typee*'s literary godfather. In importing his urbane, witty style to the Marquesas, Melville was seizing Irving's American legacy.

That legacy spread its influence through the genteel New York press and its writers. Not wanting to appear crass provincial boors like the ones Dickens satirized in *Martin Chuzzlewit,* editors like Clark of *The Knickerbocker* used "The Editor's Table," his column of rambling, often sentimental observations of urban life, to create a world of civilized discourse through which to instruct readers in urban taste. Evert Duyckinck identified "a peculiar style of book, genial, humorous, and warm-hearted, which a race of New Yorkers seems sent into the world specially to keep up." At least among journalists and the merchant bourgeoisie to which Allan Melvill belonged, these writers canonized "a world where taste was respected, wit admired, erudition praised."[19] Melville would certainly have known the spectator literature inside out and would have understood its centrality to the literary culture of New York.

This is not to say that he did not see it and its pretensions satirically. In his first known appearance in print, the "Fragment from a Writing Desk, No. 1," published in the Lansingburgh *Democratic Press and Lansingburgh Advertiser* in 1839, Melville presents himself as a spectator in the "metropolis" of Lansingburgh writing to his friend M— in the city. Melville extravagantly mocks the spectator's manners, morals, and especially his self-satisfaction: "Pollux! what a comfortable thing is a good opinion of one's self!" (*PT*, 192). But the essay is most interesting in what it shows that Melville felt comfortable satirizing long before writing *Typee*. Rather than seeming, as Perry Miller and William Gilman imply, an anxious outsider trying to imitate Knickerbocker style and at the same time work his way into Democrat Young America literary circles, Melville appears here a self-confident literary persona, able to mock himself and the dominant literary conventions.[20]

The essay first makes fun of the scholarly M—; L.A.V. urges him to put down his "musty and withered" book and read his letter, which, in true Addisonian style, he has made "the vehicle of so much good sense, sterling thought, and chaste and elegant sentiment" (191). Then L.A.V. launches into a description of his own social graces, which, with some help from Lord Chesterfield, he has begun to improve:

> [I have come to] the conclusion that in this pretty corpus of mine was lodged every manly grace; that my limbs were modeled in the symmetry of the Phidian Jupiter; my countenance radiant with the beams of wit and intelligence, and my whole person, the envy of the beaux, the idol of the women, and the admiration of the tailor. And then my mind! why, sir, I have discovered it to be endowed with the most rare and extraordinary powers, stored with universal knowledge, and embellished with every polite accomplishment. (191–2)

Hence he not only conceives of himself as "a *distingue* [*sic*] of the purest water, a blade of the true temper, a blood of the first quality," but also re-creates provincial Lansingburgh as "my own metropolis," where he promenades "the Broadway of our village." Whereas the provincials "shuffle along the walk, with a quick, uneasy step, a hasty clownish motion," L.A.V. applies Chesterfield's advice by adopting "a slow and magisterial gait, which I can at pleasure vary to an easy, abandoned sort of carriage, or, to the more engaging alert and lively walk, to suit the varieties of time, occasion, and company." Calling himself "beautiful as Apollo, dressed in a style which would extort admiration from a Brummell, and belted round with self-esteem as with a girdle," he goes on to display his elegance in a lengthy paean to various unnamed beauties of Lansingburgh (192–3).

This pose, that of the most urbane citizen in a provincial society, lampoons the spectator's confidence in himself. It is very similar to the attitude Melville was to adopt for his urbane narrator Tommo, in *Typee*. The self-mockery suggests that, ably as Melville could employ the spectator's urbane diction and narrative technique, he also saw its silliness and affectation. The spectator in Melville's early novels becomes an urban type to criticize as well as a model to imitate.

More than literary tradition defines the spectator's characteristic style, however; he grows out of a particular urban form. For Irving, Clark, and Melville, the spectator conducts his travels within a world modeled on the structure of the old Walking City of Knickerbocker New York. This was the town Melville grew up in, and although it had changed noticeably by the time he returned in 1844, New York still had its heart in the area bounded by Fourteenth Street on the north, intersected by Broadway and the Bowery, and containing the Wall Street district, the Five Points, City Hall and the Park, Union Square, Washington Square Park, and Greenwich Village. Within this compact structure, working people still lived in or near their places of work; the middle class mingled in working-class districts; shops, shipping, and an active street life of scavenging and peddling made for a variety of commercial enterprises; the grid structure allowed travel along both axes through the city, north–south and east–west between the rivers, to flow directly, if not always rapidly, through the congested streets; business had not yet isolated itself from commerce, and much investing and Wall Street activity still took place in a busy coffee-house culture.[21] Journalists like Lydia Maria Child, Walt Whitman, or Edgar Allan Poe celebrated a city where one could stroll to the Battery and find fresh breezes, wander into picturesque streets, roam through a dense, exciting urban crowd, or sit at a distance and observe it from a cafe window.

The grid plan grew out of an urban ideology of growth and speculation. It expressed the city's confidence in that growth and in rational plans to contain and organize it. The spectator literature of New York also celebrates the city's expansive spirit and the flow of people and goods through an accessible, navigable terrain. Melville's *Typee*, written in the wake of his travels abroad and in the flush of his reacquaintance with the burgeoning cosmopolitan city of his youth, partakes of the spectator's joyous progress through a rich and stimulating landscape. But it is also deeply critical of the civilization the city represents and seeks to export, like its other goods, all over the world. In *Omoo* and *Mardi*, that criticism deepens until it seems that Melville's characters have not left the city behind but are traveling in

a Pacific landscape contaminated by urban life. Melville's narrators have
the spectator's freedom of movement and speculation, but these novels
evince only cautious optimism about his prospects.

A word about terminology. I have chosen in this chapter to maintain
the older word "spectator" for Melville's urbane ramblers, rather than
the term widely used in recent critical theory, the "flaneur."[22] The spectator and others of his fraternity – the lounger, idler, dandy, rambler,
bachelor, tattler, loafer, man-about-town, citizen of the world, cosmopolitan, observer, man in the street, bohemian, loiterer, amateur detective –
may appear to be aspects of one single urban type, different versions of
the flaneur.[23] This figure, the subject of Charles Baudelaire's poetry and
of Walter Benjamin's brilliant criticism, embodies modern fascination with
the city as a structural maze, a chaos of humanity, a noisy carnival, a
glittering market of modernity, and capitalism incarnate.[24] The flaneur,
as he appears in the wonderfully rich and varied literature on the subject,
is the poet of that city, representing the possibilities for an urban man
and an urban aesthetic.

Despite the wealth of material on the subject of the flaneur, I do not
find its application to antebellum American literature entirely satisfying.
It is not just that "flaneur" as a term is applied in contradictory ways, so
that he is seen on the one hand as a critic of modern capitalism and on
the other as a product of commodity culture like the wares in the arcades
he loves. But also, although "spectator" and "flaneur" seem to mean the
same thing, they come from different literary traditions and urban structures. The spectator belongs to the older world of the Walking City; he
can master his urban environment in a day's walk. The flaneur comes
from the Paris of Napoleon III and Baron Haussmann, who designed Parisian boulevards to accommodate the new traffic in horse-drawn vehicles.
Pedestrians had the use of wide sidewalks, but the arcades came more and
more to provide the experience of intimacy that had previously been offered by the streets. There the flaneur finds the crowds that delight his
intellect and senses. These differences in urban form do not signify much
for the second half of the nineteenth century, when New York made Fifth
Avenue its own version of the Champs Elysées, but for the New York of
Melville's youth, the spectator's London is more apt as a model. Furthermore, although the flaneur shares many of the spectator's characteristics,
the spectator lacks some of the flaneur's. Both present themselves as masters of the city, urban adventurers who seize the chance opportunities the
city provides. But the flaneur also has a strong romantic element that seeks
surrender to the city's aesthetic and sensual pleasures. Especially in America, where the moral-reform press held tremendous influence, much urban literature of the antebellum period explicitly warned seekers after
pleasure to mend their ways or go home to the suburbs. Given certain
exceptions, such as Poe's notable "The Man of the Crowd," Fanny Fern's

sketches, and Whitman's poems, the American sensibility resisted flaneurial tendencies until later in the century.

In relation particularly to Melville, the term is not useful. Melville's works contain many urban men, some of whom resemble the flaneur, many of whom do not. He has dandies like Harry Bolton and John Paul Jones; cosmopolitans like Dr. Long Ghost, Benjamin Franklin, the Cosmopolitan, Rolfe, and Jack Gentian; urban gentlemen like Redburn, Pierre, and Derwent; urban wanderers like the narrators of the sketches, Israel Potter, and Clarel; urbane sailors like Jack Chase, Ishmael, and Captain Vere; and urban underworld characters like Bland, Jackson, Claggart. A single term does not begin to cover this variety of urban characters, and instead diminishes the richness of Melville's irony, his attention to class distinctions, and the depth of his responses to a spectrum of urban forms, literary and literal.

Furthermore, Melville's early narrators simply do not have the flaneur's maturity and sophistication. They are, as this chapter will show, figures from an earlier tradition whom, even as he began to commit himself to a career as a writer and to an urban audience of readers, Melville held up for criticism. In *Typee*, the spectator and his urban culture can still be said to contain certain ideals. Probably as early as *Omoo*, however, and certainly by the time he wrote *Mardi*, Melville was prepared to satirize the self-confidence of the capital and its spectators with savage energy.

Typee: *The Polynesian Spectator*

Melville's use of the spectator in *Typee* allowed him to accomplish two of his goals. One was to pass among genteel readers in London and New York as one of them. Another was to create a witty and entertaining narrative. But clearly his bold seizure of this popular figure for his South Seas narrative produced some strain, which he did not foresee or adequately control. The narrator, Tommo, brings his urban habits of lounging, observing, and interpreting to the Marquesas. But he finds, as the narrator of "Man of the Crowd" discovers of his subject, that *"er lasst sich nicht lesen"* – it cannot be read.[25] The novel, then, in a sense unfolds the failure of the spectator, or of his philosophy, to read others in a dense cultural milieu. Nevertheless, Melville's narration remains anxious, rather than clearly resolved in its criticism of the spectator's failures.

Melville's choice of a narrator who speaks like a gentleman rather than a common sailor, who adopts the position of an insider in urban culture rather than a social interloper, deliberately brings the class assumptions that underlie the spectator's persona to the foreground. For Melville, these class issues profoundly influenced his survival in the literary marketplace; and, after all, he *was* a gentleman and not a common sailor. The reviews on both sides of the Atlantic testify that this theme found constant play. "When, too," said the review for *John Bull*, "we consider the style of composition, so easy, so graceful, and so graphic, we own the difficulty we feel in believing that it is the production of a common sailor." The *Critic* agreed that "[t]he author is no common man," and the *Times* found Melville "a very uncommon sailor, even for America, whose mariners are better educated than our own. His reading has been extensive . . . his style that of an educated man." The same writer made the next step by recommending the book as ideal for a sophisticated urban audience, "full of the captivating matter upon which the general reader battens . . . endued with freshness and originality . . . that cannot fail to exhilarate the most enervated and *blasé* of circulating library loungers." While denouncing Melville's evident admiration for cannibals, the review for the *London Quarterly Review* summed up the almost universal appraisal of the book: "With regard to the literary merits of the work, there can be, we apprehend, but one opinion. The style is clear, manly, and lively; the vivacity of the author is combined with the refinement of the gentleman."[26]

It was precisely this gentlemanliness, one suspects, that alienated the religious press in America, some of whose writers accused the book of being *too* urban. Said the reviewer for the *New-York Evangelist*, "The work was made, not for America, but for a circle, and that not the highest, in London, where theatres, opera-dancers, and voluptuous prints have made such unblushing walks along the edge of modesty as are here delineated." In the secular press, however, Nathaniel Hawthorne, Margaret Fuller, Charles Fenno Hoffman, and even Lewis Gaylord Clark, Mr. Knickerbocker himself, united in praising the book, and especially its style. Clark confessed, "We had perused this very entertaining work with a great deal of pleasure, from the easy, gossiping style of the author, and his constant and infectious *bonhommie*." In what seems to represent the critical consensus, Hiram Fuller's piece in the *New York Evening Mirror* concluded: "The style has a careless elegance which suits admirably with the luxurious tropical tone of the narrative, and we cannot read the book without suspecting the author to be at least as well acquainted with the London clubhouses as with the fore-castle of a merchant-man."[27]

It seems clear that Melville intended his narrative of life among the cannibals to capture and amuse a London audience. The state of contemporary copyright laws made it necessary that he appeal to English readers before he could sell the book in America. It had to have a lively and "racy" quality that was lacking in most travel narratives of the day. As Melville later pointed out in his own review of J. Ross Browne's *Etchings of a Whaling Cruise*, "of late years there have been revealed so many plain, matter-of-fact details connected with nautical life that at the present day the poetry of salt water is very much on the wane" (*PT*, 205). Even though Melville depended upon a library of "plain, matter-of-fact" books in the writing of *Typee*,[28] he did not imitate the style of these, nor of the sea narratives of Dana or Cooper. Indeed, much as he admired both these writers, they lacked the stylistic flair to which he aspired: "The perusal of Dana's Two Years Before the Mast, for instance, somewhat impairs the relish with which we read Byron's spiritual address to the ocean" (205). Melville was determined to avoid a "book of unvarnished facts," as he called *Etchings of a Whaling Cruise* (205).[29] He must seem to his readers to know the inside not only of a vessel but of a club, to understand and share the tastes of urban readers. Fortunately for him, during the time he was writing *Typee* he had for literary advisor and model a young gentleman living in London and observing the habits of its readers – his brother Gansevoort Melville.

Combined in Gansevoort were the graces and affectations of the true Knickerbocker type. Although it was Herman whom Allan Melvill described as "an honest hearted double rooted Knickerbocker of the true Albany stamp" (*Log*, 25), Gansevoort had the advantage of the true New York stamp. At an early age, he impressed his family with his looks and charm, his grace in dancing, and his abilities as a "distinguished classical scholar" and orator (*Log*, 43). Although forced to take over his father's fur and cap shop after his death, he did not long remain a merchant. When the fur business failed he went to New York, where he rather reluctantly studied law. His diary and letters, however, show that he pursued a variety of literary interests, reading and writing down his opinions of Byron, Scott, and "Watts on the Improvement of the Mind" (*Log*, 62). In 1842, while Herman was at sea, Gansevoort commenced making political speeches in New York and in 1843 began campaigning for candidate Polk. The reviews of his speeches, like those of *Typee*, indicate that critics admired his style, which they seemed to find witty and urbane, as much as what he said: "His language was chaste, refined and humorous withal, which like a charm, enlisted the undivided attention of the audience. . . . the audience were perfectly electrified." "[H]e held the attention of his audience for two hours and a half . . . embellishing his discourse with all the graces of oratory, the keenest wit, and passing alternately 'from grave to gay, from lively to severe.' " He gave "an address sparkling with wit, and interspersed with vehement and startling appeals which went like a shock of electricity through every breast" (*Log*, 183–4, 185, 186). Although Horace Greeley bluntly called Gansevoort Melville's speeches "too much gas and glory" – their Tammany politics did not agree with him (*Log*, 186) – President Polk rewarded his labors with a position in the American legation in London, where the young orator settled in and bought *The Canons of Good Breeding: or The Handbook of the Man of Fashion. By the Author of "The Laws of Etiquette."*[30] There also he met Washington Irving, showed him Melville's manuscript, and with him "walked arm in arm to Wiley and Putnams" (*Log*, 202).

Since Gansevoort never wrote anything except letters and journals, he has not generally been considered as a literary influence on Melville,[31] but probably no one made a more direct impression on Herman's early writings. Five years before Melville wrote the "Fragments," Gansevoort was reveling in Byron and using the kind of heightened language that his brother would later satirize (*Log*, 60); it is possible, in fact, that the M— of the first "Fragment" is an exaggerated portrait of Gansevoort. Herman probably learned from and shared Gansevoort's early appreciation of Scott (*Tales of a Grandfather*) and Cooper (*The Prairie*). Because of Gansevoort's membership in the Albany Young Men's Association, Herman was able to join at fifteen and use the library there.[32] Most important, though, is the fact that Gansevoort was a trusted and active partner in the preparation of *Typee*. Melville gave him full authority not only to act as his agent with Murray but also to correct proofs, approve revisions, and see the copy through the press. Whether or not Gansevoort made suggestions for the later chapters that Herman sent on after Murray accepted the book, his remarks show that he had strong opinions about them: "The bulk of the new matter consists of three new chapters, numbered respectively 20 – 21 – & 27, which are in my humble opinion less amenable than the others to the faults you have pointed out, and from their subject matter, especially that of Chapter 27, will go far to give a more life-like air to the whole" (*Log*, 200–1). Gansevoort was responsible for obtaining Wiley and Putnam as Melville's American publisher, and arranged and rearranged the terms. During the long hours when he corrected the proofs he noted the "intrinsic merits" of the book and worked tirelessly to represent Herman's wishes to Murray: "He seems to regard them [certain corrections] as of importance & I should be sorry to have them overlooked" (*Log*, 203, 201). Melville later depended on his sisters as copyists and on his brother Allan as agent, but Gansevoort's letters and diary indicate a much closer literary sympathy, bordering on a collaboration between them, than Melville achieved with anyone else except his wife, Elizabeth. Perhaps when he offered Hawthorne the materials for the "Agatha" story in 1852, he had in mind something like the literary partnership he and Gansevoort had briefly enjoyed.

Gansevoort Melville was an urbane young man who, in the years his brother spent at sea, developed his political and oratorical skills so far as to win a brilliant consular post in London, something which Herman spent much of his maturity trying to achieve. Although Melville certainly contributed to and cultivated the myth that he was something of a savage, as Gansevoort himself implied several times (*Log*, 110, 187), he did not hesitate to make use of so convenient a model of the urban gentleman and spectator. The characteristic narrative pose and language of *Typee* show Melville consciously, even ostentatiously, imitating the spectator's voice.

That voice assumes the gentlemanly diction of the spectator, adopts a panoramic view, and speaks from the vantage point of urban civilization. Tommo reminds the reader that the book was written right in New York: "Even now, amidst all the bustle and stir of the proud and busy city in which I am dwelling, the image of those three trees seems to come as vividly before my eyes as if they were actually present" (244). Many of the reviews, in fact, played on the notion of the sailor-hero completely at home in the city, spinning his nautical yarns to a group of friends. One characteristic account conveys the myth that Melville worked assiduously to spread:

> after five years wandering, on the ocean, he landed "one fine day," some six years ago at the Battery, walked to his brother's office in 14 Wall street, and after being reintroduced to his family and friends, amused his leisure by writing down the recollection of his adventures; when finished, he gave the manuscript to his brother Gansevoort, who was about proceeding to London as Secretary of Legation, and from his hands it got into those of Murray, the well known publisher of Albemarle st., who finally printed it in the Colonial Library. We believe this to be the simple history of one of the most charming semi fictions of the present times. Written without effort, it carries the reader along by the grace of its composition, the piquancy of its anecdotes, and the apparent truthfulness of its narrations.[33]

We know, of course, that Melville arrived at Boston, not New York; that Allan worked at Number 10, not Number 14, Wall Street; that Melville wrote some of the book in Lansingburgh; that, as Gansevoort's letters show, he took considerable care and felt great anxiety in the writing of it. He wrote the book probably, not so much to "amuse[. . .] his leisure" or, as Willis put it, to "beguile[. . .] the long winter hours of his own home circle," but because, as his biographer J.E.A. Smith said, writing aside, "One could not well see to what profession he was adapted" (*Log*, 188). The style of *Typee*, however, convinced readers that Melville was an unencumbered, casual narrator, writing effortlessly and freely of his travels. Indeed, although the book contains action and adventure, the bulk of it is static and nostalgic: a series of reflections made by a spectator obviously detached in time and place from the events. Tommo never fully abandons his panoramic distance, never succumbs utterly to the Typee point of view. Maintaining, or seeming to maintain, the spectator's distance helped Tommo to "pass" among genteel urban readers.

Tommo seems to relish the role of spectator in Polynesia, however, with some of L.A.V.'s delight in impressing the provincial inhabitants of his little village. This role-playing and the urban-centered language Tommo uses produce much of the book's genial humor, which so charmed his readers. For example, he describes three inmates of his Marquesan house as "dissipated, good-for-nothing, roystering blades of savages" and others as "lovely damsels, who instead of thrumming pianos and reading novels, like more unenlightened young ladies" (85), pound tappa into cloth. The allusions to civilization are meant to establish the superiority of Typee life, but they insistently remind urban readers of their own world. A woodland path is "the grand thoroughfare of Typee" (90), much as the main street of Lansingburgh, in Melville's first "Fragments," was a Broadway. Marheyo, a Polynesian man about town, resembles an "English squire [who] . . . regales his friends at some fine old patrimonial mansion" (96). While granting that the Typees are cannibals, Tommo declares that "a more humane, gentlemanly, and amiable set of epicures do not probably exist in the Pacific" (97). Numerous urban references surround his descriptions of the Ti, "a sort of Bachelors Hall," a "savage Exchange, where the rise and fall of Polynesian Stock was discussed" (157). Tommo attends the dinners there, "like those gentlemen of leisure who breakfast at home and dine at their club" (151). Mehevi presides "like a gentleman doing the honors of his mansion" over the sumptuous meals, and Tommo reflects "that bachelors, all the world over, are famous for serving up unexceptionable repasts" (158). Kory-Kory, Tommo's "valet," appears "like a dandy at a ball-room door" (161), and even Tommo, again like the narrator of the Lansingburgh "Fragments," joins the festive crowd "with the slow and dignified step of a full-dressed beau" (162).

These remarks indicate that the genteel world of leisure and fashion is never far from Tommo's mind. He draws on it again and again, as L.A.V. did, to make fun of a provincial society where he sees himself as the most urbane inhabitant. More than the jokes, however, his characteristic language and observations show his essential detachment from the islanders. He distances himself even physically, as when he describes the sound of the tappa hammers: "When several of these implements happen to be in operation at the same time, and near one another, the effect upon the ear of a person, *at a little distance*, is really charming" (148; emphasis mine). More often, through the use of words like "scene," "sketch," and "spectacle," Tommo frames events, becoming Addison's spectator or Irving's scene painter, and an essentially noncommittal, even at times unconscious, observer: "forgetful alike of my own situation, and the vicinity of my still slumbering companion, I remained gazing around me, hardly able to comprehend by what means I had thus suddenly been made a spectator of such a scene" (49). The act of contemplating a scene immediately stops action, confuses consciousness, and makes the narrator "forgetful." In a particularly striking image, Tommo compares a French admiral to a Polynesian king, with adverse reflections on the "splendid Frenchman." Yet he immediately withdraws from the visual image into "the thoughts that arose in my mind as I gazed upon the novel spectacle before me. In truth it was an impressive one, and little likely to be effaced. I can recall even now with vivid distinctness every feature of the scene" (29). Nevertheless, he gives few details, and such a remark almost always indicates a reluctance to describe the "spectacle" or "scene" with any distinctness at all. "I will not recount every hair breadth escape, and every fearful difficulty that occurred before we succeeded in reaching the bosom of the valley" (65). After a particularly vague description of Fayaway – "strange blue eyes," skin "inconceivably smooth and soft" (86) – he asserts defensively that "[t]his picture is no fancy sketch; it is drawn from the most vivid recollections of the person delineated" (86). Yet the word "scene" or "sketch" usually indicates a startling *loss* of memory: "Amidst these novel scenes a week passed away almost imperceptibly" (97).

This habit of viewing life in scenes displays Tommo's urbane cast of mind. For all his protestations, he does not join fully in the passions and desires of the islanders. Rather, he expects to be entertained: "I felt in some sort like a 'prentice-boy who, going to the play in the expectation of being delighted with a cut-and-thrust tragedy, is almost moved to tears of disappointment at the exhibition of a genteel comedy" (128). Like the London or New York spectator, Tommo sees the world as a theater for his private viewing, for his voyeurism and consumption. In many ways *Typee* does resemble a genteel comedy, a spectacle of island life wrought for urban bachelors. Similarly, as Tommo remarks, it is an exhibition, like the urban panoramas or those exhibitions of natural history viewed by city dwellers in museums. Kory-Kory, the prime example of such an exhibition, is "covered all over with representations of birds and fishes, and a variety of most unaccountable-looking creatures, [which] suggested to me the idea of a pictorial museum of natural history, or an illuminated copy of 'Goldsmith's Animated Nature' " (83). Tommo, presenting himself here in the guise of a literary anthropologist, verges at times on voyeurism, framing the islanders as pictures in an exhibition.

These references, however, are still conventional, casual, and humorous. They would not point to a darker side of Tommo's spectating, nor would they intrude themselves on the reader's notice, except that Tommo himself reveals anxiety. Tommo's observation comes to an important and for him dangerous turning point when he meets Marnoo, the Polynesian spectator. This "taboo" man appears midway through the novel and also midway through a chapter on "taboo" itself. Tommo has just succeeded in breaking one of the tribe's gender taboos by getting the priests to allow Fayaway to travel around the inland lake with him in a canoe. This act appears as a gesture of male feminism on his part: "for the life of me I could not understand why a woman should not have as much right to enter a canoe as a man" (133). Tommo believes, as he has read in the "Young Men's Own Book," in the uplifting influence of "the society of

virtuous and intelligent young ladies" (132) and would like to allow Fayaway to exert her influence even further by joining him in the boat. He
hopes to secure her "emancipation" as well as his own improvement:
"Ridiculous, indeed, that the lovely creatures should be obliged to paddle
about in the water, like so many ducks, while a parcel of great strapping
fellows skimmed over its surface in their canoes" (133). At the same time,
his emancipation of Fayaway produces greater leisure and pleasure for
him. Kory-Kory rows the boat while they recline; and, in the book's most
famous and erotic moment, Fayaway makes her body into a mast for a
tappa sail, displaying herself for Tommo's ecstatic spectating. Truly, at this
moment, Tommo would seem to have raised spectating to an unprecedented height; never has it appeared so successful.

At just this moment Marnoo arrives. The ensuing scene produces an
extraordinary reversal, as Tommo sees in Marnoo a man far more urbane
and successful than himself. Marnoo is, first of all, tremendously popular,
"Some distinguished character, I presume, from the prodigious riot the
natives are making" (135). Tommo's first feeling is one of damaged vanity: "So vain had I become by the lavish attention to which I had been
accustomed, that I felt half inclined, as a punishment for such neglect, to
give this Marnoo a cold reception" (135). His pique, however, gives way
to admiration when he sees that Marnoo is "one of the most striking
specimens of humanity that I ever beheld" (135). Marnoo is physically
beautiful, a "Polynesian Apollo" whose ringlets curling around his head
and neck, an oval countenance, beardless cheeks, and skin of "feminine
softness" (136) resemble far more the surviving portrait of Gansevoort
Melville than a typical Marquesan (Figure 15). And, like Gansevoort's,
"the effect he produced on his audience was electric" (138). Marnoo also
possesses all of Gansevoort's skill in the verbal arts: "He had a word for
everybody; and turning rapidly from one to another, gave utterance to
some hasty witticism, which was sure to be followed by peals of laughter"
(138). He is steeped in the politics of the island and has arrived with news
of recent developments among the French at Nukuheva, the island's capital, bringing much fresher intelligence than Tommo's. Although Tommo
cannot understand what Marnoo says, he is impressed by his oratory: "The
grace of the attitudes into which he threw his flexible figure, the striking
gestures of his naked arms, and above all, the fire which shot from his
brilliant eyes, imparted an effect to the continually changing accents of
his voice, of which the most accomplished orator might have been proud"
(137). Whipping up the passions of his audience, he "exhorted the Typees to resist these encroachments [of the French]; reminding them, with
a fierce glance of exultation, that as yet the terror of their name had
preserved them from attack, and with a scornful sneer he sketched in
ironical terms the wondrous intrepidity of the French, who, with five war-
canoes and hundreds of men, had not dared to assail the naked warriors

Figure 15. Miniature portrait of Gansevoort Melville, 1836. (Courtesy of Gansevoort-Lansing Collection, Rare Books and Manuscripts Division, The New York Public Library: Astor, Lenox and Tilden Foundations)

of their valley" (138). No less than Gansevoort, the fiery spokesman for the Mexican War, does Marnoo stir his listeners, who "stood regarding him with sparkling eyes and trembling limbs, as though they were listening to the inspired voice of the prophet" (138).

A brilliant speaker, a passionate politician, Marnoo also sways the crowd in an area where Tommo felt himself in command: "I am, indeed, very much inclined to believe that Marnoo, with his handsome person and captivating manners, was a sad deceiver among the simple maidens of the island" (138). Tommo has congratulated himself on his popularity and success among the islanders, but Marnoo puts him completely out of countenance: "I easily perceived that he was a man of no little consequence . . . ; that he possessed uncommon talents; and was gifted with a higher degree of knowledge than the inmates of the valley. For these reasons, I therefore greatly feared lest having, from some cause or other, unfriendly feelings toward me, he might exert his powerful influence to do me mischief" (138). It turns out, however, that Marnoo has contrived to produce exactly this reaction in Tommo by deliberately ignoring him until his presence among the Typees has created a favorable impression. Then he explains the meaning of his extraordinary status and special knowledge of the island: "me taboo" (139).

Tommo has learned about taboo from his own experience of being frustrated by the tribe's prohibitions. He also knows that certain men, by nature of their "friendly relations with some individual belonging to the valley, whose inmates are at war with his own, may, under particular restrictions, venture with impunity into the country of his friend" (139).[34] Marnoo has acquired this special status and hence may travel freely throughout the island, protected from harm and "held as sacred" (140). He has also managed to voyage among the whites and learn their language because of his "natural quickness" and other advantages. He thus has it in his power to negotiate among the varied social groups of the island and at the same time to maintain a privileged distance. He is, then, the Polynesian spectator, a true citizen of the world.

Tommo reacts to the challenge Marnoo presents with misgiving, a great loss of confidence. From the time of Marnoo's departure, a good deal of the zest seems to go out of his island holiday: he begins to suspect the villagers of wanting to eat him; his spectating appears to give him little pleasure as he begins to toss off chapters of anthropological filler; and he redoubles his efforts to escape. These come to a head in his second significant contact with taboo, the mystery surrounding tattooing, which the natives begin to insist that he undergo. The tattooing is, he recognizes, a social custom and local art form. If "taboo," as he understands it, works something like "the canons of good breeding" (221) with which he is already familiar (a phrase that echoes Gansevoort once again), it might seem that he could politely decline. Or, as he did with Fayaway's sailing, he could prevail on the priests to make an exception. But tattooing is also invested with religious significance, and during the time he is being tattooed, a man is taboo, isolated much as is a woman "in an interesting situation" (222). Tommo reveals at this point that he himself has been declared taboo by Mehevi after Toby leaves the valley, and until now Tommo has enjoyed the privileges of his "sacred investiture" (222). But now he finds that his taboo cannot protect him; instead of being able to live as spectator among the islanders indefinitely, enjoying the exhibition of their genteel comedy, he must face the fact that they now mean to make an exhibition out of *him*. The Typees see tattooing as art on a "hu-

man canvas" (218), for them a serious and literal counterpart to Tommo's scene painting. Tommo, however, recoils at the idea that "I should
be disfigured in such a manner as never more to have the *face* to return
to my countrymen" (219). Furthermore, the tattooing means conversion.
It is a religious rite intended to make him one of them. From this point
on, Tommo's position as privileged spectator is vitally threatened and
threatening. He realizes that he is on the point of being incorporated into
the tribe in an act of symbolic cannibalism that would make a spectacle
of him, and he resolves to escape as soon as possible.

In the end, Tommo is saved by the institution of taboo. Marnoo organizes a rescue mission led by taboo islanders, and under their protection Tommo gets away. For all the book's trenchant criticisms of
Civilization and the missions, for all Tommo's assertions that the Typees
"enjoyed an infinitely happier, though certainly a less intellectual existence, than the self-complacent European" (124), his urbane narration
reveals that he prefers being in a place where he is the number one spectator. In fact, the enthusiastic response Melville received to his South Seas
yarns, his discovery that back in New York his life among the cannibals
made him a Marnoo in civilization, surely propelled the writing of *Typee*
in the confident style he gave it. In the writing of *Omoo* and *Mardi*, however, he was not able to hold on to his magic taboo. In these books, the
spectator's mastery of his subject is challenged not only by the Pacific
islanders but by the narrator's own increasing self-doubts.

Omoo: *The "Man About Town" Sort of Life*

> The title of the work – Omoo – is borrowed from the dialect of the
> Marquesas Islands, where, among other uses, the word signifies a rover,
> or rather, a person wandering from one island to another, like some of
> the natives, known among their countrymen as "Taboo kannakers."
>
> (*Omoo*, xiv)

Such a rover was Marnoo, and Tommo admired his intelligence, charisma,
and freedom to move among the hostile tribes of the valley. But Tommo
is not himself a rover in *Typee*. In spite of his daring escape from the *Dolly*
and his intrepid journey through the mountains, he does little traveling
once he arrives. His roving takes the form of leisurely strolling through
the settlement, and for most of the novel he is held captive, partly by the
natives, partly on account of a mysterious injury in his leg. His rambling
occurs more in the manner of his narration, which moves dilatorily over
the subject of Polynesian society, than in any physical journeys. In *Omoo*
the same character, now called Typee, has the opportunity for more vig-
orous and sustained travel once he escapes from his captivities, first on
board the *Julia* and later in the Tahitian prison, the Calabooza Beretanee.

But the nature and meaning of his spectating is quite different in *Omoo* from what he encountered in *Typee*, and his roving takes on an entirely different significance in relation to urban civilization and his urban readers. For now the narrator assumes the point of view of the Polynesians, witnessing the rovers and their depredations of native culture, rather than that of New York. He sees the rovers, white sailors cruising through the islands of Tahiti, as degenerates rather than as gentlemen or taboo kannakers. The rovers have lost the aura that invested Marnoo, and *Omoo*'s spectators – Dr. Long Ghost and Typee himself – fall far short of the Polynesian ideal.

Melville appears in *Omoo* to have moved far away from the urban-centered gentility of *Typee*. The book contains few of the jocular references to New York blades and damsels, clubmen and stockbrokers, ballrooms and boudoirs. The style is far less ingratiating, making less effort to seduce urban readers with the charms of Polynesian groves, island maidens, and quaint barbaric customs. Even less than *Typee* does *Omoo* concede to the moral concerns of its readers, continuing the attack on missionaries mounted in *Typee* and displaying a wanton disregard of genteel notions of temperance or chastity. Nor does Typee completely disassociate himself from the wickedness being practiced around him. He does not succumb to the drunkenness and brutality of the sailors nor to Doctor Long Ghost's lasciviousness, but he does not distance himself from these goings on either, and he stoutly declares his solidarity with the men during the mutiny. Only by a slight degree of decorum and wit in his narration does Typee avoid falling into the debased condition of his subjects, the broken-down white parasites of the Pacific. Only a very fine line seems to separate the civilized from the savage in his narration.

That fine line, however, is exactly Typee's point. As he would ask rhetorically in *Israel Potter,* so Melville seems to ask in *Omoo:* "What separates the enlightened man from the savage? Is civilization a thing distinct, or is it an advanced stage of barbarism?" (*IP*, 130). At every point in the narrative Typee implicitly tests the boundaries of *civitas* by showing the disastrous condition of both natives and whites in Polynesia. His urbanity always in danger of being destroyed by contact with savage sailors, immoral cosmopolitans, reckless beachcombers, and corrupted islanders, Typee finds that he no longer has the protection of his urban taboo. The danger now is not, as it was in *Typee*, that he will be eaten, but that he will simply lose his identity, or the positive value of that identity, as a member of urban white society.

Typee is at risk because city and wilderness are no longer distinct realms. In *Typee* the city is a defined environment where the book is written, bought, and read, where terms like "Stock Exchange" and "dandy" have clear references, and where the spectator-narrator feels himself at home. In *Omoo*, however, the Edenic world of the South Seas has become urbanized, contaminated by its contact with white civilization, degraded, not raised, by the Wall Street spirit of colonization. As a result, the wilderness is no longer a wilderness, and the city no longer contained within its boundaries. It has spread all over the world, so that wherever Typee roams he cannot escape the evidence of civilization. Even when he visits a seemingly untouched kingdom like the vale of Tamai, his cosmopolitan companion, Long Ghost, comes along to corrupt the maidens and exploit his opportunities. At one point, when the two men consider a longer stay in Tamai, Long Ghost mocks his own citified accomplishments and the uses to which they might be put: "Ha! ha! I'll put up a banana-leaf as physician from London – deliver lectures on Polynesian antiquities – teach English in five lessons, of one hour each – establish power-looms for the manufacture of tappa – lay out a public park in the middle of the village, and found a festival in honor of Captain Cook!" (245). But as Typee has shown throughout the novel, just such improvements, just such entrepreneurial visions on the part of white settlers, have destroyed the native economies and societies. Long Ghost's very urbanity is at the heart of the devastation brought on by the whites.

Typee, then, to some extent distances himself from the spectator's urbanity, plays second fiddle to Long Ghost, and avoids direct contact with the natives in *Omoo*. There is no dalliance with a Tahitian Fayaway, no devoted friendship with someone like Kory-Kory – the only male friendship, with Kooloo, is a hypocrisy – no convivial social life such as he enjoyed with Mehevi and the men of the Ti – in fact, no prolonged contact of any sort; he spends the first half of the novel among his own kind, in irons, and the second half wandering throughout the region making only brief sojourns in any one place. It is hard to understand, then, why *Omoo* seemed to so many of its readers to have recaptured the successful urbanity of *Typee*. In London the *Spectator* hailed its "fluent vivacious style." As before, reviewers could not believe that such prose could come from a common sailor: "From his narrative we gather that this literary and gentlemanly common-sailor is quite a young man. His life, therefore, since he emerged from boyhood, has been spent in a ship's forecastle, among the wildest and most ignorant class of mariners. Yet his tone is refined and well-bred; he writes like one accustomed to good European society, who has read books and collected stores of information, other than could be perused or gathered in the places and amongst the rude associates he describes" (*Log*, 249). The *Times* reviewer wondered if Melville were really American, because of his "many easy references to English literature and to London."[35]

Although American reviewers fretted over the book's morals and its veracity, many found *Omoo* as enjoyable as *Typee*, if not more so. Evert Duyckinck enthused at length: "It is not altogether the truthfulness of these sketches, however, that constitutes their great charm – a daguerreotype could be merely accurate; it is the warmth, the tropical luxuriance, the genial flow of humor and good-nature – the happy enthusiasm, gushing like a stream of mellow sunshine from the author's heart – all these, and a thousand nameless beauties of tone and sentiment, are the captivating ingredients of 'Omoo' " (*Log*, 245). Walt Whitman praised the book's judicious moderation: "not so light as to be tossed aside for its flippancy, nor so profound as to be tiresome." Horace Greeley, though voicing doubts about the moral tone of the book, had to say that "[f]ew living men could have invested such scenes, incidents and persons as figure in 'Omoo' with anything like the charms they wear in Melville's graphic pages" (*Log*, 248).[36]

Just as puzzling as these nineteenth-century effusions is the strain of twentieth-century readings of *Omoo* as light, insubstantial humor. D. H. Lawrence, himself a rover, remarked: "Perhaps Melville is at his best, his happiest, in *Omoo.*" Newton Arvin spoke of the book's being "written in a period of emotional freedom and effervescence," as an "easy and emotionally liberating current of humorous narrative," lightened by "Long Ghost's jolly philandering." Both critics, however, added significant qualifiers that indicate, I think, the fundamental ways in which the book has been misunderstood. Lawrence went on to say of Melville that, "For once he is really reckless. For once he takes life as it comes. For once he is the gallant rascally epicurean." By this, Lawrence means that in *Omoo* Melville finally springs loose from the restraints of civilization, reveling in bacchanalian freedom. Clearly, however, Melville's recklessness is of another order entirely. He is far more reckless of his urban readers than he was in *Typee*, far more direct in his attacks on genteel white society. And Arvin, too, unwittingly missed the point when he took another common view of the book, that it represents a journey into primitivism: "Taken together they [*Typee* and *Omoo*] tell the story of a quest or pilgrimage . . . from the world of enlightened rationality, technical progress, and cultural complexity, backward and downward and, so to say, inward to the primordial world that *was* before metals, before the alphabet, before cities." Perhaps that statement works for *Typee*, but *Omoo* clearly shows the world that comes after cities, in the wake of civilization.[37]

Melville's letters on the subject do little more than keep these conflicting readings in tension. In his first letter to Murray on *Omoo*, he calls it "a comical residence on the island of Tahiti" (*Correspondence*, 58), clearly hoping that his London publisher will find the spectator's rambles through scattered Tahitian villages with the comical Long Ghost an entertainment as "racy" as that of *Typee*. On finishing the work, however, he had a rather different set of concerns to present to Murray:

> I think you will find it a fitting successor to "Typee"; inasmuch as the latter book delineates Polynisian Life in its primitive state – while the

new work, represents it, as affected by intercourse with the whites. It also describes the "man about town" sort of life, led, at the present day, by roving sailors in the Pacific – a kind of thing, which I have never seen described anywhere. – The title of the work, may be thought a curious one – but . . . I desire the title (as it now appears) to remain untouched – its oddity, or uniqueness, if you please conveys some insight into the nature of the book. It gives a sort of Polynisian expression to its "figurehead." (*Corr*, 78)

First, Melville makes clear the difference in his intentions from *Typee*, namely, that the book is *not* about primitivism but about intercourse with whites, a far less "comical" topic than his idle sojourn in the Typee valley. Next he indicates, with his telling phrase, that these are "man about town" whites – gentlemanly spectators but also rather tougher, less privileged rovers. As the book demonstrates, there is not much difference between the rough sailors of the *Lucy Ann* and the careless beachcombers Typee and Long Ghost, except that the latter have a certain degree of education and charm that the others lack. But the most significant detail of the letter is Melville's insistence on his title. He had indeed had trouble with *Typee*, which Murray published under the more prosaic title, *Narrative of a Four Months' Residence among the Natives of a Valley of the Marquesas Islands*. In keeping the "Polynisian expression" Omoo, Melville was also pressing his claim for a Polynesian point of view. The Polynesian rover, the "taboo kannaker," represents the ideal according to which the white rovers must be judged. Against this standard of ideal spectating, Melville's sailors appear debased, vicious, and contemptible, not urbane.[38]

There is no Marnoo in *Omoo* and no moment when the white spectator sees himself in the Polynesian mirror as clearly as in *Typee*. Instead something more subtle occurs: the long, slow process by which Typee becomes disgusted with Long Ghost. This cosmopolitan, "as entertaining a companion as one could wish; and to me in the Julia, an absolute godsend" (12), stands, at the beginning of the novel, for all the best urban civilization has to offer:

> And from whatever high estate Doctor Long Ghost might have fallen, he had certainly at some time or other spent money, drunk Burgundy, and associated with gentlemen.
>
> As for his learning, he quoted Virgil, and talked of Hobbes of Malmsbury, beside repeating poetry by the canto, especially Hudibras. He was, moreover, a man who had seen the world. (12)

Typee values the Doctor's learning, conviviality, and leisurely spectating. He also sees in him the qualities of mellowness and raciness that most reviewers recognized in Melville. During the first half of the novel, Doctor Long Ghost, with his good breeding and good humor, contrasts strongly with the sordid sailors and the hypocritical Tahitian whites who oppress the islanders while living in idleness and splendor.

In the second half of the novel, however, Typee begins to see Long Ghost more and more in contrast with himself. The Doctor's evasion of hard work during their period of potato farming on Imeo begins to annoy him, and in time he is "not a little pleased to see the doctor's reputation as an invalid fading away so fast; especially, as on the strength of his being one, he had promised to have such easy times of it, and very likely, too, at my expense" (225). Long Ghost's popularity with the farmers and the natives loses its appeal for Typee: "I quickly perceived, that in the estimate formed of us, Long Ghost began to be rated far above myself" (231). With Marnoo, such a perception caused Tommo anxiety and jealousy, but Typee fights back: "To tell the plain truth, things at last came to such a pass, that I told him, up and down, that I had no notion to put up with his pretensions; if he were going to play the gentleman, I was going to follow suit; and then, there would quickly be an explosion" (231). Long Ghost agrees to leave, and they patch up their quarrel. But when Typee sees his behavior among the unspoiled inhabitants of Tamai, Loohooloo, and Partoowye, where he pursues his "jolly philanderings" among the young women, or gets drunk on "detestable liquors" while making "such a fricassee of vowels and consonants, that it was enough to turn one's brain" (274–5), Typee's patience wears thin. For although he too admires island beauties and enjoys Tahitian hospitality, he recoils at the Doctor's hypocritical urbanity. No further explosions occur, but in the end Typee's delight in getting back on board a whaler and his lack of regret in leaving the doctor behind, although he shakes him "long and heartily, by the hand" (316), indicate that he has had enough of Long Ghost's kind of spectating.

Melville certainly maintains a gentlemanly spectator-narrator in *Omoo*. Typee longs to get back to the city and, as in *Typee*, clearly feels most at home there. But in *Omoo* the city of New York, of Typee's audience, no longer seems the center of the world. Queen Pomaree in Tahiti also has a capital, a throne and crown sent her by Queen Victoria, and a train of white followers, "gentlemen pensioners of state, basking in the tropical sunshine of the court, and leading the pleasantest lives in the world" (247). New York is not the only attraction for gentlemen spectators; the cosmopolitan Long Ghost has decided to "tarry awhile" (315) in the Pacific. As Melville will show in *Mardi*, the South Seas is full of capitals, where an imaginative spectator may tarry indefinitely, seeing as much of the city as he could possibly desire.

Mardi: *Cities of Beryl and Jasper*

In *Mardi*, Melville raises spectating to metaphysical heights. Calling the reader to join him in his rambles – "We are off!" (3) – he presents himself at first as another Tommo or Typee, a gentleman sailor in the Pacific. One of the "brethren of the order of South Sea rovers" (7), the as yet unnamed narrator is an Omoo of the ocean, but he dreams from the beginning of traveling in a city – a celestial city. He ends the first chapter with a vision of a city in the clouds toward which he yearns: "In the distance what visions were spread! The entire western horizon high piled with gold and crimson clouds; airy arches, domes, and minarets as if the yellow, Moorish sun were setting behind some vast Alhambra. Vistas seemed leading to worlds beyond. To and fro, and all over the towers of this Nineveh in the sky, flew troops of birds. . . . My spirit must have sailed in with it" (7–8). This city, its exotic architecture of the East appearing improbably in the West, seems both a real place where the birds fly and also a City of the Imagination, an allegorical city where the philosophical spectator will satisfy his thirst for knowledge by roving its full extent. *Mardi* itself, with its cosmopolitan philosophers traveling around the world visiting great capitals, appears as such an allegorical city, repository of the history, poetry, and philosophy of human kind. "We are fuller than a city" (594), says Babbalanja.

The narrator's Nineveh, however, is not just a city in the clouds, an allegorical representation of the mystical wonders awaiting the mind in its sweeping travels. It is also a reminder of great cities, and the empires of which they are capitals. As Melville does in future works, by comparing New York to Nineveh and Babylon, ancient cities evoke modern capitals, though with an ominous warning: these too will fall. Thus, in *Redburn*, Melville speaks of "the New York guide-books . . . now vaunting of the magnitude of a town, whose future inhabitants . . . will regard all our Broadways and Bowerys as but the paltry nucleus to their Nineveh" (*R*,149). *Mardi*, too, is full of ancient cities from the fallen empires of Assyria, Babylonia, Egypt, Greece, Persia, Macedonia, and Rome. In *Typee* and *Omoo*, Melville mentions but a few cities: Byzantium, Damascus, Sparta, Naples, Sicily, Rome, and Thebes. *Mardi* contains references to Arbela, Argos, Babylon, Damascus, Denderah, Edessa, Enna, Ephesus, Luxor, Naples, Persepolis, Petra, Rome, Susa, Tadmor, Troy, and Tyre, as well as the veiled allusions to modern cities like Washington, Paris, London, Rome, Naples, and the Vatican. It also refers to the ancient kingdoms or empires of Assyria, Babylonia, Bactria, Egypt, Etruria, Greece, Latium, Libya, Macedonia, Parthia, Persia, and Sicily, not to mention the modern countries of Spain, Germany, Austria, France, England, Russia, Scandinavia, and America, all of which he portrays as empires. And finally, Melville includes a number of kings, conquerors, and founders of cities – notably, Aeneas, Alexander, Antigonus, Antiochus, Antony, Artaxerxes, Attila, Aurelian, Belshazzar, Belus, Brutus, Caligula, Cambyses, Cleopatra, Darius, Domitian, Hannibal, Julius Caesar, Nebuchadnezzar, Nero, Pilate, Pisistratus, Sardanapulus, Semiramis, Sesostris, Tarquin, Titus, Verres, and

Xerxes. The title of the book refers to an Asian and later a Persian domain, south of Bactria, and Mardi's king, Media, shares his name with the ancient kingdom of the Medes.[39]

Nothing in his earlier books prepares a reader for the outpouring of learning that Melville displays in *Mardi*, the expanded reach of his urbane spectator, and especially the broad panoply of cities he offers to view. In some ways, his reaching back in time to suggest the origins of cities anticipates his references to the ancient cities of Carthage, Jerusalem, and Rome in "Bartleby" or "The Encantadas," and later in *Clarel*. By superimposing these cities and their modern equivalents on a Polynesian terrain, he implies that cities arise naturally out of the most untouched, inviting landscapes. As in *Typee* and *Omoo*, the beauty of the South Seas islands attracts kings and emperors; soon the whole archipelago becomes a sprawling empire, similar to that which Thomas Cole portrays in his famous series of paintings, *The Course of Empire* (1836).

The real empire in the novel, according to Wai-chee Dimock's compelling argument, is Melville's fiction, the author the only emperor. In his freedom to name and dispose of characters, in the authoritative way he demands and inhabits a large narrative space, in his desire not simply to create but to dominate his fictional world, and in the resulting "spectralization of the actual reader into an ideal one," Melville exercises his imperial power, his imperial self. Once the unnamed narrator becomes Taji, Melville treats him like any other character. Taji is no longer a narrator but a piece of narrative property. The real journey is that of Melville the author as he pursues his quest for narrative freedom.[40] Especially given what we know of Melville's sense of himself as author of *Moby-Dick* and *Pierre*, this reading of Melville is a forceful one.

But that imperial self grows within an urban ideology of unbounded space and opportunity to which Melville, in *Mardi*, gives his most sustained and critical attention to date. Taji, I would argue, is an *urban* imperial self, one of many in the book, but ultimately he brings the course of empire to a destructive conclusion that Melville sees as deranged. The book asserts the freedom of the creative artist, but it also meticulously describes how that assertive freedom is implicated in the city's crimes against nature and the people of the earth. We have seen how Tommo and Typee bring with them to the South Seas their urban habits of walking, lounging, idling, rambling, and viewing panoramically from a traveler's distance. The freedom of movement that a great capital city like New York provides for an unencumbered gentleman gives them tremendous confidence in their own power and locomotion. For them, the Polynesian landscape resembles the ideal urban form, threaded by "thoroughfares," populated with hospitable hosts providing delectable refreshments, and offering a wide variety of "characters," "scenes," and "spectacles" for their amusement and pleasure. Melville deliberately invokes this idle urban stereotype in order to show its damaging effects on the Polynesian people, who have suffered, as many of the poor in New York did, from the intrusions of governments, reformers, and tourists into their realm. In *Mardi*, however, Melville takes the spectator even further in his urban rambles and shows his damage as universal in its implications.

Mardi begins with the spectator-narrator of *Typee* and *Omoo*. He is bored with life on the ship, where no one can "talk sentiment or philosophy" with him, where he is "pining for some one who could page me a quotation from Burton on Blue Devils" (5). He longs for a society of intellectual cosmopolitans, one where: "No custom is strange; no creed is absurd; no foe, but who will in the end prove a friend. In heaven, at last, our good, old, white-haired father Adam will greet all alike, and sociality forever prevail" (13). This vision, similar to the champagne-drinking sociality in heaven that he later proposed to Hawthorne, suggests a paradise of bachelors. Indeed, the narrator tires of the ship as of a marriage – "[h]e has taken the ship to a wife, for better or for worse, for calm or for gale; and she is not to be shuffled off" (10) – and is ready for the society of his own kind. This narrator appears to be the most gentlemanly of Melville's sailors, more like Redburn than Tommo: "And thus aboard of all ships in which I have sailed, I have invariably been known by a sort of drawing-room title." He hastens to add that he has not "put hand in tar bucket with a squeamish air, or ascended the rigging with a Chesterfieldian mince," but nevertheless, "it had gone abroad among the Arcturion's crew, that at some indefinite period of my career, I had been a 'nob.' " He even convinces his companion Jarl that he could be "one of the House of Hanover in disguise; or, haply, . . . bonneted Charles Edward the Pretender" (14). On all his previous ships, the sailor-narrator had a very good reason to revolt against an oppressive captain. On the *Arcturion*, however, he is simply fed up, and when he complains, the captain offers him a reasonable way out: "you may leave her if you can" (6).

Until the narrator reaches land at Mardi, his early adventures remain within the pattern of the spectator narrative. Drifting in an open boat gives him an opportunity to comment on the scene in typical spectator fashion: "we often encountered the dandy Blue Shark, a long, taper and mighty genteel looking fellow, with a slender waist, like a Bond-street beau, and the whitest tiers of teeth imaginable. This dainty spark invariably lounged by with a careless fin and an indolent tail" (40) – much the same style in which Dickens described the pigs of New York. He observes Jarl's quaint habits and jokes about the comforts of their little boat. Their coming upon what seems to be an abandoned ship allows him to shift into a Gothic mode, as they wonder about strange noises, dead bodies, and spirits; with the discovery of Samoa and his wife Annatoo, he moves to a parody of domestic sentimentality and delivers himself of various bachelor prejudices against women. Telling Samoa's story, he becomes a racy raconteur; taking over the ship, he plays the part of a captain with distinct satisfaction. Although he describes Samoa as a "coxcomb" (98), he is by far the greater coxcomb of the two.

However, the encounter with Aleema, the priest who with his sons is abducting the beautiful Yillah, changes the course of the spectator's journey irrevocably. In *Typee* Tommo committed an act of violence against Mow-Mow, the island chief, but he did so reluctantly and in what he considered self-defense. In *Omoo* he witnesses Bembo's murderous attempt to dash the ship against the rocks, but beyond joining in the mutiny participates in no violent behavior of his own. In murdering Aleema, however, he acts without thought or reason on the sudden impulse to protect the unseen Yillah. Although certain that he has done the right thing, he feels tremendous guilt over the murder and, just as Pierre later questions his motives in pretending to marry Isabel, so *Mardi*'s narrator wonders if he had a "selfish purpose; the companionship of a beautiful maid" (135). For the rest of the novel, the narrator is only partly a spectator as he travels through Mardi as Media's guest; he is also a refugee from Aleema's avenging sons, and soon he becomes Yillah's pursuer, and eventually Hautia's as well.

Once he touches land at Mardi, he also becomes Taji, a demigod. In assuming the character of a "half-and-half deity" (164), a "gentleman from the sun" (165), a member of a band of "strolling divinities" (166), Taji takes on some of the privileges and delights of spectatorial taboo. Like Marnoo, he will have the run of the country, and like the rover of *Omoo*, he will be feasted and entertained everywhere. His divinity gives him the same status as the demigod-king, Media, who with his "city in the woods" (171), his palace that "invited all loiterers to lounge" (171), and his "free, frank bearing" (166) and love of good food and wine, is a cosmopolitan prince and noble companion. Taji inwardly counsels himself not to be a "snob" (177), but clearly this kind of elevated intercourse with kings, and soon with poets, philosophers, and historians as well, is exactly what he was looking for when he jumped ship. Spectatorship once again appears as a kind of ideal, an urbane, intellectual state of taboo.

In that state of blessed taboo, Taji wanders throughout the Mardian archipelago, observing in a Swiftian panoply all the realms of the earth, all stories of the past and systems of thought, all lyrics, wisdom, and nonsense that the world and his talkative companions Babbalanja, Yoomy, Mohi, and Media have to offer. His search for Yillah and his flight from Hautia and his pursuers occupy little of his time and attention, as he turns his thoughts to both studious spectating and studied conviviality. Indeed, as Dimock points out, he almost seems to disappear from view, especially in volume 2; here the book opens out into one enormous panorama wherein, it seems, the reader becomes a spectator, seeing at first a series of fictional realms, then Europe (Dominora, Franko, Romara, etc.), and at last, as in a mirror, America and slavery. Through their inspired discourse, the travelers also make their way through the worlds of religion, politics, philosophy, art, and literature, finding no subject taboo.

But there is another, less exhilarating sense in which Taji is taboo, one that eventually drives him from polite society. After some desultory visits to the Tapparians and the isle of Pimminee, Aleema's avengers strike again, and Taji, perhaps unintentionally, reveals what he has not mentioned before, that he has murdered the priest. "All started," but Babbalanja is the only one to respond with a moral statement: "'tis true, then, Taji, that an evil deed gained you your Yillah: no wonder she is lost." King Media, however, reacts "unconcernedly," more the diplomat than the moralist: "Perhaps better, Taji, to have kept your secret; but tell no more; I care not to be your foe." Yoomy, however, produces the most puzzling rejoinder of all, as it refers to a completely inexplicable sign: " 'Ah, Taji! I had shrank from you,' cried Yoomy, 'but for the mark upon your brow. That undoes the tenor of your words' " (423). Characteristically, Yoomy the poet concerns himself with Taji's words and signs as much as their meaning. The mark on Taji's brow, heretofore unmentioned and after this also unmentioned, appears to tell him that Taji is somehow blameless. This taboo mark recalls the sign on an earlier character's brow, the tattoo of a blue shark imprinted on Lem Hardy of *Omoo*: Hardy, a "renegado from Christendom and humanity," has adopted native dress and made himself a "sovereign power" among the islanders. As a sign of his warlike fierceness and at the same time his willingness to join the natives, he has "voluntarily submitted" to being tattooed: "What an impress! Far worse than Cain's – *his* was perhaps a wrinkle, or a freckle, which some of our modern cosmetics might have effaced; but the blue shark was a mark indelible." Hardy's "campaigns beat Napoleon's"; and as a reward for his efforts, he wins a Tahitian princess, a munificent dowry, and "the sacred protection of an express edict of the Taboo, declaring his person inviolable forever." This form of taboo differs widely from the ideal taboo embodied in Marnoo. Hardy is the epitome of the Pacific rover, "uncared for by a single soul, without ties, reckless, and impatient of the restraints of civilization" (27–8). If Marnoo's taboo makes him seem the most urbane of men, Hardy's establishes that he is the most urban; for although he has fled civilization, he embodies the reckless, predatory spirit of the modern metropolis. Like Cain, he goes to the city as a founder. Having shed blood, he seeks refuge among the mob.[41]

Taji, too, bears the mark of Cain. He has shed blood, and his journey through Mardi is just as much desperate flight as urbane ramble. Cain's mark protected him from further reprisal and made it possible for him to wander among men. Taji's can do the same. But from this point on in the narrative, the terrain becomes increasingly threatening, as they leave behind the fanciful island paradise and embark on a journey around the world, visiting the domains of the bloodthirsty Piko and Hello, who use war games for population control, King Bello of the imperialist Dominora, the combustible isle of Franko, the slaveholding regions of Vivenza, until, exhausting the world's empires, they return to Doxodox, Hooloomooloo, and Serenia. It would seem that Taji's travels have taken him to the heart of civilization rather than away from it. His taboo protects him from harm, but not from anguish.

In all this, Melville mocks the assumption of civilized man, an assumption held by Cain, of his superiority to the natural world. This unnatural hubris, this longing for cities in the clouds, has proven to be man's most destructive illusion. The story of the king of Hooloomooloo, Isle of the Cripples, makes this point especially clear. King Yoky, the current leader of the Cripples, asks if any of the visitors is a Comparative Anatomist and can help him with a problem. It appears that an ancestor of his discovered "an old gray-headed Chimpanzee, one day . . . meditating in the woods." This chimpanzee, named Rozoko, looks "very grave, and reverend of aspect; much of a philosopher. To him, all gnarled and knotty subjects were familiar; in his day he had cracked many a crabbed nut." Loving his "Timonean solitude" in the woods, he "needed many bribes and bland persuasions, to induce him to desert his mossy, hillside, misanthropic cave, for the distracting tumult of court" (571).

The first oddity in this story, of course, is that the chimpanzee has a name, as fanciful as any of the human names in the book, and that his philosophy and his preferences seem perfectly reasonable. His Timonism and misanthropy are not, as they would be in a human, a sign of deviance or wickedness, but the natural preference of one species for his own habitat over that of another. Yet the king loves this ape as a friend and wants to bring him to court, where he is "promoted to high offices, and made the royal favorite." Again this friendship seems natural on both sides. Rozoko "forgot his forests; and, love for love, returned the aged king's caresses." They eat and drink together and commiserate with each other on the experiences they have in common, holding "discourse of palsies, hearses, shrouds, and tombs." Two old graybeards, they see that "the world's great bubble bursts" and look to heaven. But, not always gloomy, they also walk out together, taking "slow, tottering rambles in the woods" with walking sticks made by Rozoko. They straddle their canes, Rozoko's "hobby," and go off to count the "mystic rings" of trees, which, they both know, mark their own long lives (571–2).

In the end, the king asks that Rozoko be buried with him; and when he dies, Rozoko stays by the body until, "at last, slowly going round it thrice, he laid him down; close nestled; and noiselessly expired." Odd as the story is, Melville's narration remains faithful to what could be considered natural in the tale. Humans and chimpanzees are close enough to sympathize, and Melville is careful not to imply that the king and Rozoko actually exchange words. Rozoko's preferences, talents, and observations are credible, and the king's love for this handsome gray animal also seems entirely believable. The story becomes ridiculous, however, once the two friends die; for "the people of the island became greatly scandalized, that a base-born baboon [the islanders have already diminished the great chimpanzee's stature and status] should share the shroud of their departed lord; though they themselves had tucked in the aged Æneas fast by the side of his Achates" (572). The allusion to Aeneas and Achates reminds the reader of the great founder of cities and his bosom friend. In using it, the people acknowledge the dignity of the king's love for a chimpanzee. Yet because they want to build a monument, they decide to dig up the monarch's body and separate his remains from those of Rozoko. Unfortunately, the bones are as lovingly united as "Saul and Jonathan," as similar as "the literary remains of Beaumont and of Fletcher," and so King Yoky hopes a Comparative Anatomist will come along and help him take them apart, "lest the towering monument they had reared, might commemorate an ape, and not a king" (572).

Monuments, we do not need Lewis Mumford to tell us, stand at the heart of city building, which is "first of all, the expression of power."[42] The early king of Hooloomooloo had little of this lust for power, but his descendants want above all to assert his superiority over the gentle, thoughtful animal, Rozoko. This anthropocentrism disturbs the philosopher Babbalanja, and in the next chapter he challenges it through the words of his guru, Bardianna: "My supremacy over creation, boasteth man, is declared in my natural attitude: – I stand erect!" (574).[43] Man's sense of lordship convinces him of his right to reign over "the bat and the brute." But, says Bardianna, "we are the least populous part of creation. To say nothing of other tribes, a census of the herring would find us far in the minority." Despite his insignificance in nature, man still aspires to rule. Bardianna admonishes him: "Oh men! fellow men! we are only what we are; not what we would be; nor everything we hope for" (575). Human aspirations toward transcendence have little to do with reality and ignore the glorious possibilities of the present world. Why not be happy with this world rather than seeking cities in the clouds?:

> "Already, in its unimaginable roamings, our system may have dragged us through and through the spaces, where we plant cities of beryl and jasper. Even now, we may be inhaling the ether, which we fancy seraphic wings are fanning. But look round. There is much to be seen here, and now. Do the archangels survey ought more glorious than the constellations we nightly behold? Continually we slight the wonders, we deem in reserve." (576)

The city men seek, like the Nineveh in the clouds, is an illusion, a monumental architecture of human pride, an expression of power, an "empire for liberty." But the world, says Bardianna, has its own cities of beryl and jasper; nature is itself a New Jerusalem, a miracle of revelations.[44] Man's desire to subdue nature by building cities makes him a Cain; better to be a Rozoko, reading one's life in the circles of trees.

Taji, however, is "fixed as fate" (638). Whereas his friends seemingly take Bardianna's advice by seeking their destinies at home, Taji flies onward toward the celestial Nineveh, or, as he discovers when he reaches Hautia, "all Venice" (650). Yillah is gone, and he decides to continue his journey "over an endless sea" (654). Yoomy sees once again the sign of Cain in this last effort: "Nay, Taji: commit not the last, last crime!" (654). But Taji, becoming his "own soul's emperor," plays out Cain's logic to the last, accepting suicide and the "realm of shades!" as his destiny. His insane flight, "pursuers and pursued" (654) rushing on, brings to its conclusion Taji's first visions of the Nineveh in the sky, with its "vistas . . . leading to worlds beyond" (8).

Melville does not, then, endorse the spirit of ruthless, imperial individualism that distinguished Cain, Alexander, Attila, Caesar, Nebuchadnezzar, Xerxes, and the rest. What begins as a seemingly harmless spectatorial stroll through a visionary city ends as a mad, criminal launch into other worlds that most of the other characters have learned to find less valuable or absorbing than their own.

In one of his philosophical ramblings, Babbalanja derides the imperialist impulse to found cities: "have to annex one of the planets; invade the great sun; colonize the moon; – conquerors sighed for new Mardis; and sages for heaven." How foolish, he says: "All we discover has been with us since the sun began to roll: and much that we discover, is not worth the discovering." Knowledge brings nothing new: "In the books of the past we learn naught but of the present; in those of the present, the past. All Mardi's history – beginning, middle, and finis – was written out in capitals in the first page penned" (580–1). In a sense, Melville, by the end of *Mardi*, has written himself *out of*, not *in*, capitals. His next books will not speak from the point of view of the spectator at the center of civilization but through narrators who are outsiders, provincials. The world will not seem a Walking City, a rational grid of streets through which the spectator moves at his ease, but rather a dense maze where he may get lost. And his characters will not be trying to conquer distant Ninevehs but merely to survive in Liverpool, London, and New York.

3

Provincial in a Labyrinth

Yes, here I had come to seek my fortune! A mere boy, friendless, unprotected, innocent of the ways of the world – without wealth, favor, or
wisdom – here I stood at the entrance of the mighty labyrinth, and with
hardly any consciousness of the temptations, doubts, and dangers that
awaited me there.   Walter Whitman, *Franklin Evans*[1]

Ah, thou rash boy! are there no couriers in the air to warn thee away
from these emperilings, and point thee to those Cretan labyrinths, to
which thy life's cord is leading thee?   *Pierre* (176)

The Walking City of Knickerbocker New York, as cultural construction,
provided the urbane spectator an ideal terrain. Its rational plan, closely
knit physical and social structure, and the shared democratic ideology of
a fairly homogeneous population made it, in Raymond Williams's phrase,
a "knowable communit[y]."[2] Within a clearly defined geographical area
and a seemingly unified social order, the city offered subjects for the spectator's continual observation and opportunities for seemingly endless wandering. But even when Melville wrote *Typee, Omoo,* and *Mardi,* the novels
responding to that model of urban space, New York had vitally changed.
As the city became more truly a capital in the commercial sense, it lost its
cohesive, rational structure. Unprecedented growth, deepening class divisions, rising land values, the flight of the wealthy from the urban center,
the tearing up and rebuilding of the streets, the pressure of immigration,
all made the old city unrecognizable.[3] In its place evolved a changing
urban structure, one difficult to navigate or to comprehend – one that
writers, artists, and city dwellers described as a labyrinth. Getting through
that labyrinth became a new challenge in urban life and literature in the
1840s and 1850s.

The idea of the city as a labyrinth was already well established in European literature by the time New York writers applied it and had a wealth

of ancient and contemporary associations.[4] Although an actual labyrinth is a highly organized and indeed rational structure, nineteenth-century British authors often used it to represent psychological disequilibrium, the anxiety and fear associated with moving *through* a labyrinth. As an image of the city, it describes perfectly the Londoner's experience of confusion in a complex urban environment. "Doubtless," said Thomas DeQuincy in *The Confessions of an English Opium-Eater* (1822, 1856), "we must have been sometimes in search of each other, at the very same moment, through the mighty labyrinths of London; perhaps even within a few feet of each other – a barrier no wider, in a London street, often amounting in the end to separation for eternity!"[5] To many, Charles Dickens's description of Todgers's in *Martin Chuzzlewit* stood for other parts of great London as well: "Nobody had ever found Todgers's on a verbal direction, though given within a minute's walk of it. . . . Todgers's was in a labyrinth, whereof the mystery was known but to a chosen few."[6] As a much older and structurally more complex city than New York, London might logically appear to be a labyrinth. It is perhaps surprising that New York, too, produced the same impression when it still had comparatively less population and density. But in fact, because of a democratic ideology that refused to acknowledge class divisions, New York's social and physical changes produced as great a cultural shock as the growing complexity of London. The visible evidence of class difference violently ruptured the old framework and produced a widespread sense that the city had become mysterious to its dwellers. Thus, no less saturated in "mystery" than that of England was the urban literature of antebellum New York – guide books, travel accounts, temperance tracts, letters, novels, pamphlets, and journalistic sketches – as well as Melville's mid-century urban novels: *Redburn* (1849), *White-Jacket* (1850), and *Pierre* (1852).

But, as we shall see, whereas much of the popular urban literature of New York attempts to penetrate the physical and social labyrinth of the changing city, revealing the city's mysteries and miseries, Melville's novels present characters who fail in this attempt.[7] Certainly many urban fictions portray sensational failure for unwary provincials who succumb to the "temptations, doubts, and dangers" lurking in the urban labyrinth. But the failures of Melville's heroes point, not to their own moral weaknesses, although they have many, but to the power of the labyrinth myth to mystify city dwellers about the misery in which they dwell. Melville's novels resist the middle-class mystification of poverty that the urban novels typically enact.

This mystification has been described by many writers as the logical outgrowth of urban capitalism and the basic condition of urban men and women. Carolyn Porter's discussion of reification in American literature describes the writer as immersed in "a social reality breeding an extreme form of alienation." In her reading drawing from Lukács, she shows how in American culture Marx's definition of alienated labor extends beyond the working class to include a whole bourgeois society alienated from the world of commodities it has created. The middle class "seem to themselves to stand outside that reality because their own participation in producing it is mystified."[8] In antebellum New York, the story of a provincial's descent into the labyrinth claims to reveal the labyrinth's hidden mysteries to bourgeois outsiders yet obscures the middle-class reader's own complicity in urban poverty and wretchedness. To understand this "strategy of mystification,"[9] we have to understand how writers used the structure and myth of the labyrinth, not only to explain but also to contain social change in New York.

For the anxiety over New York becoming a labyrinth has an immediate political context – American democratic individualism – that gives its own nuances to the general conditions of capitalist alienation, reification, and mystification. As the city attracted provincials and immigrants, as the old districts became more crowded, as rising land values forced ordinary people into less desireable living spaces, as speculation and greed drove landlords and business owners to exploit new arrivals, as poor city management failed to meet the needs of citizens, the city clearly began to challenge the ideology of liberty and justice for all – or, as Thomas Butler Gunn called it, "[t]he right to do 'as you d—n please' – to quote the democratic phraseology of the aborigines."[10] Perhaps the issue of liberty – that is, liberty to live and work in comfort – meant more to middle-class city dwellers than did justice for all, especially now that justice was meant to extend to refugees from the famines and revolutions of Europe. But in any case, the American ethic of individualism faced a serious threat as more individuals competed for its benefits. Many New Yorkers chose to escape the pressure by moving north. As a result, the old town where people had lived and worked side by side became the domain of commerce, industry, and low-rent housing. No wonder, then, that it looked unrecognizable to the middle class, to people like Melville who had grown up in the old, prosperous, unified town. The process of mystification, then, by which the older town came to seem a labyrinth, a place of mystery and misery, grew directly out of a bourgeois ideology of unlimited freedom, space, and growth. When writers came to represent their own city, they felt they were being truthful when they described it as a mystery.

But Melville was less interested in representing urban mystery and misery than in criticizing the practices of those who did. In his novels, the failure of the provincial hero implicates the culture that led him to expect success in the great city. Getting through the labyrinth is, in Melville's version of the story, a dubious achievement, implying not heroic intelligence and courage but rather naiveté and misplaced idealism. Melville's questing provincial becomes trapped in a labyrinth, one that is not only outside him in the physical and social system of the city but also inside him, culturally imprinted on his own mind and imagination, and thus harder to escape.

The Labyrinth of New York

In recognizing alienation as a fact of nineteenth-century urban life, and urban literature as an attempt to assuage middle-class anxiety over rapid social change, we may make the mistake of assuming that New Yorkers did not know or want to know about the sufferings of the poor. If the labyrinth trope made it easier for readers to explain the complexity of urban life, and if the mystery-and-misery fiction allowed them to sensationalize and sentimentalize urban poverty, one might conclude that New Yorkers created these myths to obscure social reality. In fact, the success of these popular tropes suggests that they clarified urban experience especially well, made visible the plight of the working class and indigent, expressed public outrage over social injustice, aroused compassion among middle-class readers, and produced significant reforms. The problem lay not so much in lack of accuracy – New York, especially in the older parts of town, did indeed resemble a physical and social labyrinth, a domain of mystery and misery – but in the popular conception of the labyrinth itself. For the idea of the labyrinth allowed New Yorkers to map the city's class, racial, and ethnic differences and contain them within the limits of a tight, though intricate, order.[11] Although certain parts of the town might seem labyrinthine, one could enter and leave them easily, with the help of a guide, often the police or the keen-eyed writer. And so, the labyrinth as image of mystery, fear, and disorder served, paradoxically, to prescribe boundaries to areas of social disorder and offer a model of extrication for the middle class.

For many New York writers and their readers, the urban labyrinth had a specific locale: the old Walking City. This, the lower part of town, centered on the Five Points district, which by its proximity to the infamous Tombs prison, as well as to Wall Street, Trinity Church, the lower reaches of Broadway and the Bowery, and even Pearl Street and the wharves, where Allan Melvill had his shop, epitomized the graphic contrasts between rich and poor and symbolized the changes the city had undergone within living memory. In the old Knickerbocker city, streets looked unfamiliar and, in some cases, hostile. Indeed, as a writer for *Putnam's* said, "though you may with some assurance navigate the instep, and are not wholly beyond hope in the heel, yet none but an old-fashioned New-York pig or policeman can ever be perfectly at home in the sole of the metropolitan foot."[12]

Although the older streets had resisted the efforts of planners to create an orderly gridiron – "The lower part of the city has . . . narrow zigzagging cow-path streets," said one visitor[13] – the streets were not in themselves so difficult to find or to follow. Rather, an outmoded and corrupt political system helped to make them a dangerous, frightening, nauseating terrain. Most noticeably, there was no consistent municipal policy on garbage removal. In the 1840s, an inefficient and poorly managed city government alternated between legislating street cleaning itself, or, when the money ran out, contracting with private carters to remove the waste.[14] An anonymous account written in 1837 makes the government's delinquency clear:

> The scavengers and carters must be paid; and the means must be provided by the common council. We cannot ask them to forego their annual two-thousand dollar dinner; we cannot deprive them of the pleasure of an occasional lunch at the alms house; for these are the only solid fruits of all their official toils and exertions. But we should just ask them to appropriate money to do, thoroughly, what they undertake to do; and what the world shames them for not doing: that is, keep the streets clean – habitually clean – and thoroughly clean.[15]

Even after a reform charter in 1849 reorganized the government and sought to control street cleaning, paving, and repair, old habits of patronage made any real reforms impossible.[16] The streets remained filthy, not only because of insufficient municipal efforts, but also because increased trade and traffic clogged them beyond relief. Open markets produced mounds of rotting vegetables tossed into the gutters; animal offal filled the streets; dead animals lay where they fell. And although shop- and homeowners were responsible for sweeping the streets in front of their doors, the piles of garbage lay for days waiting for the carts to come. Naturally the city's cleanliness problem became a health problem as well. Dr. Stephen Smith, reporting to the Council of Hygiene in 1864, quotes with clinical accuracy and perhaps fascination a typical description of the streets in the 1840s and 1850s:

> As a rule, the streets are extremely dirty and offensive, and the gutters obstructed with filth. The filth of the streets is composed of house-slops, vegetables, decayed fruit, store and shop sweepings, ashes, dead animals, and even human excrements. These putrifying organic substances are ground together by the constantly passing vehicles. When dried by the summer's heat, they are driven by the wind in every direction in the form of dust. When remaining moist or liquid in the form of "slush," they emit deleterious and very offensive exhalations. The reeking stench of the gutters, the street filth, and domestic garbage of this quarter of the city, constantly imperil the health of its inhabitants.[17]

When Pierre falls into the gutter and finds himself "dabbled with mud and slime" (341) he might well hurry home for a cold-water bath. Simply getting through the street mud risked one's life, limbs, nose, and lungs.

The only visible help came from an army of poor children who filled the vacuum left by the city, sweeping the crossings for a pedestrian's penny. However, because, in the minds of many reformers, this occupation was the entry-level position for a career of prostitution and theft, the condition of the streets was seen to have terrible social consequences: "The first thing I can remember is being cold and hungry, and half naked and ragged, and sent out in the rainy mornings into the streets barefooted, to sweep the crossings and beg for pennies."[18] The physical condition of the streets became a sign of political indifference and corruption, as well as of threats to social order, health, and the pleasure of walking through the old town.

Even if one could navigate the sidewalks, crossing the street exposed one to further risk. In the absence of traffic controls, horse- and human-drawn vehicles coursed promiscuously through the streets: "all sorts of horse-carts, hand-carts, dog-carts, goat-carts, meat-carts, bread-carts, wood-carts, ash-carts, swill-carts, and dirt-carts, together with cars, wheelbarrows, sleds, sleighs, jumpers, &c" (Ross, 165). William Bobo describes two young ladies trying vainly to cross Broadway:

> They made repeated attempts, but failed; and as for 'a Jehu' making any halt for you, unless given to understand that you want a ride, it is a thing unknown in the history of a Broadway Omnibus driver. They seemed timid – I presume were strangers – and therefore did not like to venture. After a while *one* made an effectual trial, but the other met with her usual disappointment; – I became interested; now the case was worse than before – they were separated; this was too bad. They remained in this predicament for nearly an hour, when 'a jam' occurred between a 'bus and a dray, which stopped the current, and the girls got together.[19]

One must assume that Bobo, who calls himself "A South Carolinian (who had nothing else to do)," was as helpless as the women to make a crossing or come to their aid; how else was he able to observe them for nearly an hour? An incident in Solon Robinson's *Hot Corn*, however, suggests that the women were right to hesitate as long as they did; the alternative could be deadly, as for the drunken father in Robinson's novel:

> [H]e heeded not the tripartite crush of carriages coming up and going down these streets, all meeting in a sort of vortex at that point. He heard, or heeded not, the drivers, "hi, hi, hi, get out of the way, you drunken son of a _____." and down he went among the horses' clattering feet among the slippery stones, and the wheels passed over him, crushing bones – human bones, and mangling flesh, and mixing human blood with street dirt.[20]

The man's fall mingled his own flesh with the animal wastes already rotting in the gutter, but when he was raised from his repugnant pool of offal, "the drivers looked down coolly" and drove on. Joel Ross reports another hit-and-run accident, which the victim luckily survived, but "the rascal of a driver never checked his horses, nor turned his head to see whether the boy was dead or alive; and I could have seen the big key 'of Sing Sing' turned upon him with an excellent relish" (168). Clearly, then, city dwellers daily experienced the streets as dangerous, if not fatal, to their safety.

Finally, and ironically, the streets became difficult to navigate as improvements took place. Constant renovation and repair, tearing down and rebuilding, revealed a labyrinth of subterranean levels and contributed to the sense that the streets were becoming an intricate maze. Starting from beneath the surface, inhabitants might see a complex network of utility pipes. These were, in fact, the pride of reformers, city officials, and historians of New York, who pointed approvingly to the excavations: "Having glanced at the external appearance of the city, let us descend beneath the surface, and see what underground New York presents," announced one guidebook. The larger of two sets of iron pipes carried water from the Croton Water Works, inaugurated with a great festival on October 14, 1842.[21] A banner at the festivities, representing "on the one side Neptune as having achieved a victory over the Demon of Fire, and on the other the Queen of Cities pointing to the noble work that had just been completed" (Belden, 39), attested to the joy citizens felt over the long overdue improvements in health, hygiene, and fire safety that the waterworks promised. The engineering achievement it symbolized bolstered civic pride as well: "In magnitude of design and solidity of construction, the Croton Aqueduct throws into shade all similar structures of modern times, and even rivals the Aqua Marcia and the Anio Novus of ancient Rome" (Belden, 41). A second set of pipes, running from the New York Gas Light Company (incorporated in 1823) and the Manhattan Gas Light Company (1830), produced the improvement in illumination that made Foster's *New York by Gas-Light* (1850) and a revolution in how the city saw itself by night, possible.[22] And finally, "at some distance below the surface of the ground, a covered canal . . . constructed of hard brick, with the joints laid close and filled with mortar . . . about thirteen feet below the surface" (Belden, 43), carried *some* of the city's sewage out to the river.

This labyrinth of pipes and sewers, these modern wonders of engineering, served ideologically to convince urban inhabitants of the "noble work" being done to improve their lives. "To us, who in more modern times and in a more practical age, look at the City of New-York through our editorial windows, and recall by the aid of History the barren plain, the marshy hollows, and the stony slopes which but yesterday, as it were, offended the eyes that are now delighted by her growing magnificence, the story of Aladdin seems hardly a fable" (*Putnam's* I, February 1853, 121). The excavations also uncovered the layers of history that revealed

how much the city had changed. Yet the construction involved in laying
the pipes, in putting down the new Russ pavement (considered superior
to the old cobblestones) and widening the streets, and in building new
houses and stores over the districts ruined by fire, created a chaos of dust,
rubble, and noise. Although the *Putnam's* series of articles, "New-York
Daguerreotyped," generally adopts an exultant tone, it often depicts the
gloomy side effects of urban renovations. For example, the author describes the widening of Liberty Street as a disturbing upheaval:

> Our artist, Döpler, has admirably represented the confusion into which
> the wholesale repairs and alterations going on in this street have
> plunged it. One after another the old tenements have disappeared, the
> bricks painted and unpainted have gone the way of all clay, the narrow
> windows have been looked out of for the last time, and the small doors
> have followed the high steps into oblivion, and that "undiscovered
> bourne" to which all the rubbish of this great city is carried. (*Putnam's*
> I, February 1853, 128)

The accompanying engraving, and a similar picture of the laying of the
Russ pavement in Broadway (I, April 1853, 368), show streets made forbidding and completely unnavigable by the excavations.

There were ample reasons, then, for New York pedestrians to feel that
the city's streets presented a considerable challenge to forward motion.
This model of urban space – a dense, dangerous maze – permeated structures of thinking and narration. In particular, the language used to describe streets and gutters carried over into descriptions of the underclass,
which in its apparent filth, neglect, degradation, dangerousness, offen-
siveness, and lack of political organization or moral control, presented a
social environment as threatening as the streets themselves. Similarly, the
responses of fear and anxiety translated into a need for reliable guides to
the labyrinth. Urban literature representing the city as a labyrinth adopted
narrative forms intended to meet the challenge in different ways. One
strategy, used by moral reformers, temperance writers, travel writers, and
journalists, sought to diminish the impact of the city's labyrinthine complexity by minimizing its scope. This tactic, often described as a "plunge
into Five Points," offers just enough exposure to urban misery and vice
to make its case but also instructs the middle-class reader in how to escape
the labyrinth or avoid entering it in the first place. A second strategy, less
overtly moral in tone, breaks down the labyrinth into parts, offering a
taxonomy of urban social types or experiences so that a reader may recognize and understand the city's social structure. And a third, rather than
minimizing the effect or complexity of the labyrinth, expands its significance, making it an emblem of a whole social system, and suggesting that
the hapless wanderer in the labyrinth may never, or only with difficulty,

escape. The reader, then, experiences the provincial's bewilderment and turns to the urban writer as guide. These tactics appear in a tremendous variety of urban narratives and sometimes mingle within the same work, but they have a common purpose: to mediate between the bewildering labyrinth and the uninitiated reader, often assumed to be a provincial and outsider to the city's secrets. They express, then, a certain confidence in the power of narrative to make sense of or give form to the city's complexity and to contain social disturbance; in that fashion they themselves enact the strategy of mystification. By steering the reader safely and vicariously through the urban labyrinth, they assert their faith in a larger moral or social order. The reader, at least, will avoid the traps into which the provincial protagonist falls, and may ignore, if he or she chooses, their moral or political implications.

In focusing on these particular strategies, I have selected from the mass of popular literature of antebellum New York the narrative structures most pertinent to Melville's mid-century urban novels. The first, the sensational plunge into urban poverty, appears in a large body of urban writings examined by Stuart Blumin, David Reynolds, Adrienne Siegel, and Janis Stout, among others. However, it is worth reviewing the characteristics of this literature.

As in so many aspects of urban literature, Dickens supplies the model, even for the conventional visit to Five Points: "Let us go on again; and passing this wilderness of an hotel with stores about its base, like some Continental theatre, or the London Opera House shorn of its colonnade, plunge into the Five Points."[23] His use of the word "plunge" signifies the suddenness, if not violence, of the change in scenery. It also suggests the physical and social descent required to enter this lower world: "Let us descend into the subterranean world, sunken somewhere in the vicinity of Five Points and the Tombs," says George Lippard in *New York: Its Upper Ten and Lower Million*.[24] Many writers openly acknowledged disgust: "Have you got a good supply of cigars? – if not, get some, as we shall need them while prowling among the filthy cellars and the malaria which envelopes that region of the city" (Bobo, 93). Again, this disgust is seen as the natural reaction to a social plunge from respectability into degradation, even when viewed, as in Robinson's *Hot Corn*, with irony: "I suppose there are some who will turn away in disgust from the double title of this chapter. What, they will say, can 'Life at the Five Points' have in it that is interesting to me, who lounge on silk brocatelle, and look down upon beggar girls and rag-pickers – disgusting objects – through lace curtains" (192). Even expressed ironically, the first effect of the plunge shocks the whole physical and moral system.

Dickens also provides an example by choosing guides. Many writers debated whether or not such guides were necessary. As a foreigner, Dickens clearly appreciated professional help: "it is needful, first, that we take as our escort these two heads of the police, whom you would know for sharp and well-trained officers if you met them in the Great Desert" (76). The officer who accompanies William Bobo claims, "there is no sort of danger in visiting the Points now-a-days," but the author begs him nevertheless to "Please show us what is to be seen, and protect us from harm" (95). Joel Ross takes the Reverend Louis M. Pease, the founding minister of the Five Points mission as his guide.[25] Pease, who began as a temperance minister and went on to establish the Five Points House of Industry, shows a good deal more sensitivity than the typical police officer does to the feelings of Five Pointers being scrutinized by a middle-class visitor: "you will hardly want to tell the people that you have come to see how *bad* they look, and so I will give you a bundle of *Tracts* to take along with you" (Ross, 90–1). More typical is the anonymous clergyman author of *Life in New York* (1847), who refused to visit the Five Points himself but sent a friend: "Of course you would never expect me to make a personal investigation of such localities, but a few nights ago a friend of mine, accompanied by a friend of his, and under the escort of a well-known police-officer, a terror to the sons and daughters of crime, and a frequent visitor in their domains, made the tour of the regions to which I have referred, and I propose to give you, very briefly, an account of *some* things they saw." This author states, incidentally, that Dickens is inclined to exaggeration – "he is altogether better at fancy than fact" – and claims that *his* account, though vicarious, will offer the truth about "the lowest and darkest dens of pollution on the continent of America!"[26]

Many writers made similar protestations, though seldom so farfetched, but the general similarity in language and tone of these accounts suggests how fully prepared they were to view the Five Points area as a moral as well as a physical labyrinth. Again Dickens's account was both characteristic and influential in the way it linked the physical terrain with moral judgment: "Poverty, wretchedness, and vice, are rife enough where we are going now. This is the place: these narrow ways, diverging to the right and left, and reeking everywhere of dirt and filth." Even the houses bear marks of the general moral decay: "See how the rotten beams are tumbling down, and how the patched and broken windows seem to scowl dimly, like eyes that have been hurt in drunken frays." The difficulty of penetrating the streets and houses is emblematic of the depths of vice and crime: "Here too are lanes and alleys, paved with mud knee-deep . . . ruined houses, open to the street, whence, through wide gaps in the walls, other ruins loom upon the eye. . . . all that is loathsome, drooping, and decayed is here" (76, 78).

George Foster was not the first American writer to recognize that the physical layout and conditions of the Points constituted a "moral geography" (120).[27] But his lengthy description of the district, which he calls "the Core of Civilization" in *New York by Gas-Light*, makes especially clear how entering the labyrinth may ensnare one's moral as well as bodily self. "Those . . . whose purposes are honest, had better walk a mile round the spot, on their way home, than cross through" (121). Like Dickens, Foster sees the darkness, ruin, and complexity of the Points emblematically. "Here, whence these streets diverge in dark and endless paths, whose steps take hold on hell – here is the very type and physical semblance, in fact, of hell itself" (120). In line with his title, Foster uses light as a crucial image in carrying through his moral scheme. Rather than taking a po-liceman or a missionary as his guide, Foster relies on the help of a "large gas-lamp" placed just across from the Old Brewery, "which throws a strong light for some distance around, over the scene where once com-plete darkness furnished almost absolute security and escape to the pur-sued thief and felon, familiar with every step and knowing the exits and entrances to every house" (121). Just as the gaslight illuminates the streets and makes them safe, so his *New York by Gas-Light* shines the light of truth on this "dark sea of licentiousness and dissipation" (124).[28]

Many accounts, attempting to portray the sea of licentiousness and dis-sipation effectively, transfer the labyrinth image from the streets to the houses themselves. Buildings contain cellars or hidden rooms where gam-blers, drunkards, and prostitutes meet in nightly orgies. Hence, at one dwelling, "the door was cautiously opened, and we stood enveloped in darkness. . . . We groped our way to a flight of stairs *down* which we marched [to an] infernal ball-room door, and there, as sure as life, was a sight [of night-time revelers] such as the disordered brain of a madman might conjure" (*Life*, 176). Dickens invites the reader to "grope your way with me into this wolfish den" to visit the "low tavern" and the "miserable room" (77). Lippard's narrator takes us through a "narrow door," into a bar where "an orgie of crime, drunkenness and rags" takes place, then into a room of gamblers, and finally, "groping your way in the darkness, over an uneven floor, and between narrow walls; after groping your way you know not how far, you descend a second ladder, ten feet or more, and find yourself confronted by a door. You are at least two stories under ground" (*Upper Ten*, 116). Lippard's Monk Hall is the epitome of the labyrinthine house of sin in Philadelphia, but when he came to write a novel about New York, he chose the Five Points as the locale for a similar place. Here the houses, as well as the streets, conveniently conceal and nourish crime.

Perhaps the most striking feature of the Five Points accounts, however, is the way the labyrinth contains and makes possible an almost unthink-able, to these observers, casual proximity between people of different families, genders, and races. Inside the tenements, the disorderly arrange-ment of the rooms, the piling up of stories, the rickety walls, and the lack of plan attest to the general wretchedness of tenement housing itself, but even more alarming are the sleeping arrangements, which promote every imaginable vice. Solon Robinson reports a black man and white woman living together. "Not sleeping together?" exclaims his interlocutor. "No, not exactly that – there is no bed in the room – no chair – no table – no nothing – but rags, and dirt, and vermin, and degraded, rum degraded, human beings" (71). Robinson, a temperance writer, shows considerably more compassion for these sufferers than Dickens, who is most struck by the fact that they don't seem to be human. Seeing what looks like a great heap of rags, he remarks: "Then the mounds of rags are seen to be astir, and rise slowly up, and the floor is covered with heaps of negro women, waking from their sleep" (77). Foster speaks for many in condemning the way tenement housing encourages the breakdown between the usual boundaries of propriety: "In this one room, the cooking, eating and sleeping of the whole family, and their visitors, are performed. Yes – *and their visitors*: for it is no unusual thing for a mother and her two or three daughters – all of course prostitutes – to receive their 'men' at the same time and in the same room" (*Gas-Light*, 122). Joel Ross visits one of these rooms where a single proprietor, "with that evident consciousness of being exalted to a rank so much above that of many others" (95), claims to pay his rent by taking in lodgers, bedding them all together on piles of rags. Clearly, in the minds of the visitors, these arrangements do not promote habits of personal decency or sexual continence.

But for many visitors the epitome of licentiousness was the dancing saloon of Pete Williams, which along with all the familiar vices of gambling, drinking, and prostitution, contained the hidden threat of an even greater violation: interracial mixing. Dickens visited Pete Williams's place and made it famous in 1842. Mainly interested in the dancing, which he found uncommonly athletic, Dickens also observed closely the racial variety among the customers: a "corpulent black fiddler," "two young mulatto girls, with large, black, drooping eyes," and a "lively hero," who, "having danced his partner off her feet, and himself too, he finishes by leaping gloriously on the bar-counter, and calling for something to drink, with the chuckle of a million of counterfeit Jim Crows, in one inimitable sound" (78–9). Why he considered them "counterfeit" remains a mystery. To many visitors, the only thing counterfeit about this description is Dickens himself. Foster was to challenge it as an "elaborate and artistic picture . . . [for] while the great artist has summoned the aid of all his well-prepared colors to fascinate the imagination with harmonious hues, graceful proportions and startling contrasts, the unambitious reporter contents himself with sketching human nature as it is and as all may see it" (*Gas-Light*, 146). But, like Dickens, Foster is fascinated with Williams's place, claiming that it will "puzzle you" (*Gas-Light*, 141). Many visitors plainly found it horrifying. The anonymous clergyman who did not actually visit the place describes a "motley multitude of men and women, yellow and white, black and dingy, old and young, ugly and – no not

handsome ... giggling and laughing in a style peculiar to the remote descendants of Ham, and making 'night hideous' with their lascivious orgies" (*Life*, 175). Bobo describes "a cellar, where we see a few males and
females, black, yellow, and white, seated or swaggering about the room.
... The music commences, and out sally two or three cotillions of this
piebald party, and away they whirl in a most disgusting and revolting manner. The negroes seem to attract the most attention" (96). E.Z.C. Judson
also emphasizes the range of skin tones: "Not less than two hundred negroes, of every shade, from the light, mellow-cheeked quadroon, down to
the coal-black, were there."[29]

Behind this fascination with skin color, in fact with many physical attributes of the blacks, including their style of dancing, their clothing, and
even their smell, runs a deep anxiety about racial mixture. Whereas Melville was to write in *Redburn* of a black American "walking arm in arm
with a good-looking English woman. In New York, such a couple would
have been mobbed in three minutes" (202); and in *Billy Budd* of the
beauty of "a native African of the unadulterate blood of Ham" (43); the
more common descriptions show the disgust, or at best humorous contempt, that the blood of Ham inspired.[30] True, some writers did not find
"the descendants of *Ham*" any worse than "their neighbors, who claim
for their ancestors Shem and Japheth" (Ross, 96), but the slurs cast upon
Jews in the Five Points are as invidious as those upon blacks, and Foster
ridicules Jewish pawnshops and Yiddish accents (*Gas-Light*, 126–7). Foster
does remark of the black women who patronize the establishment that,
"on the whole, they are more tidy and presentable – or rather less horribly
disgusting – than their white companions" (142). Such faint praise suggests better than anything else how very disturbing white middle-class visitors found Pete Williams's place.

As the proprietor of this notorious establishment, Williams himself is a
kind of local celebrity, who draws similarly mixed assessments from his
visitors. He is described in varying terms as "a rascally-looking wretch who
dealt out the liquors to the frequent calls of his customers" (*Life*, 176),
as "a middle-sized man – of course a colored one ... with a broad grin
that showed at least four inches' width of ivory" (Judson, 90), and as a
"middle-aged, well-to-do, coal-black negro, who has made an immense
amount of money from the profits of his dance-house – which, unfortunately, he regularly gambles away at the sweat-cloth or the roulette-table
as fast as it comes in" (*Gas-Light*, 145). It is of course not openly stated
but nevertheless significant that Pete Williams is a successful property
owner and businessman, as important in his community as his counterparts among the Upper Ten and on Wall Street just a few blocks away.
Foster nevertheless prefers to emphasize his sexual prodigality – "there
are something under a dozen 'yellow-boys' in the neighborhood who have

a very strong resemblance to Pete" (145); and he also alludes to his strong opinions on the theater: "He of course abominates Macready but 'hollers' on Forrest" (145), a reference to the Astor Place riots that Melville participated in on the opposite side. Foster, though giving perhaps the fullest description of Pete Williams available, does not leave us with a satisfying portrait. He offers instead his conflicted explanation of this establishment's character – "you cannot, however, begin to imagine *what* it is" (142) – as a puzzle.

And then moves on. No matter how many disturbing reflections – on morality, race, sexual license, drunkenness, poverty, tenements and landlords, filth, and crime – a visit to Five Points inspires, the authors of these accounts generally exit in good order. Dickens, after meditating on human wickedness, ends with a weary farewell: "let us say, Good night, and climb upstairs to bed" (80). The South Carolinian gives up in disgust, enigmatically expressed: "But enough, let us go home; it is frozen music; it won't pay; the bitter overbalances the sweet" (Bobo, 97). And the clergyman who didn't really visit the Five Points himself breathes a sigh of relief: "But we were glad to emerge from this den, and breathe again the pure air of heaven" (*Life*, 177). The plunge concludes with a return to one's proper element.

In its closure and containment, such a narrative would seem to imitate the anecdotal structure of the spectatorial essay: an excursion into a different part of town that produces a set of new impressions and some old moral reflections. In fact, however, the visit to the labyrinth, as we have seen, is rather more disturbing than the typical spectator sketch. Although the author often dismisses the experience with a joke or a pious statement, he has generally made considerable effort to record what he thinks is the truth about a genuinely distressing place. The vividness of the descriptions, while it often seems sensational, reveals a level of awareness and anxiety that clearly communicated directly with middle-class readers' anxieties about the city. And the graphic reminders of moral, racial, and ideological difference make these accounts very different from those of the spectator, who travels through the city to find out what makes humans everywhere the same.

A second strategy for organizing urban experience – one that appears less commonly than the sensational plunge but has a similar function – creates a taxonomy of urban types. Growing out of the guidebooks and histories of New York and drawing heavily, often self-consciously, on the language of Linnaean classification, this strategy allows the writer to adopt the tone, not of the moralist but of the scientist, guiding the reader through a labyrinth, not of experience but of knowledge.[31] In an early example, the writer of *A Glance at New York* (1837) offers to describe the "genus dandy."

> Like other great cities, New York has her share of this class of the biped
> without feathers. The whole number, after a careful estimate, is believed
> to be about 3000; or one to every hundred of the population. They
> abound more or less in every part of the city, from Corlaer's Hook to
> the Battery, and from Blooming Dale to White Hall. But they are mostly
> to be seen in public places – at the corners of streets, on the door-steps
> of hotels, and in the various public walks.[32]

The author goes on to divide the dandies into three types: "*chained*
dandies, *switched* dandies, and *quizzing-glass* dandies," according to which
"harmless pieces of ornament . . . they severally wear about their persons
or carry in their hands" (80). The supreme form of the breed, "a dandy
of the first water," combines all three; "and his head is found, on dissec-
tion, to possess three times the vacancy of the single, simple, or uncom-
pounded dandy" (81). As a group, dandies *seem* to be multiplying in New
York. But, "the truth is, the race is not particularly admired, and especially
by the ladies. The consequence is, that they have little chance of getting
married and thus propagating the species. It is believed, therefore, that
in time they will run out. That the race will become extinct; and like the
mammoth, leave nothing behind them but their bones: *de mortuis nil nisi
bone-um*" (83). The mock-scientific tone, of course, creates a very different
effect from the horror or puzzlement of the labyrinth sketches. But it is
trying to do something similar, namely, to make sense, to construct an
order of things, out of a new urban phenomenon. Foster does the same
thing when he tries to organize the "classes of eating houses. . . . Linnaeus
would probably classify them as Sweenyorum, Browniverous, and Delmon-
ican" (*Gas-Light*, 216); or, in another essay, he attempts to classify the new
bowling saloons. With these, the issue is one of language: "we used to
have bowling 'alleys' and billiard 'rooms,' in abundance" (84). Now, under the pressure to become genteel, the old alleys and rooms have become
saloons, and "[e]very steamboat is a 'floating palace,' every muddy Daguerreotype is a 'magnificent specimen of the fine arts' – and every grog-
shop harangue is pronounced by the 'intelligent and independent press'
to have been a 'thrilling and masterly effort of genuine eloquence' " (84).
It becomes the task of the writer, then, to sort out these labels and clarify
them for the reader.

Perhaps the most celebrated examples of urban taxonomy appear in
Poe's stories, where the urban detective, working out of his knowledge of
urban types, uses scraps of information to reconstruct the whole character.
In "The Man in the Crowd," the narrator distinguishes between different
classes of people on the street: the businessmen, the "tribe of clerks," the
"swell pick-pockets," the gamblers, peddlers, and beggars, "the women
of the town," and other assorted "ragged artizans and exhausted laborers
of every description."[33] From "an abstract and generalizing turn," his

thoughts "descended to details, and [I] regarded with minute interest the innumerable varieties of figure, dress, air, gait, visage, and expression of countenance" (507). These details include the set of an ear or a thumb, microscopic observations that locate individuals precisely in their classes and places. The whole plot turns on his encountering a specimen that defies his capacity "to form some analysis of the meaning conveyed" (511) by this new species, the man of the crowd. As Melville would do in *White-Jacket*, Poe suggests the epistemological limits and social injustice of such efforts at classification.

Such an awareness does not appear in Thomas Butler Gunn's *The Physiology of New York Boarding-Houses* (1857), an extended example of the taxonomic method. This book humorously addresses itself to the "half a million of human beings" (11) inhabiting New York and also to the future "student, curious in antiquarian knowledge" (14). "The subject is so vast, so comprehensive," however, and the different types so peculiar, that "[c]lassification, therefore, becomes impossible. We shall only endeavor to place them under appropriate titles" (15). And so he describes "The Fashionable Boarding-House Where You Don't Get Enough to Eat," "The Boarding-House Wherein Spiritualism Becomes Pre-Dominant," "The Boarding-House Where There Are Marriageable Daughters," "The Boarding-House Where You're Expected to Make Love to the Landlady," or "The Vegetarian Boarding-House (As It Was)." The catalogue of houses eventually evolves, or rather degenerates, into a racial and ethnic catalogue as well, as he describes the English, French, German, Irish, and Chinese; this is a descending order, with the Chinese at the bottom, "a class of wretched and degraded beings, thoroughly pagan in faith, in vices, in ignorance and misery" (276). As in the labyrinth sketch, the taxonomy allows the writer to establish class and racial differences. Nevertheless, the author claims that "our book is pretty honestly written" (296), just as other urban writers claimed to be presenting only the truth in their pictures of urban misery. Furthermore, he claims to have a serious purpose in exposing the evils of boardinghouse life, though he cannot see any way of doing without them (299). Although it is clear, then, that the taxonomy is intended primarily for amusement, it does address a new, expanding area of knowledge and experience that many city dwellers found threatening. The boardinghouse exposes the middle-class observer to complexities of class and ethnic differences in New York; Gunn's book obligingly guides him through a perplexing new order.

Other taxonomies – George Ellington's *The Women of New York* (1869) or parts of Charles Sutton's *The New York Tombs* (1874), a catalogue of famous criminals – appeared throughout the nineteenth century, but they never achieved the celebrity of the mystery-and-misery fiction, the third variety of urban literature most prevalent in this period. Such works as Joseph Holt Ingraham's *The Miseries of New York* (1844), the anonymous

The Mysteries of New York (1845), E.Z.C. Judson's *The Mysteries and Miseries of New York* (1848), Harrison G. Buchanan's *Asmodeus* (1848), James Rees's *Mysteries of City Life* (1849), George Thompson's *City Crimes; or Life in New York and Boston* (1849) or *New York Life* (1849), Ingraham's *The Beautiful Cigar Girl, or the Mysteries of Broadway* (1849), and George Lippard's *The Empire City* (1850) and *New York: Its Upper Ten and Lower Million* (1853) represent just some of the mystery-and-misery fiction in New York that Melville might have encountered. These novels, sensational portrayals of life in the city often as popular with working-class readers as with the middle-class audience, seem quite similar to the "plunge" literature in portraying the poverty and humiliation of the city's most wretched inhabitants. They differ from the urban sketch, however, in making the labyrinth an image, not just of decay in certain sections of town, but of the systematic corruption of the whole city. Often this expanded labyrinthine scheme dominates the structure of the fiction as well, and we begin to have the labyrinthine plots of Judson and Lippard.

George Foster, in *New York Naked* (1850), announced the sensibility that informs the labyrinth literature:

> Heretofore a thick pall has been spread over the crumbling skeletons and rotting ulcers of civilization, which by the common consent of philosophers, moralists, and political economists, had never been raised to permit anything but the briefest glance at the horrors that lay beneath. But more recently, the juster and braver theory has obtained that truth and light are always good, and that in order to cure the terrible maladies that afflict humanity, first of all it is necessary that they should be clearly examined and deeply probed. So help me Heaven, as I am a living soul, and have an immortal destiny to expect, this has been the one only object of all the developments of misery, destitution, filth, and crime, in the dark labyrinths of this metropolis that ever I have made![34]

As we have seen, Foster's faith in truth – the journalist's pen – and light – the gaslight that reveals the night world to the daytime citizen – sustains him in his probing of the urban ulcers. But in much of the mystery-and-misery literature, that faith is sorely tried, as one character after another comes to grief in the threatening city. Nevertheless, the popular urban fiction offers the reader a number of ways to understand, and to avoid, this fate. This approach, by advising youthful provincials to eschew the city's temptations rather than seek social change, works to sustain rather than to destroy the myth of an urban labyrinth.

Like the urban "plunge" and the urban taxonomy, the mystery-and-misery novels have certain structural characteristics in common. The first of these is the jarring contrast, usually between the wicked city and the innocent countryside. Whitman's *Franklin Evans* begins in rural Long Island and varies the hero's urban adventures with two forays into the country, one in a small inland town and another on a southern plantation. Lippard's *New York: Its Upper Ten and Lower Million* uses the childhood retreat of his dangerous female, Frank Van Huyden, to show the depths of infamy into which she has fallen from her youthful pastoral innocence. The countryside may also seem to reside within characters themselves, who preserve their pastoral innocence in the city; Judson, for example, uses the contrast between Isabella Meadows, a "child of nature," and her brother Charles, the gambler and debauchee, to epitomize the country–city dichotomy. That contrast often seems to fall along gender lines, with the women retaining pastoral virtues while trying to protect their menfolk from urban vices. The story of "Henry Newton and his Sister," for example, shows the "devoted sister" pursuing her erring brother to the city in order to save him (*Life*, 31–54). But in other cases, the woman is the fallen one, as, abandoned by her provincial suitor, she flees to the city for solace or a livelihood or refuge from her stern or brokenhearted parents. The country, however, serves almost unfailingly as the standard of virtue against which urban vice is measured.

But contrasts abound within the city as well, principally between the luxuries of the rich and the miseries of the poor. These differences are obvious in titles like *New York: Its Upper Ten and Lower Million*, or in Matthew Hale Smith's *Sunshine and Shadow in New York* (1869), which is not actually a novel but contains the paradigmatic frontispiece contrasting Stewart's mansion with the Old Brewery.[35] Such contrasts are also mapped, as we have seen, on the surface topography of the town, causing inhabitants to see social and cultural differences in their daily travels through the city. Many stories begin with the lament that "it has been well and often said, that one half of the world know not how the other half live" (*Life*, 7), but in fact the streets constantly expose people to the sufferings of others. Even Broadway, the city's most glamorous thoroughfare, has two sides: the fashionable side where the people promenade to be seen, and the other side, the East side, where people conduct their business: "the west side is known as the 'Dollar' and the east as the 'Shilling Side,' from the fact, I suppose, that all the fancy stores are upon that side" (Bobo, 13). Melville, of course, did not let the opportunity to exploit this irony pass him by in *Pierre*, where, "[m]ixing with neither of these [the West or East side of Broadway], Pierre stalked midway between" (359).

Furthermore, the proximity of Broadway to the Five Points makes forays into the labyrinth relatively simple and convenient: "Extremes are always coming into contact. It is but a step from the mansion where wealth gathers its luxuries, to the cellar or garret where hunger gnaws and cold pinches: from the gorgeous temple where worship goes up from purple cushions, to the cell where guilt and wretchedness curse and groan" (*Life*, 234). Often this contact appears in the urban literature as casual, benign, or even comic. Judson, for example, exploits for comic purposes the episode when his confidence man Frank Hennock accompanies a naive, wealthy merchant, Peter Precise, on a tour of Five Points. Mr. Precise can hardly believe that such sights exist: "My God! Can all this *be*, in a Christian city?" (78). Nevertheless, in spite of having his pocket picked several times during his visit (once by Hennock himself), Precise insists on spending his last cash on food and supplies for the poor, risks catching their diseases, and persists in his investigations long into the night. The contrast between his fussy, middle-class benevolence and the Five Pointers' wretched but generally good-natured condition produces a comic effect.

The more typical social contrast, however, places wealthy vice opposite virtuous poverty in a much more sinister relationship. Lippard's *Empire City* throws countless beautiful, innocent, and defenseless women into the clutches of men whose money gives them the power to take what they want. Virtue is no defense against men like Gabriel Godlike, the sensual, powerful senator, or Beverly Barron, the man of fashion and despoiler of wives. But again, gender lines may shift. Madame Resimer, the abortionist, is just as wealthy, powerful, and corrupt as her male colleagues,[36] and Frank Van Huyden, habituated by her father and lovers to wealth and luxury, takes full advantage of available males. The contrast becomes even more striking when it is embodied in one person, as when the fascinating, corrupt Frank tells of her youthful innocence or when the beautiful wife and mother Joanna is, at the same time, the mistress of Beverly Barron.

A second narrative structure in the labyrinth literature, just as potent as the moral and social contrast, is the rush toward ruin. For although most urban authors express sympathy for the sufferers in the city, and often recognize how the greed of the wealthy exploits the poor, they tend to blame human weakness and sensuality for the degradation of their characters. Particularly in relation to sexuality, the rush to ruin explains such anomalies as Frank and Joanna. Virtuous women must, of course, strenuously resist the sexual advances of men; but once they do submit, for whatever reason, they unleash powerful passions within themselves and can never be pure again. Foster's prostitute in *New York by Gas-Light* falls naively into the hands, first of her equally naive cousin and then of a hypocritical minister, who sees an opportunity and seizes it. "Thus, by my instinctive trust in love and my natural veneration for religion and its minister, was I, while yet a child, perverted to shame" (99). But as a result, she becomes a sexual monster: "What are men to me, but as victims to pluck, or food for my insane and fierce appetites?" (99) Similarly, Frank Van Huyden, once sacrificed to her mother's schemes for prostituting her, displays her own latent corruption by living the life of the wealthy courtesan with fierce and desperate pride.[37]

Drinking has a similar effect on people. Once having taken the first sip, the unprepared young man or woman can seldom avoid complete destruction. And that swift, sure onrush into disaster comes to stand for the experience of entering the city itself:

> I would rather speak of NEW YORK, under a figure drawn from the borders of our own state. The youth who enters it glides smoothly along, as on a gently descending stream, whose banks are clothed with verdure and gemmed with flowers; onward and downward he floats his bark; he is in the rapids now, but he loves his danger, hears with mad joy the roar of the mighty cataract below; laughs at the mists that rise like pillars of cloud to warn him that destruction is near; he plies the oar with fiercer strength, as if the lightning speed of the dashing current were too slow for him; on, on, down, down; the brink is gained; one wild *hurrah* rises above the torrent's voice, and the young voyager makes the final, fatal, returnless plunge. (*Life*, 13)

In just such terms do the seduced woman and the drunken man rush toward ruin, often taking in every other possible vice and crime along the way. And yet, although the torrent seems a resistless force and the labyrinth an impossible maze, the author often blames the youth for succumbing to their influence. Either weak in virtue or strong in passion, the provincial innocent risks all by entering the city in the first place.

The moral-reform authors, then, would seem to want to have their virtuous men and women and their labyrinths too. Even when authors bemoan the fate of poor sewing girls forced into prostitution or young clerks into gambling, they imply that although perhaps initially honest, these provincials too easily forgot or neglected their parents' teachings. They mystify the power of sexual drives and alcoholic influence to sway young hearts. Exposing human evil in the mass, these novels offer moral but not social or political solutions. "Oh, reader! – if it is your determination to follow us through the many checkered paths that it will be our purpose to walk, you will have revealed to you a knowledge of things done in this great city, that you never knew, and little dreamed of before. . . . Reflect well upon this – reason as you ought, and abhor these plague-spots upon the fair face of society."[38] The effect of much labyrinth literature is to explain the misery of the poor and the mystery of urban life as built in to the structure of the city itself, with its striking contrasts, its display of vice, its seductive pressures, and the certainty of complete destruction if one gives in to temptation. Yet that structure is viewed not as social or political in nature but almost always as moral. The provincial in the labyrinth, the reader of the novel, has but one choice: to avoid the plague spots of the city, to refuse to enter the labyrinth at all.

Clearly, though, if provincials did not go to the city there would be no urban novel, and so the urban novelist must strengthen the reader's virtue so that he or she can traverse the city safely. Herein lies the strategy of mystification. The urban mystery novel attempts to guide the provincial reader and protagonist through the labyrinth by revealing the mysteries and miseries to avoid. And yet the graphic depiction of those secret horrors and temptations, according to the logic of the labyrinth literature itself, is bound to draw the provincial into the labyrinth inexorably, from the first sip of urban experience. The urban novelist, then, must convince readers that they alone can resist the attraction of the labyrinth; the vicarious experience will, in a sense, innoculate them against its dangers. If readers believe, however, that they can resist the pull to inevitable ruin, then they must believe in the power of individual virtue, not of collective action, to triumph over the social challenges of the city. The hidden promise of the labyrinth literature is of success for the middle-class city dweller and failure for the miserable, who because of their individual weaknesses – they were warned, after all – or racial or ethnic characteristics, have brought their terrible fates upon themselves. This distinction is important, because it is too easy to see the urban literature only as trying to attract provincials through its sensational portrayals of a dazzling underworld. The moral warnings, like the labels on cigarette packets, may appear the necessary gloss on a literature intended to seduce provincials into the city. In fact, people like Foster, Lippard, and Judson are doing something more sincere than this cynical explanation would suggest. They are serious in warning people away from the city's dangers and temptations. The problem, or contradiction, lies in the fact that, although they may be willing to recognize the full scope of urban poverty, they continue to uphold bourgeois virtue as the solution to it. Even Lippard, who goes the furthest in indicting the city as a social and economic system, stops short of recommending social change. His hero, Giulian Van Huyden, does recognize the evils of property: "Wealth, after all, call it what you will, let it appear in the shape of coin, or take the form of land, or manifest itself in paper money, splendid edifices, or luxurious apparel, is but the representation of so much sweat, so many tears, so much blood."[39] Yet his complicated will, intended to extricate *him* from the responsibility of administering his wealth, entangles his descendants in a maze of sorrow and crime. His good intentions help to build an urban labyrinth; and although Lippard exposes them in the end, the harm is done.

Lippard, however, is problematic in that he does emphatically draw attention to the economic structure of crime and misery.[40] His breathtaking description of New York emphasizes its labyrinthine complexity, its immense commercial power, and the evil effects of its success. It also gathers together and heightens many of the strategies we have seen so far: the country–city contrast, shown here in a vision of New York's pastoral landscape swallowed up by the "wilderness of stone and brick and mortar, dissected by streets, and encircled by forests of masts"; and the contrasts between wealth and poverty, vice and virtue, in an "Empire of

wealth that blinds you with its glare, and misery, that strikes you dumb
with its anguish, an empire of palaces and hovels, garlands and chains,
churches and jails" (42). But Lippard goes beyond the conventional contrasts by examining closely the economic structure that creates them; and
in this endeavor he embarks on a deeper social analysis than the labyrinth
literature typically attempts. The opening to *New York: Its Upper Ten and
Lower Million* makes Lippard's social and political consciousness especially
clear in a contrast between the economies of Europe and America:

> In the Old World twenty-one years glide by, and everything is the same.
> At the end of twenty-one years, two millions would still be two millions.
> Twenty-one years in the New World is as much as two centuries to the
> Old. The vast expanse of land; the constant influx of population; the
> space for growth afforded by institutions as different from those of Eu-
> rope (that is from those of the past), as day from night – all contribute
> to this result. . . . Thus in twenty-one years, by *holding on to its own*, the
> Van Huyden Estate has swelled from TWO MILLIONS to ONE HUNDRED
> MILLIONS OF DOLLARS. The age moves on; it remains in its original pro-
> prietorship, swelled by the labor of millions, who derive but a penny
> where they bestow upon the estate a dollar. It works not; mankind works
> for it. Has this wealth no duties to mankind? Is there not something
> horrible in the thought of an entire generation, for mere subsistence,
> spending their lives, in order to make this man, this estate, or this cor-
> poration, the possessor of incredible wealth? (viii, ix)

Lippard's whole plot, in fact, depends on this economic structure, for as
the fortune has increased, Van Huyden's heirs are now willing to commit
every conceivable crime in order to eliminate their rivals. Thus Lippard's
city is a labyrinth of money and property; and it is greed, not the temptations of sex and liquor, that drives men and women to ruin.

There is no mistaking Lippard's sincerity or political energy in the
novel. At the climax, in a repudiation of popular plot formulae, Van Huyden's virtuous heir refuses to "touch one dollar of the Van Huyden estate!
. . . Have you been a father to me? It would be very striking, and altogether
like the fifth act of a melodrama, no doubt, for me to overlook your
twenty-one years of silence, and with love and tears consent to be your
heir. But you have not been my father" (278–9). The heir, called Nameless throughout, has himself been one of the miserable poor and recognizes that his father's wealth has created a labyrinth from which he must
extricate himself. But in the end, Lippard leaves the matter of the one
hundred millions unresolved. Nameless retires to a pastoral life, Giulian
Van Huyden goes to Rome, and the last remaining heir, the socialist Arthur Dermoyne, leads a party of homesteaders West. The virtuous characters, then, leave the labyrinth but refuse to take responsibility for the
wealth that keeps others in its thrall. Having created the labyrinth and

condemned its effects, they depart from the city, which remains a labyrinth still. Thus Lippard's opening question, "Has this wealth no duties to mankind?" (ix), remains unanswered at the end. And although Lippard offers a radical critique of the economic structure of the city, he mystifies the labyrinth just as much as the temperance writers do.

Nevertheless, we can see how successfully the labyrinth literature performs, in Jane Tompkins's phrase, its "cultural work."[41] This work is to explain to people living in a city that has become unrecognizable how they may navigate its new terrain. It does not suggest that they may change the terrain. One can choose whether or not to enter the labyrinth, and one can learn, with the help of the author, how to get through it safely; one can even hope to help individuals in distress. But even as acute an observer as Lippard does not try to imagine how to make the city *not* a labyrinth.

Nor, in that particular sense, does Melville. All of the protagonists of his mid-century urban novels are provincials trying to move through an urban labyrinth. Redburn seems the least equipped to enter, the one most prone to take a quick plunge and retreat. White-Jacket, far more adventurous and cunning, attempts an urban taxonomy in his quest for knowledge of urban secrets and crimes. And Pierre commits himself fully to an exploration of an overwhelming labyrinth he cannot hope to escape. In large part, then, Melville's provincials undergo the trials of their urban counterparts in historical and literary New York. But Melville suggests, through his creative use of this literary trope, the ways in which his provincials have mystified themselves and their experience. In his novels, the labyrinth becomes a cultural construction allowing the hero to imagine that his urban quest will end successfully. In fact he fails, not because of moral weakness, as many of the urban narratives might conclude, but because he foolishly trusts in the mystifications of urban literature.

Redburn: *A Plunge into Urban Poverty*

Redburn is an especially clear example of Melville's ironic demystification of urban myths, because the youthful protagonist so studiously adheres to the standard moral frame of the urban plunge narrative. Thoroughly schooled in temperance and reform literature, anxiously nurtured by provincial, virtuous women, and immature as the standard provincial heroes, Redburn enters the labyrinths of New York, Liverpool, and London to seek his fortune. In the end he fails to make a cent, but he also avoids the conventional rush to ruin, not because he is especially virtuous or has met a kindly urban guide, but because his provincial caution and anxiety prevent him from engaging fully in the urban experience. Like the visitors to Five Points, he sees just enough of the urban labyrinth to satisfy him that he would rather not see more. He returns to the provinces at the end, seemingly little wiser than when he left; at least, his abandonment of the destitute Harry Bolton suggests that he has learned only prudential wisdom in the city.[42]

Yet this reading of Redburn's character leaves out the very real gains he has made in his compassion for and understanding of different classes of people,[43] and it ignores the rich humor and sympathy with which Melville endows his narration. The evident affection of Melville's narrator for his erring protagonist reveals that the real target of his irony is less the boy than his literary and moral culture.[44] And Melville's use of the urban plots and tropes suggests not so much an attempt to reach a popular audience by filling the book with "diverting dark-temperance and city-mysteries images"[45] as it offers a new way to understand the provincial as one who remains mystified by the city's mysteries because of his indoctrination in the literature of mystery. Melville's narrator, however, possesses the understanding that Redburn lacks and thus corrects for his faulty vision. It is very clear, then, how the process of mystification is taking place.

To begin with, Redburn is unusually unprepared for life in the labyrinth, unusually inclined to be mystified. For unlike the typical working- or even middle-class provincial like Franklin Evans or Charlie Meadows, Redburn is a product of an older urban environment, the city of the elite spectator. Redburn is the "Son-of-a-Gentleman" (as are White-Jacket, Ishmael, and Pierre) who was born in New York; he grew up reading the *Spectator* and hearing his spectator father tell stories about his journeys to Europe's great cities. His father's ruin has forced provinciality upon him, and he is truly a "boy disappointed" (10). He enters the city, then, with a certain proprietary self-righteousness, pointing his gun threateningly at the cabin passengers on the river boat and nourishing desperate schemes: all very different from the humble hopes that a hero like Franklin Evans expresses on arriving in the city ("God . . . has planted in our bosoms the great sheet-anchor Hope!" [148]). For Franklin Evans the journey to the city represents a rise in his class expectations; for Redburn it signals a fall. And although educated from an early age in the ways of the city, he knows only the old European city "full of mossy cathedrals and churches, and long, narrow, crooked streets without side-walks, and lined with strange houses" (5). Thinking himself an urban native, a spectator by rights, he undergoes an even greater social fall than the typical provincial youth.

Nevertheless, although Melville makes Redburn in some ways an unconventional provincial, he subjects him to the humbling experiences of the greenhorn by exposing him to foreign cities – Liverpool and London – and the ship itself, where his provinciality makes him the target of sailor abuse. He also constructs the novel's various urban environments as versions of a moral labyrinth. By breaking up the urban experience into parts, however, he prevents Redburn from hurtling into ruin. Rather, *Red-*

burn follows a more episodic structure as the boy makes the plunge into one urban environment after another. In a sense, his experience is repetitive, yielding always the same limited moral wisdom. But Redburn does in fact gain insight; and although he does not recognize how his cultural conditioning has shaped his responses to the city, the narrator's humorous irony makes it evident. Furthermore, the narrator emphasizes that Redburn learns to read social signs that challenge his former readings of the city. As in the plunge literature, he enters the foreign element and returns to the native one externally unchanged, but in fact his whole orientation has subtly altered. The repetitive, episodic structure shows how gradually, though not sensationally, Redburn has changed.

The novel divides unevenly into five urban expeditions: Redburn's first visit to New York, his outbound journey on the *Highlander*, his explorations of Liverpool, the brief nocturnal visit to London, and his return on the *Highlander* to New York. In each of these, Redburn's experience of finding himself in an urban labyrinth of vice and poverty causes him to test his conventional reading of the city. And in each encounter, the ironic narrator makes it clear that Redburn's way of seeing the city as a labyrinth relieves him of social responsibility, even as he sheds some of his moral conventionality. In the end, it seems that Redburn's successful negotiation of the labyrinth has implicated him unwittingly in the mystification of urban poverty.

Redburn's first visit to New York, his briefest urban experience, nevertheless establishes two important points: his conditioning in the spectator tradition, and his capacity for keen yet detached observation of urban life. The opening chapter reveals his childish admiration for the cities his father traveled and the genteel literature his father read: "There was a fine library edition of the Spectator in six large volumes with gilded backs; and many a time I gazed at the word '*London*' on the title-page" (7). In his mind he connects these volumes with a bookcase that resembles an Old World house: "It had a sort of basement, with large doors, and a lock and key" (7). Cities appear to him in the context of urban literature, and literature in the image of European cities. His genteel urban background, however, causes him to misread Captain Riga's behavior when he gets to New York. The captain, seeing an opportunity to cheat an inexperienced youth, tells Redburn's friend, "I hope he's a country lad, sir ... these city boys are sometimes hard cases" (16). Riga, simply reinforcing Redburn's own provincial prejudices, swindles him out of an advance on his wages. Redburn does recognize that it would have been better not to tell Riga of his genteel connections, but he still feels mystified enough by his gentlemanly dress and demeanor to ship with him.

Nevertheless, that brief encounter seems to make him more alert in his excursion into the Five Points area, namely Chatham Street, where he finds the pawnshops. Foster describes these as the haunts of "the descendants of Israel . . . the human kite, formed to be feared, hated and despised, yet to prey upon mankind" (*Gas-Light*, 127–8). Redburn adopts an automatic racism too, seeing the pawnshop owner as evil, "a curly-headed little man with a dark oily face, and a hooked nose, like the pictures of Judas Iscariot" (19). He does not seem entirely surprised, then, when the man offers him only half what he thinks his gun is worth; energetically Redburn seizes the gun and goes on. But although Redburn is prepared to see the pawnshops as dens of infamy, "like a great seine, that caught every variety of fish" (21), he also takes a rather more detached and detailed view of the owners and customers than Foster does. Foster sees the shopkeepers conventionally as villains, but Redburn offers a surprising note of empathy when he describes them standing behind their counters like "prisoners looking out of a jail" (20). Foster describes only the "felon" who brings in his stolen goods, but Redburn records vignettes of "a thin woman in a faded silk gown and shawl, holding a pale little girl by the hand" (20) and of "a young man in a seedy red cravat and a pimply face" (21), whom Redburn describes as "martyrized" by the shop-owner's accusations of theft. On the whole Redburn avoids the sentimentality and moralizing of the Five Points sketch.

This plunge into a picturesque urban underworld gives Redburn his first and most direct experience of the city. But the long journey to Liverpool extends his exposure by throwing him among a crew who live primarily in the city. As a packet ship, the *Highlander* is a much more domestic craft than Melville's whalers and naval vessels. Indeed, the story of Max, the sailor with a wife in New York and another in Liverpool, shows that the maritime life of these men represents a brief interlude in their onshore, urban lives. They may have cosmopolitan habits – they "talked about Gibraltar, and Canton, and Valparaiso, and Bombay, just as you and I would about Peck Slip and Bowery" (46) – but they are not essentially travelers: "sailors only go *round* the world, without going *into* it" (133). They inhabit primarily the working-class districts of the cities where they dock. In allowing Redburn to enter into this life, the voyage helps him understand a class he has never known before and prepares him for the great social labyrinth of Liverpool.

Until now, Redburn has "never thought of working for my living" (36); the sailors, however, teach him the culture of the working man.[46] The first and most painful lesson he learns is class hostility, for the sailors see Redburn as competition: "They asked me what business I, a boy like me, had to go to sea, and take the bread out of the mouths of honest sailors and fill a good seaman's place." Redburn interprets this complaint as personal abuse: "how could I help seeing, that the men who could thus talk to a poor, friendless boy, on the very first night of his voyage to sea, must be capable of almost any enormity," and consequently he "loathed, detested, and hated them with all that was left of my bursting heart and soul" (52).

When he learns more about the sailors' lives, however, he comes to see them not as wicked individuals who hate him but as members of a class whose structure he begins to comprehend.

Redburn understands and enters the sailors' world first through the medium of alcohol. Unlike the naval sailors of *White-Jacket*, who receive their daily tot of liquor, the *Highlander* sailors must get their liquor in the city. And like the characters in urban temperance novels, they are perpetually addicted to drink, loading up while on shore and bringing on board their jugs and cigars for *"tapering off"* (46) at sea. When they get to Liverpool, the drinking will start again at Danby's saloon; they ship for New York dead drunk or, in the case of Miguel Saveda, just dead, and arrive in the city ready to drain their glasses and purses again. Having taken the temperance pledge and read the *Sailors Magazine*, Redburn is prepared to see the sailors' drinking in the light of moral urban literature. Yet he himself becomes a drinker on the voyage. At first, he accepts the liquor out of "necessity," to cure his seasickness. But, as he remarks, this event launches a career of similar episodes, about which he seems to feel little remorse; "it insidiously opened the way to subsequent breaches of it [the temperance pledge], which though very slight, yet carried no apology with them" (44).[47] Later Redburn has no trouble enjoying a sociable glass of beer with the skipper of a salt drogher or some wine with Harry Bolton at the gambling palace. For all his horror, then, at the condition of the sailors, he does not himself undergo the rush to ruin. Unlike Franklin Evans or Solon Robinson's Jim Reagan, both of whom must renew their pledges when they find they cannot drink even a little without becoming drunk, Redburn adopts a policy of moderate temperance. In this way he is able to join the sailors' alcoholic culture while still maintaining his own sobriety. He is, in other words, able to negotiate successfully the labyrinth of drink.

Redburn also learns to deal with the racial diversity he encounters on board the ship. Whereas many visitors to the Five Points area fled in horror from the spectacle of blacks mixing with whites and all sorts of strangers with each other, Redburn learns to accept the range of racial and social types he meets on the ship.[48] Partly he is able to do so because he can make fun of them, especially the blacks; but also, the two blacks on board, Mr. Thompson the cook and Lavender the steward, occupy a special status that makes it possible to like and to condescend to them at the same time, much as George Foster does with Pete Williams. For the blacks are not sailors competing with the whites for their jobs but instead serve in menial positions; Redburn feels safe making jokes at their expense. So Mr. Thompson appears as a comic religious old man who studies his Bible among the cooking pots, entertains "reverend looking old darkies, who besides their natural canonicals, wore quaker-cut black coats," and "notwithstanding his religious studies and meditations . . . used to use some bad language occasionally" (82). Lavender the steward is a "handsome, dandy mulatto, that had once been a barber in West-Broadway." He perfumes himself, cherishes a "lock of frizzled hair" that he carries in his vest pocket, and is "a sentimental sort of darky, and read the '*Three Spaniards*' and '*Charlotte Temple*.' " Redburn uses the contrast between them, and their paradoxical friendship, for comic purposes, making them objects of curiosity; when they sit together on the cook's narrow shelf, they look like "the Siamese twins" (83).

Redburn's humor, however, uses the racial stereotypes in subtle ways. On the one hand, he seems to adopt a tolerant, mildly condescending tone:

> And sometimes Mr. Thompson would take down his Bible, and read a chapter for the edification of Lavender, whom he knew to be a sad profligate and gay deceiver ashore; addicted to every youthful indiscretion. He would read over to him the story of Joseph and Potiphar's wife; and hold Joseph up to him as a young man of excellent principles, whom he ought to imitate, and not be guilty of his indiscretion any more. And Lavender would look serious, and say that he knew it was all true – he was a wicked youth, he knew it – he had broken a good many hearts, and many eyes were weeping for him even then, both in New York, and Liverpool, and London, and Havre. But how could he help it? . . . It was not he, but the others, that were to blame; for his bewitching person turned all heads and subdued all hearts, wherever he went. And then he would look very serious and penitent, and go up to the little glass, and pass his hands through his hair, and see how his whiskers were coming on. (83–4)

This passage exploits in full its comic possibilities: the contrast between grave Mr. Thompson and the "gay deceiver"; the satire on religious literature, which would condemn the erring Lavender; and the implied contrast between the way this potentially serious scene would play between two white men and its rendition here in literary blackface. Redburn seems to have used humor to neutralize whatever might seem challenging about the black presence on the ship.

At the same time, however, Redburn's tone draws attention to the way Melville is breaking down racial stereotypes even as he seems to reinforce them. For in the detail with which he describes the two men, Redburn offers a tribute to their individual characters that dignifies the racial humor. His portrait of Mr. Thompson in particular suggests a depth of character beyond the stereotype So, although he makes fun of the cook's belabored attempts at reading, he takes his project seriously:

> But on the day I speak of, it was no wonder that he got perplexed, for he was reading a mysterious passage in the Book of Chronicles. Being

aware that I knew how to read, he called me as I was passing his premises, and read the passage over, demanding an explanation. I told him
it was a mystery that no one could explain; not even a parson. But this
did not satisfy him, and I left him poring over it still. (82)

Perhaps Redburn is poking fun at the idea of anyone reading the Book
of Chronicles seriously; the beginning, at least, with its long genealogical
lists, offers little for "a serious old fellow, much given to metaphysics"
(81) to chew on. But Mr. Thompson's dedication to his task makes him
nevertheless a worthy character. In a novel little given to character analysis, the attention devoted to him and to Lavender suggests Redburn's
willingness to observe closely and sympathetically, even when echoing certain prejudices.

Mr. Thompson of *"Fore-castle-square,* opposite the *Liberty Pole"* (82),
Lavender formerly of West-Broadway, are just two of the characters who
remind Redburn that he is living in an urban environment. In fact, he is
most struck by the sailors' behaving as if maritime travel meant only a
slight interruption of their ordinary lives. Even on board, the sailors pursue their urban occupations, which Redburn finds ridiculous. Jack Blunt,
for example, spends most of his time, as Lavender does, worrying assiduously about his hair. The fact that there is no one on board to admire
Blunt's efforts does not discourage him; he is preparing himself for im-
minent social activity. Captain Riga, too, treats the voyage as an interlude
during which he can wear his "shabby clothes, very different from the
glossy suit I had seen him in at our first interview, and after that on the
steps of the City Hotel, where he always boarded when in New York."
Redburn is shocked to see him rush "out of the cabin in his nightcap,
and nothing else but his shirt on; and leaping up on the poop . . . [begin]
to jump up and down, and curse and swear, and call the men aloft all
manner of hard names, just like a common loafer in the street." Like the
men, though, Riga behaves as if the ship were an extension of the city;
except that, unlike Blunt and Lavender, he neglects his hair, which "by
a sort of miracle, began to grow of a pepper and salt color, which might
have been owing, though, to his discontinuing the use of some kind of
dye while at sea" (71).

The most peculiarly urban character, however, and the most disturbing
to Redburn, is Jackson, who "was a native of New York city, and had a
good deal to say about *highbinders,* and *rowdies* whom he denounced as
only good for the gallows; but I thought he looked a good deal like a
highbinder himself" (56). Where Redburn would have gained the experience required to form this judgment is anyone's guess, but clearly he is
perplexed by Jackson's association with urban working-class gangs. For
although Redburn sees Jackson as evil, a "Cain afloat" (104), a fiend
(62), he also sees him as part of a recognizable urban subculture, the

working men of the Bowery: "He dressed a good deal like a Bowery boy; for he despised the ordinary sailor-rig" (56). With his blue overalls, red woolen shirt, and broad white hat, Jackson announces the independent republican spirit of the American b'hoy. To writers like Foster, Judson, and Whitman, the b'hoy represents the best and most characteristic urban type.[49] Foster racistly claims that the b'hoy expresses the *"free development to Anglo-Saxon nature"*; and, to him, "[t]here can be no doubt that, thus far, the Anglo-American is the highest and most perfect specimen of the human being" (*Gas-Light*, 170). He admits that "in the boisterous roughness, the rude manners and the profanity of the b'hoy there is little, truly, to elicit our admiration" (170). But the b'hoy is also the true working man:

> his cheerful and patient performance of the labor to which he is allotted and by which he lives – his constancy and faithfulness to his domestic duties and responsibilities – his open abhorrence of all "nonsense" – the hearty manner in which he stands up on all occasions for his friend, and especially his indomitable devotion to fair play – bespeak for him and his future destiny our warmest sympathies and our highest hopes. (170)

More importantly, however, the b'hoy embodies American political ideals:

> His hatred of the self-styled "aristocracy" – what is that but an exaggeration of a virtuous contempt for coxcombry, affectation, sham and snobbery? For well he knows that the only aristocracy in such a country as his is composed of its men of genius and intellectual power. . . . He is on intimate terms with men like Walsh and Leggett, whom he knows to be far superior in every respect to the shallow-pated, milk-hearted sucklings of foppery and fashion. How can he fail, under these circumstances, to imbibe a thorough dislike of an aristocracy he believes to be absolutely his inferiors – who possess no natural nor political rights over himself – and whose one solitary point of distinction is that they have more money than he? (171)

Jackson, with his claim of kinship with the great general and president, seems to assert the same kind of radical-democratic politics as the b'hoys.[50]

Clearly, however, Redburn sees none of these attractive traits in Jackson. Instead he sees him as a bully, full of "brass and impudence," "a marvelously clever, cunning man, though without education; [who] . . . understood human nature to a kink, and well knew whom he had to deal with" (57). Jackson certainly seems to know whom he has to deal with in Redburn, for more than ridiculing his greenness, as the other sailors do, he takes him in deadly earnest: "if ever I crossed his path, or got into his way, he would be the death of me, and if ever I stumbled about in the rigging near *him*, he would make nothing of pitching me overboard" (52). Redburn attributes these remarks to Jackson's evil nature, his sickness, perhaps his jealousy of Redburn's health and good looks. But Foster explains the b'hoy's temper in political terms that seem more relevant to Jackson:

> [H]e sees that by the mere accident or perhaps dishonesty or oppression and defrauding his class which has enabled them to amass a little money, they live in ostentatious idleness and ease, – producing nothing yet enjoying all, – while he produces all and enjoys nothing. Is it not natural that all this should rankle in his heart until he becomes impatient, unjust and reckless, and sometimes even is led to wreak personal vengeance upon the obnoxious class? (*Gas-Light*, 171–2)

Jackson's taking a particular dislike to the genteel Redburn suggests an irritation of this kind; and Redburn's seeing that hostility as stemming from Jackson's mental disorder, his evil nature, or his "moody madness" (58) offers a good example of the process of mystification at work. Redburn knows enough of the b'hoy and highbinder culture to recognize Jackson's independence in clothing and attitude. Yet he fails to see the political dimensions of Jackson's behavior and persists in judging him morally. At first he prays not to end up like Jackson – "I began to feel a hatred growing up in me against the whole crew – so much so, that I prayed against it, that it might not master my heart completely, and so make a fiend of me, something like Jackson" (62) – but then masters his own heart enough to pity him: "though there were moments when I almost hated this Jackson, yet I have pitied no man as I have pitied him" (105). As the urban reform literature repeatedly indicates, this attitude of virtuous pity helps to mystify rather than expose the causes of human wretchedness.[51]

Redburn's uncharitable attitude toward Jackson represents a blind spot in his social vision. But in other ways, his experience on board the *Highlander*, by submerging him in an urban subculture, challenges and to some extent softens his prejudices. Redburn sheds certain genteel provincialisms – his idea of visiting the captain, for example, or his fussiness about getting his feet wet – and abandons to some degree his racial and social preconceptions. He also learns enough of the sailor's art to perform his job creditably and to blunt the worst of the sailors' criticisms. He stops talking about the sailors in the mass, either as "cruel and black-hearted" (52) or, in sentimental terms, as "men of naturally gentle and kind dispositions, whom only hardships, and neglect, and ill-usage had made outcasts from good society" (47). When he describes the privileged captain and cabin passengers, or the men turning in after a night watch, his tone suggests unquestioned solidarity with the working-class crew.

It may seem surprising, then, that when Redburn reaches Liverpool, he reverts to many of his genteel attitudes, especially toward the city. But Liverpool is much more an urban labyrinth than the *Highlander*. And in this city, which includes a far wider range of classes than exists on the *Highlander* and a much greater social diversity, Redburn becomes newly provincial. Yet in repeating the plot of a provincial plunge into a labyrinth, Melville has new opportunities to display Redburn's ignorance of this complex social system that, "away from the docks, was very much such a place as New York" (202). And Redburn shows in new ways his tendency to mystify urban poverty through pious disclaimers of individual responsibility.

The Liverpool sections of *Redburn* appear to most readers to establish the urban themes of the novel. Redburn's wanderings through town, his discovery of vice in the "Corinthian haunts" of the port, and his attempts to relieve a dying mother and her children in a cellar have been extensively discussed as evidence of Melville's awareness of social ills and his capacity to represent the city and its mysteries.[52] It has, however, not been viewed in the more specific context of New York's urban form, its growth, ideology, and cultural construction as a labyrinth. Placed in that context, Liverpool appears a faithful portrait of New York and a strident challenge to Redburn's provincial thinking. In Liverpool, Redburn shows an awareness of the city's social structure and a defiance of reform ideology that he was not willing or able to display in New York. In the Liverpool sections, Redburn develops a social consciousness; and this urban awareness makes his forays into London, and later New York, where he reverts to provincial attitudes, especially surprising and unexpected.

Redburn's first question – "And this is England?" – establishes that Liverpool, rather than being the elegant upper-class city that he was expecting, and that his father experienced, has become like New York a confusing mixture of peoples and classes: "[f]rom the street came a confused uproar of ballad-singers, bawling women, babies, and drunken sailors" (133). Intending to tour the city as a spectator, Redburn finds himself a new arrival trying to find his way in an urban labyrinth. Ironically, that understanding arises from his misguided attempts to use his father's guidebook. And, in a further irony, he describes one of those family guidebooks as stamped with "an intricate coat of arms on the cover, looking like a diagram of the Labyrinth of Crete" (142). To Redburn it is the quaint old guidebooks, with their heraldic devices and pedantic titles, that seem labyrinthine at first. And in fact, the old town his father visited has some characteristics of a labyrinth: "there seems little plan in the confined and crooked looking marks for the streets, and the docks irregularly scattered along the bank of the Mersey" (144–5). His father's pen-marks, inscribed on the old map of Liverpool, show that he "penetrated . . . into the narrowest courts" (145). Redburn fondly hopes that the guidebook will allow him, too, to penetrate the city: "Great was my boyish delight at the prospect of visiting a place, the infallible clew to all whose intricacies I held in my hand" (151). But, because of the changes in the physical and social terrain of the town, Redburn finds to his sorrow "to how few is the old guide-book now a clew" (157).

The structural changes in Liverpool closely resemble those in New York in the 1840s, and Redburn's observations of them echo the anxiety these changes produced in New Yorkers. Redburn makes this connection explicitly when he refers to the New York guidebooks:

> And even as this old guide-book boasts of the, to us, insignificant Liverpool of fifty years ago, the New-York guide-books are now vaunting of the magnitude of the town, whose future inhabitants, multitudinous as the pebbles on the beach, and girdled in with high walls and towers, flanking endless avenues of opulence and taste, will regard all our Broadways and Bowerys as but the paltry nucleus to their Ninevah. From far up the Hudson, beyond Harlem River, where the young saplings are now growing, that will overarch their lordly mansions with broad boughs, centuries old; they may send forth explorers to penetrate into the then obscure and smoky alleys of the Fifth Avenue and Fourteenth-street; and going still farther south, may exhume the present Doric Custom-house, and quote it as proof that their high and mighty metropolis enjoyed a Hellenic antiquity. (149)

This passage first gives an accurate assessment of the preoccupation of many contemporary guidebooks with New York's population. E. Porter Belden, for example, estimates that "New-York and its vicinity, at the close of the nineteenth century, will contain nearly three millions of souls" (125), although he acknowledges that "[t]o penetrate the arcana of the future, is impossible" (123). Joel Ross guesses that "in 1860 [the population] will probably be, including Brooklyn and Williamsburgh, at least 1,000,000," although "[p]robably the day will come when New-York will have outstripped all the cities of the old, as she has already those of the new world" (13). Mid-century guidebooks seemed to vie with each other in statistical calculations of New York's future population and land mass. But Redburn's description of their "vaunting" secondarily draws attention to the anxiety they betray over that unbridled growth, as it surges "beyond the Harlem River" and reduces proud Fifth Avenue to "obscure and smoky alleys." Redburn exposes New York's pretensions to grandeur by suggesting ironically that future archaeologists will mistake the neoclassical Custom House for a genuine antiquity. And in implying that "they may send forth explorers to penetrate" the old streets, Redburn projects the labyrinth into the future, as New York's eventual destiny.

Redburn's sense of disorientation in Liverpool is described in terms for which New Yorkers could have found local referents. For example, when he looks for the Old Fort and finds the Old Fort tavern instead, he discovers the same paradox that visitors to New York observed in finding that the Battery, the old Revolutionary fort, was now a public promenade. When he looks for his father's hotel and encounters a man whose father helped to tear it down, he feels the wonder expressed by many New York journalists over their changing city: "It is startling to enumerate the number of churches which have been pulled down and displaced to make room for the great business which spreads with such astounding rapidity over the whole lower part of the city, prostrating and utterly obliterating every thing that is old and venerable, and leaving not a single land-mark, in token of the former position of the dwelling-places of our ancestors" (*Putnam's* 1, April 1853, 357–8). Perhaps the greatest shock comes when Redburn seeks the Old Dock, which once held *"so great a number of ships afloat in the very heart of the town"* (158), and finds instead the Custom House. He learns that the old pool that gave the city its name served as a dock but was later filled in: "here the doom of Gomorrah seemed reversed, and a lake had been converted into substantial stone and mortar" (158–9). Many New York guidebooks made similar remarks about the filling in of Collect Pond, whose history seemed emblematic of the city itself. Once a home for the Indians and a source of water and recreation for the early town, it became poisoned by tanneries and slaughterhouses along its banks and also stood in the way of the streets that ambitious planners envisioned. It seemed to Lydia Maria Child and others an appropriate irony that this site should have furnished a spot for the Tombs: a crime against nature produced a place to incarcerate criminals.[53]

Redburn, then, implicitly registers his culture's anxiety about urban change. This anxiety starts with the experience of finding the streets difficult to travel or comprehend and extends into a sense that the whole city is a frightening labyrinth. "This world, my boy, is a moving world," reflects Redburn. Just as New York was seeing its waterfront filled in to create new streets to accommodate wharves and businesses, "[t]his very harbor of Liverpool is gradually filling up." It is practically trite for Redburn to conclude that the city "never stands still; and its sands are forever shifting" (157).

It is also, as we have seen, predictable that Redburn would extend his feeling of physical alienation into a judgment about the moral character of the city as well. Even before he has seen the town, he recognizes its moral landscape; before long he can judge that the bad beer, the swipes, "is drunk in large quantities by the poor people about Liverpool, which, perhaps, in some degree, accounts for their poverty" (135). Quickly he recognizes the "land-sharks, land-rats, and other vermin, which make the hapless mariner their prey"; he expects to find "notorious Corinthian haunts in the vicinity of the docks, which in depravity are not to be matched by any thing this side of the pit that is bottomless" (138). And

perhaps the reader expects that Redburn will refrain from a full description of the worst parts of Liverpool, supplying the conventional Dicken-
sian language of the plunge literature in its place:

> The pestilent lanes and alleys which, in their vocabulary, go by the names
> of Rotten-row, Gibraltar-place, and Booble-alley, are putrid with vice and
> crime; to which, perhaps, the round globe does not furnish a parallel.
> The sooty and begrimed bricks of the very houses have a reeking,
> Sodom-like, and murderous look; and well may the shroud of coal-
> smoke, which hangs over this part of the town, more than any other,
> attempt to hide the enormities here practiced. . . . Propriety forbids that
> I should enter into details. (191)

All of the details, after all, would be perfectly familiar to New York readers.

It is all the more remarkable, then, that Melville manages to use Redburn's conventional moral language to expose the mystifications of urban
literature. It is also remarkable that, in spite of his mystification, Redburn
manages at points to break through it toward an understanding of the
social structure of poverty. Melville accomplishes this subtle task by using
the physical structure of Liverpool – its streets, docks, and walls – to impress on Redburn a notion of a similarly massive and oppressive social
structure that creates walls between the classes. The way Redburn both
sees and fails to see this connection produces a tension in the narration
– Redburn is at times hopelessly mystified, at others strikingly observant
and active – but that tension is necessary to create a true understanding
of how Liverpool functions as a labyrinth.

The docks give Redburn a physical sense of the way the city contains
and classifies social groups, allowing a maximum amount of commercial
activity and growth while controlling and minimizing social disorder. He
begins by admiring their size and construction, which seem superior to
"the miserable wooden wharves, and slip-shod, shambling piers of New
York" (161), and he links them with the wonders of nature and antiquity:
"I beheld long China walls of masonry; vast piers of stone; and a succession of granite-rimmed docks, completely inclosed, and many of them
communicating, which almost recalled to mind the great American chain
of lakes: Ontario, Erie, St. Clair, Huron, Michigan, and Superior. The
extent and solidity of these structures, seemed equal to what I had read
of the old Pyramids of Egypt" (161). In his extended tribute, he claims
that the docks stand as a more fitting monument to the heroes "who by
their valor did so much to protect the commerce of Britain" (162) than
the ignoble obelisks and towers raised in their memory: "[t]hey are but
tomb-stones" (162). A living monument, a dock bearing a hero's name,
would emphasize that "true fame is something free, easy, social, and com-

panionable" (162); and so the docks would commemorate the social rather than the individual benefits that arise from military heroism.

Redburn, then, emphasizes from the first that the docks represent social organization and effort. Like the Pyramids, they have required enormous labor, "the earth and rock having been laboriously scooped, and solidified again as materials for the quays and piers" (163). Each covers a huge area, "about fifteen or twenty acres," and contains so many ships that when a new vessel enters the dock, all the others must move to make room: "[a]nd so it runs round like a shock of electricity; touch one, and you touch all" (164). It is logical, then, for Redburn to see each dock as a city, and as representing the larger city whose commerce it serves: "Surrounded by its broad belt of masonry, each Liverpool dock is a walled town, full of life and commotion; or rather, it is a small archipelago, an epitome of the world, where all the nations of Christendom, and even those of Heathendom, are represented" (165). And it is not surprising that this great urban enclosure should remind him of New York: "A Liverpool dock is a grand caravansary inn, and hotel, on the spacious and liberal plan of the *Astor House* " (165).

What is surprising, or rather illogical, however, is that Redburn should simultaneously admire the docks and pity the beggars who line their streets. Although Melville makes this irony abundantly clear, Redburn misses the connection between Liverpool's commercial dominance and the poverty of its citizens. Melville's narration of Redburn's observations, however, indicates the degree of his character's mystifications. He fails to recognize that the same power that built the walls around the docks built the walls surrounding the wretchedness in Lancelott's Hey. In that sense, then, though he loses some of his provincial innocence about poverty and vice in the great city, he never fully penetrates its social labyrinth.

This mystification begins with Redburn's tribute to the Genius of Commerce, which he claims creates an ideal community among the docks: "Here are brought together the remotest limits of the earth; and in the collective spars and timbers of these ships, all the forests of the globe are represented, as in a grand parliament of masts.... Here, under the beneficent sway of the Genius of Commerce, all climes and countries embrace; and yard-arm touches yard-arm in brotherly love" (165). As on the *Highlander*, Redburn experiences a degree of that brotherhood himself as he encounters men of different classes and, now, different countries. His descriptions of a cozy dinner on board a salt-drogher with "an old ruby of a fellow" (167), of listening to the sober Germans sing their hymns, of visiting an Indian vessel and conversing at length with a talkative Lascar, and of observing a brigandlike slaver mooring alongside a Floating Chapel, all ring with exultation over the varieties of human fellowship. This experience of brotherhood, enacted under the influence of the Genius of Commerce, "should forever extinguish the prejudices of national dislikes" (169), Redburn decides. More than that, it nullifies the hatred he once felt for the sailors, lifting him to ecstatic heights of cosmopolitan enthusiasm: "our blood is as the flood of the Amazon," not as the blood of Ham, Shem, and Japheth, flowing in mutually exclusive lines. "We are the heirs of all time, and with all nations we divide our inheritance. On this Western Hemisphere all tribes and people are forming into one federated whole." His rhapsody concludes with a Pentecostal vision: "Then shall the curse of Babel be revoked, a new Pentecost come, and the language they shall speak shall be the language of Britain. Frenchmen, and Danes, and Scots; and the dwellers on the shores of the Mediterranean, and in the regions about; Italians, and Indians, and Moors; there shall appear unto them cloven tongues as of fire" (169). Naturally, although Redburn neglects this point, the language of Britain will be spoken by all, as the Genius of Commerce emanates from New York and Liverpool, closely connected by the packet lines.

It is, of course, an advance in Redburn's thinking for him to find the conversation of a Lascar as useful as his father's guidebook once was. Now, instead of consulting Adam Smith or his *Spectator*, he turns to the sailors for enlightenment: "If you want to learn romance, or gain an insight into things quaint, curious, and marvelous, drop your books of travel, and take a stroll along the docks of a great commercial port. Ten to one, you will encounter Crusoe himelf among the crowds of mariners from all parts of the globe" (172). But his romanticizing the sailors and the commerce that federates them into one whole causes him to misunderstand how commerce also creates walls around them. To him, the commercial activity has a romantic charm: "Nothing can exceed the bustle and activity displayed along these quays during the day; bales, crates, boxes, and cases are being tumbled about by thousands of laborers; trucks are coming and going; dock-masters are shouting; sailors of all nations are singing out at their ropes; and all this commotion is greatly increased by the resoundings by the lofty walls that hem in the din" (164). Redburn sees the walls as enhancing commercial activity within rather than as containing or oppressing human beings.

Melville heightens this mystification even further. Redburn, encountering other walls away from the docks, sees how society closes off its potentially disturbing elements, yet he does not connect that social problem with the economic structure of the docks. The incident in Lancelott's Hey, while opening his eyes to the profound misery of the starving woman and children, does not make sense to him in anything but the rhetorically compromised terms of the moral-reform literature. And yet this encounter forces him, more than anything else he sees in the city, to question the whole structure of society itself. And the chapter shows Melville exploiting the ironies of reform literature to the fullest. The first impression Redburn receives is of an oppressive physical terrain: a street with "a strip of crooked sidewalk," "dingy wall[s] . . . on every side, converting the mid-day into twilight," and in a cellar fifteen feet below the level of the street, a hole where the mother and children crouch, making a "soul-sickening wail" (180). This walled space makes a horrifying contrast with the walled spaces of the docks, full of communal activity and brotherhood; Redburn finds the cellar completely cut off from the social body. One beggar in a nearby street does not know the woman at all, others know her but blame her for her misery – "was she ever married? tell me that" (181) – the local policeman says it's not his street, Redburn's landlady says she has already given food to all the beggars on her own street, and finally, when Redburn does manage to give them comfort, he realizes that he can't perform the one truly charitable act of putting them out of their misery, because "the law, which would let them perish of themselves without giv-ing them one cup of water, would spend a thousand pounds, if necessary, in convicting him who should so much as offer to relieve them from their miserable existence" (184). There seems to Redburn no social or legal context for such extreme suffering.

As a result, he falls back on a moral appeal: "Ah! what are our creeds, and how do we hope to be saved? Tell me, oh Bible, that story of Lazarus again, that I may find comfort in my heart for the poor and forlorn. Surrounded as we are by the wants and woes of our fellow-men, and yet given to follow our own pleasures, regardless of their pains, are we not like people sitting up with a corpse, and making merry in the house of the dead?" (184). Redburn's allusion to Lazarus suggests that he sees a religious miracle as the only possible solution to such misery as this. And although his questions cast doubt upon the efficacy of the Bible or such a miracle, he offers no other. Yet Melville, by rendering the incident hor-rifying and by showing Redburn's strenuous attempts at charity as ulti-mately futile, shows how little choice Redburn has but to echo the pieties of his culture. The walls erected by the city of Liverpool, under the be-neficent sway of the Genius of Commerce, have the staying power of the Pyramids to keep people in their misery.

The whole Liverpool section, then, enacts the tension between Red-burn's developing social consciousness, as he learns to navigate and un-derstand the labyrinth of Liverpool, and his continuing mystification as he celebrates the Genius of Commerce, which he serves and hopes to profit by. This tension climaxes with a fourth urban plunge, his journey to London with his new friend, Harry Bolton. In turning to the genteel Harry for inspiration and reviving his longings for aristocratic company, Redburn in this episode reveals his provincialism anew. Liverpool, once so fascinating to him and full of dock life, now appears as "[s]moky old Liverpool" (212); London is the "metropolis of marvels" (237), and to London he turns his hopes. Curiously, although Redburn is now experienced enough to see the holes in Harry's stories, stories that "began to breed some suspicions concerning the rigid morality of my friend, as a teller of the truth" (223); and although he can now instruct Harry in the ways of the ship ("be not deceived by the fascinating Riga" [220], he tells him); yet his eagerness to see London overcomes all his suspicions of Harry's character. That provincial eagerness, and his mystification in the London palace of vice to which Harry conducts him, suggest that Melville intends to keep exploiting his naiveté.

For the London sections seem almost comic in their parody of scenes of aristocratic dissolution in novels by Judson and Lippard. This is a plunge, not into a real city, but into labyrinth literature, and Redburn plays the innocent as if he were reading a script. London itself he sees as a confused glimpse from the window of a cab: "As we rattled over the boisterous pavements, past splendid squares, churches, and shops, our cabman turning corners like a skater on the ice, and all the roar of London in my ears, and no end to the walls of brick and mortar; I thought New York a hamlet, and Liverpool a coal-hole." Arrived at the Aladdin's Palace, "with the purple light," he finds a stage set of urban and urbane decadence: trompe-l'oeil colonnades, "galaxies of gas lights," mahogany tables, "knots of gentlemanly men, with cut decanters and taper-waisted glasses, journals and cigars, before them" (227–8). Then a melodramatic plot worthy of the sensational urban writers unfolds in which the young men drink wine, Harry goes off to gamble away his fortune, Redburn contemplates the scene of "metropolitan magnificence," which convinces him that, "though gilded and golden, the serpent of vice is a serpent still" (234), Harry returns in despair, and they leave at dawn, Harry having extracted from Redburn an oath of secrecy. The only thing missing from the conventional plunge into corruption is Redburn's seduction, betrayal, and descent to ruin.

But Harry accomplishes it for him, and Redburn's response shows the insufficiency of his urban education, as well as his sexual naiveté. Rather than probing or understanding the mystery of Harry's predicament, although he certainly has a clue of what has happened, Redburn accepts the situation with ill grace: " 'And this, then,' said I, 'is your showing me London, is it, Harry? I did not think this.' " When Harry holds him to his oath, Redburn tries to bury the episode: "Now lie down, and let us forget ourselves as soon as we can; for me, you have made me the most miserable dog alive" (235). Unable to understand Harry's misery, unable perhaps to conceive that an English aristocrat could *be* miserable, Redburn removes himself from the challenge to his charity.

The question may be why Redburn should show as much charity to Harry as he does to the woman in Lancelott's Hey. Harry is indeed a privileged young man who has squandered his resources; the woman more truly calls out for pity. Yet Redburn feels, somehow, that Harry deserves his friendship, and he seems to exhibit much more guilt and remorse over having betrayed him than over having failed to alleviate the unknown woman's suffering. After all, he cannot solve the social problems that cause the woman to suffer; he can perhaps extend friendship to Harry. But whatever his reasons for behaving as he does, his judgment is clearly affected by his vision of London as a magnificent city. It clouds his perceptions of Harry's true character, seduces him with its promise of aristocratic pleasures, and leads him astray from his working-class solidarity with the sailors. The London episode, by demonstrating the extent to which Redburn allows his urban imagination to mystify him as to the city's real character, shows the flaws in his moral and social vision.

Redburn to some extent redeems himself on the voyage home, where his sympathy toward the emigrants shows the compassion he has acquired from his experience in Liverpool. His evident love for the emigrant boy Carlo is a sentimental attachment, but in his analysis of the emigrants' poverty, sickness, and oppression, brought on by unscrupulous agents and captains, he displays the full range of his social awareness. This exhibits itself in anger against the rich cabin passengers: "Lucky would it be for the pretensions of some parvenus, whose souls are deposited at their banker's, and whose bodies but serve to carry about purses, knit of poor men's heart-strings, if thus easily they could precisely define, ashore, the difference between them and the rest of humanity" (242). But even more remarkable is his understanding of their misery as coming from the dominance of the wealthy: "For the emigrants in these ships are under a sort of martial-law; and in all their affairs are regulated by the despotic ordinances of the captain" (263). They may suffer from certain ethnic characteristics – Redburn is not above mocking Irish habits of slovenliness – and he does emphasize the ways in which they have brought misery upon themselves: "the very hardships to which such beings are subjected, instead of uniting them, only tends, by imbittering their tempers, to set them against each other; and thus they themselves drive the strongest rivet into the chain by which their social superiors hold them subject" (264). And yet the captain's handling of the epidemic among the emigrants, the callousness with which the cabin passengers protect themselves while shunning the sick, and especially the care with which the captain cleanses the vessel of all evidence before it reaches port, offer a vivid model of the way those in power deal with urban problems. Melville makes the connection between the ship and a city obvious by comparing the steerage to a "crowded jail" (287) similar to the Tombs. But since it is clear that the emigrants come chiefly from the poorest sections of Liverpool and are bound for the poorest parts of New York, Redburn cannot escape the obvious conclusion that the problems of New York start in the exploitation of the emigrants. These provincials, unlike the hardy farmers and workers of the temperance literature, seem to have no chance at all of making it through the urban labyrinth; and Redburn sees that most New Yorkers won't care if they do or not.[54]

The other sign of Redburn's developing vision displayed on the homeward voyage appears in his contrast with Harry, who now replaces him as the greenhorn of the ship. He arrives at the morning watch in his dressing gown, just as Redburn had begged to be excused from wetting his feet, and he inspires the same ridicule and disbelief among the sailors that Redburn had. But as in London, Redburn seems mostly to stand by and let Harry take the abuse, even when he discovers that Harry will never succeed as a sailor. The recognition of his own competence is gratifying to Redburn but does little to help Harry, who once again seems to Redburn an innocent victim of the sailors' wickedness rather than a deluded aristocrat who perhaps deserves their scorn. Redburn's inability either to condemn Harry's foolishness or to help him out of his predicament suggests, again, that he continues to be mystified by the spectacle of Harry's supposed wealth.

Redburn ends with the *Highlander*'s arrival in New York, the humiliating discovery that Harry and Redburn will not be paid for their labor, Redburn's hurried return to his provincial family, and Harry's desperate and suicidal decision to ship on a whaler. It has struck many readers as an abdication of Redburn's maturing vision that he abandons Harry to his fate and resumes his own provincial life and attitudes. What has he accomplished after all? Melville's satirical display of the moral hypocrisy of the labyrinth literature, especially in the London sections, suggests that he considers Redburn a product of that culture, a permanent provincial whose intervals of understanding of the city's corrupt social system surface only briefly during a disturbing urban immersion. Redburn is glad to see the sailors go and seems to have few fond memories of his voyage. He appears to regret only the embarrassment of being exposed for having left Harry to his certain death: " 'Harry Bolton was not your brother?' cried the stranger, starting" (312), and Redburn feels himself revealed as a moral hypocrite, a Cain who has failed his brother.

It should be stressed, however, that Redburn has always harbored secret misgivings about Harry. Aside from his melodramatic gestures and spurious stories, Harry throws away a perfectly good dollar and a half with a gambler's carelessness. It may be that Redburn's experience in the working-class world of the *Highlander* and his travels through the labyrinth of urban poverty in Liverpool have lessened his patience for the genteel mode. Although Redburn extricates himself from the labyrinth at the end of his story and returns to the provinces, he has demonstrated his capacity to read the signs of urban life with greater acuteness than before. It is hard to believe that he will remain in his mother's village for long; and, indeed, the ending of the novel shows that he too ships on a whaler, returning once more to the sailors. Although he seems to have dipped only briefly into the world of urban mystery and misery, Redburn has substantially changed in the way he reads that world; given his cultural conditioning, that accomplishment may be a great one indeed.

Redburn suffers financial failure in the novel rather than moral ruin. In his own mind he has traveled safely and successfully through the urban labyrinth. Yet cities remain mysterious to him, and he prefers to escape to a provincial retreat. Melville's ironic narrator makes it clear how Redburn has failed to understand the social and economic structure of urban misery. In *White-Jacket*, where there is far less distance between the narrator and protagonist, Melville constructs an urban labyrinth on board a naval ship and a protagonist who successfully creates a taxonomy, an order of things, to explain the labyrinth's structure. Unlike Redburn, however, White-Jacket finds himself trapped in the labyrinth, which he can neither fully penetrate nor escape.

White-Jacket: *An Urban Taxonomy*

Jack Chase exults in the urbanity of a naval ship: "a man-of-war is to whalemen, as a metropolis to shire-towns, and sequestered hamlets" (16). Jack, of course, is a gentleman, and he speaks for the members of the main-top, the gentry of the crew. But Melville's narrator also repeatedly insists that the ship is a "city afloat" bringing together "men of all callings and vocations" (74); "[w]ith its crew of 800 or 1000 men, a three-decker is a city on the sea" (144).[55] White-Jacket, a provincial in the underworld of the ship, seeks to find the "infallible clew to this mystery" (48), the mystery of the ship's hidden structure of power that oppresses the sailors. But White-Jacket, though socially an outsider to the ship's order, shares the sailors' oppression and comes to identify with their misery. Thus he speaks sometimes as a provincial looking for clues to the labyrinth and at other times as a true native who can offer intimate knowledge of its depths. Indeed, the structure of the novel and of his narration gradually pulls him from the heights of the main-top, with its genteel urbanity, into the depths of the ship and its vices, enacting a provincial journey into the labyrinth. But White-Jacket has the advantage of maturity and special knowledge of the ship's mysteries and hence can offer something the naive Redburn cannot – namely, a taxonomy of the city-ship's social structure. With this taxonomy he hopes to make sense of a body of knowledge and experience that is essentially beyond comprehension, as it represents, on the one hand, an almost unimaginably rigid social hierarchy and, on the other hand, a potentially dangerous, rebellious, and wicked mob ready to ignite at any time. White-Jacket is to some extent at home in this explosive environment, but at the same time he is baffled by its mysteries. In the end, he finds he cannot penetrate the labyrinth nor adequately extricate himself from it. The taxonomy offers clues to a provincial reader but ultimately mystifies him.

White-Jacket's urban taxonomy depends primarily on the ship being understood as a city, and Melville is almost heavy-handed in the numerous reminders of New York. This is a New York imagined most vividly in terms of catastrophe. "The occasional phosphorescence of the yeasting sea cast a glare upon their uplifted faces, as a night fire in a populous city lights up the panic-stricken crowd" (106). During the naval exercises, the sailors rush about like "Bowery-boy tars," and "the entire ship is in as great a commotion as if a whole city ward were in a blaze" (67); during a battle "our bulwarks might look like the walls of the houses in West Broadway in New York, after being broken into and burned out by the Negro Mob" (69). When the men run out of grog, the whole ship is undone: "the ship was like a great city, when some terrible calamity has overtaken it" (54). But White-Jacket also evokes the less turbulent world of the city. When the decks have been washed, they look "clear and unobstructed as the sidewalks of Wall Street of a Sunday morning" (87). When covered with snow, they resemble "Broadway in winter, the morning after a storm, when rival shop-boys are at work cleaning the sidewalk" (117). And the wide decks make possible the New York promenade: "during the early part of the evening, the main-deck is generally filled with crowds of pedestrians, promenading up and down past the guns, like people taking the air in Broadway" (50). On the face of it, many of these images seem conventional and even accidental. But White-Jacket's subject, the rigidly ordered world of the naval vessel, and his narrative structure, a journey into a labyrinth that requires a taxonomy of knowledge, reveal that New York offers a necessary model for the ship's social and physical order.

White-Jacket's investigation of "The World in a Man-of-War" enacts a descent into a labyrinth of knowledge. In this endeavor he somewhat resembles Redburn in his genteel provinciality. White-Jacket does not actually start his journey outside the urban ship, as Redburn does, nor does he undergo Redburn's experience of initiation into the sailors' harsh life. He begins his journey on the ship itself, but he does have an air of social superiority that he must relinquish if he is to learn its secrets. This sense of his own gentility is heightened by his friendship with Jack Chase, a gentleman who knows many languages and can discourse freely on Byron, Scott, Shakespeare, Homer, and Camoens. Chase creates a social club of spectators in the main-top, where the men lounge idly, wear the distinctive dress of their class, and "literally looked down upon the landlopers below, sneaking about on the deck" (15). White-Jacket exhibits the prejudices of his class when he refers to the crew as "nothing but a mob" (9); when he goes among the men, "[i]n vain I kept clapping my pockets like nervous old gentlemen in a crowd; that same night I found myself minus several valuable articles" (37). Often he uses the condescending tone of the genteel outsider: "sailors, as a class, entertain the most liberal notions considering morality and the Decalogue; or rather, they take their own views of such matters" (38). Sailors appear to him in the mass, inseparable and impenetrable: "so thick is the mob, that not one thief in a thousand is detected" (39). White-Jacket's direst statements on the physical and moral state of the men reflect his righteous disdain; so he calls the ship "the asylum for the perverse, the home of the unfortunate. Here the sons of adversity meet the children of calamity, and here the children of calamity meet the offspring of sin" (74). In his most solemn pronouncements, he certainly echoes Redburn's judgments of Liverpool: "[t]he sins for which the cities of the plain were overthrown still linger in some of these wooden-walled Gomorrahs of the deep" (375–6).

But to identify White-Jacket as a genteel outsider, a Victorian moralist among the sailor mob, only establishes his readiness to see the ship as an impenetrable labyrinth, a deep respository of the sins of the earth, or of the ocean. White-Jacket, however, comes down from the rigging to essay a description of this labyrinth, and when he does, he finds himself a provincial drawn into the labyrinth's depths. In order to penetrate the ship's hidden mysteries, White-Jacket must surrender his aristocratic prejudices, as Redburn did, and enter into the fraternity of the crew.[56] White-Jacket's taxonomy of the ship helps him to make this journey by leading him into the ship's inner world.

White-Jacket's taxonomy, like Thomas Butler Gunn's physiology of boardinghouses or Poe's ordering of urban types, categorizes the men of the ship in a descending order, beginning with the commodore and moving down to the men below decks, whom he calls the Troglodytes. But unlike Gunn's structure, which casts contempt upon the lower classes, White-Jacket's classification works in reverse. The officers elicit his contempt, whereas among the men he seeks the knowledge of nautical secrets he craves. Of course, the whole taxonomy is, like Gunn's, basically a comic device, and he pokes fun at the below-decks men as well as at the commodores. But as the taxonomy, and the novel itself, progress, it becomes clear that White-Jacket's sympathies move away from the upper class and toward the lower orders, until he comes to identify himself with the crew, against the officers.

White-Jacket also invests the taxonomical enterprise with the suspense of the urban labyrinth literature. The descent into the depths of class and knowledge begins to take on the excitement of a plunge into mysterious areas of the city. And there is clearly a contrast between the world of the officers, which contains little mystery, and that of the hidden men, which does. The commodore, for example, being remote and lofty, excites little interest. White-Jacket presents him as a kind of naval form on feet, a man whose only function is to issue orders about the men's pickles. Most of the other officers merit only the briefest mention, and the midshipmen

come in for considerable scorn, as they are privileged boys with the trap-
pings of officialdom but none of the experience: "something like colle-
giate freshmen and sophomores" (26). The master-at-arms, Bland, is the
only one of the officers to receive description, but as eventually becomes
evident, he grows more interesting as he himself penetrates and dwells in
the labyrinth world of vice and crime.

White-Jacket makes similar social judgments of the men, too, whom he
divides by watch and by mess. "[T]he necessity of precision and discipline" (8) on the ship produces a perfect symmetry in these divisions
among the men: "Now the fore, main, and mizen-top-men of each watch
– Starboard and Larboard – are at sea respectively subdivided into Quarter
Watches" (9); these divisions determine where one works, where and
when one sleeps, and with whom one eats, works, and sleeps throughout
the cruise. It also determines one's character. Hence the Sheet-Anchor-
men are "an old weather-beaten set ... hearty old members of the Old
Guard; grim sea grenadiers" (9). By contrast, the After-Guard's-men are
"composed chiefly of landsmen; the least robust, least hardy, and least
sailor-like of the crew" (10). White-Jacket sails off into poetic exaggeration
in describing them as "mostly slender young fellows ... [who] lounge
away the most part of their time, in reading novels and romances; talking
over their lover affairs ashore; and comparing notes concerning the melancholy and sentimental career which drove them – poor young gentlemen – into the hard-hearted navy" (10). These dandies are neither as
pitiable nor as doomed as Harry Bolton; they have a secure place in the
navy, in spite of their being *"silk-sock-gentry"* (10). The "waisters," on the
other hand, are the true provincials of the ship, *"sons of farmers"* who tend
to the pigs and sheep and who are "good for nothing else" (10). But
below them, below the decks in fact, live the most mysterious group, the
"Troglodites or '*holders*,' who burrow, like rabbits in warrens, among the
water-tanks, casks, and cables" (10). White-Jacket compares them to
"Cornwall miners," "Jonah ... in the whale's belly," or "the mysterious
old men of Paris, during the massacre of the Three Days of September"
(10–11). Later White-Jacket will devote considerable energy to seeking
out these mysterious old men, but at the beginning of his investigation
he emphasizes their strangeness and unknowableness: "after a three years'
voyage, they still remain strangers to you. ... everyone marvels who they
are, and whence they come; they disappear as mysteriously; and are seen
no more" (11). From the beginning of the novel, then, White-Jacket
evinces the provincial's fascination with the hidden areas of the ship and
the taxonomer's skill in inscribing boundaries to them.

As White-Jacket's investigation proceeds, it becomes clear that the
above-board world of the vessel is oppressively organized and restricted;
but the below-decks world contains all the ship's disorganized and explosive elements. The taxonomy, then, and the narrative as well, begin to

move from a hierarchical order toward a labyrinthine one, a structure that just barely contains its own confusion, fear, and tension. Above the decks, White-Jacket describes the ship as "something like life in a large manufactory" (35) or as a "lofty, walled, and garrisoned town, like Quebec, where the thoroughfares are mostly ramparts, and peaceable citizens meet armed sentries at every corner" (75). The "uppermost deck" most forcefully reminds the sailor of this martial order: it is "the Police-office, Court-house, and yard of execution, where all charges are lodged, causes tried, and punishment administered" (131). But as one descends below decks, that image of military order degenerates into images of social disorder: "it is like the lodging-houses in Paris, turned upside-down; the first floor, or deck, being rented by a lord; the second, by a select club of gentlemen; the third, by crowds of artisans; and the fourth, by a whole rabble of common people" (75).[57] White-Jacket clearly sees the criminal and revolutionary implications of this descending order: "And with its long rows of port-hole casements, each revealing the muzzle of a cannon, a man-of-war resembles a three-story house in a suspicious part of the town, with a basement of indefinite depth, and ugly-looking fellows gazing out at the windows" (75). The social levels of the ship, so clearly marked, give ample warning of potential trouble.

Besides classifying the various social levels of the ship, White-Jacket offers a theory of character that in some sense locks these levels into place; that is, "this theory about the wonderful influence of habitual sights and sounds upon the human temper" (46). Quoin, the quartergunner, gets his "very cross, bitter, ill-natured, inflammable" (44) nature from "consorting with those villainous, irritable, ill-tempered cannon" (45). The top-men are "more liberal-hearted, lofty-minded, gayer, more jocund, elastic, adventurous, given to fun and frolic" (47) than their earthbound comrades; the sheet-anchor-men, living in the outdoors, are "free, generous-hearted, charitable, and full of good-will to all hands" (47). But the Troglodytes, "who lived down in the tarry cellars and caves below the berth-deck, were, nearly all of them, men of gloomy dispositions, taking sour views of things" (47). Although this theory helps White-Jacket to explain the ship's social divisions in terms of environmental influence, it mystifies the real power structure of the navy. Eventually he learns from his own experiences of oppression not to adopt such sweeping classifications.

Instead, as he begins to explore the ship's hidden regions, White-Jacket finds himself drawn into a realm of mystery that enables him to see the other world in the man-of-war. This journey of discovery leads him away from his elitist attitudes toward a more sympathetic kinship with the men. Having weathered the crisis of Cape Horn, he pauses to take "A Peep through a Port-hole at the Subterranean Parts" of the ship. Here he departs from his urban taxonomy to plunge into the *Neversink*'s "subterra-

nean depths" (123). Following a "dim, devious corridor," he enters a
"gloomy apartment, lit by a solitary lamp"; here he finds the "mysterious
store-rooms" of the vessel, described in labyrinthine terms: "Through low
arches in the bulk-head beyond, you peep in upon distant vaults and cat-
acombs" (124). Here the "Yeoman is to be found burrowing in his underground store-rooms," a Troglodyte of "unaccountable bachelor oddities"
(125). This mysterious character whets White-Jacket's appetite for mystery,
and he undertakes a more thorough investigation of the "several parts of
the ship under hatches shrouded in mystery, and completely inaccessible
to the sailor" (127).

The most mysterious areas of the ship contain the explosives, presided
over by the Gunner. The whole chapter describing White-Jacket's visit
makes it clear how the taxonomic quest works to initiate a bourgeois outsider into the secrets of the labyrinth. He begins by remarking once again
that the ship may contain regions unknown and mysterious to the above-
decks world: "Among such a crowd of marked characters as were to be
met with on board our frigate, many of whom moved in mysterious circles
beneath the lowermost deck, and at long intervals flitted into sight like
apparitions, and disappeared again for whole weeks together, there were
some who inordinately excited my curiosity" (127). White-Jacket regrets
"that there was no public printed Directory for the Neversink, such as
they have in large towns" and thinks of "compiling a *Hand-book of the
Neversink*, so that the tourist might have a reliable guide" (127). Implicitly
appointing himself as guide, he leads the way "into regions full of interest
to a successful explorer" (127). But because these regions contain the
living quarters of the commodore and the captain, they present literal
barriers to the enterprising traveler that make them even more mysterious. "Night and day armed sentries guarded their sacred portals, cutlass
in hand" (128), and so the casual passerby cannot hope to penetrate the
secret depths. This experience of mystery makes White-Jacket aware of the
military structure that keeps him in his place; for the first time he explicitly identifies himself with the rest of the mystified crew:

> Thus, though for a period of more than a year I was an inmate of this
> floating box of live-oak, yet there were numberless things in it that, to
> the last, remained wrapped in obscurity, or concerning which I could
> only lose myself in vague speculations. I was as a Roman Jew of the
> Middle Ages, confined to the Jews' quarter of the town, and forbidden
> to stray beyond my limits. Or I was as a modern traveler in the same
> famous city, forced to quit it at last without gaining ingress to the most
> mysterious haunts – the innermost shrine of the Pope, and the dungeons
> and cells of the Inquisition. (128)

The experience of penetrating the labyrinth only so far reminds White-
Jacket of his powerlessness and removes him from the privileged position

of the maintop. Now he feels himself ghettoized, a member of a despised class, trying to "gain ingress" to a forbidden place.

The fact that these regions house the arms of the vessel gives White-Jacket some sense of the revolutionary potential of its hidden recesses. The Gunner, "a short, square, grim man, his hair and beard grizzled and singed, as if with gunpowder" (128), is the very image of combustion, and White-Jacket thinks nervously of Guy Fawkes and the Bastille. His domain is so dangerous that "before penetrating further than that vestibule, every man of the gunner's-gang silently removed his shoes, for fear that the nails in their heels might possibly create a spark" (128–9). The gunners are overwhelmed both by their barrels of powder and by their power over a mighty force: "it was a business full of direful interest, to be buried so deep below the sun, handling whole barrels of powder, any one of which, touched by the smallest spark, was powerful enough to blow up a whole street of warehouses" (129). The ceremony and mystery with which the navy shrouds its own guns emblematically reveals how a social structure mystifies its own complicity by creating a labyrinth to hide its secrets. It recalls the myth of Minos, who built the Cretan labyrinth to conceal the evidence of his wife's adultery and his own shame; the naval labyrinth, an embodiment of political power, similarly works to mystify and conceal official wrong and weakness.

White-Jacket himself comes to this conclusion as he begins to consider ever more closely the ship's structure and methods of authority. His protest against flogging reveals the language and legal fiction by which the navy makes war on its own men. His experience of traveling through the labyrinth brings him into close kinship with other oppressed sailors, until he is prepared to enact a revolutionary impulse of his own; faced with flogging, he determines to hurl himself and the captain into the sea. He arms himself for political battle against the oppressors by descending to the world of the decks: "But White-Jacket is ready to come down from the lofty mast-head of an eternal principle, and fight you – Commodores and Captains of the navy – on your own quarter-deck, with your own weapons, at your own paces" (147), whence follows his long, passionate defense of the sailors against floggings. His new sense of solidarity with his shipmates, "all under lock and key; all hopeless prisoners like myself; all under martial law; all dieting on salt beef and biscuit; all in one uniform" produces a new "love and affection for them, grounded, doubtless, on a fellow-feeling" (174).

White-Jacket, then, affirms that he has traveled through the labyrinth and given up his genteel pretensions to join the sailors. Yet there is one deeper layer to the labyrinth that challenges his assertion of democratic fraternity with the men. This is the true underworld of the ship, the world of crime that flourishes under the noses of the unsuspecting sailors. White-Jacket explains how the power structure of the ship creates the drive toward and the opportunity for crime. Because the navy provides each sailor with a daily drink, it offers the stimulus for smuggling, gambling, and further drinking. But, even more reprehensible, it makes possible the undercover operations of the corrupt master-at-arms, Bland, who smuggles liquor on board and distributes it through a network of his spies. More than hammering home the temperance theme, White-Jacket makes the ship and its labyrinth of hidden vice an image of urban life. He does this twice by calling attention to the connection between Bland and the master French detective, Eugène François Vidocq (1775–1857). Vidocq, like White-Jacket, is a taxonomer of urban mysteries; but his equivocal moral nature suggests to White-Jacket the ethical problems of creating an urban taxonomy.

White-Jacket calls Bland a "very Vidocq in vigilance" (27) and then, after Bland has disgraced himself by involuntarily disclosing his participation in a liquor smuggling ring, invokes Vidocq ironically to explain the captain's decision to restore Bland to his former position: "Perhaps Captain Claret had read the Memoirs of Vidocq, and believed in the old saying, *set a rogue to catch a rogue*" (189). The allusions to Vidocq, whose supposed *Memoirs* were published in 1828, evoke this self-consciously urban man, who, as both criminal and detective, knew all the mysteries and miseries of Paris. In fact, his life inspired Sue's *The Mysteries of Paris* (1844), as well as the character Vautrin in Balzac's novels. But Vidocq is more interesting in connection with White-Jacket because his *Memoirs* offer an urban taxonomy, a science of urban classification.[58]

Vidocq's knowledge of the city came from intimate experience of its underworld. Although he himself, a second son and soldier, was from the countryside, he went to the city to find or seize his fortune. In the aftermath of the Napoleonic Wars, hordes of unattached soldiers, adventurers, younger sons, dispossessed farmers, and brigands converged on Paris, where these men and women found a secure refuge. Just as Israel Potter was to reason later, Vidocq became "persuaded that I could nowhere be so safe as in the heart of a capital, where it is easy to lose oneself amid the crowded population" (2:122). Just so does Bland carry out his criminal enterprises at the very heart of military authority.

After years spent as a thief and convict, Vidocq turned his expertise to professional advantage by becoming the founder of the secret, or detective, police of Paris. Using disguise, thieves' patois, and extraordinary persistence, he mingled freely with the robbers, often participating in their crimes up to the point of discovery and arrest. It was this direct participation in crime that many citizens criticized and that almost cost him his job. But more than the excitement of the chase, or vicarious capture, Vidocq seems to have thoroughly enjoyed the intellectual challenge of his job, which required him to bring into play his skills in recognizing and classifying criminals:

I have been able to distinguish the character proper to each species [of thief]; the physiognomy, language, habits, manners, dress, arrangement, and details. I have studied all, remembered all. . . . Frequently from the inspection of a single article of clothing I would more quickly describe a thief from head to heel than our celebrated Cuvier, with two maxillaries and half-a-dozen vertebrae, can distinguish an antidiluvian animal or a fossil man. (4:6–7)

Vidocq carries through his scientific metaphor in the spirit of reform. The criminals, he claims, are poor and ignorant. Punished harshly for minor offenses, they live by their wits, but many are so inept at crime that they get caught again and again. Vidocq proclaims the importance of science and castigates the society that keeps these people in the criminal class rather than putting their energies to better use: "Science is abroad, but she walks alone; she advances for the privileged classes; she progresses for the rich. She illumines only the upper regions, the lower are still in darkness; the poor go on hap-hazard and blindly: woe to him who errs and mistakes the right road!" (4:2). Having exposed the politics of science (and of gaslight), Vidocq proposes a reformed science, offering himself as a taxonomer of criminals, proposing his own methods of classification: "I must renounce the Linnaean system" (4:8) and use one more appropriate for thieves: "let us call things by their right names" (4:9). As their linguist, and more importantly their comrade, Vidocq can accurately read their actions, classify their traits, and analyze their characters. At the same time, he performs a humane act. Once exposed, once read, the criminals may be rehabilitated. Taxonomy will motivate charity, science bring light.

Only in the city can such a study take place. "In a small town a thief is completely out of his element" (4:35). But in Paris, he is "at his ease in the midst of tumult, confusion, bustle, embarrassment, disorder, and a troubled and muddy stream of affairs" (4:36). The urban thief has certain social advantages over the provincial thieves, who "have no urbanity" and are "destitute of that sharp wit, which under certain circumstances, gives to the indigenous thief a decided superiority" (4:37). In short, Vidocq implies that, like his respectable counterparts, the provincial thief is "generally less civilized than those whose education has been carried on in Paris" (38). In Vidocq's urban myth, then, the Parisian thief shares in the cosmopolitan and social virtues of the city's better citizens; "They all regard each other as the members of one large family" (4:38). The city educates and socializes criminals, gives them a "code which they study, [and] perpetually reminds them, 'Thus far shalt thou go, and no farther' " (4:38). Under this humane system, the city supplies its own ethic for the provincial ethic so soon forgotten. Like the crew of the *Neversink*, urban criminals find themselves a home in the mob.

Vidocq's tolerance for and understanding of the urban criminal gives him some of the cosmopolitan equivocalness of Bland, in whom "vice *seemed,* but only seemed, to lose half its seeming evil by losing all its apparent grossness" (187). Yet Vidocq is serious in wanting to catch and study criminals. The intimate relationship he proposes between detective and criminal – both men of the night, both men of courage, wit, and adventure, both urban scientists of mystery and misery – clearly fascinates White-Jacket. Bland's "snaky, black eye, that at times shone like a dark-lantern in a jeweler-shop" (187) leaves no doubt in White-Jacket's mind of the "accomplished scoundrel within" (187). But at least during the period of Bland's public disgrace, "I admired his heroism in sustaining himself so well under such reverses" (188). White-Jacket, a taxonomer of the mob himself, recognizes another man who, like Jackson, knows human nature to a kink.

But White-Jacket is not completely comfortable with Bland's Vidocqian vigilance, nor with the world of crime that he inhabits. Beneath the hammocks where the men sleep at night, gamblers carry on their activities by the light of sinister lanterns, "like burglar's dark-lanterns in the fifty-acre vaults of the West India Docks on the Thames" (306). The location of the gambling, under the very buttocks of sleeping sailors, suggests the labyrinth that exists just beneath their consciousness: "It may well be imagined, therefore, how well adapted is this mysterious and subterranean Hall of Eblis to the clandestine proceedings of gamblers, especially as the hammocks not only hang thickly, but many of them swing very low, within two feet of the floor, thus forming innumerable little canvass glens, grottoes, nooks, corners, and crannies, where a good deal of wickedness may be practiced by the wary with considerable impunity" (306).[59] Over this labyrinth of vice Bland is supposed to exercise his moral and military authority; but White-Jacket's statement that he "reigns supreme in these bowels of the ship" (306) suggests that he is more complicit in the gambling himself than otherwise. White-Jacket shows nothing but contempt for these undercover activities. The mysteries of the gamblers do not offer the romantic possibilities he is seeking in his journeys through the labyrinth, and in the latter part of the novel he returns to the main-top and to his more lofty view of the ship. Although he continues to condemn war, to sympathize with his mates, and to side with rebels like Ushant, White-Jacket makes no more forays into the labyrinth of the vessel. Instead he moves back toward the provincial morality with which he began his investigations: "But we have seen that a man-of-war is but this old-fashioned world of ours afloat, full of all manner of characters – full of strange contradictions; and though boasting some fine fellows here and there, yet, upon the whole, charged to the combings of her hatchways with the spirit of Belial and all unrighteousness" (390).

White-Jacket seems, then, to have entered the labyrinth, explored its depths with considerable appreciation for its Vidocqian ambiguities, and then extricated himself, using taxonomy as a device for ordering his experience. But the conclusion to the novel indicates that White-Jacket has not left the labyrinth or its mysteries behind him. On the contrary, he claims he cannot end the novel on land because he must not depart from the mysteries he has explored: "Let us leave the ship on the sea – still with the land out of sight – still with brooding darkness on the face of the deep. I love an indefinite, infinite background – a vast, heaving, rolling, mysterious rear!" (396). Rather than having explored and then extricated himself from the mysteries of human existence, he finds that they have entered his soul: "There are no mysteries out of ourselves" (398). He claims to have found on the ship a kind of ideal brotherhood among his mates, but now the ship has cut loose from home and become an image of the earth itself, a "world-frigate" (398) bound for an indeterminate destination. Now the whole world is a ship, with its hidden miseries carried along inside of her: "Outwardly regarded, our craft is a lie; for all that is outwardly seen of it is the clean-swept deck, and oft-painted planks comprised above the water-line; whereas, the vast mass of our fabric, with all its store-rooms of secrets, forever slides along far under the surface" (399). In spite of the hopeful message that "Life is a voyage that's homeward-bound!" (400), it seems more likely that White-Jacket sees himself as caught in a floating labyrinth he can never escape.

Although the labyrinth metaphor makes it possible to see White-Jacket as permanently entrapped in an urban ship, it is more difficult to determine how far the strategy of mystification has succeeded with him. Unlike Redburn, White-Jacket does not return to the provinces, or to a naive or genteel distance from urban problems. But he does become mystified by the mysteries and miseries of the ship, failing to recognize how his own main-top point of view has produced an oppressive classification of the sailors and their vices. In the end, he extends fraternal love to his comrades of the maintop, not to the ship as a whole; like Redburn, he retreats from his own social criticism into a moral statement, that God, "Our Lord High Admiral, will yet interpose" (400) in the affairs of miserable sailors. Having penetrated the labyrinth as far as he has, then, it seems that White-Jacket can neither retreat nor go farther. Instead he moves off onto a metaphysical plane.

Pierre, too, loses himself in a metaphysical labyrinth. His journey into the city will bring him to the heart of the mysteries White-Jacket was seeking to uncover; but they are located not in a metaphorical city-ship but in the heart of New York. *Pierre* is the most labyrinthine of Melville's urban novels, the one most daring – and least successful – in its penetration of an urban labyrinth.

Pierre: *The Mysteries and Miseries of New York*

The popular urban literature of antebellum New York conceived of the city as a physical and social labyrinth whose construction appeared a mystery to city dwellers. Perhaps the labyrinth seemed an appropriate metaphor for the rapidly growing city, not just because it suggested the mystery of urban life, but also because its very creation was a mystery. How did it get there? Who built it? Why did it exist? These were not questions that urban fiction routinely asked. Rather, writers like Judson and Lippard assumed that the city became a labyrinth naturally as it grew. As we have seen, many writers and their characters – Redburn and White-Jacket among them – concentrate on getting through the labyrinth, not on examining or understanding its construction. But Pierre has this knowledge forced upon him; he is the first of Melville's characters to discover that he has constructed a labyrinth of his own. He learns, or rather Melville's mocking narrator reveals, that the labyrinth he seeks to penetrate originates in his own mind and imagination; he mystifies himself.

In this emphasis on the labyrinth as a philosophical construction, a product of an urban mind, Melville does not in *Pierre* press a reading of the labyrinth as a social construction, a cultural artifact or myth shared by a whole society. He does, it is true, suggest a political reading of the city's class structure, a critique of democratic individualism, but he does not enter, as many popular urban writers did, into the social labyrinth of New York.[60] In fact, Melville has been criticized for making his New York unsocial, unreal, unnamed. The landmarks that in any other contemporary work would have the conventional associations given to Broadway, Five Points, the Tombs, and City Park, he leaves abstract and unidentified. The mysteries and miseries that in other labyrinth literature would be embodied in specific plots – the contrast between aristocracy and poverty, the plunge into urban poverty, the descent to ruin – appear in *Pierre* in their most disembodied form, as the vaguely rendered mystery and misery of Isabel herself, and Pierre's own rush to disaster. Thus, whereas in *Redburn* and *White-Jacket* Melville seems to work ironically with the conventions of labyrinth literature, showing the ways his characters have been mystified by the social construction of the city as labyrinth, in *Pierre* he seems to turn away from popular conventions.[61] Whereas *Redburn* and *White-Jacket* examine the mysteries and miseries of the urban and oppressed poor, exposing as they do the mysterious operations of power, *Pierre* seems remote from real people and real suffering.[62]

But in seeing the labyrinth in *Pierre* as a construction of the self, Melville implicitly examines its social and cultural meanings as well. It is true that Pierre is alone in his discovery that he has been mystified by the myth of the labyrinth; but his ruin implicates the urban culture in which he was bred. Like Redburn and White-Jacket, Pierre falls from an aristocratic-provincial height into urban depths. Like them, he discovers that his dream of achieving success, of penetrating the labyrinth, of finding knowledge and truth in the city is a delusion. That he makes this discovery by encountering not only the mysteries of class but those of gender – the

inchoate mystery and misery of Isabel – renders his quest no less significant. Unfortunately, once trapped in his own labyrinth, he cannot escape
the urban labyrinth either, and he dies in prison.[63]

Pierre makes a remarkable journey through a labyrinth that is conceived,
not just in terms of the contemporary city, but in terms of the ancient
sources of the modern labyrinth – that is, the labyrinth of Crete. Melville's
narrator evokes this labyrinth specifically in the passage that introduces
this chapter. It is one of the most puzzling passages in the novel. Pierre,
in the midst of making his fateful decision to enter a pretended marriage
with his illegitimate sister Isabel, meditates on his extraordinary choice.
The narrator suggests that because of his youth Pierre lacks the calm
resolve that would foresee the dangers of what he is doing: "That all-
comprehending oneness, that calm representativeness, by which a steady
philosophic mind reaches forth and draws to itself, in their collective en-
tirety, the objects of its contemplations; that pertains not to the young
enthusiast" (175). Instead, Pierre rushes enthusiastically into his "new
and momentous devoted enterprise, [ignoring] the thousand ulterior intricacies and emperilings to which it must conduct" (175). With supreme
confidence in the rightness of his choice, "this hapless youth [is] all eager
to involve himself in such an inextricable twist of Fate, that the three
dextrous maids themselves could hardly disentangle him, if once he tie
the complicating knots about him and Isabel" (175).

Certainly the narrator's tone warns of the dire consequences of Pierre's
entering the moral labyrinth of an assumed marriage with his sister. But
in the next sentence, the narrator implies that there are other labyrinths
toward which Pierre could or ought to move: "Ah, thou rash boy! are
there no couriers in the air to warn thee away from these emperilings,
and point thee to those Cretan labyrinths, to which thy life's cord is leading thee? Where now are the high beneficences? Whither fled the sweet
angels that are alledged [*sic*] guardians to man?" (176). This passage
implies that Pierre's guardian angels, in directing him *away* from the intricacies and emperilings of his fateful decision, would lead him *toward*
another labyrinth, the Cretan labyrinth to which his life's cord is leading
him. Whatever path Pierre chooses, then, he is in a labyrinth.[64] The labyrinth depends on his choice.

The emphasis on choice, even a choice attended and aided by fates,
angels, and "gods of woe" (179), suggests what for Melville defines the
experience of traveling through a labyrinth. A labyrinth is a landscape of
choice. The Cretan labyrinth tested a hero's skill and nerve by offering a
structure of winding and roundabout paths among which he must find
the right way to the center, or heart, of the labyrinth. These paths are
called, in the works of Ovid and other classical writers, *ambages*, from the
word *ambo*, meaning "two" or "both"; the *ambages* give the traveler a
choice between two possible paths. *Ambages* is both a technical term for a

labyrinthine structure and also a metaphor for labyrinthine forms of speech or experience:

1. (*a*) A roundabout or circuitous path, course, etc., meanderings, twists and turns; (*b*) a roundabout or circuitous movement, wandering to and fro
2. Long-winded, obscure or evasive speech, a circumlocution, digression, evasion
3. Mental confusion or uncertainty. (Doob, 53)

As this definition of the Latin term makes clear, the English "ambiguity" bears a direct linguistic relationship with the structure, experience, and language of the labyrinth. "Ambiguity" in this context means not simply mystery but doubleness, causing doubt or uncertainty about choice. In calling his novel *Pierre, or the Ambiguities,* Melville suggests that Pierre is a man in a labyrinth – wandering, uncertain, and forced to choose between two paths.

It is no accident, then, that Pierre's two great sources of inspiration are Hamlet, who stands on the brink of a choice between being and not-being, and Dante, who begins his *Divine Comedy* by losing his way in the woods and turning to Virgil, himself a poet of the labyrinth, to guide him through the labyrinths of Hell. Both give him courage for "[h]igh deeds" (171); both invite him into the "city of Woe" (168). It is also no accident that Pierre's mind and tongue follow the ambages through which he has chosen to travel. A man of ambiguity, he speaks, as does Melville's narrator, the language of ambiguity – the "long-winded, obscure or evasive speech" of the labyrinth. Clearly, Melville meant his labyrinth to suggest, not just a particular place like the city of New York, but also an ongoing existential condition in a man who makes a momentous decision that involves him thereafter in a perpetually ambiguous state.

But Melville also make it clear that Pierre's labyrinth, the one to which his life's cord is leading him, is the Cretan labyrinth, and hence invokes the myth of Daedalus, Minos, Theseus, Ariadne, Pasiphaë and her son, the Minotaur. This myth reminds us that someone built the labyrinth, that it did not simply appear. This human agency in the building of the labyrinth is important for our understanding of Pierre's agency in building his, and so I shall review the myth.[65]

The first difficulty in locating human agency in the building of the labyrinth is identifying the builder. Daedalus, of course, designed the labyrinth; but Minos commissioned it, and if Pasiphaë had not loved a bull, Minos would not have wanted one in the first place. The labyrinth Minos had in mind served as a prison, foremost, for the dangerous Minotaur; but Minos also sought to hide the Minotaur, evidence of his cuckoldry and shame, from public view. Later, when he devised the idea of feeding his enemies to the Minotaur, the labyrinth became a slaughterhouse as well. Its intricacy, then, served several purposes: to protect the Minotaur from intruders, to protect the public from the Minotaur, and eventually to create a grisly game or ritual out of the Minotaur's meals. This is the labyrinth that Minos had built, a structure to bolster and protect his own power. But the labyrinth Daedalus built attests to his creative genius in being able to design a structure of wondrous intricacy, a structure that seen from the air rather than from the ground might appear beautiful rather than terrifying. Daedalus also created the labyrinth as a test of heroic skill; the hero who can find his way in the labyrinth deserves a kingdom. Finally, Daedalus made the labyrinth an artifact of desire. It houses the offspring of Pasiphaë's desire for a bull, and it brings Ariadne and Theseus together in their successful conquest of the Minotaur. It suggests Daedalus's alliance with feminine genius, for he gives Ariadne the thread by which she saves Theseus.

At the heart of Minos's labyrinth is power and death; at the heart of Daedalus's, creativity and desire. Both forces are morally ambiguous, however. Minos represents the patriarchal power of the state oppressing young men and maids, but he also upholds marriage and family by punishing Pasiphaë and her son, and strengthens Crete by subjugating Athens. Daedalus represents heroic ingenuity and unfettered desire, but at the same time he is powerless to prevent the human sacrifices and the disasters that threaten Theseus's and Ariadne's love. The labyrinth, then, embodies (among its many meanings) the uneasy union between pure urges – hunger, anger, lust, predation – and social structures: political order, family, and artifice. It is double doubleness.

Without referring again specifically to the Cretan labyrinth, Melville nevertheless implies throughout *Pierre* that the labyrinth – the labyrinth of the city, the novel's labyrinthine plot, Pierre's quest for truth in a labyrinth of experience – has been constructed out of conflicting impulses: it is both a creation of the imagination and an imposition of human choice. Pierre is generally confused about his motives, but at every juncture he makes his choices and creates his labyrinths for himself. By choosing Isabel, Pierre creates a moral, legal, and sexual labyrinth; by attempting a novel that will shatter moral and literary conventions, Pierre constructs a literary labyrinth that he can never get through or beyond; and in entering enthusiastically into a condition of ambiguity, mystery, and misery, he becomes mystified by his own creations. Only when Pierre can see that mystery is something *created*, not accidental, can he penetrate the mystification that surrounds him. By then, however, he has wandered into the path that leads to the prison, the house of crime and passion, rather than into the heart of the labyrinth.[66]

Although in *Pierre* Melville reaches back to mythic and literary labyrinths for inspiration, he also employs some of the narrative structures of the contemporary urban literature, in particular the country–city and artistocrat–pauper contrasts, the rush to ruin, and the ideas of mystery and misery used to represent the city as an overwhelming labyrinth from which the provincial protagonist can never escape. In *Redburn* and *White-Jacket*, Melville used these conventions innovatively, criticizing the provincial protagonist who allows himself to be mystified by the city's mysteries. *Pierre* complicates and deepens this mockery by making it ambiguous, by giving the reader many choices. Thus we see that the conventions are being used, but their meaning is unclear.[67]

Melville announces the complicated use he plans to make of urban literary conventions in the opening sentences of *Pierre*, where he sets up the country–city contrast.

> There are some strange summer mornings in the country, when he who is but a sojourner from the city shall early walk forth into the fields, and be wonder-smitten with the trance-like aspect of the green and golden world. Not a flower stirs; the trees forget to wave; the grass itself seems to have ceased to grow; and all Nature, as if suddenly become conscious of her own profound mystery, and feeling no refuge from it but silence, sinks into this wonderful and indescribable repose. (3)

In the eyes of the visitor from the city, nature appears strange. Accustomed perhaps to the petrifaction of the urban landscape, the urban sojourner sees the country as still, silent, artificial. Unable to comprehend rural quiet after the noises of the city, the urban viewer attributes to nature a consciousness of her own mystery, which sinks her into repose. It is clear from the opening words of the novel how a perception of mystery has been imposed and composed by an imaginative urban spectator – the mysterious and ambiguous narrator. Later comparisons between the country and the city also will be undermined by this narrator, who reveals all judgments as imaginative constructions.

Pierre, however, considers himself an urban man, able to frame experience in an unambiguous urban perspective. Although a child of the patrician pastoral landscape of Saddle Meadows, he has from an early age made "annual visits to the city; where naturally mingling in a large and polished society, Pierre had insensibly formed himself in the airier graces of life" (6). Like Redburn and White-Jacket, then, he privileges urbanity without penetrating the urban labyrinth of class difference. In fact, true to his aristocratic upbringing, he, or the narrator speaking for him, distrusts the social mobility and turbulence of the city: "In our cities, families rise and burst like bubbles in a vat. For indeed the democratic element operates as a subtile acid among us; forever producing new things by corroding the old" (9). Pierre prefers continuity with the past, status and privilege, to the vital, corrosive energies of the city. In his view of the world, nature is aristocratic, the city democratic and therefore fallen: "the town is the more plebeian portion: which, besides many other things, is plainly evinced by the dirty unwashed face perpetually worn by the town; but the country, like the Queen, is ever attended by scrupulous lady's maids in the guise of the seasons, and the town hath but one dress of brick turned up with stone" (13).

Melville's narrator, however, stresses that Pierre's inherited urbanity brings with it a provincial naiveté about urban life, especially its vices. For when Pierre learns that his urbane father may have indulged in some urban temptations, his provincial upbringing makes it difficult for him to comprehend the facts. Compared to his father, and later his cosmopolitan cousin Glen Stanly, Pierre has been "secludedly nurtured, ... never ... thoroughly initiated into that darker, though truer aspect of things, which an entire residence in the city from the earliest period of life, almost inevitably engraves upon the mind of any keenly observant and reflective youth of Pierre's present years" (69). The narrator, then, early associates the city with truth and knowledge, and gradually Pierre does too. Once aware of his father's true nature (or what he surmises of the truth), Pierre sees his past "as suddenly lighted up as a midnight city by a burning building, which on every side whirls its reddened brands" (71). His love for his mother and his reverence for his father, built upon falsehood, seem to him a sacred construction, but the narrator ironically indicates its weakness: "Love is built upon secrets, as lovely Venice upon invisible and incorruptible piles in the sea" (81). As Ishmael reminds us in the "Town-Ho Story," nothing about Venice is incorruptible, and Pierre himself knows that his hiding away the chair-portrait violates the trust between his mother and him. Even before Pierre goes to New York, then, he has some notion that he cannot naively dismiss the city as a plebeian town. It contains secrets and mysteries of potent significance for him.

Just as Pierre learns that his conventional understanding of the country is false, so he must learn also that his conventional reading of the city is wrong. Melville's narrator skillfully develops the country–city contrast by bringing Pierre into New York at night with the inexperienced Isabel and Delly. The shock of their first exposure to the city resembles the conventional plunge into the labyrinth, but the narrator suggests that Pierre's reactions misconstrue the environment in much the same way the sojourner from the city miscontrues nature. In particular, the language used to describe the city conveys Pierre's implicit moral judgment. The town is seen in the "unequal light reflected from the windows"; Broadway appears as "a long and very gradual slope running toward the obscure heart of the town"; its lights "seemed not so much intended to dispel the general gloom, as to show some dim path leading through it, into some gloom still deeper beyond" (229). The cobblestones make the carriage jolt so that Pierre jokes bitterly that "the buried hearts of some dead citizens have perhaps come to the surface." Pierre seems to take grim delight in frightening the provincial girls with sentiments drawn straight from reform literature: "Milk dropt from the milkman's can in December, freezes not more quickly on those stones, than does snow-white innocence, if in poverty, it chance to fall in these streets" (230). And the hidden streets of the town's haunts also appear in conventional language, though heightened indeed: "they come from the far-hidden places; from under dark beetling secrecies of mortar and stone; through the long marsh-grasses of villainy, and by many a transplanted bough-beam, where the wretched have hung" (231).

But Pierre's first encounters with the city show that unconsciously he creates his own experiences of urban alienation. For example, he accuses the hack driver of infamy when the man fails to bring him to the right house; but the house is not lighted, and the driver has made an honest mistake. Nevertheless, Pierre unleashes a torrent of abuse on the man, whom he sees as one of the "Charon ferry-men to corruption and death." In fact, the whole class of cabdrivers appear to him "[f]letchers and carriers of the worst city infamy . . . professionally familiar with the most abandoned haunts; in the heart of misery, they drive one of the most mercenary of all the trades of guilt" (232). Only the intervention of a police officer prevents Pierre from damaging the driver and his carriage in an ill-conceived leap at the horses' heads. Similarly, Pierre is shocked to come back to the police station, where he has deposited Isabel and Delly, to find them in the midst of a brawl. Yet he blames the officer instead of himself for exposing the women to an "in-door riot" (241). Again he reveals his conventional distaste for the "mob" he finds there, a crowd worthy of Foster's most vivid descriptions of Pete Williams's place: "In indescribable disorder, frantic, diseased-looking men and women of all colors, and in all imaginable flaunting, immodest, grotesque, and shattered dresses, were leaping, yelling, and cursing around him" (240). Speaking "that dialect of sin and death, known as the Cant language, or the Flash" (240) (some of which Judson tried to reproduce accurately in *The Mysteries and Miseries of New York*), reeling and dancing about, and threatening the two frightened maidens with lewd insinuations, the crowd seems an inhuman mass of noise and confusion. But the narrator explains that Pierre is prepared to understand the scene in the terms of labyrinth literature: "Though the hitherto imperfect and casual city experiences of Pierre, illy fitted him entirely to comprehend the specific purport of this terrific spectacle; still he knew enough by hearsay of the more infamous life of the town, to imagine from whence, and who, were the objects before him" (241). Hearsay, which we have to imagine consists in large part of urban journalism and labyrinth literature, has taught him to see these people as conventional props in the provincial's plunge into a threatening city.

The most dramatic, though brief, instance of Pierre's tendency to view the city in conventional terms is his encounter with the prostitute. After he leaves Isabel and Delly in the police station, Pierre ventures into Broadway, where a female voice beckons him:

> Pierre turned; and in the flashing, sinister, evil cross-lights of a druggist's window, his eye caught the person of a wonderfully beautifully-featured girl; scarlet-cheeked, glaringly-arrayed, and of a figure all natural grace but unnatural vivacity. Her whole form, however, was horribly lit by the green and yellow rays from the druggist's.
>
> "My God!" shuddered Pierre, hurrying forward, "the town's first welcome to youth!" (237)

Pierre's remark indicates that he has understood thoroughly the meaning of the encounter as a close brush with temptation and sin. But the narrator emphasizes how unconventional the prostitute actually is. She herself is "beautifully-featured" and "all natural grace." But lighted by the apothecary's brilliant lights, she seems evil. As the description makes clear, it is the "flashing, sinister, evil cross-lights of the druggist's window" – New York by gaslight – that make her appear glaring and unnatural, "horribly lit by the green and yellow rays." Once again, then, Pierre has recombined the elements of his experience to fit his preconceived notion of the city as an evil terrain. It is his cross-lights that are sinister and evil.[68]

After these preliminary conventional encounters, which like Redburn's visit to the gambling palace seem a deliberate parody of the exaggerations of Lippard and Judson, Pierre settles into a more accommodating mood, as he takes up life as an Apostle and seems to abandon disturbing urban encounters. He does, however, see the decayed part of town where the Apostles stands as a "wilderness of tiles, slate, shingles, and tin; – the desolate hanging wildernesses of tiles, slate, shingles and tin, wherewith we modern Babylonians replace the fair hanging-gardens of the fine old Asiatic times when the excellent Nebuchadnezzar was king" (271). This passage reminds us of the country–city contrast by juxtaposing the gardens with the wildernesses of tiles, slate, and so on. But Pierre had earlier associated Babylon with Saddle Meadows, "whose wooded hills . . . stood before them like old Babylonian walls, overgrown with verdure; while here and there, at regular intervals, the scattered peaks seemed mural towers; and the clumped pines surmounting them, as lofty archers, and vast, outlooking watchers of the glorious Babylonian City of the Day" (35). The paradoxical way in which the country seems like a Babylonian city, whereas New York, the true modern Babylon, appears as a wilderness, shows once again how the ironic narrator works to undermine and confuse the conventional structures of the urban narrative. The country–city contrast can hardly function when the same terms apply to both sides.

As in the urban novels, Pierre also encounters disturbing social contrasts within the city, primarily between the Upper Ten, represented by the urbane Glen Stanly, and the Lower Million, represented by Pierre, who is now part of the wretched rather than the privileged classes. Although Glen has grown up in the same pastoral environment as Pierre, he left to travel abroad; nor "had the thousand nameless fascinations of the then brilliant paradises of France and Italy, failed to exert their seductive influence on the previous feelings of Glen" (218). Glen's experiences have spoiled him, for foreign travel, as it did perhaps for Pierre's father, "dislodges some of the finest feelings of the home-born nature; replacing them with a fastidious superciliousness" (218). The climax of Pierre's first night in the city, Pierre's impetuous meeting with Glen after he finds that his cousin has abandoned him, derives its tension from the contrast between Pierre, all "dusty, travel-stained, and ferocious," and Glen, "carelessly lounging in a half side-long attitude upon a large sofa" (238). The "dandy" Glen could not be more different from the "savage" Pierre. And even more remarkable is Pierre's swift transformation from someone schooled in "the airier graces of life" (6) into a leaping madman, issuing murderous threats in his cousin's drawing room. Again it is clear that Pierre's encounter with Glen, like his moment with the prostitute, is conventional and parodic. But it serves, as the other paradigmatic episodes have done, to commit Pierre to provincialism rather than urbanity and to place him at a disadvantage in the world of the labyrinth-city.

In his use of two other common structures, however, the rush to ruin and the journey into the city's mysteries and miseries, Melville shows how Pierre reverses the typical outcome of the urban plot.[69] For although Pierre does rush into ruin, he is not undone by the usual urban temptations of alcohol, gambling, or miscellaneous dissipation. Although he has committed certain improprieties by entering into his unorthodox relations with Isabel, and later Lucy, he initiated those practices before entering the city. His urban trajectory involves his metaphysical intoxication with finding and writing the Truth. This is what, ironically, turns him from the sober path of strict virtue and brings him finally to incest (possibly), murder, and death in prison. In his headlong, impetuous surge toward self-annihilation, Pierre is as heedless as Harry Bolton, but he knows that he is gambling with his own soul. Pierre's ruin comes from his desire for truth, not from anything the city does to him. In that sense, the city provides a convenient plot structure but not the moral structure that informs much urban reform literature. On the contrary, Pierre's rush to ruin indicts the whole moral system that would prefer him to lie rather than perform an unconventional act.

Ultimately, the rush to ruin is most useful in reminding the reader that Pierre has chosen his path in the belief that he was doing the right and only thing. Once he makes the choice, ruin inevitably results. But since Pierre actively chooses and seeks his ruin, rather than live a lie or submit to social convention, his demise has the opposite effect of the ruin of the weak youths of temperance fiction. His death signifies the failure not of a sinning youth but of a corrupt city.

This reading of Pierre's ruin as something willed and chosen in a critical ambage suggests a rather simple and linear journey through the urban labyrinth. Pierre goes to the city, then, to await the results of his suicidal decision to marry Isabel. In this reading, the city seems incidental, simply the locale where events unfold, or rather, fold themselves around Pierre. But the city is more than a stage for Pierre's progress toward annihilation; it is the domain of mystery and misery and the place where Pierre works out his struggle to understand both. He has already contemplated mystery and misery in Saddle Meadows, in his reading of Dante and Homer, in his defense of the abandoned Delly, and in his acceptance of Isabel. In the city, however, he must face the recognition of his own complicity in, his own desire for, creating the structures of mystery and misery. Only in the city can he demystify mystery.

Pierre's experience of mystery begins with Isabel – "that mysterious, haunting face" (37) – but even before he hears her mysterious story he feels that she beckons him to greater mysteries beyond herself: "For me, thou hast uncovered one infinite, dumb, beseeching countenance of mystery, underlying all the surfaces of visible time and space" (52). He also reflects that Dante "had first opened to his shuddering eyes the infinite cliffs and gulfs of human mystery and misery" (54); the ground has been prepared for Isabel's arrival. When he has read her letter exposing his father's youthful indiscretion, he rushes into a mystery he conceives as Truth: "From all idols, I tear all veils; henceforth I will see all hidden things; . . . Now I feel that nothing but Truth can move me so. This letter is not a forgery" (66). In a kind of labyrinthine logic, Pierre asserts that the greater the mystery, the more the truth. As the fragments of Isabel's story emerge, as his fragments of memory and speculation fill them out to make a whole cloth, Pierre makes her mystery a truth in his mind.

Melville's ironic narrator, however, repeatedly stresses Pierre's mistaken enthusiasm. Urging Pierre to rebuild the inner shrine to his father's memory, the narrative voice reminds him that "Such a note as thine can be easily enough written, Pierre; imposters are not unknown in this curious world; or the brisk novelist, Pierre, will write thee fifty such notes, and so steal gushing tears from his reader's eyes" (69–70). This is a statement worthy of the narrator of *The Confidence-Man*, but it could also come from Hamlet in his advice to the players. The narrator's mocking cynicism underscores Pierre's naive eagerness to believe Isabel's sensational story. In the light of her mysteries, his own past and its mysteries begin to assume a shape for him: "Pierre saw all preceding ambiguities, all mysteries ripped open as if with a keen sword . . . [a]nd now, by irresistible intuitions, all that had been inexplicably mysterious to him" (85) begins to make sense. More than that, her story suggests to him the bottomlessness of mystery in the self: "Is it possible, after all, that spite of bricks and shaven faces, this world we live in is brimmed with wonders, and I and all mankind, beneath our garbs of common-placeness, conceal enigmas that the stars themselves, and perhaps the highest seraphim can not resolve?" (138–9). This discovery convinces Pierre that the literature of mystery falsely construes mystery's truth; and now we find out that he has been reading more than Dante and Shakespeare. He has been immersed in popular labyrinth literature as well, and has "read more novels than most persons of his years; but their false, inverted attempts at systematizing eternally unsystemizable elements; their audacious, intermeddling impotency, in trying to unravel, and spread out, and classify, the more thin than gossamer threads which make up the complex web of life; these things over Pierre had no power now" (141). Pierre, steeped in the literature of mystery, sees it now as an empty taxonomy, a falsehood; and "while the countless tribes of common novels laboriously spin vails of mystery, only to complacently clear them up at last," Pierre feels himself to be moving through a labyrinth of the "profounder emanations of the human mind . . . [that] never unravel their own intricacies, and have no proper endings" (141).

While still in the country, then, Pierre feels that he has experienced the depths of mystery, the mystery not of urban suffering but of the soul's truth. But he also encounters misery for the first time. First he discovers the profound woe of Isabel, which opens up to him a vision of complete isolation and despair: "while thou, my brother, had a mother, and troops of aunts and cousins, and plentiful friends in city and in country – I, I, Isabel, thy own father's daughter, was thrust out of all hearts' gates, and shivered in the winter way" (158). But there is also the "affair of that infamous Ned and that miserable Delly" (103), as his mother describes it. This is a more conventional story of betrayal and ruin than Isabel's, but it stimulates Pierre's compassion and, more than that, leads him to ask the kinds of questions that demystify and uncover his mother's and clergyman's attempts to suppress Delly and her misery. "*How* is she to depart? *Who* is to take her? Art *thou* to take her? *Where* is she to go? *Who* has food for her? *What* is to keep her from the pollution to which such as she are every day driven to contribute, by the detestable uncharitableness and heartlessness of the world?" (163). These are the conventional questions of moral reform literature, but in asking them himself Pierre for the first time shows that he recognizes the operations of genteel power in keeping the poor in their place. The collusion between his mother and

Mr. Falsgrave appears to him evidence of a larger corruption in the social body. What he fails to recognize, however, is the way he too colludes in keeping Delly oppressed; for, though he kindly removes her from her negligent parents, he makes her Isabel's maid in a situation that Delly herself will later find oppressive when she discovers that she may be living in a nest of sin (321). Nevertheless, in Isabel's cottage, Delly reminds Pierre of the depths of human suffering, and her misery strengthens his resolve to go to the city.

In the country Pierre encounters mystery and misery with an intensity he has never experienced before. He recognizes their outlines from the novels of mystery he has read, but also feels sure that in Isabel and Delly he has discovered the truth of human suffering, a bottomless well of mystery and misery that makes all previous fictions false. This discovery reverses the usual movement of urban novels, in which the provincial protagonist goes to the city to find the mysteries and miseries that will educate him in the truths of human experience. For Pierre, however, the city where he hopes to discover, live by, and write about the truth turns out to be a gigantic fraud. All he discovers is the "everlasting elusiveness of Truth" (339), and it seems to him that he wanders in a maze of doubt.

Whereas the country bred and reinforced Pierre's faith in mystery, the city tests that faith in one ambage after another. At each of these junctures, Pierre comes face-to-face with his own choices and recognizes that he may have been wrong, that he has mystified himself about the truth. As he moves through the labyrinth, he finds repeatedly that he has taken a wrong turn, has created a fiction that he suddenly sees as a mystification.

One of the most disturbing of the challenges to his attempts at penetrating the labyrinth of mystery is the mocking philosopher Plotinus Plinlimmon. His pamphlet casts doubt upon the efficacy of Pierre's actions, not their rightness; Pierre has always taken the opposite position, that his actions must be right whether or not they were expedient. Plinlimmon is also a spiritual quack, a con artist, who never reads or writes but who accepts Curaçao from his abstemious followers, because "Mohammed hath his own dispensation" (291). Most disturbing of all to Pierre, however, is his intuition that, although Plinlimmon is a master of falsehood, he knows the truth about Pierre: His "face knows that Isabel is not my wife! And that seems the reason it leers" (293). Plinlimmon's scrutiny of Pierre's inner life, his peeping in on Pierre's "miserable condition" (292), makes Pierre aware that the story he has constructed of his relation to Isabel is a fiction that someone else, not a particularly admirable person either, can easily penetrate. Plinlimmon exposes to Pierre the ridiculousness of his own situation. For some time now, Melville's narrator has mocked Pierre's attempts to write a great book, to sustain his enthusiastic commitment to Isabel, to succeed in the great city; but Plinlimmon mocks Pierre to his face.

Pierre faces a similar challenge from Isabel herself. She does not mock him, but she makes him question his motives in protecting her and his means of doing so. First, when Isabel asks him about his early poems, which he has described to her as "precious things, readily convertible into silver and gold" (272), he is forced to admit to her that his previous work is useless. Next, when she grasps his hand and beckons him to her arms, calling him brother, Pierre exposes that fiction too: "Call me brother no more! How knowest thou I am thy brother?" (273). Pierre for the first time rejects his own notions of virtue – "Virtue and Vice are trash" – and dares the gods to "look after their own combustibles" (273). Isabel's response, however, is to sink back into her old attitude of mystery: "I am a poor girl, born in the midst of misery, bred in mystery, and still surviving to mystery" (273). Her experience has taught her that virtue and vice are mysteries as well. To her, then, Pierre's insistence on Virtue is incomprehensible; only when he slinks away from clearly defined boundaries between right and wrong, only when "thou wouldst be lunatic to wise men, perhaps – now doth poor ignorant Isabel begin to comprehend thee" (274). In the country Isabel's mystery seemed to make her wise, but now it veers off into lunacy. Pierre sees his construction of their relationship as a fiction that has allowed him, perhaps, to indulge in the greatest sin rather than to exercise the greatest virtue. When she calls him brother again and he corrects her – "I am Pierre" (274) – he suggests that he recognizes his own impure motives in making the journey with her to the city. That recognition begins the process by which his extreme actions come to lose their mystique for him.

This process comes to a head when Lucy arrives and shines the light of her pastoral innocence on Pierre's domestic arrangements. Pierre becomes hyperconscious of his role-playing as Isabel's husband, comically insisting before all that she is his wife. But Lucy, like Plinlimmon, seems to have divined the truth, to have penetrated the mystery. Unfortunately, she has decided to adopt the same attitude of enthusiastic virtue that Pierre has and so does not offer to interfere in his domestic life or to expose its inner workings. But in her presence Pierre sees Isabel as a jealous, anxious woman who behaves more and more badly. In the inevitable denouement, Pierre decides to scrutinize Isabel's mysteries more closely. Her coincidental resemblance to a picture in a portrait gallery causes him to ask the question he refused to contemplate in Saddle Meadows: "How did he know that Isabel was his sister?" (353). Now he begins to see that his conviction of her identity came from a "nebulous legend," "his own dim reminiscences of his wandering father's death-bed" and, most damaging of all, "his own manifold and inter-enfolding mystic and transcendental persuasions, – originally born, as he now seemed to feel, purely of an intense procreative enthusiasm: – an enthusiasm no longer so all-potential with him as of yore" (353). Perhaps he could see this enthusiasm tolerantly, as a youthful spasm. But Pierre understands that he has undergone something much more serious: a professional inoculation against mystery. His own experience of wandering in a philosophical and literary labyrinth, immersed in bottomless mysteries and miseries, has made him suspicious of amateurs of mystery and misery:

> especially since he had got so deep into the inventional mysteries of his book. For he who is most practically and deeply conversant with mysticisms and mysteries; he who professionally deals in mysticisms and mysteries himself; often that man, more than any body else, is disposed to regard such things in others as very deceptively bejuggling; and . . . more than any other man, is often inclined, at the bottom of his soul, to be uncompromisingly skeptical on all novel visionary hypotheses of any kind. (354)

Finally Pierre has acquired the skepticism of the narrator.

Pierre's professionalism in the marketing of mystery now surpasses Isabel's skill. In some ways, his recognition that his writing of mystery now gives him an advantage over Isabel, now allows him to see into her mysteries, creates the novel's most ironic moment. At the same time, however, although Pierre finally perceives his complicity in Isabel's power to mystify him, he remains mystified still, convinced as he is of his own power to delve into and write about mysteries. After all, he has staked his life and the support of three women on the writing of a book that purports to tell the truth to humankind. He has rejected his own earlier writing as commercial and mystifies to himself his present endeavors, which he considers pure of commercial motives and executed in the strictest and most virtuous poverty. If, however, his writing has professionalized mystery for him, how does he expect to keep it free of the false motives and practices he has despised in others? In secularizing his worship of Isabel's mysteries, he has unknowingly stripped mystery from his own life and work.[70] Yet he remains mystified by his own struggle in the labyrinth, seeing himself as "a mind, which by becoming really profound in itself, grew skeptical of all tendered profundities" (354). Rejecting Isabel's story allows him to demystify her but remystify his own fiction-making.

Pierre's bloody finale in a sense forces him out of the labyrinth of his self-mystification by allowing him to act decisively. No longer swimming in the sea of Isabel's mysteries, he takes action against his enemies, Glen Stanly and Frederic Tartan. The double murder seals his doom but also releases him from the false situation in which he has been living with Lucy and Isabel. Still, Isabel has the last word, and in her final statement – "All's o'er, and ye know him not" (362) – and her final action of concealing his body with her hair – "arbored him in ebon vines" – she asserts her power to make Pierre's story a mystery. Just as she had earlier twisted him in the "complicating knots" from which "the three dextrous maids themselves could hardly disentangle him," so her hair catches him in a great net of mystery and mystification, claiming him for her version of the truth.

Nevertheless, as Melville's earlier reference to the Cretan labyrinth has made clear, Isabel cannot shroud Pierre's choices in mystery. Melville's narrator has shown that Pierre made his own decisions at each juncture of the labyrinth; he also comes to see his participation in his own ruin. It is the novel's great irony that Pierre's wanderings in the urban labyrinth should lead him to penetrate certain mysterious fictions and yet fail to penetrate the labyrinth itself; or perhaps he learns that the only way to reach the center of the urban labyrinth, to expose its real structure, is to commit a crime and end up in the Tombs. There one finds that the city is Minos's labyrinth, a structure that enforces and conceals its own power, rather than Daedalus's labyrinth, a structure that celebrates genius and love, even when they violate social norms.

It might seem that, for his novel of the labyrinthine city, Melville did not particularly need or even intend New York. Pierre's fall into the gutter in what must certainly be some hidden corner of the Five Points could have happened anywhere, and when he stalks into Broadway, seeking the "very proscenium of the town" (359) as the place to stage his murder, he could as easily be in Rome or Boston as in New York. The themes of mystery and misery, the urban labyrinth, the rush to ruin, are not re- stricted to or defined by New York, and Pierre might have tried to become an unsuccessful writer in any number of cities. Melville's allusiveness and yet elusiveness in identifying his city as New York suggests as much a desire to universalize the great city as to hint that his novel takes place in a recognizable locale.

Yet nowhere but in New York does one find a Broadway, where one "pavement was well nigh deserted, save by porters, waiters, and parcel- carriers of the shops," whereas on the other, "for three long miles, two streams of glossy, shawled, or broadcloth life unceasingly brushed by each other, as long resplendent, drooping trains of rival peacocks brush" (359). Only of New York, with its astronomically high population figures, could an author make such a statement as this: "One in a city of hundreds of thousands of human beings, Pierre was as solitary as at the Pole" (338). And yet, paradoxically, that same density of population produces a strange kind of comfort, too: "he had found some relief in making his regular evening walk through the greatest thoroughfare of the city; that so, the utter isolation of his soul, might feel itself the more intensely from the incessant jogglings of his body against the bodies of the hurrying thousands" (340). New York is one of the few places where a Pierre, a Plinlimmon, and a Charlie Millthorpe, Pierre's cheerfully provincial friend, could live under one roof. In New York, America's largest and most impersonal city, three such iconoclasts as Pierre, Isabel, and Lucy might suppose that they could succeed in their journey through its labyrinths.

But *Pierre* also shows the fatuousness of the urban quest. Melville savagely attacks the literature and mythology of an urban labyrinth, at the same time giving the labyrinth serious, considered, and extensive representation. In mocking the moral impulses of the labyrinth literature and yet refusing a social reading of the city's labyrinthine structure, Melville locates the labyrinth in the mind and heart of a misguided provincial. Pierre's urban imagination brings him closer to the heart of the urban labyrinth than either Redburn or White-Jacket dared to go – perhaps, after all, he reached it – but Melville offers no strategy of mystification, no model of extrication for the provincial reader. Primarily for its mockery of the moral urban quest, *Pierre* escaped the labyrinth of commercial popularity.

PART TWO

Escaping the City

4

Town Ho

===

"[A] man-of-war is to whalemen, as a metropolis to shire-towns."

White-Jacket, 16

"By art is created that great Leviathan, called a Commonwealth or State
– (in Latin, Civitas) . . ."

Opening sentence of Hobbes's *Leviathan,*
Moby-Dick (xx)

There now is your insular city of the Manhattoes, belted round by
wharves as Indian isles by coral reefs – commerce surrounds it with her
surf.   *Moby-Dick* (3)

In this chapter I will argue that *Moby-Dick* is the most pro-urban of Melville's books.

The term "pro-urban," of course, is not particularly descriptive or useful and suggests the limits of the term "anti-urban," typically used until
quite recently to describe Melville's position in relation to the city. Common sense would suggest the absurdity of applying broad labels to the
range of Melville's urban writings and practices. Furthermore, as the work
of what Frederick Crews has called the "New Americanists" has focused
on the problem of whether a writer *can* speak outside his or her culture,
the debate over Melville's anti- or pro-urbanness becomes difficult to sustain.[1] But, most important for this discussion, the city is, as Spiro Kostof
has argued, in *process.* When we talk about cultural constructions of the
city, urban forms as they appear on the landscape or in artifacts that
represent the city, we are talking about changing, dynamic structures:
"Cities are never still; they resist efforts to make neat sense of them. We
need to respect their rhythms and to recognize that the life of city form

must lie loosely somewhere between total control and total freedom of action.''[2] Attempts by New York planners to develop the city for speculation encountered obstacles, first the rocky terrain and later the immigrant and middle-class tenants who did not share the interests of speculators.[3] In the popular urban fiction of the antebellum period, efforts by writers to make sense of the emerging city met with resistance, not only from the subject of representation itself, but from the writer unable to master his or her subject completely. Melville's narratives similarly display the conflicts between "total control and total freedom of action" that urban form and its literary constructions try to contain.

I have been speaking of Melville's city not only as the place New York but also as a web of narrative strategies of representation. These conventional modes – the city as panoramic capital or as challenging labyrinth, the urban protagonist as urbane spectator or questing provincial, urban travel as lounging or as searching for clues – appear throughout the urban culture in a variety of literary and graphic forms. In adapting them to his early travel and nautical narratives, Melville seized upon some handy literary tools, using them, as he would so many of his sources, with the characteristic élan and "all-fusing spirit" (*CM*, 9) of his creative imagination. Isolating his use of urban motifs, styles of discourse, patterns of movement, and points of view allows us, primarily, to *see* these formal principles as they work in his art. It becomes easier, then, to speak precisely of how Melville engages in his urban culture's rituals of representation, even when he does not locate his characters primarily in a city, as in his novels (*Redburn* excepted) before *Pierre*.

Moby-Dick, then, could be seen in this context as employing many of the urban modes we have seen in Melville's other early novels. Although most of the story takes place at sea, it launches itself from Manhattan and an extended period (twenty-two chapters) on land. As in *Typee* and *Omoo*, the narrator's departure from urban civilization allows him to reflect on that civilization from a critical, spectatorial distance. As in *Redburn* and *White-Jacket*, a socially and racially diverse sailor population challenges the narrator's tolerance of others. And as in *Mardi*, a survey of another world leads the narrator on a speculative quest that ends in disaster. In his narrative style and discourse, Ishmael fuses spectatorial wit, criticism, and panoramic vision with the meditative, digressive methods of the wanderer in a labyrinth. At times he brilliantly masters his subject, displaying intellectual dexterity and courage. At others he surrenders, in a masthead reverie or communal squeezing of sperm, to ecstatic, spiritual, or emotional waves. Most of all, a heteroglossic language reminds the reader of his or her own urban culture while revisioning it in the nautical context. The whale as subject becomes as diverse, contentious, populous, dangerous, exciting, and unfinished as the city itself: a *civitas* in the making.

Whatever *Moby-Dick* may share with its urban culture, however, has al-

ready received extensive attention.⁴ In terms of urban *form*, the novel remains unexplored. I see *Moby-Dick* as both a culmination of and a
transition in Melville's lifelong engagement with urban form. Of his early
novels of escape, it signals his most complete break. In no other novel
does his narrator travel so far from the city, the proud city of growing
New York. Yet what does he escape to? Although he is literally at sea for
most of the novel, Ishmael inhabits, bodily and mentally, a world that he
often describes as a town – a walled town, like the early settlement of
Manhattan, the medieval walled towns of Europe, and even the colonial
outposts of South America. This town, while "insular" and ultimately
doomed, represents a thriving community and a form that protectively
encloses its social diversity and heteroglossic Babel. In escaping the city,
Ishmael does not find solitude in a wilderness. Instead, he finds community in a series of towns, from New Bedford to the *Pequod* and the *Town-
Ho*, to the proudest towns of all, Lima and the Manhattan of his
imagination. This book, then, celebrates the Town in Town Ho. It also
shows that that Town is threatened by the new world of the City, or conversely, the City of the New World.

Walls, Whales, and Towns

Moby-Dick displays the differences, and at points the conflicts between urban forms at various stages of their evolution. Towns and cities appear
throughout the book, not in polarity but, in Kostof's terms, in process.
They also surface repeatedly in metaphors for the whale and the ship,
suggesting a significant partition in point of view. Looked at from the
outside, a walled town – Quebec, Ehrenbreitstein, Lima, or New York –
appears forbidding and oppressive. Viewed from the inside, however, as
in the wooden-walled ships the *Pequod* or *Town-Ho*, or the enclosure of
space that the whales form around their babies, or the interior space of
the whale itself, the walled town appears full of vitality, community, and
love. Ishmael moves back and forth between these different vantage
points, at times appreciating the vital spirit of the walled town and at
others decrying its "exclusiveness" (*MD*, 543).

The urban form of the walled town differs from the gridiron plan of
growing New York and other emerging North American cities in being
closed, protective, and in many cases antidemocratic. It implies a military
function, to protect the populace from attack, and a social structure based
on feudal hierarchies. In the colonial outposts of the New World, it
worked, as the medieval walled town had, to create an orderly, stable base
for conquest, commercial activity, and the building of culture.⁵ In terms
that might have been congenial to Melville, Lewis Mumford describes
both the pleasures and the liabilities of walled towns, especially the advantages in uses of public space: "as far as usable open spaces go, the

medieval city had at its foundation and through most of its existence a far higher standard for the mass of the population than *any later form of town.*"[6] Because of low population density, a "vital social environment" (49), and ample public space for gardens and markets, the lack of plumbing and modern comforts produced less inconvenience, paradoxically, than many Victorian reforms. Furthermore, "the psychological import of the wall must not be forgotten" (54) as a guarantee of safety. "As in a ship, the wall helped create a feeling of unity between the inhabitants: in a siege or a famine the morality of the shipwreck – share-and-share-alike – developed easily" (54). The only problem, Mumford notes, was that the wall also created a "fatal sense of insularity" (54). And as economic considerations made it important for cities to trade and cooperate, the protective walls had to come down. Mumford's concluding statement on the walled town captures the mixed sense of regret and relief as this old urban form passed away:

> There is little more to be said about the medieval city. Its economic and its social basis had disintegrated, and its organic pattern of life had been broken up. Slowly, the form itself became dilapidated, and even when it continued to stand, its walls enclosed a hollow shell, harboring institutions that were also hollow shells. It is only, as it were, by holding the shell quietly to one's ear, as with a sea-shell, that one can catch in the ensuing pause the dim roar of the old life that was once lived, with dramatic conviction and solemn purpose, within its walls. (72)

Although Mumford realizes the futility of preserving that older urban form, he regrets its passing and the vision of social unity and cooperation that it implies. Melville was to express similarly ambivalent responses in *Moby-Dick.*

Openness and closure, the twin possibilities of urban space, appear in the towns with which Melville opens the book, New York and New Bedford. Both towns remind Ishmael of the early days of town building, when colonial settlers came into conflict with native populations; both show the pleasures and dangers of containment and expansion; both suggest the influence of urban form on their inhabitants' lives and movements.

In spite of his celebratory tone, Ishmael's first description of New York refers directly to its history and development as a fortress imposing its culture on an alien land: "There now is your insular city of the Manhattoes, belted round by wharves as Indian isles by coral reefs – commerce surrounds it with her surf" (3). The reminder of the island's original inhabitants, the Manhattoes, is not so subtly doubled by Melville's reference to other Indian isles. The story of the first sale of Manhattan land appeared in nearly all guidebooks of the period and received gleeful treatment in Washington Irving's *A History of New York from the Creation of the*

World to the End of the Dutch Dynasty by "Diedrich Knickerbocker." Without explicitly referring to the walls of the original settlement, Melville economically delineates their significance by showing that the city is insular, belted, and surrounded. The wharves and commerce that belt the city round suggest more forgiving walls than those of the embattled medieval town. Even the Battery, the last reminder of the town's early history as fort, appears here in its benign aspect as a "noble mole . . . washed by waves, and cooled by breezes" (3–4). But the city still functions to confine as well as protect its inhabitants; and that task becomes more obviously strained as the city grows beyond its original limits.

For Melville's Manhattan is an old walled fort adapting itself somewhat uneasily to commercial expansion. His language emphasizes the tension between an older urban form – the walled town, a walking city – and the new demands of capitalist entrepreneurship, which opens up urban space for growth but also controls the city's inhabitants. Melville underlines the tension between people and urban structure through an image of streets that move people toward the water: "Right and left the streets take you waterward" (3) toward the Battery. Yet when people get to the water they stand in motionless reverie, held in by the city's natural and man-made boundaries. They are, then, urban prisoners: "of week days pent up in lath and plaster – tied to counters, nailed to benches, clinched to desks" (4). And they are prisoners within the old city walls: the southern limit of the Battery, the old military fortification at "the extremest limit of the land," where they stand "[p]osted like silent sentinels all around the town" (4); and the northern limit of the old wall, now called Wall Street, which hems them in not with a military enclosure but with a line defining the city's new identity as a financial capital, clinching clerks to desks. They seem to move toward the water through some volition of their own, but Melville suggests compulsion rather than desire: "Inlanders all, they come from lanes and alleys, streets and avenues – north, east, south, and west. Yet here they all unite. Tell me, does the magnetic virtue of the needles of the compasses of all those ships attract them thither?" (4). Unlike the "robust healthy boy with a robust healthy soul in him, at some time or other crazy to go to sea" (5), the dwellers of New York seem like entranced lemmings: "crowds, pacing straight for the water, and seemingly bound for a dive" (4). The walls surrounding New York, then, create an island, uniting the inhabitants into a mindless crowd, a frame that the economic forces working from within the city threaten to tear open with sudden violence.

In contrast, the seaport town of New Bedford seems open and embracing. Although Melville refers humorously to Nantucket and New Bedford as cities, Nantucket being "the Tyre of this Carthage," they appear quite different as urban forms from "the good city of old Manhatto" (8). Not that there are no sinister reminders of a grim urban landscape. The "hard, asphaltic pavement," the "dreary streets," the references to "ashes from that destroyed city, Gomorrah" (9) and to "Lazarus there, chattering his teeth against the curbstone for his pillow, and shaking off his tatters with his shivering" (10) call up the same menacing urban world as the mystery-and-misery fiction. New Bedford has imposed its form on "this once scraggy scoria of a country" (32) in as determined a way as New York leveled the island of Manhattan: "So omnipotent is art; which in many a district of New Bedford has superinduced bright terraces of flowers upon the barren refuse rocks thrown aside at creation's final day" (33). Much as in New York, commerce has taken over the town and created its wonders: "all these brave houses and flowery gardens came from the Atlantic, Pacific, and Indian oceans" (32). At the same time, the town's shipping gives it a diverse everchanging population of mariners from all over the world. Constantly receiving new infusions, from the "wild set of mariners" coming off each new whaling vessel (15), to the "green Vermonters and New Hampshire men, all athirst for gain and glory" (31), the town remixes itself every day. The most important aspect of this diversity for Ishmael, besides the opportunity it provides to observe "Feegeeans, Tongatabooans, Erromanggoans, Pannangians, and Brighggians" (31), is that he meets Queequeg and "marries" him. Sharing his landlord's connubial bed with the tattooed island prince provides Ishmael with an experience of delight, intimacy, and privacy that no ship can match. At the Spouter Inn with Queequeg, Ishmael enjoys the keenest pleasures of life in a "civilized town" (31).

Paradoxically, New York, which has expanded far beyond the fort New Amsterdam, seems more closed and contained than the smaller seaport town of New Bedford. In fact, Ishmael suggests that New Bedford, with its large foreign population, is as cosmopolitan as New York or London: "Even in Broadway and Chestnut streets, Mediterranean mariners will sometimes jostle the affrighted ladies. Regent street is not unknown to Lascars and Malays; and at Bombay, in the Apollo Green, live Yankees have often scared the natives. But New Bedford beats all Water street and Wapping" (31). Whereas in *Typee* Melville brought the city to the savage, in *Moby-Dick* he brings the savage to the city: "actual cannibals stand chatting at street corners; savages outright; many of whom yet carry on their bones unholy flesh. It makes a stranger stare" (31). But it also makes this stranger, Ishmael, feel that he has entered a far more open and tolerant world than that of the landsmen pent up in lath and plaster. It also suggests the intimate connection, developed at later points in the novel and in Melville's work after *Moby-Dick*, between savagery and civilized life, between barbarism and culture, between the city of Cain, who killed his brother and founded a fortress, and the city of Abel, the settler. The presence of savages on the streets of New Bedford, like the Manhatto ghosts inhabiting the streets of New York, reminds Ishmael that cities grow out of conflicts between founders and barbarians, colonizers and natives; but in New Bedford that conflict is in large part defused because of the democratic, racially diverse throng of sailors that populate its streets, wharves, and taverns.[7]

Even in New Bedford, however, Ishmael encounters the darker implications of urban form. When he turns away from the docks and sailor hangouts to enter Father Mapple's church, he finds evidence that New Bedford is not only an open seaport but also a walled town full of walled-in people. The memorial plaques for dead whalemen appear on the chapel walls, "masoned into the wall on either side the pulpit" (34), the mourners are each "purposely sitting apart from the other, as if each silent grief were insular and incommunicable" (34), and when Father Mapple ascends to his crow's-nest pulpit, he faces his congregation "impregnable in his little Quebec" (39). Yet in pausing over this anomaly, Ishmael reflects on the spiritual needs fulfilled by building walls, which gather people together to celebrate community, honor the dead, and protect each other from the dangers outside. Cities and towns keep "the horrors of the half-known life" (274) at bay, for "the rumor of a knocking in a tomb will terrify a whole city" (37).[8] Within city walls, men and women face their fears in company, not alone. When Father Mapple retreats to his citadel, then, he offers an example to his parishioners of provident preparation for the sieges of life: "for replenished with the meat and wine of the word, to the faithful man of God, this pulpit, I see, is a self-containing stronghold – a lofty Ehrenbreitstein, with a perennial well of water within the walls" (39). That sustaining well suggests that, though the walled town contains "insular" grief, it also nurtures life.

In his sermon, Father Mapple alludes to many of the urban terms that Melville employs later in the book. The story of Jonah begins in "wicked Nineveh" (47), the proud city that Melville showed in *Mardi* as the epitome of human dominion over the earth and its creatures. In escaping the city, Jonah flees to a ship, where he finds God (not at the masthead, as Ishmael will do, but in the depths of the hold) and a community of sailors who, though "appalled [at Jonah's confession], . . . still are pitiful" (46). Ejecting Jonah from the ship saves both the community and him, but only after he has spent some time in the hold of another ship, the living vessel of the whale. Redeemed by his travels through the underwater world of the whale, Jonah emerges to tell his story, "to preach Truth to the face of Falsehood" (48). Ishmael, too, escapes the proud city to enter the walled towns of whalers and whales, emerging later to tell his story in the face of falsehood.

It should come as little surprise that the *Pequod* appears in the novel as a town, not a city. As Jack Chase remarked in *White-Jacket*, "A man-of-war is to whalemen, as a metropolis to shire-towns" (16). He suggests that whalers are provincial in comparison with the sophisticated, up-to-date naval vessel, but White-Jacket's irony makes room for the second obvious reading, that whalers lack the warship's terrifying machinery of subjugation and destruction. What seems distinctive about Melville's use of the trope is Ishmael's shifting point of view. For in his analogies between the *Pequod* and medieval walled towns, he implicates the whaleship in a feudal structure that oppresses the common sailor under a heavy weight of aristocratic privilege. At other times, however, he suggests that the solidarity among shipmates creates an experience of democratic fraternity that one cannot find in the class-divided city.[9]

According to the logic of Jack Chase's metaphor, the *Pequod*, a whaler, is not a metropolis but a town, a wooden-walled town like the New York of the first settlers. Melville reinforces that connection through a number of other such analogies, particularly to medieval European towns. The appearance of the *Pequod*, for example, makes Ishmael think of the "kings of Cologne" and "the pilgrim-worshipped flag-stone in Canterbury Cathedral where Becket bled" (69). Equipping the *Pequod* for its voyage resembles preparations for a medieval siege, as the sailors supply their needs for "three-years' housekeeping upon the wide ocean" (95). The many references to medieval knighthood and warfare suggest the feudal hierarchies in force on the *Pequod*. Ahab appears as a king of his fiefdom, his mates are knights, and the harpooneers are squires. The trying out of the whale, refining its flesh into oil, resembles, as many critics have seen, the operations of a medieval workshop or guild, with an extensive lore and ritual attached to the work, a spirit of cooperation among the workers, a preindustrial use of hand tools, and a precapitalist sense of satisfaction in seeing the work completed.[10] Whaling itself appears comparable, not only to the medieval hunt but also to medieval warfare between walled towns: "I know a man that, in his lifetime, has taken three hundred and fifty whales. I account that man more honorable than that great captain of antiquity who boasted of taking as many walled towns" (111). There is even a ship called the *Town-Ho*, a name that means, as Melville's note tells us, "the ancient whale-cry upon first sighting a whale from the mast-head, still used by whalemen in hunting the famous Gallipagos terrapin" (242); in "The Encantadas," Melville refers to the same Galapagos tortoises as "walled towns" that, like whaling vessels, have the "known capacity of sustaining life, while going without food for an entire year" (*PT*, 131). The *Pequod* as structure and enterprise, then, suggests a tightly organized community led by a king dedicated to warfare and the hunt. In stark confirmation of this, Ishmael describes Ahab as a fortress that has turned in on itself: "his special lunacy stormed his general sanity, and carried it, and turned all its concentred cannon upon its own mad mark" (185). And in his own acknowledgment of the same fact, Ahab near the end of the novel laments "this life I have led; the desolation of solitude it has been; the masoned, walled-town of a Captain's exclusiveness, which admits

but small entrance to any sympathy from the green country without"
(543).

Ishmael complicates this analogy between the ship and medieval towns
by suggesting that as much as walls may mason up the self in grim, insular
grief they also create a safe haven from the howling universe outside, an
enclosed ground where one may find peace, pleasure, and fellowship with
others. Ishmael finds this fulfillment partly in his communion with his
shipmates, which is far deeper and more satisfying than what either Redburn or White-Jacket finds on shipboard. As the chapter "A Squeeze of
the Hand" indicates, Ishmael is inspired by a vision of democratic, spiri-
tualized, and erotic comradeship with his fellow workers: "Come; let us
squeeze hands all round; nay, let us all squeeze ourselves into each other;
let us squeeze ourselves universally into the very milk and sperm of kindness" (416). As I will show in my reading of "The Town-Ho's Story," a
similar sense of comradeship and solidarity, though not so ecstatically expressed, binds the sailors of the *Town-Ho*. In the chapters where the men
are away from Ahab, whose commanding presence automatically converts
them into an undifferentiated mob, the sailors work in the joint-stock
spirit of equality that Allan Melvill, in an earlier generation, found so
disturbing in the city of New York. Queequeg saves a fool from drowning,
complacently proving that " 'It's a mutual, joint-stock world, in all merid-
ians. We cannibals must help these Christians' " (62).

Like Jonah, Ishmael travels through the world of the whale as well as
the ship, and it is there, in his imaginative construction of the whale, that
he experiences the purest delights of enclosure: "herein we see the rare
virtue of a strong individual vitality, and the rare virtue of thick walls, and
the rare virtue of interior spaciousness" (307). Ishmael makes the connection between whales and walled towns when he refers to the captain
of antiquity who captured three hundred and fifty of them. But, as the
whale draws to it all manner of significations throughout the narrative, it
also includes the spectacle of city and town. The quotation from Hobbes's
Leviathan links the whale with *civitas*. In other examples from Melville's
"Extracts," the whale appears in connection with London – " 'The aorta
of a whale is larger in the bore than the main pipe of the water-works at
London Bridge' " (xxiii) – and Berlin – " 'The papers were brought in,
and we saw in the Berlin Gazette that whales had been introduced on the
stage there' " (xxv). In the cetology chapters, Ishmael looses an outpouring of urban and architectural analogies for the whale. The whale's lower
jaw is a "terrific portcullis" (332), his blood vessels are a "remarkable
involved Cretan labyrinth" (371), his tail resembles "old Roman walls"
(375) and a "Lima tower" (439), and the spine looks like "the great
knobbed blocks on a Gothic spire" (454). The whale's head, especially,
evokes images of towns, walls, and buildings. The forehead is a "dead,
impregnable, uninjurable wall" (337) containing a "great Heidelburgh

Tun" (339) of oil. Like "the great dome of St. Peter's" (307), as impressive as "the Dome of the Pantheon" (345), it conceals the brain "hidden away behind its vast outworks, like the innermost citadel within the amplified fortifications of Quebec" (348). The whale's bones also often literally serve as architecture, as in the "Extracts" quotation from Hawthorne, where the character says, "I built a cottage for Susan and myself and made a gateway in the form of a Gothic Arch, by setting up a whale's jaw bones" (xxiv); and at the Spouter Inn, where guests enter the bar through "the vast arched bone of the whale's jaw" (14). (The "Etymology" reminds us that the Scandinavian word for whale, *hval*, means "arched or vaulted" [xv].) The most magnificent example of the whale as architecture is the woodland temple, in the Bower of the Arsacides, created by a beached whale's skeleton. A similar phenomenon, the skeleton in Sir Clifford Constable's collection, is a true museum piece: "Sir Clifford thinks of charging twopence for a peep at the whispering gallery in the spinal column; threepence to hear the echo in the hollow of his cerebellum; and sixpence for the unrivalled view from his forehead" (451). Although these references are just a few of the many analogies Ishmael makes between the whale and civilized life, they suggest that his investigation of the whale takes him on a journey through towns as well as over the ocean.

The whale also creates its own walled spaces that give Ishmael intimations of the combined danger and pleasure of a walled town. When a wounded whale pulls Ishmael's boat in among a large herd of whales, he is at first aware of "the density of the crowd of reposing whales" and the danger of "no possible chance of escape" unless "a breach [occurred] in the living wall that hemmed us in; the wall that had only admitted us to shut us up" (387). Yet within the enchanted circle of the living wall, Ishmael observes the domestic life of the whales – the nursing infants, the frisking youngsters, and the "young Leviathan amours in the deep" (388). This image of "dalliance and delight" (389) provides one of the treasured experiences of joy in the novel, matched only by the sperm-squeezing, Ishmael's communion with Queequeg, and his vision of the "insular Tahiti" (274) of the soul. It is enough, however, to convince Ishmael that walls can enclose space in a way that nurtures rather than represses life. It sustains him through the long destructive trajectory of Ahab's walled-town madness.

As all these references suggest, when Ishmael escapes the city, he travels among towns, within walls. The fuller significance of that encounter emerges when he discovers the town in Town Ho.

The Town-Ho's Story

Although images of walled towns appear throughout *Moby-Dick*, they do not in themselves offer more than an interesting metaphorical web. The most significant exploration of the cultural meaning of urban form appears in Ishmael's narration of the *Town-Ho*'s story in chapter 54. In the way he presents this story, Ishmael makes it clear that *where* the story gets told influences *how* it is told. The *Town-Ho* story is the novel's clearest example of how urban form influences literary form. It also celebrates the multiplicity of urban forms and the literary forms they generate.

The *Town-Ho*'s story is told at three different sites, each one identified with a particular city or urban form. The first is on the planks of the two ships, the *Pequod* and the *Town-Ho*, whose meeting place at sea is compared to a sociable gathering at a working-class tavern in any major port. The second takes place in Lima, where Ishmael tells the story to a group of Spanish cavaliers gathered at an inn on the plaza. And the third is the story's publication in New York, where he proposes "to put on lasting record" (243) a story that has circulated orally for some time. Although each of these sites differs markedly as urban form and each narrative form differs as well, they all have one thing in common: at each site Ishmael subtly emphasizes the contact, indeed the conflict, between cultures, one "civilized," one "barbarian." One might say that the linking theme of the three narrative occasions is the presence of the hidden Indian who challenges the civilizers and their pretensions. At each point Ishmael questions whether the founders of cities are not more barbarian than the "savages" they have displaced.

Even without the complications of these multiple tellings, the *Town-Ho*'s story is complex. A tale of mutinous rebellion by the heroic, reckless mariner Steelkilt against the cruel mate Radney and his obtuse captain, it shows Moby Dick, who intervenes at an opportune moment to destroy Radney, as "a certain wondrous, inverted visitation of one of those so-called judgments of God which at times are said to overtake some men" (242). Ishmael treats it as a "tragedy" (242), elevating the events to cosmic significance; yet the meaning is obscure. Does the story show Steelkilt's heroism or his fall? Does it portray Radney as a villain or as an unfortunate victim, mourned by a grieving widow? Is Moby Dick the agent of a wise or vengeful God? Or is he merely a random, "mysterious fatality" (255)? Ishmael swears at the end of the tale to the truth of what he says – "I know it to be true; it happened on this ball; I trod the ship; I knew the crew; I have seen and talked with Steelkilt since the death of Radney" (259) – yet his story raises many doubts about its authenticity, not least among his credulous Spanish listeners, to whom he makes an oath on the largest Bible they can find.

If the story itself seems dark and mysterious, its multilayered narration complicates it even further by showing that its meaning changes with each site, each teller, each audience. The story becomes a mirror of culture, a product of its narrative location.

We do not witness the narration of the first story, but it is the most authentic source, told by the white sailors of the *Town-Ho*, who observed the mutiny directly, to Tashtego, the "unmixed Indian from Gay Head" (120) and harpooneer of the *Pequod*. This narrative site would not appear to be urban, as it is in one of the most remote corners of the globe, the Cape of Good Hope. Yet as Ishmael describes it the Cape greatly resembles the urban working-class haunts of sailors: "The Cape of Good Hope, and all the watery region round about there, is much like some noted four corners of a great highway, where you meet more travellers than in any other part" (242). The two ships are engaged in a gam, which Melville describes as the "friendly and sociable contact" (239) at which whalers excel; "Whereas, some merchant ships crossing each other's wake in the mid-Atlantic, will oftentimes pass on without so much as a single word of recognition, mutually cutting each other on the high seas, like a brace of dandies in Broadway" (239), whalers abound in "godly, honest, unostentatious, hospitable, sociable, free-and-easy" (240) geniality. The first urban site of the story, then, is the broad highway, not the high-and-mighty Broadway, of the ocean. The narrative is part of a social exchange between the men of two ships swapping news, gossip, and stories. And, in a remarkable aberration, the gam with the *Town-Ho* is the only gam, among the ten that take place in *Moby-Dick*, in which a real exchange occurs between the sailors, not just the captains and officers. In fact, in most of the gams no exchange occurs at all, as Ahab repeatedly refuses fellowship with other whalers. The *Town-Ho* gam, then, offers a rare opportunity for the kind of communal socializing that the working-class sailors seek in their seaport taverns.

At this site, the narrative takes place in secrecy and within carefully observed class boundaries. In particular, the story of Steelkilt's plan to murder Radney and Moby Dick's timely intervention remains the "property" of the sailors and never travels beyond them to Ahab and the officers:

> the secret part of the tragedy about to be narrated, never reached the ears of Captain Ahab or his mates. For that secret part of the story was unknown to the captain of the Town-Ho himself. It was the private property of three confederate white seamen of that ship, one of whom, it seems, communicated it to Tashtego with Romish injunctions of secresy, but the following night Tashtego rambled in his sleep, and revealed so much of it in that way, that when he was wakened he could not well withhold the rest. Nevertheless, so potent an influence did this thing have on those seamen in the Pequod who came to the full knowledge of it, and by such a strange delicacy, to call it so, were they governed in this matter, that they kept the secret among themselves so that it never transpired abaft the Pequod's main-mast. (242–3)

The mystery of the story, "this darker thread" that the men keep from Ahab and the mates, is itself unknown. For Ishmael does not make it clear whether it has to do with Moby Dick's intervention in the events on the *Town Ho*, which would have appalled Ahab by reminding him of the whale's fury, or whether it concerns the mutiny by Steelkilt and the sailors, which might have made Ahab aware of the rebellious crew. Ishmael's narration, then, while seeking to enlighten his listeners about what would have caused the sailors to show "such a strange delicacy," as well as about what would have disturbed Tashtego's sleep, remains opaque.

But if the meaning of the story is mysterious to Ishmael's readers, its cultural context suggests why it had meaning for the sailors. The name "Town-Ho" offers an etymological clue, which Melville jokingly obscures by defining the word in a footnote. Aware that many of his readers might think that the name means something like, "Oh, look! There's a town!" he explains that "town-ho" is "the ancient whale-cry upon first sighting a whale from the mast-head, still used by whalemen in hunting the famous Gallipagos terrapin." He fails, however, to add a fact that he would surely have known, namely, that the word is not, as it appears, an English usage but has its source in a Native American word, "townor": "the boys, as soon as they can talk, will make use of the common phrases, as townor, which is an Indian word, and signifies that they have seen the whale twice."[11] Early in the novel, Ishmael has described the "Red-Men" who were the first to "sally out in canoes to give chase to the Leviathan" (8), but here he indicates the presence of the same Red Man through Tashtego, who admits the story into his imagination, where it disturbs his sleep and blurts itself out to the other sailors. The deeper connection between the "cannibal of a craft" (70), the *Pequod*, named for "a celebrated tribe of Massachusetts Indians, now extinct as the ancient Medes" (69) and the *Town-Ho*, named for the Indians who first hailed whales, remains submerged. Although the Town in *Town-Ho* would seem to refer a New York reader to the civilized world, the name shows the brotherhood between *Pequod* and *Town-Ho*, both savage craft. It is appropriate, then, that the white sailors of the *Pequod*, Ishmael among them, receive the story from Tashtego rather than directly from the white *Town-Ho* sailors.

But class distinctions define the story's narration as much as racial difference.[12] On the *Town-Ho*, the story is at first "private property." It belongs to the white sailors who took part in the mutiny, only a few of whom remain, as many defected and the rest are Polynesians hired on by the desperate captain. Sailors, as Melville shows in his other nautical fiction, do not own much property, but they do assert proprietary rights to their small holdings. Once they entrust this bit of their private property to Tashtego, however, it becomes part of his imagination, which owes little to white notions of property. In Tashtego's savage consciousness, and on the savage *Pequod*, the story becomes alienable property, circulating among the sailors from whom Tashtego "could not well withhold the rest." At the same time it stays among the sailors, who make sure that the story "never transpired abaft the Pequod's main-mast." Thus, although

Tashtego's savage imagination liberates the story from its white masters, it remains the property of the working-class sailors, who declare their solidarity with each other and with the *Town-Ho* mutineers by keeping it secret. In their trust of Tashtego, the sailors indicate that class loyalty matters more than racial difference.

As one of the sailors, Ishmael acquires the story along with the rest; but he does not keep it secret, nor does he seem to honor the sailors' trust: he tells the story at its second urban site, in Lima, "to a lounging circle of my Spanish friends, one saint's eve, smoking upon the thick-gilt tiled piazza of the Golden Inn" (243). Here, instead of being property to be guarded with "Romish injunctions of secresy," the story becomes entertainment for a group of "fine cavaliers" who prefer drinking to attending mass. Here, too, the reader shares in the story, hearing the substance of the mutiny for the first time and observing the befuddled Spanish cavaliers as they strive to understand its puzzling American phrases. Whereas the first narration shows the story's impact on the savage and working-class imagination in an underworld tavern, the second shows its reception among aristocrats and colonizers, and also how the urban setting and audience work to create Ishmael's urbane narrative style. Still the story remains, as it was during the gam, a social exchange, not a written record. It takes place in the spirit of gossip, "free-and-easy" sociality, passing the time. In telling the story, however, and seeing that its effect on Spanish cavaliers is as powerful in its way as it had been on Tashtego and the sailors, Ishmael recognizes his obligation to preserve the story in its third form, publication, and at its third urban site, New York. So he resolves that, "[i]nterweaving in its proper place this darker thread with the story as publicly narrated on the ship, the whole of this strange affair I now proceed to put on lasting record" (243).

In Lima, however, his main objective is to amuse his friends with an absorbing tale. The setting of the lavish urban inn and the audience of wealthy gentlemen determines the form – a straightforward, mostly linear narrative recounted in colorful style, full of humor yet faithful to the facts and respectful of conventions. Ishmael makes it clear that he is shaping the tale for particular listeners: they are Spanish, and therefore do not understand all the local American references; and also they are Catholic and therefore take seriously the religious suggestions – "the wondrous, inverted visitation of one of those so called judgments of God" – in the story. It is important that they are not practicing Catholics and have decided to escape from the city's religious festival by staging their own festivities instead. When Ishmael utters a faintly blasphemous remark – "sinners, gentlemen, most abound in holiest vicinities" (249) – Don Pedro responds with a religious joke of his own: " 'Is that a friar passing?' said Don Pedro, looking downwards into the crowded plaza, with humorous concern" (129). Nevertheless, they are peculiarly susceptible to Ishmael's tale of Moby Dick's almost supernatural agency in killing Radney, and Ishmael plays on their superstition by calling for a Bible and a priest so that he may swear to the tale's veracity. Like the *Town-Ho* sailors, then, Ishmael resorts to "Romish injunctions" not because he fears spreading the tale but for the opposite reason, in order to inspire belief.

The choice of city is as important as Ishmael's particular audience. Lima, as a colonial city with a long history of European subjugation of native populations, reminds American readers of their own colonial history. Just as the gam brings together savage and civilized, Pequod and town-bred, Tashtego and confederate whites, so Lima associates Incas and Spain, native and colonial empires, infidels and autos-da-fé. Earlier, in "The Whiteness of the Whale," Ishmael emphasized Lima's great age, "Old as Pizarro," and its being "the strangest, saddest city thou can'st see" (193) – an image of the urban sublime. But in the telling of the *Town-Ho* story, Lima stands for urban corruption, as his listeners recognize:

> "In the name of all us Limeese, I but desire to express to you, sir sailor, that we have by no means overlooked your delicacy in not substituting present Lima for distant Venice in your corrupt comparison. Oh! do not bow and look surprised; you know the proverb all along this coast – 'Corrupt as Lima.' It but bears out your saying, too; churches more plentiful than billiard-tables; and for ever open – and 'Corrupt as Lima.' So, too, Venice." (249)

The cavaliers display their urbanity and cosmopolitanism in recognizing the corruption of their own city and their own place in this corruption. "'I see! I see!' impetuously exclaimed Don Pedro, spilling his chicha upon his silvery ruffles. 'No need to travel! The world's one Lima'" (250). "Lima" as symbol of European wickedness grows naturally out of its history of domination and oppression.

Ishmael's narration reveals its urban setting much as the confederates' revealed theirs. During a gam at sea, the men express their class solidarity in an intimate social interchange that is potentially subversive. Theirs is the domain of the street and the tavern, a working-class underworld that conceals secrets and revolts.[13] Their narratives bind the sailors together so closely that one man's nightmare becomes the other men's shared property. In Lima, Ishmael enters the isolated world of aristocratic privilege where narrative is an artifact. His story, like the gold of the Incas, is an object to be revered, carried back to Spain for others to admire. Rather than the unquestioning solidarity of the sailors, Ishmael experiences the polite exploitation of the conquistadors. They mine Ishmael for knowledge of the exotic foreign realm he describes; and he, an obliging narrator, gives them what they desire. His social position in relation to them is ambiguous, for he is at once a gentleman and a sailor. The cavaliers are his friends, but he is not one of them – by nationality, religion, or mode of life. Ishmael offers to share his riches with the Spaniards, but in the end his story is hostile as well; for he seeks to terrify these genial gentlemen by subtly reminding them of the barbarism, violence, and terror at the heart of urban society. Although the story of the mutiny promises his listeners that force if not law will prevail, the heart of the story attacks his audience's faith in civilized order and authority – in urban form itself.

The choice of Lima, then, is significant for a second reason, as a model of urban form. Unlike New York, which white settlers founded on land that had not previously been developed, Lima and other South American cities had a long history of urban growth before the Europeans came. Impressive capitals like Mexico City had large central plazas, flourishing markets, beautiful buildings, and wide, straight streets radiating from the urban center or neatly organized in a planned grid. Some cultural historians have questioned whether Spanish settlers brought the gridiron-plaza design to the New World or imported what they found there back to their own cities, which were more often based on the labyrinthine, unplanned layouts of Islamic cities.[14] More significant for Ishmael's narration, however, is that, regardless of whether the plaza already existed as a ceremonial center for native civilizations or a symbol of European domination, it implies an urban structure quite different from that of New York, which in the 1850s did not have such a symbolic center. In the original settlement of which Wall Street was the northern boundary, the town centered on the fort. As the city became a more self-conscious trading center, City Hall and the park around it seemed to many observers and guidebook authors the town's plaza. But to fulfill the specific social functions a large central plaza provides – buying and selling, religious rituals and processions, social display – New York had many sites: Broadway for the fashionable promenade, Astor Place for cultural consumption, Wall Street and Trinity Church for Mammon and God, the Battery for recreation, and so on. Part of the drive behind the movement to design Central Park came from the perception that New York had no common public space for a variety of cultural and social functions. The "heart of proudest town" that Melville would evoke in Clarel's Jerusalem did not seem to exist in mid-century New York.

The meaning of the heart of a Spanish-American city, however, lies in a history of cross-cultural influence, a mingling of two old and highly developed cultures. The model of the plaza – a multifunctional space where a wide variety of people may meet and participate in the city's activities – suits this culture's needs exactly, and so do the literary forms it generates. Hence Ishmael's story, in "the style in which I once narrated it at Lima" (243), contains all the cultural diversity, richness, and colorfulness of the plaza just steps away from the inn where he recounts it.

At the same time, Ishmael's covert attack on the genteel Spaniards cloaks itself in an urbane language that mediates between his listeners and another world, the North American wilderness. He suggestively brings together savage and civilized, native and colonizer, on common ground. Just as the plaza permits an easy interchange between contending cultures, so Ishmael's language allows cultural exchange to take place through its interweaving of native American terms that he continually interrupts his story to explain. Part of the story's urbaneness, in fact, consists of its tolerance of interruption. Ishmael alerts the reader to the coming breaks in his narration: "Of those fine cavaliers, the young Dons, Pedro and Sebastian, were on the closer terms with me; and hence the interluding questions they occasionally put, and which are duly answered at the time" (243). So genial, relaxed, and intimate are these gentlemen that narrative and conversation intermingle. Ishmael takes the questions in good part, and he designs his story so as to accommodate and make effective use of them. Yet they afford him another opportunity as well, that of going outside the narrative to include the world of the American frontier and wilderness. This wild landscape, from which the *Town-Ho* rebels come, brings the barbaric, rude underworld of the sailors into the urbane gentlemen's consciousness and reminds them of an urban underworld which, like the native populations of Peru, they have suppressed and ultimately forgotten in colonial Lima.[15]

Ishmael's narration works steadily and ruthlessly to emphasize the connections and conflicts between barbarians and civilizers. He begins by defining the Lakeman and the Nantucketer for the benefit of Don Sebastian, who breaks into the story to exclaim, "Lakeman! – Buffalo! Pray, what is a Lakeman, and where is Buffalo?" (244). Ishmael's answer is both an explanation and a declaration of American pride and superiority. For to explain the Lakeman's character – "Thus, gentleman, though an inlander, Steelkilt was wild-ocean born, and wild-ocean nurtured; as much of an audacious mariner as any" – he has to describe the Great Lakes. And here he goes on at length about the vast size of the lakes, and "their rimmed varieties of races and of climes," the great nations on both sides, the fierce naval battles of their past, the forests and the "wild barbarians, whose red painted faces flash from out their peltry wigwams." He appears to be wandering far from the story for no particular reason. Yet many of the details support the theme he will develop throughout the story, the links between barbarism and civilization. Hence, the remote forests and wild animals and men bear a close relationship with cities of Europe and North America:

> for leagues and leagues [the lakes] are flanked by ancient and unentered forests, where the gaunt pines stand like serried lines of kings in Gothic genealogies; those same woods harboring wild Afric beasts of prey, and silken creatures whose exported furs give robes to Tartar Em-

perors; they mirror the paved capitals of Buffalo and Cleveland, as well
as Winnebago villages; they float alike the full-rigged merchant ship, the
armed cruiser of the State, the steamer, and the birch canoe. (244)

Although "Borean and dismasting blasts" sweep the lakes, sending to the
bottom "full many a midnight ship with all its shrieking crew" (244),
although the lake is as wild as an ocean, it is also a cosmopolitan landscape, with ties to Europe, Africa, Buffalo, and Cleveland.

In the second interruption, Ishmael develops this theme more fully
when Don Pedro begs him to explain the meaning of "Canallers." Ishmael mockingly replies, "Canallers, Don, are the boatmen belonging to
our grand Erie Canal. You must have heard of it" (248), but agrees to
elaborate. His answer gives a picture of urban wilderness and cosmopolitan barbarians:

> "For three hundred sixty miles, gentlemen, through the entire breadth
> of the state of New York; through numerous populous cities and most
> thriving villages; through long, dismal, uninhabited swamps, and afflu-
> ent, cultivated fields, unrivalled for fertility; by billiard-room and bar-
> room; through the holy-of-holies of great forests; on Roman arches over
> Indian rivers; . . . and especially, by rows of snow-white chapels, whose
> spires stand almost like milestones, flows one continual stream of Ve-
> netianly corrupt and often lawless life. There's your true Ashantee, gen-
> tlemen; there howl your pagans; where you ever find them, next door
> to you; under the long-flung shadow, and the snug patronizing lee of
> churches. For by some curious fatality, as it is often noted of your met-
> ropolitan freebooters that they ever encamp around the halls of justice,
> so sinners, gentlemen, most abound in holiest vicinities." (248–9)

In this landscape the country provides no refuge from the city; the Canal
urbanizes 360 miles of territory, making it all Venetianly corrupt. Ishmael
makes a special point of the religious anomalies: the forests, not the
churches, are "holy-of-holies"; the churches, on the other hand, simply
provide a shelter, a "snug patronizing lee" for, not protection from, the
lawless life and metropolitan freebooters. Both points challenge the cavaliers directly, for as pioneers of an advancing European civilization they
place their faith in Roman arches and populous cities, and as representatives of the Spanish church they claim to cast a benign light, not a "long-
flung shadow," over Peru. In *Israel Potter*, Melville will describe John Paul
Jones, the pirate dressed in laces and rings, as a "jaunty barbarian in
broad-cloth" (63). In this passage he offhandedly asserts that the barbarian Canallers are the most urban of men and, by implication, that Spanish
gentlemen are the most barbaric freebooters in broadcloth.

Clearly his listeners to some degree grasp the hint, as one rueful member of the audience thanks Ishmael for naming Venice when he might

have substituted Lima. Ishmael continues in this vein by describing the Canaller's splendid decadence:

"Freely depicted in his own vocation, gentlemen, the Canaller would make a fine dramatic hero, so abundantly and picturesquely wicked is he. Like Mark Antony, for days and days along his green-turfed flowery Nile, he indolently floats, openly toying with his red-cheeked Cleopatra, ripening his apricot thigh upon the sunny deck. But ashore, all this effeminacy is dashed. The brigandish guise which the Canaller so proudly sports; his slouched gaily-ribboned hat betoken his grand features. A terror to the smiling innocence of the villages through which he floats; his swart visage and bold swagger are not unshunned in cities." (249)

At this point Ishmael's meaning becomes entirely clear, as at least one of his listeners sees the analogy between the indolent but lethal Canaller and the lounging gentlemen of Lima. Don Sebastian spills his chicha and declares, "The world's one Lima!" (250). Country and city, savage and civilized, jaunty barbarian and metropolitan freebooter meet under one city's name, within one urban form.

Ishmael tells the rest of his story – Steelkilt's resistance, his confrontation with the Captain, Radney's continued provocations, Steelkilt's stealthy plans to kill the mate, and finally the providential appearance of Moby Dick – with but one brief interruption: " 'Moby Dick!' cried Don Sebastian; 'St. Dominic! Sir sailor, but do whales have christenings? Whom call you Moby Dick?' " (256). Ishmael has no patience for explanations now, and furthermore seems to be overwhelmed by his own story: "Nay, Dons, Dons – nay, nay! I cannot rehearse that now. Let me get more into the air, Sirs" (250). Recovering from a brief swoon, Ishmael concludes his tale of Radney's death in the whale's jaws, Steelkilt's escape to freedom, and his final image, that of "the widow of Radney [who] still turns to the sea which refuses to give up its dead; still in dreams sees the awful white whale that destroyed him" (258).

The story ends, then, as it began, with a bad dream, a dream that tells a terrible tale. Don Sebastian begs to know if the story is true, and Ishmael, calling for a Bible and the most solemn priest to be had, swears his impressive oath: "So help me Heaven, and on my honor, the story I have told ye, gentlemen, is in substance and its great items, true. I know it to be true; it happened on this ball; I trod the ship; I knew the crew; I have seen and talked with Steelkilt since the death of Radney" (259). The cavaliers are silenced, convinced by this demonstration of faith. Nor does it seem that Ishmael would tolerate an interruption now. The story has effected its hostile purpose in silencing the Spanish cavaliers.

But Ishmael's conclusion, intended to silence enquiry, arouses more

doubts than it settles. Although the story is over for the Spanish gentle-
men, it is still active at its third urban site of narration, the world of his
American readers. For them the story has another form, one suited to
New York: the form of "lasting record" (243).

New York is an island "belted round by wharves" (3), and the "Town-
Ho's Story" is a narrative belted round by literary form. Whereas in Lima,
Ishmael's telling partakes of its sociable milieu and aristocratic audience,
where its open form, like that of the plaza, invites comments, interrup-
tions, oaths, drinking, and fainting fits, in its written form the story
achieves enclosure. Although he agrees to tell the story in "the style in
which I once narrated it at Lima" (243), he also declares his serious aims:
"Interweaving in its proper place this darker thread with the story as publicly narrated on the ship, the whole of this strange affair I now proceed
to put on lasting record" (243). No such preamble prepares the Lima
gentlemen for the horrific conclusion, but Ishmael's New York readers
will be searching for the darker thread in the story. And they will have
the opportunity, which the cavaliers lack, of examining Ishmael's words
closely and seeing their many-layered ironies and nuances. They will enjoy
the humor of his descriptions of Lakemen, Nantucketers, and Canallers;
they will appreciate Ishmael's mocking portrait of the effete aristocrats;
and they will understand how much the story of violence and revolt undermines the haughty empire the Spanish gentlemen represent. By en-
closing his narrative in written form, Ishmael makes it subtly pleasurable
to a different kind of urban audience, the socially diverse, sophisticated,
discerning readers of New York.[16]

But although Melville encloses the story with meaning, as wharves enclose Manhattan, he still leaves room for considerable mystery. The same
statement that is supposed to quell the cavaliers' doubts raises many more
for his home audience; they would recognize the basic insincerity of the
oath, having presumably detected Ishmael's satiric view of Spanish Catholicism and the gentlemen's credulity.[17] And as soon as the oath calls
itself into question, Ishmael's facts do too. When, that is, did Ishmael see
Steelkilt? When was he in Lima? Admittedly, Melville may not have noticed
the chronological anomalies in his story, but they do seem indicative of a
basic desire to deceive. Whenever Ishmael told the story in Lima, he
claims that the mutiny took place "some two years prior to my first learning the events which I am about rehearsing" (243). In the order of events,
then, the mutiny happens sometime before the gam; then the events of
Moby-Dick occur, leaving Ishmael alone to tell the tale; then, during his
cruise on the *Rachel* or another ship, he encounters Steelkilt once again;
and finally he ends up in Lima, about two years after the mutiny but still
some time before he returns to New York to publish his narrative; for he
originally shipped "[s]ome years ago – never mind how long precisely"

(3). Even at that unspecified long-ago time, however, Ishmael had already had a career as a country schoolteacher and considerable experience as a sailor, enough, at least, to find that whenever he gets the hypos, "I account it high time to get to sea as soon as I can" (3). In Ishmael's "lasting record," then, the events he refers to cover an untold number of years and experiences, which he has belted round with narrative to make a more compact form.

Ishmael also seems deliberately to efface the one unknown but crucial fact in the story: what Steelkilt told the Captain and Radney. Various scholars have speculated on what Steelkilt might have said,[18] but it seems equally worthwhile to determine why Ishmael did not put it in the "lasting record." His final, firmly stated claim that he has "seen and talked with Steelkilt since the death of Radney" inspires belief, but the first speculation must be that Ishmael has not in fact met Steelkilt, or that if he has Steelkilt did not tell all. But Ishmael has shown deep sympathy for his character throughout the narrative and equally strong admiration for his beauty and heroism: "Steelkilt was a tall and noble animal with a head like a Roman, and a flowing golden beard like the tasseled housings of your last viceroy's snorting charger; and a brain, and a heart, and a soul in him, gentlemen, which had made Steelkilt Charlemagne, had he been born son to Charlemagne's father" (246). It seems likely that a meeting did take place for such strong visual images to have made an impression on Ishmael, and even more likely that Steelkilt's charismatic temperament exerted its power over Ishmael as well. In preserving Steelkilt's privacy, then, Ishmael answers the question raised by his telling the *Town-Ho* story to the cavaliers in the first place – namely, whose side is he on? His loyalty to Steelkilt indicates that although he was willing to betray Tashtego's secret to the Spanish aristocrats, his true sympathies lie with the sailors. That message would have eluded his Lima audience but would not have escaped his New York readers.

Ishmael seems, then, to place his faith in his New York audience, in the enclosed but democratic city of Manhattan rather than the open, Europeanized city of Lima. New Yorkers can tolerate the story's mystery, whereas the Spaniards cannot. They understand the social nuances of the story, the peculiar names, whereas the cavaliers need to be guided through its intricacies. They need no "Romish injunctions" to prevent them from either misusing the story's content or abusing its narrator. And they appreciate Ishmael's subtle wit, his sympathy with the urban underworld, and his good-humored urbanity. In *Moby-Dick*, then, Melville assumes an open dialogue between the world of the narrative and the world of the city. No matter how vigorously Ishmael seeks to leave New York behind in his journey through the "wonder-world" (7) of the whale, his devotion to the "lasting record" encloses the book in a vision of urban form. In that sense of New York as a place where the narrator may repose his story in its lasting form, *Moby-Dick* seems the most pro-urban of Melville's books.

Even New York, however, originally one of those "Indian isles," has betrayed its earliest inhabitants by imposing urban form. If the *Town-Ho*'s tale allows Ishmael to show how the city gives lasting meaning to a free-floating loose fish of a story, it also shows that all cities are filled with metropolitan freebooters, "terror to the smiling innocence" of America.

* * * * * *

Moby-Dick suggests a way of traveling the town by escaping the city. In his narratives after *Moby-Dick*, Melville locates that town not in a seagoing vessel or the belly of a whale but often on the same site as the city itself; or in a domain slightly apart, like the home, theater, or church; or even somewhere geographically distant but structurally similar, like London, Paris, or Jerusalem. Whereas distancing town from city in *Moby-Dick* allows Ishmael to retain his trust in New York, enabling him to return there to tell his story, his later narratives exhibit the strain of trying to find the heart of town within a burgeoning city. But Melville's different strategies of creating urban space for characters unable to find a place to live in the city suggest that he did not see the city only as an empty, heartless place but as a dynamic ground of cultural conflict out of which new, more encompassing cultural forms might emerge.

5

Sojourner in the City of Man

He had neither trunk, valise, carpet-bag, nor parcel. No porter followed him. He was unaccompanied by friends. From the shrugged shoulders, titters, whispers, wonderings of the crowd, it was plain that he was, in the extremest sense of the word, a stranger.   *The Confidence-Man* (3)

In Melville's earlier novels, characters negotiate urban space by traveling through it. The city on display, as capital or labyrinth or even Ishmael's good old city of the Manhattoes, offers numerous opportunities for the urban traveler, even when, as in the labyrinth, he must struggle to find his way. In Melville's fiction of the 1850s, the city often appears, in contrast, as a wasteland similar to the landscape he evokes at the beginning of "The Encantadas": "Take five-and-twenty heaps of cinders dumped here and there in an outside city lot" (*PT*, 126). This urban form resembles not a splendid panorama of civilized life or a romantic urban maze but a flat, desolate plane over which the urban man or woman drifts in an aimless manner – a sojourner, rather than a dweller, in the modern city. Instead of seeking human mystery in a fascinating underworld, the sojourner seems to be looking for a place to rest, a home. Nor does Melville suggest, as he does in the earlier novels, that such a home will have the healing domestic comforts of the provincial home left behind. The city has no home for the urban sojourner.

Melville's early novels imply that his maritime travelers *can* find a home away from home on the fraternal ship. His most notable example, *Moby-Dick*, portrays a domestic paradise of bachelors. Although the men of the *Pequod* are far from home, they create a domestic haven from a heartless world on its well-scrubbed decks. In the separate sphere of the vessel, they "try out" the whales in maneuvers more like Catharine Beecher's exercises in domestic economy than what takes place in a factory, mine, or office. The men, masters of cooking and preserving, as well as expert seamsters, launderers, and tenders of the fire, operate an efficient cottage industry on the model of the eighteenth-century farm or early urban work-shop home.[1]

In his narratives after *Moby-Dick*, however, in *Pierre*, many of the maga-zine stories, and *Israel Potter* – the fiction most immediately concerned with the city and with his New York readers – Melville's protagonists signally fail to find homes, secure refuges where men or women may work or find repose.[2] Pierre lives in an urban tenement, a converted church with few if any domestic comforts. Bartleby finds a narrow space in a lawyer's office to lay his "lean, reclining form" (27). Hautboy the fiddler lives "in the fifth story of a sort of storehouse, in a lateral street to Broadway . . . curi-ously furnished with all sorts of odd furniture, which seemed to have been obtained, piece by piece, at auctions of old-fashioned household stuff" (266). The narrator of "The Two Temples" occupies a church tower and the Tombs for a night but seems to have only meager quarters of his own; in London, penniless, he is in an even worse predicament – "My landlady wont receive me in her parlor" (309) – and he looks for temporary refuge in a theater. The Bachelors have a luxurious club to dine at and sleep in, if they choose, but it provides a cloister from the world, not a home. Jimmy Rose dwells miserably in an "untenanted" (341) old house on a deserted street, "once the haunt of style and fashion, full of gay parlors and bridal chambers; but now, for the most part, transformed into counting-rooms and ware-houses" (336). And Israel Potter drearily passes forty-five years in London's slums, in "his Moorfields' garret" (166), or, more often, trudging the streets, peddling and scavenging. The city has no homes for these men, most of whom are failures. They know not the comforts of domestic, private space.

Even more remarkable, the characters who live outside the city – the narrators of "The Piazza," "The Lightning-Rod Man," "Cock-a-Doodle-Doo," "I and My Chimney" – have houses, but houses contaminated or threatened from within. None has a home, a domestic space filled, as Melville's Arrowhead was, with family, servants, and animals.[3] Rather, the narrator of "The Piazza" mentions no other inmates of his house. In lofty solitude from family or neighbors, he builds his porch on the north side, an act that at best makes his house a "cool elysium," but in winter a place where "I pace the sleety deck, weathering Cape Horn" (3). The narrator of "The Lightning-Rod Man" stands his ground firmly on the domestic hearth but suffers the intrusion of a cynical salesman who threatens him and his house with awful destruction: "Will you order? Will you buy? Shall I put down your name? Think of being a heap of charred offal, like a haltered horse burnt in his stall; – and all in one flash!" (124). The salesman's visit reminds the narrator of his danger, even in a house: " 'Are you so horridly ignorant, then,' he cried, 'as not to know, that by far the most dangerous part of a house during such a terrific tempest as this, is the fire-place?' " (119). The narrator of "Cock-a-Doodle-Doo" enjoys his domesticity rather more comfortably, greeting his creditor "in an arm-chair, with my feet on the table, and the second bottle of brown-stout handy, and the book under eye" (273), the very picture of domestic ease. But as in "The Piazza," his prosperity is all show, for he owes money all around the country. In fact, he finds more real domestic cheer in Merrymusk's shanty than in his own comfortable "plantation" (286).

"I and My Chimney" and "The Apple-Tree Table" are the only ones of Melville's house stories to contain families. In both stories, however, the family's happiness and peace are undermined by something from within, the wife's renovating ambitions in "I and My Chimney," and the mysterious ticking beetle in "The Apple-Tree Table." In each case, the narrator positions himself in opposition to his family, seeking domestic peace by alienating himself from them: the "mossy old misanthrope . . . standing guard over my mossy old chimney" (377) has declared war on his family, and the owner of the apple-tree table takes pleasure in exposing his wife's and daughters' superstitions.[4] Even though these men have comfortable houses, there is little suggestion of the domestic pleasures of home.

The absence of women, of inviting domestic space, of female domestic power, in narratives often concerned with men finding themselves a home, or finding themselves at home, is striking for several reasons. First is that, although Melville himself had a comfortable home at Arrowhead filled with women concerned with domestic affairs, he wrote most of his stories about men who fail to find homes, especially in the city. In fact, New York was undergoing the crisis in housing and open space that culminated in the efforts to create Central Park in 1857. His protagonists undergo trials in searching for a home similar to those of other New Yorkers during this period. Melville's focus on the problem of finding space in which to live and work suggests his awareness of the changes in the city. More than that, his work, especially *Pierre*, "Bartleby, the Scrivener," and "Jimmy Rose," protests against the power of property owners in New York to deprive, even in a sense unman, the propertyless.

Second, however, Melville's homeless protagonists appear in the context of the literature of domestic ideology. In popular novels and magazines often written by or for women, the culture of domesticity and the feminine sphere was achieving a central place.[5] Melville's selection of characters who fail in the domestic sphere might seem to suggest a deliberate rejection of that ideology.[6] In fact, it suggests something more complicated, the doubts that both male and female authors shared about the possibility of anyone finding a home in the city. The confidence expressed in middle-class domestic literature in women's power to resist urban evils and reform erring men by building a safe domestic haven arises from and balances against a widespread fear of the city. Like labyrinth literature, domestic literature offers a way to map the city's social geography along the lines of gender as well as of class and offers, too, a model of escape from the city's mysteries and miseries. But much of the domestic literature enacts deep uncertainty about the possibility of finding a real home in the city. And Melville's narratives, particularly *Pierre* and his paired sketches, make that anxiety a central issue.

Homelessness, vagrancy, or even rental transiency represented a threat to middle-class security and social order in New York; domestic literature responded to that threat by superimposing a new ideological map over the city's changing geography; both these developments reflect the changes in housing and property relations in New York. But there is another discursive realm in which these anxieties displayed themselves – namely, that of religion and reform. Under the pressure of immigration and the problems blamed on the propertyless classes – disease, prostitution, alcohol, and the moral and social ills that wrecked families and homes – many middle-class city dwellers might respond, as Bartleby's lawyer does, "with assumed tranquility, but an inward tremor," by saying "really, the man you allude to is nothing to me – he is no relation or apprentice of mine, that you should hold me responsible for him" (39). The old paternalistic family and workshop structures that had provided care for the unfortunate, the vagrant, the diseased, or the unattached, had generally given way to social structures like the police and the poorhouse or the various benevolent societies and missions.[7] Whereas in the older city or village one could not escape one's social obligations to the dispossessed, in the New York of the 1840s and 1850s, reformers feared that a middle-class homeowner might indeed ask Cain's question – "Am I my brother's keeper?" – and come up with the lawyer's answer. That such moral callousness could exist among the city's successful citizens made New York seem, in Melville's phrase, the domain of "Cain's city and citified man" (*BB*, 53). And in Cain's city, "the man thoroughly civilized, even . . . a fair specimen of the breed," can easily fail his brother, the sinless and homeless Abel.

The Christian myth of Cain and Abel provides the dark urban antithesis to the pastoral American myth of Eden. In Paradise, humankind's first and ideal home, there was no labor, only its fruits. Cain and Abel offered these in a votive sacrifice: the fruits of the field, Cain's produce, and of pastoral care, Abel's lamb. God's reasons for preferring Abel's offering to Cain's remain mysterious; whatever they were, he got a human, rather than an animal, sacrifice. According to Augustine, Cain fled in shame from the act and built a city where he might hide his face with its distinctive mark: Cain's city, or the City of Man, as distinguished from the heavenly Jerusalem, or City of God. In his revision of the biblical story, Augustine represented Abel's death as an entrance into the City of God, a timeless condition that makes him a sojourner, not a dweller, in Cain's city:

Of these two first parents of the human race, then, Cain was the first-
born, and he belonged to the city of men; after him was born Abel,
who belonged to the city of God. . . . When these two cities began to
run their course by a series of deaths and births, the citizen of this
world was the first-born, and after him the stranger in this world, the
citizen of the city of God, predestined by grace, elected by grace, by
grace a stranger below, and by grace a citizen above. . . . Accordingly it
is recorded of Cain that he built a city, but Abel, being a sojourner,
built none.[8]

As Alexander Welsh has thoroughly explained in his study of Dickens,
the story of Cain and Abel offers a particularly satisfying myth of cities
and human character. If "the founder of the earthly city was a fratricide"
(55), then his descendants are cursed too. The good man, of a completely
different order of being, lives "in the earthly city without being of it"
(118). It is possible in this version of the myth, and as Melville implies in
"Bartleby," *Israel Potter*, and *The Confidence-Man*, to construe underclass
vagrancy and homelessness as a sign of purity, as a state of moral exclusion
from the sins of the city.

Melville seems as familiar with this notion as Dickens, not to mention
Byron, Gessner, Coleridge, and other nineteenth-century Romantics.[9]
Aside from the numerous references to Cain that appear in his fiction,
he makes a significant link between Cain and New York in his 1850 letter
to Evert Duyckinck: "What are you doing there, My Beloved, among the
bricks & cobble-stone *boulders*? Are you making mortar? . . . There is one
thing certain, that, chemically speaking, mortar was the *precipitate* of the
Fall; & with a brick-bat, or a cobble-stone *boulder*, Cain killed Abel" (Corr.,
167).[10] Cain appears in his fiction, in descriptions not only of isolated
figures like Lem Hardy of *Omoo* and Jackson of *Redburn*, but also of dwellers in the City of Man: Pierre, rushing out into Broadway with "the murderer's mark of Cain . . . burning on the brow" (336), Bartleby's lawyer
asking if he is his brother's keeper, later Claggart of "Cain's city and
citified man."

The City of Man, then, offers a broad mythic foundation for a modern
notion of the wicked city. Cain supplies the model, not only for the obvious criminal, but also for the remote fratricide, the outwardly "good"
citizen who nevertheless harms his brother by failing to "keep" him. And
Abel stands as the prototype of the man who has no home in Cain's city,
who sojourns by virtue of his sinlessness, whose vagrancy is a mark of
unearthliness – and of freedom.

We have at least three senses, then, in which New York appears, in
Melville's fiction and in the literary culture at large, as a City of Man. The
first is the political, in which "man" is defined according to citizenship,
property, voting, political power. As property relations and the housing

market changed in the 1840s and 1850s, so too did the definition of the political man. By the curious logic of property and housing in New York, ownership made one a man; vagrancy unmanned him. The sojourner in the City of Man cannot find a home and hence has no political, and in Bartleby's case, no personal identity. He is excluded from the enclosure of private space and must inhabit the city's public spaces: denied Town, he lives in City.

If in the political sense the City of Man is opposed to the City of Not-Man, in the logic of separate spheres of gender, the City of Man stands in opposition to the City of Women. But this formulation reveals the limits of the middle-class domestic ideology. As the work of Gillian Brown, Christine Stansell, and Mary Ryan has shown, the separate spheres of male and female labor, the workplace and the home, dissolve once one leaves the middle class. Working men and women could not maintain the same divisions between home and work that middle-class women could afford. The sojourner in the City of Man protests against an oppressive middle-class domestic ideology that denies to both men and women the comforts of domestic space. Melville's *Pierre* and many of the magazine stories show that the City of Man upholds a domestic ideal that is out of the working class's reach.

In the third sense, the spiritual dichotomy of Augustine, the City of Man stands in relation to a City of God, an ideal order. In this scheme, the sojourner wanders through the City of Man on his journey toward the heavenly world. This world is not, as in Welsh's reading of Dickens, the home, but another world beyond the city. In Melville's narratives, especially *Israel Potter*, that other world suggests what he would call in "The House-Top" a "Town, redeemed." Although many of Melville's Abels travel through a City of Dis, they manage by holding their ground to find a way to live and thrive in the City's hidden Town: a vision of incorporated humanity that redeems the city's heartlessness.

All these constructions of New York as a City of Man envision urban space that is not, as it was in the labyrinth literature, mysterious, subterranean, and sensational, but rather empty and public.[11] Unlike the provincial who travels deep into the urban heart, the sojourner wanders over the surface of the streets, making them his home. In Melville's rendering of the prototype, however, this notion of urban space and urban traveler takes many forms – from Pierre's romantic wandering, Bartleby's principled transiency, and the seedsman's bewildered travels, to the essentially comic journey of Israel Potter and the Confidence-Man's cosmopolitan rambles. All fail to find a home in the City of Man; but some are happy failures who manage to create an alternative space for themselves in a redeemed town. As urban form, the City of Man presents an often inspiring challenge to the urban sojourner.

Tenancy in the City of Man

"Among us working-men," says Harry Aikin, the virtuous poor man of Catherine Maria Sedgwick's *The Poor Rich Man and the Rich Poor Man* (1836), "property is a sign of industry, temperance, and frugality."[12] Many of Melville's mid-fifties protagonists, however, do not own property; they sojourn, rather than live, in the city because they cannot find permanent homes. Their failure to find housing or employment in New York indicts a market system that promoted ownership of property and condemned transiency. Tenancy in the changing housing market of the 1850s carried with it serious implications about character: questions of worth, independence, reliability, citizenship, rights. Without the sanctification of property, a man might seem not to have a reliable identity. Melville heightens this ideological absurdity by presenting a number of men – Pierre, Bartleby, Jimmy Rose – whose transiency makes them, in the eyes of those who hold property, unstable characters. Not owning property in the City of Man makes them not-men.

The house in New York of the forties and fifties was as much a site of cultural anxiety as the home. Underlying and connected to the attention concentrated on domestic life, which I shall also consider in this chapter, anxiety over housing grew out of middle-class New Yorkers' fears about the city's tremendous growth. Too many immigrants meant not enough housing for all. John Griscom, writing in 1845, conveys the perplexity and dismay many middle-class New Yorkers felt: "The tide of emigration which now sets so strongly towards our shores, cannot be turned back. We *must* receive the poor, the ignorant, and the oppressed from other lands. . . . [But] we are parties to their degradation, inasmuch as we permit the inhabitation of places, from which it is not possible improvement in condition or habits can come."[13] Griscom's humane view accepts both the inevitable and irresistible pressure of immigration and also American responsibility for its most unfortunate consequences; many nativist New Yorkers would not so readily assume responsibility for the welfare of immigrants.

Yet the housing crisis was not simply a matter of supply and demand. New York still had a great deal of open space, some of it lying unused, until Frederick Law Olmsted saw its possibilities as a site for Central Park. Many city dwellers could find housing by moving north of the Walking City, and omnibuses and hacks made the downtown still accessible. But as land values rose and speculators saw new opportunities in the New York land market, housing prices shot out of the reach of many people, even those of the middle class. During the Panic of 1837, when new housing construction slowed down, many landlords built houses in the yards of their lots – the standard 25' by 100' lots set up by the grid plan of 1811 – and rented out the space. After the Panic, and the others that followed, these densely built sections of the city no longer appealed to contractors building for middle-class families, and landlords found they could make more profits by subdividing their properties, renting rather than selling. The social geography of the city began to reflect changes in the housing patterns, as neighborhoods decayed in the older sections of town, but as we have seen, much urban literature addressed immigration as a moral problem rather than through a systematic analysis of the housing market.[14]

Melville, however, brings issues of housing and tenancy explicitly into his fiction of the fifties: the ambiguities of proprietorship in *Pierre*, the power struggle between tenants and landlords in "Bartleby," and the volatility of fortune in "Jimmy Rose." In all of these, Melville addresses many of the housing issues found in reform and sensational literature – immigration, temperance, domestic morality, the downward spiral of social mobility – but with a particular emphasis on the subtle politics of ownership and the complexities of landlord–tenant relationships. For him, the problem of tenancy lies not in external social pressures like those of immigration, nor in particular human weaknesses like the greed of landlords or degradation of tenants. His works instead tell the story of renters and rentiers caught up in a struggle for power in the increasingly constricted space that New York had to offer. Characteristically, however, he does not oversimplify this struggle; some of his propertyless characters have at one time owned property, or they assert their proprietary rights; conversely, some of the property owners find themselves on the losing side of this battle, discovering too that they lack the property and authority they thought they possessed. Pierre, Bartleby's employer, and Jimmy Rose all find themselves conditional proprietors, transient tenants, within a heartless system of rents.

Pierre is remarkable among Melville's works, and among urban novels of the period, in embodying the landlord–tenant tension in one person, Pierre himself. In his travels from country to city, Pierre experiences both ends of the spectrum from proprietorship to precarious tenancy. Of course, many provincials of urban novels move from comfortable subsistence to urban homelessness, but not many begin as the possessors of large country estates.[15] But Melville does something further to heighten the contrast: he makes proprietorship a condition of identity, of an ontological security in the world. Pierre, and the other characters who enter a state of vagrancy or uncertain tenancy – Isabel, for example – lose their certain identities; they become blurred and ambiguous. The condition of rental tenancy, then, challenges not only a concept of ownership but also a sense of self. This intimate connection between proprietorship and selfhood rests on the logic of New York's structure of property. Pierre tests that logic in his sojourn through the complexities of the housing market.

Pierre begins as a proud proprietor.[16] Emerging in the opening pages from the "high-gabled old home of his fathers" (3), bending his steps through a village he considers his own, peopled by his own tenants, and contemplating hills and meadows "sanctified through their very long uninterrupted possession by his race" (8), Pierre seems the epitome of the land lord. His family have not only wrested the land from "three Indian kings, the aboriginal and only conveyancers of those noble woods and plains" (6), but they have also maintained their sovereignty through warfare: the Indian wars that left one Glendinning "unhorsed on his saddle in the grass, with his dying voice, still cheering his men in the fray" (6), the Revolution in which Pierre's grandfather fought, and the more recent Anti-Rent controversy of 1839–46 between the patroons and tenant farmers. Pierre's "family pride" is bound up in a history of titles, conveyances, and "haughty rent-deeds" that establish "surprising eternity for a deed, and seem . . . to make lawyer's ink unobliterable as the sea" (11).

Pierre exhibits his proprietorship in actions as well as in deeds. Like his mother, he takes a patronal interest in his servants and tenants, although his mother reprovingly reminds him "never to permit your hilariousness to betray you into overstepping the exact line of propriety in your intercourse with servants" (18). But Pierre takes his duties seriously. On the evening he first sees Isabel, he has spent most of the day "[o]n some distant business, with a farmer-tenant" (44), and he readily accepts his mother's request to look in on the Miss Pennies' sewing circle and inspect their progress. Much as he is "apt to be a little impatient sometimes, of these sewing scenes" (44), he conscientiously supports the enterprises of "the good people of the village" (44). As his mother coyly tells him, she wants him "to know who they are you live among; how many really pretty, and naturally-refined dames and girls you shall one day be lord of the manor of" (44–5). It is not likely that Pierre expects to assert any droit du seigneur, as he is already pledged to Lucy, but the hidden salaciousness of Mrs. Glendinning's comment suggests the reach of Pierre's powers over the "shy and pretty Maries, Marthas, Susans, Betties, Jennies, Nellies; and forty more fair nymphs, who skimmed the cream, and made the butter of the fat farms of Saddle Meadows" (46). We get a sense of that proprietary power over tenants' bodies in Mrs. Glendinning's disposition of the "infamous Ned and that miserable Delly" (103). Of the married Ned, she declares, "He shall not stay on any ground of mine; my mind is made up, sir" (99). Relying on "the holy rigor of our Church's doctrines," and her own absolute authority, she concludes, "as I loathe the man, I loathe the woman, and never desire to behold the child" (101). For his part, Pierre does not question his decision or power to take on Delly's plight. Acting out of sympathy for her misery, he also behaves as a conscientious master, relieving an unfortunate tenant and yet, incidentally, keeping her in his benevolent service. Without any of this mother's harshness, Pierre still knows instinctively his responsibilities to and for his tenants.

The same proprietorship that Pierre takes so much for granted, however, has been deeply undermined long before his decision to marry Isabel ejects him from his paternal house. From early in the novel we learn how tenuous is Pierre's place in the structure of property and inheritance. For one thing, Melville's narrator mocks the whole idea of an American proprietary aristocracy in the opening chapter. Referring to the titles of the patroons – their pedigrees and their title-deeds – he gravely belittles their pretensions to hereditary power and longevity:

> But whatever one may think of the existence of such mighty lordships in the heart of a republic, and however we may wonder at their surviving, like Indian mounds, the Revolutionary flood; yet survive and exist they do, and are now owned by their present proprietors, by as good nominal title as any peasant owns his father's old hat, or any duke his great-uncle's old coronet. (11)

Pierre proudly claims his hereditary rights through ownership of such tattered symbols as an old British flag and the General's baton, objects scarcely more useful to him than his father's old hat. "Unimaginable audacity of a worm that but crawls through the soil he so imperially claims!" (11).

But Pierre soon discovers for himself what an audacious worm he has been when he realizes that his father's will has disinherited him. Clearly he has never considered that he might not enjoy his privileges "so long as grass grows and water runs" (11). When his mother tries to draw his attention to legal matters – "You know, that by your father's will, these lands and—" (57) – Lucy's unexpected entrance cuts short all talk of inheritances. In frustration Mrs. Glendinning speaks of kidnapping Lucy and handcuffing Pierre to the table, "else there will be no having a preliminary understanding with you, previous to calling in the lawyers" (60). Pierre would do well to have called in the lawyers. When he decides to leave for the city with Isabel, he remembers that his father died without changing the will written before Pierre's birth. As the narrator legalistically reveals: "By that will which as yet had never been dragged into the courts of law; and which, in the fancied security of her own and her son's congenial and loving future, Mrs. Glendinning had never but once, and then inconclusively, offered to discuss, with a view to a better and more appropriate ordering of things to meet circumstances non-existent at the period the testament was framed; by that will, all the Glendinning property was declared his mother's" (179). Pierre learns, then, that his title depends not on hereditary right but on affection. For although he considers that "the law, if appealed to concerning the provisions of his father's will, would decree concerning any possible claims of the son to share with the mother in the property of the sire" (180), yet his regard for his father's reputation and his mother's feelings prevents him from entering a suit. The will, then, undermines Pierre's proprietary assumptions even before he has challenged them himself.

However, the most damaging work of "Time's tooth" (11), gnawing away at the foundations of Pierre's estate, grows out of his father's character and mistakes as an urban tenant. Mr. Glendinning has certainly kept up the Saddle Meadows property in his marriage to Mary Glendinning and his fathering of Pierre. But in his earlier life, he abandoned his proprietary responsibilities in order to court the most unstable of urban sojourners: a beautiful, dangerous emigrée from France. Unlike the immigrants of *Redburn* and of much urban fiction, this Frenchwoman is rich and aristocratic, coming from a title and property far more distinguished than Glendinning's. As a political refugee and a foreigner, however, she threatens his proprietary status. He cannot marry her and preserve his hereditary portion.

As well as undermining Mr. Glendinning's status, she also turns his head, so that he seems to lose his identity, or to take on a wholly new one. His cousin Ralph Winwood, at any rate, finds he has to resort to "stealing his portrait" (77), as Glendinning will not consent to sit for him. Rather, the man he paints, "a brisk, unentangled, young bachelor, gayly ranging up and down the world; light-hearted, and a very little bladish, perhaps" (73), looks nothing like the man his friends and family know: says Ralph, "I have painted nothing that looks as you there look" (78). Glendinning's lapse from his accustomed identity turns out, however, to be short-lived. The Frenchwoman vanishes, and "though your father and many other gentlemen moved heaven and earth to find trace of her, yet . . . she never re-appeared" (76). Her tenancy in New York has proved brief and disappointing, and Pierre's father returns to his proprietary obligations.

In the portrait that records his delight in the Frenchwoman's existence, however, Pierre's father appears, like her, a brief and unsatisfactory tenant: "He is lightly, and, as it were, airily and but grazingly seated in, or rather *flittingly tenanting* an old-fashioned chair of Malacca" (72; emphasis mine). In language that but flittingly seems to tenant the page, Melville's narrator suggests that the sitter's happiness, his joyous desire, makes him as unstable a tenant as the French emigrant. And that flitting tenancy comes back later to haunt Pierre, whose desire for Isabel makes him, too, an unsuitable tenant, and master, of Saddle Meadows. By the end of Book IV, the young man who saw the horizon as his domain now inhabits a small chamber of the house, "tenanted only by himself; and sentineling his own little closet" (84), where he contemplates his father's face in the small space still available to him. Once his mother learns the truth, "Beneath my roof, and at my table, he who was once Pierre Glendinning no more puts himself," and he finds himself "jeeringly hurled from beneath his own ancestral roof" (185).

Even before entering the city and becoming an urban tenant rather than a rural landlord, then, Pierre has had intimations of his flitting tenancy under the ancestral roof. In the crisis produced by this realization, "he dashed himself in blind fury and swift madness against the wall, and fell dabbling in the vomit of his loathed identity" (171). But once Pierre chooses, even embraces, tenancy over proprietorship, he loses that loathed identity, as his father briefly lost his, and becomes ambiguous – ambiguous, that is, in his relation to property as well as in the many other ways Melville implies. Pierre's proprietary ambiguity, like that of his father and of Isabel, makes him an unknown quantity in the world of property his mother and cousin Glen inhabit; it also makes him anonymous in New York City. In Saddle Meadows he is everywhere known as Master Pierre Glendinning, but in the city he has no title, no rights, no manhood. By implication, New York is a place where property makes the man; lack of property makes him ambiguous.

We have seen this proprietary ambiguity already in the chair-portrait, which in its depiction of the elder Pierre Glendinning as a renegade from property renders him unrecognizable to his family, and strangely disturbing: "Consider this strange, ambiguous smile" (83). Isabel's transiency makes her ambiguous too. The daughter of the sojourning French emigrant, she never finds a home of her own, dwelling conditionally and briefly in a number of unsatisfactory households: a deserted French château, an asylum, a farmhouse (only with the support of her absent father; once he dies, she is asked to leave), and in another farmhouse as hired help. By the time she moves into the New York tenement, it is clear that she has never experienced anything but transiency, which is bound up intimately with her own identity. In fact, when Pierre considers the chair-portrait in relation to Isabel, he concludes that "not Pierre's parent, as any way rememberable by him, but the portrait's painted *self* seemed the real father of Isabel" (197); she is the child, not of settled parents, but of a man's flitting tenancy in a mood, in a chair, and in a picture.

Pierre welcomes the transiency and ambiguity he sees in Isabel because it liberates him from his large proprietary responsibilities and the loathed identity as Master Pierre Glendinning that went with them. But he does not foresee that urban tenancy will not free him to write "precisely as I please" (244), to be the man he wants to be. Instead, Pierre's tenancy in the Apostles places him unwittingly at a disadvantage in an aggressively expanding housing market. Ironically, that market grows out of the very ideology of independence and individualism that he himself has pursued by moving to the city to write.

Springing from a republican tradition that defined private property as an individual right within a democratic polity, the 1811 grid plan for New York City offered "equality of access" to all potential property owners. Furthermore, with the extension of suffrage to non–property owners in 1826, Democratic politicians sought to remove the obstacle of proprietorship as a requirement for voting.[17] The city, then, promised equality of ownership, opportunity, and political participation to all free white male citizens. These moves in part reflected the undeniable fact that many people in New York, even among the middle class, did not own property. "In 1853, the *Tribune* said that only one in eight families owned a house of any kind, while no more than one-third were able to rent a dwelling exclusively for themselves. Six years later, Halliday estimated that of the city's 116,000 families, only 14 percent lived in single-family houses, owned or rented, and another 12 percent in two-family dwellings."[18] This low level of ownership was no accident. In fact, the way the grid was *developed*, not planned, produced the inequities in the housing market that the *Tribune* observed. Although the grid was even, Manhattan's topography was not. Early in the development of the city, contractors developed the more attractive, level areas for wealthy and middle-class investors, leaving the swampy district around the old Collect Pond to the poor inhabitants and new arrivals. The grid proved itself an ideal instrument for speculation, and wealthy capitalists like John Jacob Astor bought huge accumulations of land and held onto them through the various panics and depressions that rocked the market and sent many a smaller landholder under.[19] "Far from fulfilling the egalitarian potential of abundant land distributed to independent proprietors, the neutral market had carried a new class dynamic into the process of residential neighborhood formation . . . [a development that grew out of various] conditions: the artificial scarcity created by concentrated ownership of vast stretches of vacant land; the structure of the competitive housing market and particularly the purchasing power that permitted elite New Yorkers to claim particular blocks for their exclusive use."[20] The New York housing market developed in direct contradiction to the democratic, egalitarian principles upon which it was founded.

Pierre is hardly aware of this political contradiction. He thinks he is leaving the aristocratic world of rural property owning for the democratic opportunities of the city. Although he once distrusted the "plebeian" (13) town, he now seeks what it has to offer: "For indeed the democratic element operates as a subtile acid among us; forever producing new things by corroding the old" (9). In terms of housing, however, the benefits of democratic access have all accrued to the landlords, who have taken advantage of liberal housing policies to acquire properties like the Church of the Apostles and convert them into tenements. *They* have acted as the subtile acid, producing new buildings for new uses by corroding the old.

Within the old church, they have created offices, shops, and apartments; "and so well did the thing succeed, that ultimately the church-yard was invaded for a supplemental edifice, likewise to be promiscuously rented to the legal crowd" (266). In their eagerness to create and exploit more space, however, "[i]n this ambitious erection, the proprietors went a few steps, or rather a few stories, too far" (266). They build more than they can use and thus end up renting out the space to a motley assortment of "artists of various sorts; painters, or sculptors, or indigent students, or teachers of languages, or poets, or fugitive French politicians, or German philosophers" (267), when they might have preferred a more lucrative population of lawyers. Nevertheless, they have vastly increased the worth of their investment.

If Melville had simply wanted to expose the cruelties of the housing market, he could have left the matter there, or in the passages where the narrator mocks Pierre's austere life at the Apostles: "Now look around in that most miserable room, and at that most miserable of all the pursuits of a man, and say if here be the place, and this be the trade, that God intended him for. . . . Civilization, Philosophy, Ideal Virtue! behold your victim!" (302). But Melville states that Pierre is a victim, not of the housing market itself, but of the ideology of democratic proprietary individualism that underwrites it. The Apostles, on the other hand, by embracing a more communal spirit, have learned to thrive in tenement housing. Unlike the radical individualist Pierre, who observes his neighbors gloomily from afar, they are "bread-and-cheese adventurers" living like "magpies" (267), all on top of one another. Pierre sees himself as a victim, but the Apostles seem cheerfully to accept their poverty, to make a virtue of it: "these poor, penniless devils still strive to make ample amends for their physical forlornness, by resolutely reveling in the region of blissful ideals" (267). At least one of them, Charlie Millthorpe, is actually making a better living in the town than he did in the country; and between his fees for scrivening and his passing the hat at lectures, he has made enough money to pay off one of Pierre's bills at a critical moment. Although many of the Apostles, like Millthorpe's family, have been disappointed in their expectations, they gamely take in sewing or copying and somehow survive. Pierre, Lucy, and Isabel, on the other hand, trying to sell their mystical writing, portrait painting, and guitar playing, show none of these urban survival skills and fail utterly. The "Flesh-Brush" philosophers have created a communal identity for themselves as Apostles, something Pierre in his radical isolation has not been able to achieve, and they are flourishing even in the tenements of New York.[21]

Pierre, however, never adapts to or tries to join the community of the Apostles, never takes the necessary steps toward making his tenancy permanent, perhaps because of lingering proprietary snobbery or his literary ambitions. Instead he seeks even greater isolation and, eventually, a kind of total existential vagrancy. Driven from his miserable flat by his despair, he wanders the streets, first for the comfort of seeing the crowds, but soon in order to get even farther away from people and houses: "now nothing but the utter night-desolation of the obscurest warehousing lanes would content him" (341). In one of these remote corners of the city, he experiences a crisis of identity:

> one night as he paused a moment previous to turning about for home, a sudden, unwonted, and all-pervading sensation seized him. He knew not where he was; he did not have any ordinary life-feeling at all. He could not see; though instinctively putting his hand to his eyes, he seemed to feel that the lids were open. Then he was sensible of a combined blindness, and vertigo, and staggering; before his eyes a million green meteors danced; he felt his foot tottering upon the curb, he put out his hands, and knew no more for the time. When he came to himself he found that he was lying crosswise in the gutter, dabbled with mud and slime. (341)

The dabbling in mud and slime brings to mind his earlier dabbling in the vomit of loathed identity, but now he has no identity at all. All the old landmarks, the horizons that reminded him who he was, have disappeared. Lost in transiency, he has no home in the city.

Pierre has rejected his earlier proprietary notions in order to travel to the city and become a poor tenant in a market that values profits and survival over "Civilization, Philosophy, Ideal Virtue!" His grudging admiration of Charlie Millthorpe's good-natured character – "Plus heart, minus head, . . . by heaven! the god that made Millthorpe was both a better and a greater than the god that made Napoleon or Byron" (320) – indicates the distance he has traveled from his earlier aristocratic views; now he admires the democrat Millthorpe, who embodies the enterprising spirit of the city. But Pierre never becomes a permanent tenant of New York. Because of his dedication to untenable ideals, he sojourns only briefly and reluctantly in the city, traveling beyond it at the end. Melville does not show Pierre as a victim of an oppressive housing market; rather than using the setting of the tenement as an opportunity for sentimentality or melodrama, Melville makes Pierre's tenancy serve a more abstract and philosophical end, namely, to show the ambiguities of tenancy in a world where older forms of proprietorship have lost their sway.[22] In "Bartleby," however, he will address more directly the tenant–landlord relationship in a conflict between two individuals who stand on opposing sides of the class battle over property and rights.

Bartleby and the lawyer seem to confront each other across a great divide – Bartleby as dispossessed, poor, laboring employee and the lawyer as sinecured, affluent, privileged employer. Although the story seems a straightforward account of class struggle, Melville makes the conflict infinitely more complex through the way he orders housing issues in the story. The real struggle between the two men is a competition for tenancy of the same space; the problem is that the space belongs to neither of them, and their class differences do not work as expected to mark the lines between them. Bartleby can challenge the lawyer's right to the space because the lawyer essentially has only tenuous rights to it himself.

Melville, however, does not at first make this complication clear. The lawyer's proprietary description of "myself, my *employés*, my business, my chambers, and general surroundings" (13) establishes the terrain of the office as emphatically *his*, as was the landscape of Saddle Meadows to Pierre. His work, "that of a conveyancer and title hunter, and drawer-up of recondite documents of all sorts" (19), shows that he is right at home in the world of proprietorship. His appointment as a Master of Chancery would have placed him in the middle of suits over property and wills[23] and gives him so much work to do that he can count on steady employment; his financial position, at least, seems secure. He does not describe or mention his own house – a significant omission – but it is within a convenient distance from the office, and his living conditions appear to be satisfactory. In short, everything about the lawyer's life and work suggests that he has a right to act proprietary.

In fact, however, the lawyer is not, as far as we can tell, a true proprietor. Whether he owns his house or not, he definitely rents, rather than owns, his office space. He might not necessarily be expected to own his office, but, as we saw at the Apostles, many New York buildings – private and tenement housing both – contained both living and working space closely connected or combined. The old workshop system, with a master running a shop or business inside the home where apprentices, women, and children all contributed their labor, was disappearing in New York,[24] but we can see that the lawyer asserts the same kind of paternal influence over his workers that Pierre did over his tenants, and it is not impossible that a lawyer might combine his living and working space. Bartleby's employer, however, rents, and also moves his quarters when it becomes necessary to do so – that is, when he cannot disengage himself from Bartleby in any other way. He has a close enough relationship with his landlord to feel guilty when the latter queries him about Bartleby's presence in the empty office, but not close enough that he has any compunction about moving. Rental transiency is a fact of his business life.

Like Pierre, then, the lawyer asserts proprietary rights and privileges when they actually belong to others. In the world of country estates, challenges to one's proprietorship come from individuals, family members whose claims take precedence. Thus Pierre loses his estate to Glen Stanly because his father's will failed to protect his rights, and his mother, in her anger, hands his title to the next in line. In New York, however, title is a much more complicated affair, involving more levels of ownership. The hierarchy of housing begins, at the bottom, with "tenants or subtenants who paid house rents for the space they occupied to landlords, who paid building rents to a leaseholder, who paid ground rent to a rentier" (Blackmar, 10). Looked at from the other end, this system shows the advantages to rentiers of buying large pieces of land and leasing them for periods, sometimes, of up to ninety-nine years. While they were put to no expense for the improvement or maintenance of the land – that devolved to the leaseholder or landlord – the rentiers reaped the profits of a pyramid of rents. The lawyer's job, indeed, involves negotiating this complicated system of titles for the benefit of his landholding clients: doing "a snug business among rich men's bonds and mortgages and title-deeds" (14).

The fact that the lawyer enjoys a close professional relationship with New York's most wealthy and celebrated rentier, John Jacob Astor, indicates the true nature of his proprietary delusions of grandeur. For although he brags about the connection, he shows little awareness of the way in which Astor's wealth works to keep small professionals like him from advancing in the housing market. This self-mystification appears obvious, however, in his self-praise:

> All who know me, consider me an eminently *safe* man. The late John Jacob Astor, a personage little given to poetic enthusiasm, had no hesitation in pronouncing my first grand point to be prudence; my next, method. I do not speak it in vanity, but simply record the fact, that I was not unemployed by the late John Jacob Astor; a name which, I admit, I love to repeat, for it hath a rounded and orbicular sound to it, and rings like unto bullion. I will freely add, that I was not insensible to the late John Jacob Astor's good opinion. (14)

But he *is* insensible, at least to the degree that he does not recognize how his prudence and method serve Astor's ends rather than his own. Astor, an adventurer, fur trader, entrepreneur, and speculator of the most daring and ruthless kind, values precisely the lawyer's "unambitious" (14) attention to protecting the rentier's interests. His praise of the lawyer's *safety* has ensured that the lawyer will not give himself over to "poetic enthusiasm," will not, for example, indulge in a taste for "the mettlesome poet Byron" (20), rather than doing his work. Astor has seen to it, through a judicious application of "bullion," that the lawyer prefers "the easiest way of life" (14) to any activity that would compete with Astor's own dominance of New York's financial and real-estate markets.

The lawyer's tenancy, then, points to his larger insecurity in New York's economic system. That insecurity is further heightened by his loss of "[t]he good old office, now extinct in the State of New-York, of a Master in Chancery" (14). Like his work for Astor, this appointment is "not a very arduous office, but very pleasantly remunerative" (14). Luckily, there is plenty of other title work for him to do, but he has "counted upon a life-lease of the profits, whereas I only received those of a few short years" (14). Unfortunately for him, the office was terminated in the same year as Astor's death, 1848. The "sudden and violent abrogation" of two sources of his income does not appear to have impoverished him, but it does suggest why he feels drawn to write the story of another dispossessed soul, Bartleby, with whom he acknowledges nothing else in common.

They have more in common, however, than he realizes. Like him, Bartleby is a man of method, prudent and safe, particularly with his own money and that of his employer. Like him, Bartleby is unambitious, seeking the "cool tranquillity of a snug retreat" (14). And most of all, Bartleby, though possessing no rights to the property he tenants, nevertheless asserts his rights to the space in a proprietary way. The problem is that, because the lawyer sees the space as his, he does not recognize Bartleby's prerogative. Bartleby's "preference," however, implies a right to the space the lawyer occupies, not because he owns it, but because he has a prior claim. This claim he advances by occupying the space himself and through his choice of proprietary language.

Unlike Turkey, who always speaks "with submission," or the lawyer, who vacillates in his language, Bartleby simply and directly *prefers*. Aside from the powerful effect that his linguistic economy has on his listeners, aside from the undeniable challenge he raises to the lawyer's expectations that he do his work, Bartleby's preference carries with it an assertion of rights. As the lawyer unwittingly acknowledges, he is "more a man of preferences than assumptions" (34), but the difference is crucial. The lawyer congratulates himself on being a man of assumptions: he will *assume* that Bartleby has vanished from the premises, and vanish he will. He admires his own tactic because of its "perfect quietness" (33). Rather than force his position, the lawyer will assume it, as he has assumed his power over the management of the office and other employees: "I *assumed* the ground that depart he must; and upon that assumption built all I had to say" (34). As Herbert Smith has pointed out, assumption, or *assumpsit*, "a writ issued in cases of nonfeasance (non-performance) in the fifteenth century and later" (740), is a common practice in chancery law. But assumption is generally a weak strategy because the claimant takes the action upon himself, rather than relying on a formal written contract or law.

> **Assumpsit** 1. A taking upon oneself, an undertaking; *spec.* in *Law.* **a.** A promise or contract, oral or in writing not sealed, founded upon a consideration; **b.** An action to recover damages for breach or non-performance of such contract. (*OED*)

As the lawyer recognizes, an assumption is not as strong as a written contract would be: "It was truly a beautiful thought to have assumed Bartleby's departure; but, after all, that assumption was simply my own, and none of Bartleby's" (34). Indeed, *assumption* often has the meaning of a false claim: "The action of laying claim to as a possession, unwarrantable claim, usurpation. . . . The taking of anything for granted as the basis of argument or action" (*OED*). In taking Bartleby's acquiescence for granted, the lawyer has acted on extremely shaky premises, as he himself admits: "The great point was, not whether I had assumed that he would quit me, but whether he would prefer to do so" (34). And of course Bartleby prefers his claim over the lawyer's.

Bartleby generally uses the word *prefer* to imply a personal inclination or desire, in the common meaning of "To set or hold (one thing) before others in favour or esteem; to favour or esteem more; to choose or approve rather; to like better" (*OED*). Mildly and politely, he informs the lawyer that he would prefer not to read copy, to run errands, to write any longer at present. There is something he likes better, his privacy and solitude. As a legal term, however, to prefer is to "give preference to as a creditor" – that is, to honor "A prior claim to something; *spec.* priority of payment given to a certain debt or class of debts; a prior right to payment" (*OED*). Payment is not the issue for Bartleby; prior right is. To prefer is also "to put forward or advance . . . to advance oneself or one's interests," or simply "to promote (in various uses)" (*OED*). Bartleby prefers his proprietary claims. To the lawyer's peremptory knock at the door, he replies, "Not yet; I am occupied" (34), implying not just that he is busy, but that he has occupied the space. It is an interesting statement of his act of possession, for he occupies (tenants) the place where he is occupied (engaged in business). He makes the place of work his home, and he asserts his prior claim, his preference, to that place. The lawyer's assumption can have no force over such a powerful claim.

In fact, the lawyer indicates by his own choice of language that he fully comprehends the implications of Bartleby's act of possession.

> Now, the utterly unsurmised appearance of Bartleby, tenanting my law-chambers of a Sunday morning, with his cadaverously gentlemanly *non-chalance*, yet withal firm and self-possessed, had such a strange effect on me, that incontinently I slunk away from my own door, and did as desired. But not without sundry twinges of impotent rebellion against the mild effrontery of this unaccountable scrivener. Indeed, it was his wonderful mildness chiefly, which not only disarmed me, but unmanned me, as it were. For I consider that one, for the time, is a sort of unmanned when he tranquilly permits his hired clerk to dictate to him, and order him away from his own premises. (26–7)

This passage takes up all the issues of ownership and tenancy we have encountered so far. Bartleby's "tenanting" raises a direct challenge to the lawyer's tenancy, but he is "self-possessed," as his body is the only thing he really commands. Nevertheless, that self-possession asserts such a primary claim that it has the force of actual proprietorship; and proprietorship conveys manhood. His possession, then, of the space unmans the lawyer, who feels himself dictated to by *his* hired clerk ordering him away from *his* premises. The lawyer declares his ownership through words, Bartleby through his physical, manly self-possession.[25]

On what ground does Bartleby base his preference, his claim? The lawyer fears he will "claim possession of my office by right of his perpetual occupancy," a possibility that "worried me very much," as he fantasizes that Bartleby may live a long time, "denying my authority; and perplexing my visitors; and scandalizing my professional reputation; and casting a general gloom over the premises" (38), as if all these were Bartleby's reasons for living. He does not consider the political grounds for Bartleby's claim, the grounds of citizenship and franchise that were changing the political map of New York. In particular, the success of the Democratic Party in registering voters in the immigrant neighborhoods made a whole new population politically active.[26] To the lawyer, it is no matter for comment that Nippers is "considerable of a ward-politician" (17). Like many young men of the city, like Melville's own brother Gansevoort, for example, Nippers is ambitious for more glory than he can earn in a lawyer's office.[27] The lawyer calls this a "diseased ambition" (17) as, like Astor, he believes in limiting the ambitions of those who work for him. But Nippers presumably wants his share of the political process and its gifts, and he devotes considerable energy to his ambitions. The same energy and excitement infect a group of citizens debating a political question on a street corner as the lawyer passes by. When they lay bets on the outcome of that day's mayoral election, the lawyer mistakenly believes that they are betting on Bartleby's preferences. He takes little notice of the substance of their "earnest conversation" (34); it is important, however, as a sign of the high level of political activity and interest among the people of New York.

Although Bartleby does not take part in this political discussion, his quiet preference of his own claim to the office seems to partake of a similar spirit. The lawyer, of course, does not see things that way, does not see Bartleby himself, as he fantasizes about "pretending not to see Bartleby at all, walk[ing] straight against him as if he were air" (35). Their subsequent conversation brings the property issues out into the open, but the lawyer fails to get Bartleby's silent point. When Bartleby states, "I would prefer *not* to quit you," the lawyer answers with reference to the terms by which he understands occupancy: "What earthly right have you to stay here? Do you pay any rent? Do you pay my taxes? Or is this property yours?" These are not the terms, however, by which Bartleby pretends to, or prefers himself to, occupancy; and so "[h]e answered nothing" (35). His claim comes, not from the power of the proprietors like Astor and

Trinity Church to buy the land,[28] but from the power of tenants to occupy the land and by their actions to limit the landlords' power: "[T]enants found that the most effective action against landlords was voting with their feet" (Blackmar, 249), absconding without paying the rent. Bartleby, who is not expected to pay the rent but is nevertheless financially self-sufficient, votes with his whole body – and stays. Such an inversion of the conventional landlord–tenant relationship, despite the fact that the lawyer is not the landlord nor Bartleby a conventional tenant, is too much for the lawyer. In an astonishing reversal of his previous position, he is thrown back on himself – "I endeavored also immediately to occupy myself" (36) – and when other occupations fail him, he takes up the vagrant life in despair: "So fearful was I of being again hunted out by the incensed landlord and his exasperated tenants, that, surrendering my business to Nippers, for a few days I drove about the upper part of the town and through the suburbs, in my rockaway; crossed over to Jersey City and Hoboken, and paid fugitive visits to Manhattanville and Astoria. In fact I almost lived in my rockaway for the time" (42). Visiting Astoria, named after his mentor, the lawyer may be aware of the ironies of his new vagrancy, but he gives no sign.[29]

In the end it is Bartleby, the reliable tenant who has steadily occupied the building, supporting himself on his savings, who is jailed for vagrancy, not the lawyer. Even the lawyer sees the ridiculous side of this paradox: "a vagrant, is he? What! he a vagrant, a wanderer, who refuses to budge? . . . That is too absurd" (38).

The lawyer has assumed ownership of property that was not his. Bartleby has preferred not to be assumed by the lawyer's proprietary fantasies. But Bartleby could not assert his claim against the mighty powers the lawyer represents – the rentiers far away, whose reach extends over space and ninety-nine years of time. If Bartleby and the lawyer could unite in common cause against the proprietors, they might, like the renters of Upper New York State, defeat the landholders. But the lawyer cannot acknowledge the common ground between Bartleby and himself: "really, the man you allude to is nothing to me – he is no relation or apprentice of mine, that you should hold me responsible for him" (39). He can think only in proprietary terms – my apprentice, my relation, my surroundings – and so cannot see how provisionally both he and Bartleby occupy the same confined space.

"Jimmy Rose" also concerns a poor man's miserable tenancy of private space. However, the story is more sympathetic to proprietors than either *Pierre* or "Bartleby." The constant refrain of "God guard us all – poor Jimmy Rose!" and the narrator's close attention to Jimmy's heroic efforts to salvage his dignity generate pity for the old man. But another old man, the narrator, injects a degree of irony by suggesting that if Jimmy's decay is pitiable, the decay of his house is pathetic. Its age makes it, like Jimmy, a ridiculous relic of the past. In "Jimmy Rose" we see a struggle, not between proprietors and tenants but between the neighborhood and the city. As the city grows, it leaves men like Jimmy and houses like his far behind. The story shows how the expanding housing market has changed the city's physical and social geography, but the narrator names no particular villains, like the developers of the Church of the Apostles or Astor and Trinity Church. The forces of the market have become generalized, diffused through the city, embedded in its geography and architecture, so that they seem natural and remote from human action, just as the trope of the labyrinth came to seem natural to the changing shape of the city. In telling the story of Jimmy's failure, the narrator tells principally the story of the city's success, and that of its middle-class proprietors.

The story opens with the narrator moving into Jimmy's house, which he has inherited, and noticing the decay of the neighborhood: "a narrow street in one of the lower wards, once the haunt of style and fashion, full of gay parlors and bridal chambers; but now, for the most part, transformed into counting-rooms and ware-houses. There bales and boxes usurp the place of sofas; day-books and ledgers are spread where once the delicious breakfast toast was buttered" (336). As we saw in the *Putnam's* article, "New-York Daguerreotyped," such elegies for old New York competed, often within the same piece, with paeans to its growth and glory. Here the narrator treats the subject jokingly, speculating that when he comes to take possession of Jimmy's house, the neighbors – "some few strange old gentlemen and ladies" – take his advent as a positive sign: "those poor old souls insanely fancied the ward was looking up – the tide of fashion setting back again" (336). But clearly no such regeneration can take place. For some time the building has been rented out "to various shifting tenants; decayed old towns-people, mysterious recluses, or transient, ambiguous-looking foreigners" (337), like Isabel's mother, perhaps. It has lost its value on the market and is hardly useful even as a rental property.

The story he tells of the house's decay, from its days of glorious Parisian wallpaper festooned with roses and peacocks to more recent times, when landlords have made such dubious "improvements" as "removing a fine old pulpit-like porch" and putting up "frippery Venetian blinds" (337), implicates the "tide of fashion" in housing. But that tide is impersonal, as are the shifts in fortune that ruin Jimmy: "times changed. Time, true plagiarist of the seasons" (339). Jimmy's troubles occur as the result of market forces far away: "Sudden and terrible reverses in business were made mortal by mad prodigality on all hands" (339). There is no explanation for Jimmy's rise and fall; the narrator devotes most of the story to Jimmy's pathetic attempts to salvage crumbs from the tables of his former friends, trading compliments, gossip, and bon mots for tea and toast. He concludes by "meditat[ing] upon his strange example, whereof the marvel is, how after that gay, dashing, nobleman's career, he could be content to crawl through life, and peep about among the marbles and mahoganies for contumelious tea and toast, where once like a very Warwick he had feasted the huzzaing world with Burgundy and venison" (345). He seems to feel that Jimmy had some choice in the matter, that he might choose to "be content" over his fate.

But the story of the house suggests that Jimmy's fate is fashion. The "mad prodigality" of business cycles has reversed his good fortune, and the tide of fashion has swept through the lower wards, leaving them desolate, given over to warehouses and a few penurious tenants. Against those forces, Jimmy's efforts, like those of Bartleby to press his claim on the city for space to live in, are futile. Curiously, however, the story generates little real sympathy for Jimmy. The narrator's pity seems self-serving and sentimental – he, after all, has inherited the house – and his acceptance of the changes in the housing market shows that, as a proprietor himself, he has only benefited from these changes. Whereas Bartleby's actions genuinely challenge the system of proprietorship and bring the lawyer to recognize some, if not all, of its absurdities, Jimmy's gallant submission to his fate serves the narrator's sense that, except for some poetic nostalgia for the past, all is well in the city of New York. Pity for Jimmy solaces this small and complacent proprietor with the notion that he himself, at least, is secure.[30]

To be a man in the City of Man, the city of intense competition over land and space, is to test the possibilities of tenancy and transiency. All three of these characters – Pierre, Bartleby, and Jimmy Rose – live transiently and are, in the eyes of urban proprietors, miserable. But each also asserts a higher claim to a selfhood defined not by property but by the human will, by assertions of individual freedom, by the force of the body and its occupation of space. Although the narrators of these works mock or pity uncertain tenancy in miserable housing, the characters stand their ground and challenge the proprietary rights and assumptions of others.

Domestic Space in the City Of Man

> Thence to the Hotel de Cluny. A most unique collection. The house is just the house I should like to live in. Glorious old cabinets – ebony, ivory carving. – Beautiful chapel. Tapestry, old keys. (*Journal*, 33)

Owning a house makes one a man in the City of Man. But that house can be a paradise only of bachelors unless the house becomes a home, a place where women *and* men can practice domestic economy, protect domestic space, and assert domestic virtue. Christine Stansell has called the world of feminine influence and female labor the City of Women. The middle-class domestic ideal is one kind of City of Women – a place where middle-class women and their men feel at home – but for the laboring man or woman such a home is often out of reach. The poor or working sojourner in the city either cannot find a home or else finds one that does not resemble the domestic ideal. His or her homelessness or lack of conventional domestic space places him or her outside the middle class, living in the city's public space.

When Melville envisioned living at the Hotel de Cluny, he did not imagine the kind of domestic space that he or most middle-class city dwellers could actually attain, nor that domestic literature, like the works of Catharine Beecher on domestic economy or those of Andrew Jackson Downing on domestic architecture, advised people to create.[31] To many readers, it has not seemed that Melville engaged in domestic issues at all, or at least with sympathy.[32] Melville's work of the mid-1850s, however, indicates as deep a concern with creating a home in the city as it does with finding a house. Most of his characters fail in this endeavor. But, as with the labyrinth literature, Melville attributes their failure to an ideology that oppresses men *and* women with its demands. As a system designed to help the middle class improve its urban advantages, domestic economy contains an implicit class bias; the home as "separate sphere," as privileged domestic space, creates a trap for both men and women; and city dwellers who try to construct homes different from the prevailing cultural model find themselves outcasts, sojourners in the city. For many of Melville's characters, the ideal home is a luxury they cannot afford.

Pierre, for example, discovers the price of domestic happiness when he decides to create a home in the city.[33] His domestic life until this point has seemed a blissful, unending idyll, a "softened spell which still wheeled the mother and son in one orbit of joy" (16). He has enjoyed almost total immersion in maternal domestic influence, and he has also been deeply influenced by Lucy's domesticity. A visit to her bedchamber gives him visions, not of sexual license, but of domestic sanctity; when he marries her, he will "unroll the sacred secrets of that snow-white, ruffled thing" (39), her bed. His reverence for domestic purity makes him feel himself a rapist: "I am Pluto stealing Proserpine; and every accepted lover is" (59). According to the domestic ideology of his period, every mother should want such a son, every woman such a lover.

Meeting Isabel, however, exposes Pierre to the realities of domestic labor. He sees her hands hardened by toil, eats bread she baked, drinks water from the cup she brings, and feels "the real sacrament of the supper" (162). Most of all, he understands her need, not for money or recognition, but "for the constant love and sympathy and close domestic contact of some one of her blood" (174). Through Isabel, he sees that he has "habituated his voice and manner to a certain fictitiousness in one of the closest domestic relations of life" (177); his previous domesticity has been a fantasy. Pierre must go to New York, however, to see how the city organizes and defines domestic space, just as it organizes and defines public space.[34] The contrast between Glen's house and Pierre's nook at the Apostles offers a satiric view of the meanings of domestic space.

When Pierre first considers moving to New York, as Lucy's husband and the author of "The Tropical Summer: A Sonnet," he entertains extravagant and artificial notions of domestic life. His cousin Glen offers him "all the hospitalities of five sumptuous chambers, which he and his luxurious environments contrived nominally to occupy in the most fashionable private hotel of a very opulent town" (220). It is significant, of course, that although Glen can afford to own a house, he chooses to rent a large apartment; his opulent tenancy is much more suitable for a bachelor. For the newlywed Pierre, however, Glen reconsiders and decides to lend him "a very charming, little, old house, completely furnished in the style of the last century, in a quarter of the city which, though now not so garishly fashionable as of yore, still in its quiet secludedness, possessed great attractions for the retired billings and cooings of a honeymoon" (220). Naming this retreat the Cooery, Glen details the domestic arrangements he will undertake – supplying servants, obtaining crockery and silver, dusting the "venerable, grotesque, old mahoganies, and marbles, and mirror-frames, and moldings" (221), and connecting the utilities: "at the turning of the faucet in the cellar, the best of the city's water would not fail to contribute its ingredient to the concocting of a welcoming glass of negus before retiring on the first night of their arrival" (221).[35] Pierre responds with a few directives of his own, asking Glen to "store the bins with a few of the very best brands" of wine and to purchase "a small bag of undoubted Mocha coffee" (223), which, in his only reference to domestic labor, Pierre plans to roast, grind, boil, and serve himself.

The cloying language of this interchange suggests that both Glen and Pierre are caught up in a masculine fantasy of domestic life, one that has no particular place for Lucy, who will presumably spend her time billing and cooing and appreciating Pierre's efforts with the mocha. Furthermore this fantasy of a home, though combining the comforts of the past – the "venerable, grotesque, old mahoganies," the "old silver immemorially pertaining to the mansion," and the "hampers of old china" – with the modern conveniences of running water, hints that the Cooery is in fact a gilded domestic trap. Glen and Pierre both envision enjoying mostly bachelor pleasures there, with Lucy gracing the table for masculine revels. Although Pierre seems quite certain that he will find himself at home in the city, he has no notion of what domestic life entails.

When Pierre realizes, however, that he has Isabel and Delly to support and he no longer has a home in Saddle Meadows, he plans "a permanent residence in the city; not without some nearly quite settled plans as to the procuring of a competent income" (227–8). He still expects to find a home in the city, but now he understands that the Cooery will not be his, except as a temporary lodging. Instead of luxuriating in the pleasures of domestic space and its comfortable appointments, he now proposes "merely [to] take the place – for a short interval – of the worthy old clerk" (228), the "old, confidential, bachelor" (220), who previously inhabited the house. His unconventional relationship with Isabel makes anything resembling the idealized domestic sanctuary, the honeymoon cottage, a joke, and now he will never be able to afford running water and fine wines. Pierre must find a place he can tenant, where he can live *and* work, rather than a sanctified separate sphere, a domestic haven.

As we have seen, Pierre's tenancy at the Apostles signifies his new place in the housing market, but it also enacts his new relation to domestic space. Rather than achieving the urban middle-class ideal of a home separate from his place of work, he is forced to make his living in the same space he shares with women, in the domestic realm. Melville makes it clear, through his ironic narrator, that Pierre experiences his domestic situation as a double misery. The loss of domestic privacy and space subjects him to the miseries of crowding, hunger, and chill that the other Apostles suffer and reminds him of his failures to provide for Isabel, Delly, and later Lucy. But also, by writing at home he endangers the sphere of his work; he cannot keep the two separate.

Melville suggests the connection between domestic space and the space of intellectual labor in a striking architectural image. He describes Pierre's early poems as the rubbish discarded during the quest for gold; then he switches the metaphor to that of a house: "Happy would it be, if the man possessed in himself some receptacle for his own rubbish of this sort: but he is like the occupant of a dwelling, whose refuse can not be clapped into his own cellar, but must be deposited in the street before the door, for the public functionaries to take care of" (258). Publication rids the young writer of his rubbish: it is the "public functionary" who clears away the trash; and once put into a book, the rubbish "can be put into the fire, and all will be well" (258). Pierre would like to have the kind of space, both living and authorial, where he could stow his rubbish privately, but as an urban tenant he cannot so discreetly get rid of it. Pierre's status as renter deprives him of domestic privacy, the inviolate solitude of the homeowner. And without the advantage of private space, Pierre may not succeed in "digging in [his] soul for the fine gold of genius" (258). The metaphor suggests, then, another version of the domestic ideal, not the separate sphere of feminine influence, of honeymoon billing and cooing, but the separate sphere of the artist, where he may freely mine his soul for gold in the condition Gillian Brown has called "domestic individualism": the private space of the solitary male who exploits female labor in order to achieve his private ambitions.

Melville shows, however, that Pierre's desire for "domestic individualism" is another fantasy. His attempts to achieve such an ideal are under-mined from the start by his own unrealizable ambitions, which the narrator mocks, but also by the conditions of living in the city. He has no choice but to work at home unless he decides to take up another trade, and he must learn to live in the world of "public functionaries" who take care of his refuse for him. He cannot afford the luxury of "domestic individualism," nor does he seem to succeed at it. Rather than attaining "an authorship independent of domesticity" (Brown, 136), Pierre fails as an author, not simply because of an unsympathetic market but because he has chosen his isolation. In adopting a working-class mode of living and working, making his home his place of work, he demonstrates that the notion of separate spheres is a middle-class dream. Of course, he fails as a worker too, as do Isabel and Lucy. Unlike Charlie Milthorpe's family, Pierre and his women are unable to support themselves through sewing or other kinds of home industry. They fail to find a place in the urban or domestic economy, partly, as Fanny Fern's Ruth Hall similarly found, because their middle-class status excludes them from the available forms of employment the city provides to working women.[36]

Although these hapless products of gentility seem to bring their failure disastrously upon themselves, Melville blames their culture more than their characters. All have grown up in fictions of domestic life; even Isabel and Delly, who have worked for their support, have been protected from the hardest realities of domestic labor by living in the country. In the city, however, Melville's characters quickly learn that domestic bliss is a luxury only certain urban families can afford. Melville's narrator implies that the "close domestic contact" Isabel craves is a natural longing, but the city, by making privacy and domesticity matters of proprietorship, puts that dream beyond her reach. In a grim coda, Melville introduces a jailor who, like the Cutlets family in "Bartleby," produces a comic inversion of the domestic theme: " 'Oh, easy, easy, young gentleman' – jingling at his huge bunch of keys – 'easy, easy, till I get the picks – I'm housewife here' " (361). The turnkey is the only truly domestic character in the novel.

Pierre, Isabel, and Lucy sojourn in the City of Man, never managing to create a home for themselves, because they cannot separate domestic from working space, nor make the separate spheres operate as they should ac-cording to the ideal model. But only fairly recently had the culture moved toward a system that divided working from living space. In their provincial lives, the world of the farm and the sewing circle, the cottage and the manor, no such divisions existed, and their labors sustained them. But the new fashion of the city, to segregate public from private space, or-dained that the people who tried to combine them would encounter in-tolerable hardship.

This problem recurs often for the characters of Melville's magazine fiction. In his short stories, Melville frequently presents a working-class or poor character who is homeless, who has no protected private sphere to retreat to and therefore invades the city's public spaces, or who mixes the private sphere with other functions so that it loses its value as a domestic haven. Melville finds many ways to present the problem, ways that display the conflict between middle-class notions of home and the realities of homelessness.

One way to view the City of Man is as a place that created an ideology of domestic ideals in order to protect its own class status. The work of Christine Stansell and Carroll Smith-Rosenberg has shown how missionary visits to the homes of the working and indigent poor fed middle-class definitions of home values.[37] "This attention to the importance of the family came from bourgeois men's and women's own preoccupations with domesticity. When reformers entered tenement households, they saw a domestic sparseness which contradicted their deepest understanding about what constituted a morally sustaining household; material effects and domestic morality were closely connected."[38] By peopling his narratives with working and poor people struggling to make homes in the city under the now-sympathetic, now-censorious eye of a middle-class narrator, Melville makes the most of this opportunity to expose bourgeois family values. The real separate spheres in his short fiction are not so much those of gender as those of class. The middle-class characters in "Bartleby," "Poor Man's Pudding and Rich Man's Crumbs," "The Two Temples," and "The Paradise of Bachelors and The Tartarus of Maids," have homes; the working-class and poor characters either do not have homes or have homes that do not fit the middle-class definition of domestic space.

We have already seen how Bartleby's use of the office for living space affronts the lawyer's sense of proprietary claims and of propriety. We need to look again at Bartleby's domesticity for a sense of the way Melville engages domestic ideology in the story. The most remarkable aspect of Bartleby's living arrangements is how closely they fit the norm, in spite of their seeming oddity. For one thing, he makes his living space a "retreat" (20). The new literature on suburban design, whose greatest spokesman was Andrew Jackson Downing, enthusiastically outlined the virtues of domestic retreat and offered elegant architectural models of homes in which, as the lawyer does by placing a screen around Bartleby's space, "privacy and society were conjoined" (19). Bartleby stands "at the entrance of his hermitage" (21), he sits "in his hermitage, oblivious to every thing but his own peculiar business there" (23), and later he "silently retired into his hermitage" (36). So, ideally, might the middle-class householder at the end of his working day; there he might find the privacy Bartleby seeks "behind the screen" (21).

Furthermore, Bartleby meets the standards of domestic neatness, order, temperance, and virtue that home visitors demand of the objects of their charitable scrutiny. The lawyer forgives Bartleby's odd behavior because of his "steadiness, his freedom from all dissipation, his incessant industry" (25) – all the things that made some people the "deserving poor," rather than the "vicious classes."[39] He is absolutely certain that "[i]t was not to be thought of for a moment that Bartleby was an immoral person" (27). Indeed, the order Bartleby maintains in his retreat, the revealing details of his spare domesticity – "under the empty grate, a blacking box and brush; on the chair, a tin basin, with soap and a ragged towel; in a newspaper a few crumbs of ginger-nuts and a morsel of cheese" (27) – ignite the narrator's sympathy. Even more impressive than Bartleby's misery is his thrift. When the lawyer finds "an old bandanna handkerchief, heavy and knotted. I opened it and saw it was a savings' bank" (28), he feels "positively awed" (29). Now he sees not only the misery but also "all the quiet mysteries" (28) of Bartleby. Now he can, in some measure, identify with his solitude and his heroic, and economical, efforts to survive in lean domesticity.

The lawyer persists, however, in misconstruing Bartleby's domestic values and assuming they resemble his own. He expects that the scrivener has a "native place" (29) to go to, that "after reaching home" (29) he might write the lawyer for money. He wishes that "[i]f he would but have named a single relative or friend, I would instantly have written, and urged their taking the poor fellow away to some convenient retreat" (32), rather than the one Bartleby at present inhabits, which is the only really convenient retreat he has. After a while, he begins to fear for Bartleby and himself, confronting each other "alone in a solitary office, up stairs, of a building entirely unhallowed by humanizing domestic associations" (36); he assumes that Bartleby would benefit from a home, that he needs to leave the wolfish environment of Wall Street and find domestic virtues. So great is his faith, like that of the missionaries, in the power of "humanizing domestic associations" that he finally offers to take Bartleby "home with me now – not to my office, but to my dwelling" (41), although there is no reason to believe that the lawyer's home has any more humanizing domestic influences than his office does. Throughout their entire association, the lawyer sees Bartleby's problem as one of moral homelessness; "keeping bachelor's hall all by himself" (27) smacks of deviance.

Thus, although Bartleby keeps house with admirable economy, the lawyer judges him for not having a home. "I like to be stationary" (41), says Bartleby, and he is much more secure and domestic an urban inhabitant than the lawyer, who keeps "veering about" (34). Nevertheless, the lawyer sees Bartleby's only alternatives as the almshouse and the Tombs. His lack of a conventional home makes him seem "the victim of an innate and incurable disorder" (29). Although a reader might be inclined to admire Bartleby's thrifty use of space for domestic purposes, the lawyer casts doubt on his sanity.

Many of Melville's other characters try to create homes in places the middle-class homeowner would not consider habitable, but few of them raise so insistent a challenge to charitable sympathy as Bartleby does. Nevertheless, Melville's poor characters tend to be proud, to stand their domestic ground as firmly as Bartleby. The Merrymusk family of "Cock-A-Doodle-Doo!", not starving but certainly dying in their miserable shanty, claim domestic independence by virtue of the miraculous Cock: "Haven't I Trumpet? He's the cheerer. He crows through all; crows at the darkest; 'Glory to God in the highest!' continually he crows it" (286). Merrymusk is proud that he can feed his family through his own labor, and his home represents for him a victory of domestic values. In his youth he was "a wandering man; until within some ten years ago, a thriftless man, though perfectly innocent of crime; a man who would work hard a month with surprising soberness, and then spend all his wages in one riotous night" (281). Marriage and children, however, have changed all that, and now he seems, "though a very poor man, . . . nevertheless, a highly respectable one" (280). The narrator concludes that, although the family is clearly suffering, they do not need outside aid. Merrymusk, indeed, considers himself the benefactor: "I am a great philanthropist. I am a rich man" (286). With the cock as domestic angel, "bent upon rejoining instanter this whole family in the upper air" (288), the Merrymusks seem self-sufficient.

Similarly the Coulters of "Poor Man's Pudding" have achieved domestic warmth and harmony in a damp, unliveable cottage. The narrator is ashamed of the way his philanthropist friend, Blandmour, sentimentalizes their poverty, but he is also ashamed to detect certain philanthropic prejudices in himself. Thus he is tempted to pity the Coulters their hard lot when, at the same time, he recognizes that he has been privileged to witness their courage, optimism, and love for each other. He blames American "peculiar political principles" for some of their misery; for American individualism makes them resent charity and yet also resent "the smarting distinction between their ideal of universal equality and their grind-stone experience of the practical misery and infamy of poverty" (296). Even more, however, he blames the complacency of charitable observers: "Of all the preposterous assumptions of humanity over humanity, nothing exceeds most of the criticisms made on the habits of the poor by the well-housed, well-warmed, and well-fed" (296). The domestic ideology of philanthropists only adds to the cruelty of indecent housing.

The narrators of these stories, then, are forced to admire the domestic triumphs of the poor. The Merrymusks and the Coulters love each other, work together, tend their sick, raise their children, suffer and die together with complete faith in domestic values. They also make thrifty use of their domestic space and practice an efficient domestic economy. The narrators, both middle-class bachelors, hardly the best representatives of the domestic ideal, find themselves having to reconsider their domestic prejudices. But also, they, and others of Melville's narrators, have to reconsider the social meanings assigned to domestic space and public space in the city.

In the most urban of Melville's sketches – "Rich Man's Crumbs," "The Two Temples," and "The Paradise of Bachelors" – the separate spheres of urban space, public and private, competitive and domestic, appear in uneasy contention. Poor and working-class characters are forced to inhabit what the middle class has defined as public spheres, to work in private spheres, to find homes away from home, or to impose private demands on public spaces. All these varieties of contention over space fulfill the implications of Bartleby's rebellion against the domestic faith: they expose the inadequacies of an ideological map intended to change the social geography of the city. Melville shows that the most disturbing separate spheres divide the classes.

In "Rich Man's Crumbs," the "vicious poor" invade the precincts of the rich and famous, threatening social order. Only the fiction of municipal charity confines a ravenous mob within a sanctioned public space. Although the story takes place in 1814 and uses the language of mob violence to suggest the revolutions of Europe, the narrator anachronistically has the New York of the 1850s in mind as well: "The spot was grimy as a back-yard in the Five Points. It was packed with a mass of lean, famished, ferocious creatures, struggling and fighting for some mysterious precedency" (298). The narrator, though expressing horror at the misery of the "pestiferous mob" (298), also suggests the horror of a clash between public and private interests, public and private space. The banquet was a private affair among great public men; the charity converts the banqueting hall into public space, now made available for the most private of needs.

In a city where poor and working people could claim little private space, the public space of New York – streets, parks, and public buildings – became places to do business, meet friends, have quarrels, dump garbage, make love, make deals – everything refined people do behind closed doors. They also made visible the tensions between class interests, as people tried to use the streets for different purposes. "The streets of New York were the city's common ground, the place where people of all walks of life encountered one another as they worked, socialized, or simply passed by. But the streets were not common property" (Blackmar, 158). Belonging to the city of New York, whose government was dominated by property holders who wished to improve their own property values, the streets did not serve the interests of all. Merchants and homeowners were offended by the use working and poor people made of the streets – for peddling, scavenging, prostitution, theft – and their lack of privacy. As

Nathaniel Parker Willis said of the Five Points, "nobody goes in doors except to eat and sleep. The streets swarm with men, women, and children.... They are all out in the sun, idling, jesting, quarrelling, everything but weeping, or sighing, or complaining.... A viler place than Five Points by any light you could not find."[40] Reform efforts focused on clearing the streets of unsightly people and their traffic. But "New York's streets ... belonged to its working-class people. Family economies bridged the distance between public and private to make the streets a sphere of domestic life."[41] Reformers missed the point that the streets *were* the homes of working-class people, that from these uses of public space came the bonds of community life that homeowners, by moving behind closed doors, had to find elsewhere – in the club, church, or theater, as Melville shows in his sketches – if they found it anywhere. Like the walled towns of Europe, New York's streets provided a community enclosed by the larger structures built up around them: a Town within the City.

"Rich Man's Crumbs" records the middle-class narrator's confrontation with this active, contentious street life, with the population that made the streets their home, and for all his sympathy with the beggars, he is quite uncomfortable: "It was just the same as if I were pressed by a mob of cannibals on some pagan beach. The beings round me roared with famine" (298). When the crowd quickly consume the unappetizing leftovers from the great feast, they surge forward, crying for more: "The yet unglutted mob raised a fierce yell, which wafted the banners like a strong gust, and filled the air with a reek as from sewers. They surged against the tables, broke through all barriers, and billowed over the hall – their bare tossed arms like the dashed ribs of a wreck" (301). Melville uses considerably more poetry than John Griscom did with his cliché, the "tide of emigration," but the language conveys essentially the same anxiety. Like Griscom, the narrator understands middle-class complicity in the misery of the poor: "That one half-hour's peep at the mere remnants of the glories of the Banquets of Kings; the unsatisfying mouthfuls of disembowelled pasties, plundered pheasants, and half-sacked jellies, served to remind them of the intrinsic contempt of the alms" (301). Yet, while still understanding their fury, he is shocked when one of the guards mistakes him for a beggar too: " 'Surely he does not mean *me*,' said I to my guide; 'he has not confounded *me* with the rest' " (300). "Bruised and battered" (302) by his contact with "the thronged rabble" (298), he has little energy left for sympathy and understanding.

Melville has economically delineated the anxieties arising from a casual contact between two classes. The invasion of public space by private interests, of private sensibilities by public realities, produces the story's blazing tensions, which Melville leaves still smoldering at the end. Such tensions are less violent in "The Two Temples" (although they were still felt strongly enough by Charles F. Briggs of *Putnam's* to move him to reject the story), but both sketches involve a private person's use of public space for his own needs. In "Temple First," the narrator is punished for his appropriation of public space. Unlike the narrator of "Poor Man's Pudding and Rich Man's Crumbs" – who "is a *gentleman*" (301) – the man in the temple has a "rather gentlemany [*sic*] appearance" (309) but is not wealthy enough to get past the door of the fashionable New York church: "just the same as if he'd said, they did n't entertain poor folks" (303). To underscore that point, the "beadle-faced" man guarding the door "was just in the act of driving three ragged little boys into the middle of the street" (304). The narrator, having stolen into the church tower by a secret stair, feels like a criminal: "He whom he thought effectually ejected, had burglariously returned" (304). Yet, fascinated by the spectacle of urban wealth displayed below him in the church, the narrator lingers until after the service, when he finds himself locked into the church.

His experience of inhabiting the temple after everyone has left resembles that of Bartleby dwelling in a Wall Street office on Sunday: "Think of it. Of a Sunday, Wall-street is deserted as Petra; and every night of every day it is an emptiness. This building too, which of week-days hums with industry and life, at nightfall echoes with sheer vacancy, and all through Sunday is forlorn. And here Bartleby makes his home; sole spectator of a solitude which he has seen all populous" (27). The narrator of "Temple First" experiences intense isolation as well: "I was left alone and solitary in a temple which but a moment before was more populous than many villages" (307). In that emptiness, he is made aware of the vastness and hostility of public space. No longer appearing human in scale or design, the church "assumed a secluded and deep-wooded air" (308). "A Puseyitish painting of a Madonna and child, adorning a lower window, seemed showing to me the sole tenants of this painted wilderness – the true Hagar and her Ishmael" (308). The empty public space seems a wilderness and its inappropriate tenants but sojourners.

"Temple First" shows the failure of affluent New Yorkers to create community spirit in their public space. To underscore that point, "Temple Second" shows how the working-class use of public space, a theater, creates community and fellowship. The narrator is still gentlemanly, but even poorer than before, even more obviously a dispossessed sojourner in the city: "A stranger in London on Saturday night, and without a copper!" (309). Evicted for the evening by an unsympathetic landlady, he has no domestic space to return to and must "drift . . . amid those indescribable crowds" of "Babylonian London" (310). By a chance act of charity, he acquires a ticket to the theater, which reminds him, by a number of associations, of the public space of the church, but because he is now a member, not a distant observer, of the crowd, he takes comfort and pleasure in the spectacle. His encounter with a boy selling ale domesticates the scene; for although he has no money for the drink, the boy offers it to him gratis, saying "drink to honest dad" (314). In the end, "borne by that rolling billow, I, and all the gladdened crowd, are harmoniously attended to the street" (315). The tide of humanity he encountered in the Guild Hall appears here as a harmonious billow.

In a London theater, this refugee from the American city encounters the working-class community of cohesive town. His companions are "Not of the first circles, and certainly not of the dress-circle; but most acceptable, right welcome, cheery company, to otherwise uncompanioned me. Quiet, well-pleased working men, and their glad wives and sisters, with here and there an aproned urchin" (313). No one ejects him from the theater, although he is using it for a different purpose than that for which it was designed. He is able to enjoy freely the communal use of public space.

If "The Two Temples" challenges the middle-class control of public space by offering a working-class alternative community, "The Paradise of Bachelors and The Tartarus of Maids" shows communities where the boundaries between public and private space have broken down entirely. The bachelors use public space for their private ends; the maids dwell, work, and labor to produce in the same dense, urbanized, multifunctional space. Such new urban structures, the office building/apartment house or the factory/home, were celebrated in the contemporary press and literature as solutions to the problem of shrinking space in the city. Melville's story suggests, however, that in their enthusiasm for such structures, little cities in themselves, the middle class worked to obliterate the nurturing functions of the older, more organically organized communities they replaced.

Much has been written about the ideological uses of space in "The Paradise of Bachelors and the Tartarus of Maids."[42] These have focused primarily on the issue of gender, on the ways the notion of separate spheres works to create oppressive gender roles for women and men. I see the sketches also showing, however, the way class structures stand behind and validate gender relations and furthermore reveal themselves most insidiously in uses of urban space.[43] The Inns of Court is public space appropriated to the private enjoyment of the bachelors. Their control of the space, moreover, is doubled by the factory owners' appropriation of female labor for profits. In both sketches, the urban sojourner has no domestic space to retreat to and must rely on public space for an unreliable welcome. That space, even when it is not physically in the city, as with the factory, is a "city by itself" (318).

Like Bartleby, the bachelors make their home in an office building. It is, of course, a very beautiful office building with private rooms for living in and entertaining. Nevertheless, Melville makes a point of the fact that the rooms are transient residences, not homes: "If being, say, a lounging gentleman and bachelor, or a quiet, unmarried, literary man, charmed with the soft seclusion of the spot, you much desire to pitch your shady tent among the rest in this serene encampment, then you must make some special friend among the order, and procure him to rent, in his name but at your charge, whatever vacant chamber you may find to suit" (319). The bachelors are nomads with their shady tents, urban sojourners, "[a]lmost all of them ... travelers, too; for bachelors alone can travel freely, and without any twinges of their consciences touching desertion of the fire-side" (322).

Given their flitting tenancy of the Inns of Court, it is all the more remarkable that they have established themselves and their "band of brothers" (322) so firmly in the city. In fact, the property has become a city in itself, by including so many of the amenities and advantages of the larger urban environment:

> The church and cloisters, courts and vaults, lanes and passages, banquet-halls, refectories, libraries, terraces, gardens, broad walks, domicils, and dessert-rooms, covering a very large space of ground, and all grouped in central neighborhood, and quite sequestered from the old city's surrounding din; and every thing about the place being kept in most bachelor-like particularity, no part of London offers to a quiet wight so agreeable refuge.
>
> The Temple is, indeed, a city by itself. A city with all the best appurtenances, as the above enumeration shows. A city with a park to it, and flower-beds, and a river-side – the Thames flowing by as openly, in one part, as by Eden's primal garden flowed the mild Euphrates. (318)

First, it should be clear that the lawyers control a large section of prime land in the center of London. Second, that land contains all the advantages of city and country, is, in fact, even better than suburbs, which try to offer "so agreeable a refuge." Third, though a very Paradise in their natural beauty, the Inns of Court supply all private and public needs, as urban space is meant to do, by bringing together all functions in one place. The lawyers can here work, read, take a banquet or dessert, sleep, walk, and "lounge on the benches beneath the trees, and switching their patent-leather boots, in gay discourse exercise at repartee" (318). The Temple is *in* the city, taking up quite a bit of London, and it also *is* a city, supplying all the best of what the city offers in a quiet retreat.

The Paradise of Bachelors is not, however, a community. It is a city within the city, not a town in the city, like the theater of the "The Two Temples." If the irony with which Melville invests the bachelors' fictitious domesticity were not enough – "you could plainly see that these easy-hearted men had no wives or children to give an anxious thought" (322) – "The Tartarus of Maids" completes the picture. Like the bachelors' apartment complex, the maids' factory brings together public and private space, labor and living, within the same space. Yet in combining public and private space, it eliminates the possibilities for community in each. The narrator becomes aware of this similarity when he is drawn to compare the factory to the Inns of Court, especially their dense, multifunctional structure:

> So that, when upon reining up at the protruding rock I at last caught sight of the quaint groupings of the factory-buildings, and with the traveled highway and the Notch behind, found myself all alone, silently and privily stealing through deep-cloven passages into this sequestered spot, and saw the long, high-gabled main factory edifice, with a rude tower – for hoisting heavy boxes – at one end, standing among its crowded out-buildings and boarding-houses, as the Temple Church amidst the surrounding offices and dormitories, and when the marvelous retirement of this mysterious mountain nook fastened its whole spell upon me, then, what memory lacked, all tributary imagination furnished, and I said to myself, "This is the very counterpart of the Paradise of Bachelors, but snowed upon, and frost-painted to a sepulchre." (326–7)

The narrator has not even seen the women yet. He has not begun to make the gender comparisons that make this sketch so rich when placed next to "The Paradise of Bachelors." What strikes him first is the structural similarity between two institutions that create living and working space in the same place, and the immediate association between such mixed structures and the city.

This basic structural similarity between the Inns of Court and the factory makes it possible to see the city as a place that uproots and unsettles both men and women. The maids are obviously more miserable than the bachelors, more physically and visibly deprived; but the bachelors simply do not know that they are miserable too: "Pain! Trouble! As well talk of Catholic miracles. No such thing. – Pass the sherry, Sir" (322). The bachelors' drinking and conviviality is directly related to their denial of misery, their own and anyone else's, whereas the women, like the pale sewing girls of popular urban fiction, allow men like the narrator to perceive and empathize with human suffering. The narrator's "pained homage" (334) to the women shows his compassion for their anguish, but his conclusion – "Oh! Paradise of Bachelors! and oh! Tartarus of Maids!" (335) – suggests that he sees no solutions. The city, by making domestic life a fiction, an appendage to the life of work, has oppressed all those who labor. They cannot recover the town within the city.

Even when characters in Melville's mid-fifties fiction have private space, it is seldom really their own, and it rarely offers domestic comfort or a real retreat from the city. Sometimes the poor, as in the case of Merrymusk or Milthorpe, can find domestic cheer even under these adverse circumstances, but more often Melville's characters feel deprived of genuine domestic security. Lacking a domestic retreat, they seek in the city's public spaces what they lack, but the city offers little welcome to the homeless sojourner. Their failure makes many of them miserable, not just because of the physical deprivation they suffer but the spiritual disease that gnaws at them – their essential insecurity in the world.

For some of Melville's characters, however, the failure to find a home in the city can be a happy failure. Rather than feeling themselves deprived because of the insufficient space the city offers, they create for themselves a space in which to live, work, and create community. They find town by escaping the city.

Abel in Cain's City

Not all of Melville's characters are miserable in the City of Man. In fact, as we have seen, some of the misery suffered by characters like Bartleby, the Coulters, or the Merrymusks has been imposed by the narrator's intolerant view of their poverty. As their homes resemble nothing that the middle-class observer would call home, they must be miserable. The narrator often admires the protagonist's lean domestic economy, but never would he wish to imitate it. Some of Melville's urban characters, however, seem to rise buoyantly above their adversity, to make their urban sojourn a comic assertion of human resiliency rather than a depressed negation. Characters like Hautboy the fiddler, Israel Potter, and the man in cream colors appearing at the beginning of the *The Confidence-Man* travel unscathed through the dense urban world, sojourning in the city but seeming not to be of it. They are not at home in Cain's City because they are not Cains; they are Abels, innocent of the crimes and fratricides on which the modern city is founded.[44]

The sojourner's failure to find a home, then, can be seen not only in terms of class and gender, property and space, but also in terms of character and spirit. Melville's urban heroes seem not to be influenced by the city's Wall Street ethic. Bartleby, a special case, is in a sense such a character, because he so steadfastly resists the narrator's assumptions. The narrator admires his courage, though perhaps unconsciously, and recognizes that Bartleby is innocent of the city's vices. In fact, he is shocked to find him, the man so "serene and harmless in all his ways," housed in the Tombs along with "murderers and thieves" (43). Although he tries to gloss over Bartleby's misfortune, he recognizes that the forlorn scrivener does not deserve it. Almost in spite of himself, the lawyer admires this Abel in a city of Cains; he sees the justice of Bartleby's traveling on to sleep "with kings and counsellors" (45) rather than suffering more in the City of Man.

Nevertheless, the lawyer fails to see how he has contributed to Bartleby's misery. When he reflects sentimentally that "both I and Bartleby were sons of Adam" (28), he does not ask whether he is not Cain to Bartleby's Abel. He also fails to understand what Melville's narration makes abundantly and ironically clear: that Bartleby's vagrancy gives him a kind of freedom and innocence that the other urban characters lack, and might indeed envy. Bartleby does not submit to the choices urban characters commonly make. He does not allow himself to be excluded from the city's public and private spaces, does not force himself to choose between domestic and working spheres. Instead he creates his own space, an alternative space, where he stands his ground, "like the last column of some ruined temple" (33). One might see this assertion of self as "imperial,"[45] but it should be clear by now that the lawyer is the more imperial one in the story. Bartleby inhabits the space by virtue of the fact that he does *not* belong there; he belongs somewhere else.

Melville never indicates where Bartleby belongs, or what the alternative to the City of Man actually looks like. Welsh's study of Dickens's City of Man suggests that the City of God is the home, the domestic heaven; Rosenthal's work on urban ideology in America argues that the City of God is Nature as it refines man's cities and makes them New Jerusalems. Melville prefers not to define the world to which Bartleby belongs, but in *The Confidence-Man* he identifies it as the "town" where "the novelist goes for his stock, just as the agriculturist goes to the cattle-show for his" (238). No other realm could contain such an "original" being, and as becomes clear in *The Confidence-Man* and *Clarel*, Melville's imagination creates such towns for "inconsistent characters" (70) to live in.

"Bartleby" presages these sophisticated works by hinting at the metaphysical and metafictional dimensions of a modern Abel's urban sojourn. "The Fiddler," however, introduces a more comic Abel, the "nobody" Hautboy. The narrator, Helmstone, nourishing visions of his own genius, is disappointed by his failure: "So my poem is damned, and immortal fame is not for me! I am nobody forever and ever. Intolerable fate!" (262). Condemned to live in a city "where enthusiastic throngs were crowding to a circus in a side-street near by" (262), he laments that he has no such admiring audience for his tragic poem. Meeting Hautboy, a man who seems marvelously contented with his life, he assumes that he is an ordinary man of the city: "Acquiescent and calm from the cradle to the grave, he obviously slides through the crowd" (265). When he learns, however, that Hautboy is an "extraordinary genius . . . who in boyhood drained the whole flagon of glory; whose going from city to city was a going from triumph to triumph" (267), he understands his sliding though the crowd rather differently. "[T]oday he walks Broadway and no man knows him. With you and me, the elbow of the hurrying clerk, and the pole of the remorseless omnibus, shove him. He who has a hundred times been crowned with laurels, now wears, as you see, a bunged beaver" (267). Hautboy's poverty and obscurity now appear, like Pierre's and Bartleby's, a choice, an assertion of will. But Hautboy does not seem miserable in his choice, but happy: "*With* genius and *without* fame, he is happier than a king" (267).

In *Pierre* and "Bartleby," anonymity is a sign of genius; knowing the anonymous character conveys special powers. Hence, Lucy glories in knowing a Pierre whom no one else knows: "Did I only know of thee, what the whole common world may know – what then were Pierre to me? – Thou must be wholly a disclosed secret to me; Love is vain and proud; and when I walk the streets, and meet thy friends, I must still be laughing and hugging to myself the thought, – They know him not; – I only know my Pierre" (37). Isabel proudly usurps that knowledge at the end of the novel: "All's o'er, and ye know him not!" (362). The narrator of "Bartleby" acknowledges that "no materials exist for a full and satisfactory biography of this man" (13). But the lawyer is powerfully moved by the spectacle of Bartleby's anonymity: "I remembered the bright silks and sparkling faces I had seen that day, in gala trim, swan-like sailing down the Mississippi of Broadway; and I contrasted them with the pallid copyist, and thought to myself, Ah, happiness courts the light, so we deem the world is gay; but misery hides aloof, so we deem that misery there is none" (28). He credits himself with knowing something of Bartleby's life, and takes a certain responsibility for him, so that eventually he becomes the authority on Bartleby to the world at large.

Hautboy, too, has a fascinating anonymity: "he entirely baffled inquisition" (266). But he does not seem to inspire the kind of acquisitive inquisition that Pierre and Bartleby do. His anonymity is not miserable but happy. His fifth-floor flat, though "curiously furnished with all sorts of odd furniture," is "charmingly clean and cosy" (266). Hautboy's genius, then, his willful anonymity, his happy obscurity, make him a comic Abel. He is in the city but not of it by happy choice, and he succeeds in his deliberate failure. Helmstone, whose name bears ominous reminders of such principled characters as Pierre and Bulkington, in the end resigns his obsession with genius and chooses the lot of the common man. Rather than performing on the stage in city after city, he works for his living on the street and in the town.

Israel Potter also has the genius of the common man, that of sliding through the crowd, like Hautboy "exempted from all moral harm" (265). He makes his way through the world pretty much unnoticed; yet his miserable condition does not make him miserable or, as in much of the sensational urban fiction, vicious. Although he behaves like a provincial in Paris and spends forty-five years in the labyrinthine underworld of London, he does not become overwhelmed by the great city. He survives his urban experience, which was never more than a sojourn, and moves beyond the city to his final destination, dying in his native Berkshire hills. Vagrant but sinless, destitute but happy, propertyless but resourceful, Potter achieves his greatest triumph in becoming anonymous. For, as one of the "anonymous privates of June 17, 1775" (viii) Melville mentions in his punning dedication to the Bunker Hill Monument, Potter has achieved, after his lengthy sojourn throughout the world, the distinction of being a democratic American hero, a common man.

Like Bartleby, Israel Potter lives a paradoxical existence, always on the move yet always trapped. In some of the most powerful urban passages Melville ever wrote, Potter appears as a hapless waif in a City of Dis, a condition generally characterized by critics as dark and hopeless. Richard Chase remarks on the "Blakeian overtones" of the urban sections, on Israel's disappearance among the "black, lightless stones of London and the age-old rhythms of its misery." Harry Levin draws the parallel with Eliot's *The Waste Land.* John T. Frederick, in an extended consideration of imagery, concentrates on "the symbolic projection of immurement and the related proximity of death . . . now enriched and intensified" and the "imagery of immurement and confinement, of stone and mud and death, of fog and mist and darkness." Frederick W. Turner III concludes that London is a "city of the dead" and that "obviously Melville is aware of the effects of industrialism on the human spirit." After calling the novel "a work quite evidently the product of exhaustion and preoccupation with that exhaustion," Janis Stout describes Potter's London as "a scene of apocalypse," "an appalling vision of modern urban life," a "hellish city."[46] Few critics if any, however, have discussed the Cain myth and the way it structures Potter's character and experience. More than a waif, Potter is a sojourner, as industrious as and far more active than the contemplative Bartleby, but nevertheless condemned to wander Cain's city or, as he envisions London, Pharaoh's Egypt, until the proper time for his exodus. Although Potter's fifty years of urban captivity take place within a few short concluding chapters, the rest of the novel makes it clear that he has been sojourning in Cain's city for most of his life.

Potter begins as a provincial hero, bred in hardiness and resourceful spirit yet determined to leave his rural home. "It appears that he began his wanderings very early," motivated by domestic discomforts, by "the tyranny of his father, and what seemed to him the faithlessness of his love" (7, 8). Three years of rural wandering, farming, trapping, and hunting give way to several more at sea. The adventures of war call upon all his native resources yet land him, finally, in a prolonged state of captivity in London. As a prisoner of war, he can never travel freely as long as the Revolution continues, and once it ends various circumstances keep him there until he is almost too old to leave. For most of the book, then, Potter lives in an indeterminate state, constantly detained in his travels toward the desired place, his home.

Unlike Bartleby, however, Potter is able to taste some of the provincial's pleasures in encountering the great city. His tenure in Paris, as a courier between English sympathizers and Benjamin Franklin, provides him an education in the ways of the world. This capital stands out in his experience and in the whole narrative as a place of possible freedom and delight. Since France is America's ally in the Revolution, Israel Potter may wear his national identity there, "freely declaring himself an American" and receiving "kindly attentions even from strangers" (36). He has the freedom given him by his special boots, whose false heels contain secret papers for Benjamin Franklin. Horne Tooke jokingly calls these "seven-league boots," and they do indeed spirit Potter quickly over the Channel and back. Paris is not, after all, a threatening place, although in the end Israel is not allowed to enjoy its civilized pleasures.

Melville presents a Paris that Israel does not have the opportunity to see but that has considerable attractions. The Latin Quarter wears a penurious yet venerable and respectable air. Unlike the Parisian lodging houses described in *White-Jacket*, with "ugly-looking fellows gazing out at the windows" (75), the "lofty" and "imposing" lodging houses of the Latin Quarter contain eccentric scientists, rapt philosophers, and "indigent young students from all parts of France . . . ironing their shabby cocked hats, or inking the whity seams of their small-clothes, prior to a promenade with their pink-ribboned little grizzets in the Garden of the Luxembourg" (47). Some of the quarter, admittedly, appears "dreary and dim; monastic and theurgic" (47). But no "reeking, Sodom-like" scene meets the eye.

One major difference between Potter's Paris and the other cities of Melville's fiction is that plainly it is a City of Women – women who do not confine themselves solely to the domestic realm, although clearly they reign there as well: "The embellishing, or softening, or screening hand of woman is to be seen all over the interiors of this metropolis. Like Augustus Caesar with respect to Rome, the Frenchwoman leaves her obvious mark on Paris. Like the hand of nature, you know it can be none else but hers" (47). Such a tribute to female influence appears seldom in Melville's fiction; perhaps only Fayaway or Lucy has such a natural decorative touch. And the tribute comes with an acid disclaimer: "Yet sometimes she overdoes it, as nature in the peony; or – what is still more frequent – is a little slatternly about it, as nature in the pig-weed" (47). Yet these excesses of nature have undoubtedly had their effect on the most powerful men in the city. Franklin, "caressed favorite of the highest born beauties of the court" (48), with his "rich dressing-gown – a fanciful present from an admiring Marchesa" (38), and John Paul Jones with his rings and lady's gold watch, appear to have paid their homage to the women of Paris. Melville seems to draw here on the urban novels of Sue and Balzac, where men like Franklin and Jones play their respectable parts by day and at night wander into the city's labyrinths to find their entertainment.

It is important for Melville's presentation of Paris and for his characterization of Franklin and Jones that both appear, unlike Israel Potter and Ethan Allen, as men of the city, or at least as men combining urbanity with pastoral simplicity and ruggedness. Both partake of the city's labyrinthine complexity, Franklin being described as one of those "labyrinth-minded, but plain-spoken Broadbrims, at once politicians and philosophers" (46), and Jones as presenting a character like his tattoos, "elaborate, labyrinthine, cabalistic" (62). Franklin is himself a little cosmopolis, "a sort of handy index and pocket congress of all humanity, . . . [needing] the contact of just as many different men, or subjects, in order to the exhibition of its totality" (48). Jones is also a cosmopolitan, "strangely dashed with a superinduced touch of the Parisian *salon*" (56), a "jaunty barbarian in broad-cloth" haunting "the heart of the metropolis of modern civilization" (63). Remarkably enough, though, both seem outside civilization as well as in it: Franklin a man of "pastoral simplicity" (46) who has "pitched his tent" (48) in the city, Jones an outlaw and barbarian, type of the "primeval savageness which ever slumbers in human kind, civilised and uncivilised" (63). But both give intimations of the Cosmopolitan to come – Franklin with his embrace of all men and all poses, Jones with his elegantly shifting, deadly nature.

Potter learns from both these men that the city demands a certain kind of duplicity even of the honorable man. His Chesterfieldian education, however, does him little harm and in fact provides a period of relief and fellowship. Once he leaves Paris, his troubles begin, taking at first the rather comic form of his escape from Squire Woodcock's house in the dead man's clothes and his flight across the countryside dressed as a scarecrow. Captured and impressed into an English naval ship, he begins the weary period of continual roving within strict limits that defines his long captivity in London.

Potter's true experience of Cain's city begins not in London but on board ship. As in *White-Jacket*, ships throughout the novel provide analogues of the city, and Melville uses the ship as an image of urban life long before Potter plunges into London: "As running down channel at evening, Israel walked the crowded main-deck of the seventy-four, continually brushed by a thousand hurrying wayfarers, as if he were in some great street in London, jammed with artisans, just returning from their day's labor, novel and painful emotions were his" (85). Potter feels himself not just apart from the crowd but deeply antagonistic to it: "He found himself dropped into the naval mob without one friend; nay, among enemies, since his country's enemies were his own, and against the kith and kin of these very beings around him, he himself had once lifted a fatal hand" (85). The mention of kinship shadowily underscores the theme of fraternity found in *White-Jacket,* the idea of the world-frigate whose passengers share an ill-fated brotherhood. But, as in *White-Jacket, Pierre,* and "Bartleby," that fraternity among the sons of Adam is shattered by fratricidal impulses, by wars and crimes. Potter has lifted his hand against these men's brothers, and they have struck down his own. This point becomes obvious in the prose surrounding the sea battle between the *Serapis* and the *BonHomme Richard.*

The imagery dominating this battle suggests an Old Testament scene of divine wrath and human destruction. John Paul Jones has already announced himself as a destroyer like the Old Testament destroyer of cities: "Give me the *Indien* and I will rain down on wicked England like fire on Sodom" (56), and he has proved himself as good as his word by putting the town of Whitehaven to the torch. But by the end of the battle against the *Serapis,* Jones has destroyed his own vessel as well: "About ten o'clock, the Richard, gorged with slaughter, wallowed heavily, gave a long roll, and blasted by tornadoes of sulphur, slowly sank, like Gomorrah, out of sight" (130). Sodom and Gomorrah appear here, as elsewhere in Melville's fiction, as reminders of God's curse on the cities, a curse that began with Cain's murder of Abel and his building of the first city. The vessels appear simultaneously as the cursed Cities of the Plain and also in a stream of fratricidal images: "It [the battle] may involve at once a type, a parallel, and a prophecy. Sharing the same blood with England, and yet her proved foe" (120); "It seemed more an intestine feud, than a fight between strangers. Or, rather, it was as if the Siamese Twins, oblivious of their fraternal bond, should rage in unnatural fight" (125); "It was a co-partnership and joint-stock combustion-company of both ships; yet divided, even in participation. The two vessels were as two houses, through whose party-wall doors have been cut; one family (the Guelphs) occupying the whole lower story; another family (the Ghibelines) [sic] the whole upper story" (126). As the preceding passage shows, the fratricide has deeply urban implications, bringing to mind Dante's Florence and later Melville's London and Lowell. So, for example, the moon lights up the ghastly scene "like the phantasmagoric stream sent athwart a London flagging in a night-rain from an apothecary's blue and green window" (123), rather like the shop window in *Pierre.* The ships lie locked together with "a long lane of darkling water . . . between, like that narrow canal in Venice which dozes between two shadowy piles, and high in air is secretly crossed by the Bridge of Sighs" (125). And in a telling image drawn from the industrial city, "the trained men of the Serapis stood and toiled in mechanical magic of discipline. They tended those rows of guns, as Lowell girls the rows of looms in a cotton factory" (127). Finally, a treacherous attack by one of Jones's brother ships, ironically named the *Alliance,* "was like the great fire of London, breaking out on the heel of the great Plague" (128). Melville characteristically represents fratricidal violence as originating in cities – Cain's city, Sodom, Gomorrah – and as finding its natural place in cities like the modern London or Venice or the analogous military vessel. The battle partakes of the barbarous violence of that primitive encounter between Cain and Abel, but it also displays the modern sophistication, technology, weaponry, and automation that come from the center of urban industrial civilization. "In view of this battle one may well ask – What separates the enlightened man from the savage? Is civilization a thing distinct, or is it an advanced stage of barbarism?" (130). Melville asserts that the modern city rests on ancient and barbaric foundations, that it carries its fratricidal impulses and institutions beyond its own gates into its armies and battleships.

Potter survives the battle to find himself in an even more dangerous situation. Leaping aboard another ship, thinking himself a member of a boarding party, he finds himself cut off from his own ship and alone amid the enemy crew. In an extraordinary chapter, "The Shuttle," Potter makes his way among all the different messes and watches of the ship, trying with airy sociability to convince each one that he belongs there. "Jealous with the spirit of class, no social circle would receive him" (134). When the officers discover him, the men, "[o]ne, and then another, and another, declared that they, in their quarters, too, had been molested by a vagabond claiming fraternity, and seeking to palm himself off upon decent society" (136). Israel finds himself "[b]lack-balled out of every club" (136) for claiming fraternity, just as Bartleby finds himself jailed for claiming a right for space to live in and the visitor to the Temple First "for having humbly indulged myself in the luxury of public worship" (309). Yet with singular mildness, persistence, and cleverness, Potter, a bit of a confidence-man himself, sticks to his story until "he conciliated the appropriation of all the officers, as well as the captain; while his general sociability served in the end, to turn in his favor the suspicious hearts of the mariners" (141). Potter's claim of fraternity proves good.

Unlike some of Melville's other urban sojourners, then, Potter shows that he is willing to take his place among the throng, even if it means captivity in Cain's city. Beginning in the brickyards outside London, where he flees after his maritime adventures, Israel toils, like the captive nation whose name he bears, so that some distant urban Pharaoh may build enormous edifices. By making the bricks that will build the city, Israel seems to participate in the city's curse, and indeed he feels keenly his oppression: "here he was at last, serving that very people as a slave, better succeeding in making their bricks than firing their ships. To think that he should be thus helping, with all his strength, to extend the walls of the Thebes of the oppressor, made him half mad" (157). Even before he enters the city, he finds himself a captive doomed, like Pierre and Bartleby, to die behind high walls made with his own bricks. The succeeding years of his captivity in London partake of the same despair, as he dreams of a Promised Land, America, and longs for a final release.

Israel Potter, however, does not perish in Pharaoh's Egypt. He is, indeed, the first of Melville's urban men – Pierre, Bartleby, Jimmy Rose – to survive the city, and he does do with considerable spirit.[47] The odds are certainly frightening. London appears as a city of dead souls, a "gulfstream of humanity" (158) pouring over the "black besmoked bridge," "hung in long, sepulchral arches of stone," "Erebus arches," lowering over a polluted river where the coal scows drift "like awaiting hearses" (159). The river is Phlegethon, the streets tombstones worn down like "the vitreous rocks in the cursed Gallipagos, over which the convict tortoises crawl" (159), and the sky looks like volcanic smoke, "about to whelm the great town, as Herculaneum and Pompeii, or the Cities of the Plain" (159–60). Potter finds himself once again in Sodom and Gomorrah.

This vision of the city is indeed bleak and desolate but is not, in Potter's case, the terminus that New York is for Pierre and Bartleby. Melville's theme in the London sections is that, in spite of the fratricidal city – "London, adversity, and the sea, three Armageddons, which, at one and the same time, slay, and secrete their victims" (160) – Israel Potter, with his characteristic ingenuity, survives as he has always done. "[H]owever desperately reduced at times, even to the sewers, Israel, the American, never sunk below the mud, to actual beggary" (165). He avoids the fatal extremes of Pierre's passionate despair and Bartleby's numb isolation, actively working, marrying, fathering, and at all times engaging in the movements of history even at his humble level. Thus, when wars end and soldiers flood the city, Potter takes to chair bottoming. When hard times hit, he gathers rags and junk to sell. "[S]omehow he continued to subsist, as those tough old oaks of the cliffs, which though hacked at by hailstones of tempests, and even wantonly maimed by the passing woodman, still, however cramped by rival trees and fettered by rocks, succeed, against all odds, in keeping the vital nerve of the tap-root alive" (165). Potter does suffer poverty, deprivation, and illness. He loses his wife and all his children but one, and his struggles seem to avail him little. Yet in the end, through the efforts of his young son and a reluctantly helpful consul, he does get back to America. There he suffers continued privation and neglect, but he remains in some sense that tough old oak tree: "He died the same day that the oldest oak on his native hills was blown down" (169). Although most of his hopes for earthly rewards have been dashed, he has escaped his urban captivity and achieved the purpose of his sojourn in the city – an exodus that brings him home.

Potter's success derives from his anonymity. Whereas Pierre longs to cap "the fame-column, whose tall shaft had been erected by his noble sires" (8) and Bartleby stands as the last column in a ruined temple, Potter leaves no trace of himself, even in metaphor. As he himself recognizes while making bricks in a London suburb – and this is a saving recognition – men live but as the bricks built into edifices designed by a mysterious Architect: "Man attains not to the nobility of a brick, unless taken in the aggregate" (156). Israel Potter's greatest distinction, the measure of his heroism, is his humility. He alone among the book's heroes seeks no glory for himself, only the liberty to gain an honest living. Thus he ironically represents the hope of the city; he is the only man to recognize the importance of the aggregate, the only one humbly to direct his efforts toward some worthy corporate end. "As man serves bricks, so God him, building him up by billions into the edifices of his purposes" (156). Israel's philosophical acceptance saves him from the despair and confusion of Pierre, Bartleby, and the lawyer. Flexible and alert, he moves with the urban tide, pursuing his individual goals but allowing himself to bend before the irresistible facts of poverty, family, illness, war, and death.

Unfortunately, his only harvest seems to be age and neglect. But Melville, only half-joking, appropriates a monument for his hero and arranges an impressive pillar over his grave in the dedication to "His Highness, the Bunker-Hill Monument": "Israel Potter seems purposely to have waited to make his popular advent under the present exalted patronage, seeing that your Highness, according to the definition above, may, in the loftiest sense, be deemed the Great Biographer: the national commemorator of such of the anonymous privates of June 17, 1775, who may never have received other requital than the solid reward of your granite" (viii). Potter's very anonymity makes him a hero. His fraternal generosity helps to mitigate the city's savage fratricidal energies and to civilize its cosmopolitans.

At the beginning of his next novel, *The Confidence-Man*, Melville introduces another sojourner: a deaf-mute evangelist who holds up a slate on which he writes the biblical injunction, "Charity thinketh no evil." Pallid like Bartleby – "His cheek was fair" – and blond like Israel Potter – "his hair flaxen" (3) – the "man in cream-colors" offers a striking similarity to them, especially in his relation to the crowd. On the one hand, he is remarkably mild, inoffensive, "of an aspect so singularly innocent" (4) that he would seem to attract little attention. Yet his manner presents a disconcerting resistance to the swirling tide of people around him and brings him to the immediate notice of the crowd: "Stared at, but unsaluted, with the air of one neither courting nor shunning regard, but evenly pursuing the path of duty, lead it through solitudes or cities, he held on his way" (3). Simply to hold his place requires his irritating the people around him; "[a]s, in gaining his place, some little perseverance, not to say persistence, of a mildly inoffensive sort, had been unavoidable, it was not with the best relish that the crowd regarded his apparent intrusion" (4). Eventually his single-minded devotion to his task subjects him to the crowd's abuse; one man flattens his hat, the crowd pushes him, "not without epithets and some buffets" (4), and eventually he gets struck accidentally by a large trunk. That blow in a sense discharges the crowd's tension, and they leave him alone. Melville concludes the chapter by returning again to the stranger's gentle, inoffensive character: "Though neither soiled nor slovenly, his cream-colored suit had a tossed look, almost linty, as if, traveling night and day from some far country beyond the prairies, he had long been without the solace of a bed. His aspect was at once gentle and jaded" (6). A traveler from "some far country," of a nature gentle but nevertheless "evenly pursuing the path," he resembles the innocent Abel sojourning in Cain's city. At the same time, his resistance to the crowd, his immediately exciting suspicion, irritation, and abuse, suggests the dynamic underlying Bartleby's and the other Abels' interactions with the city. The gentle, innocent wanderer arouses distrust and anger from the crowd, not only because they are a wicked crowd, but also, Melville implies, because of some challenge in his manner, "the air of one neither courting nor shunning regard" (3). He seems, then, to resist the city.

With that subtle nuance, Melville steps away from a simplistic reading of the innocent, victimized Abel in an Evil City. His Abels are not passive. They do not flee their fates. They enter the city by choice, seeking a place of their own. As will become clear in Melville's later works, especially *The Confidence-Man* and *Clarel,* the decision to enter the city, to experience its full and perplexing diversity, its complex and multileveled structure, becomes an increasingly compelling choice.

6

Pilgrim in the City of God

Dusked Olivet he leaves behind,
And, taking now a slender wynd,
Vanishes in the obscurer town.

Clarel (498)

The Town Is Taken by Its Rats

The transient or homeless characters of many of Melville's narratives of the 1850s are trying to find homes in the older sections of New York, the town defined by the old walls of the Battery and Wall Street, the busy streets of Broadway, the Bowery, and Five Points. At the time Melville wrote these stories, New York City included much more, not only the new residential areas moving up Fifth Avenue, but also the suburbs of Brooklyn and Staten Island. In seeking homes in New York's old town, Melville's characters encounter the difficulties of finding space in the densely populated, disturbing City of Man that New York seemed to have become. In the interstices of his stories, however, in the descriptions of Hautboy's crowds or the working-class theater or Nippers's ward politics, one sees a community of middle- and working-class people sharing the same space in what could be a communal town rather than a divided city. At moments, the City of Man gives intimations of being a City of God – a "Town, redeemed" (*BP*, 87) occupying the same space as that which the city has claimed for itself. Entering the City of Man can bring the sojourner into the "heart of proudest town" (*C*, 496).

Melville's decision to enter the great modern city that New York became in the second half of the nineteenth century required considerable preparation. He spent years planning his move, hoping perhaps for a triumphal return to his native city, the town he had known. When the time came, however, to sell Arrowhead and relocate to New York, he was very different from the young man who, like the other males in his family,

234

had sought his fortune there.[1] New York, too, in the years he had lived at Arrowhead (1850–63), had vastly grown and changed. It seemed to many observers of its landscape and culture to have outgrown itself. Certainly its population had exploded well beyond its mid-century levels. More than that, the city seemed to have burst beyond the old models of urban form. There seemed no adequate way to describe its size, complexity, density, and power.

Melville's poem, "The House-Top," published in his *Battle-Pieces* of 1866, explores the tensions of city dwellers living in a time of riot and war. At the same time it raises the question of urban form in a city that seems to have "rebound[ed] whole æons back in nature." In the ambiguous way it positions the speaker of the poem, "The House-Top" recapitulates some of the cultural constructions of urban form we have seen so far and suggests why Melville sought to reconsider them in his later work.

Here is the poem in full:

No sleep. The sultriness pervades the air
And binds the brain – a dense oppression, such
As tawny tigers feel in matted shades,
Vexing their blood and making apt for ravage.
Beneath the stars the roofy desert spreads
Vacant as Libya. All is hushed near by.
Yet fitfully from far breaks a mixed surf
Of muffled sound, the Atheist roar of riot.
Yonder, where parching Sirius set in drought,
Balefully glares red Arson – there – and there.
The Town is taken by its rats – ship-rats
And rats of the wharves. All civil charms
And priestly spells which late held hearts in awe –
Fear-bound, subjected to a better sway
Than sway of self; these like a dream dissolve,
And man rebounds whole eons back in nature.
Hail to the low dull rumble, dull and dead,
And ponderous drag that shakes the wall.
Wise Draco comes, deep in the midnight roll
Of black artillery; he comes, though late;
In code corroborating Calvin's creed
And cynic tyrannies of honest kings;
He comes, nor parlays; and the Town, redeemed,
Gives thanks devout; nor, being thankful, heeds
The grimy slur on the Republic's faith implied,
Which holds that Man is naturally good,
And – more – is Nature's Roman, never to be scourged.

(*BP*, 86–7)

In this most puzzling urban poem, the narrator positions himself ambiguously in relation to the city. On the one hand, he appears to occupy the privileged space of the distant spectator, scanning the urban landscape from the height of his own housetop. The "roofy desert" resembles the panoramic sweep of housetops represented in early prints of New York or Lippard's description of a "wilderness of stone and brick and mortar" or lithographs illustrating LeSage's *Diable Bôiteux* or Buchanan's *Asmodeus*, where curious devils lift the tops of houses to take spectatorial peeks. The fact that Melville probably was out of town during the Draft Riots increases the modern reader's sense that he distanced himself geographically – and indeed morally, politically, and socially – from the city's most cataclysmic nineteenth-century demonstration of urban upheaval and change.[2] His convincing adoption of the conservative tone, hailing "wise Draco" and the suppression of the "rats of the wharves," suggests that Melville turned his back on his 1850s sailor sympathies and Democratic politics.[3]

Along with the view of the distanced spectator, however, Melville also suggests that of the labyrinth prowler. For in his imagination the poem's narrator is able to descend into the city's hidden recesses, where angry rioters prepare themselves for insurrection; like the rebellious sailors of the Town-Ho, they live in "dense oppression, such / As tawny tigers feel in matted shades, / Vexing their blood and making apt for ravage." Sharing their sense of oppression, unable to sleep, suffering from the "Sultriness [that] pervades the air / And binds the brain," the narrator connects his own unease and tension, by a kinetic sympathy, with those of the classes hidden below. If he does not seem exactly one of them, he does not seem fully comfortable with the Republican position of his class, either.[4] In all that follows these opening lines, a labyrinthine tension undermines the spectatorial sentiments of the speaker.

But the narrator's pessimism is unmistakable and brings to mind another of Melville's urban prototypes, Cain's city, the City of Man. The housetop observer seems radically removed from a city where "man rebounds whole eons back in nature." Melville's note, referring at this line to a quotation from Froissart – "I dare not write the horrible and inconceivable atrocities committed" – draws attention to the savage fratricidal violence at the heart of the City of Man, as he did in *Israel Potter*. His invocation of Draco and Calvin is consistent with the view that Cain's city holds no place for the innocent sojourner seeking a home. It is all public space, where "civil charms" and "priestly spells" fight for supremacy over the "rats."

In his concluding lines, however, Melville upholds another idea of the city, an urban ideal that has been profoundly violated but may, at least within the imagination of a housetop observer, be recoverable, that of Nature's Rome.[5] The paradox in his equation between "Man" and "Nature's Roman" suggests the existence of a paradoxical Rome: not the historical evil empire, nor the Rome of American nativist fantasies, the whore of Babylon, but an ideal republic, a cosmopolis where "Man is naturally good." Although Melville's speaker states that the riots, and the draconian suppression of them, produce a "grimy slur on the Republic's faith" in man's natural goodness, the last lines assert that such a faith, and perhaps such a Rome, exist.

In itself, the poem exhibits masterfully the deep tensions between these conflicting models of urban order and the people who uphold them. As Robert Levine argues in relation to "Benito Cereno," Melville's narration is "nervous" – that is, it uses contending views to seduce readers into distancing themselves from ambiguity and thereby implicating themselves in a blind and foolish certainty: "Only when we contemplate our temptation, however short-lived, to experience with the captain both his fear of conspiracy and his pursuit of tranquility can we truly come to understand the seductiveness of captaincy and, I would suggest, our similar temptations toward analogous forms of captaincy in our own time."[6] Similarly, in "The House-Top" Melville seduces the reader with the temptation to accept the view of such analogous "captains" as Draco, Calvin, and cynic kings. The reproach of the final lines, however, throws the reader whole eons back to a republican faith that asserts a belief in natural goodness, not innate depravity. Within that benign faith, one does not see man as a rat, but as a citizen of a "redeemed" town.

In reproaching his own city, Melville upholds an ideal urban form that can contain its oppositional forces, where no one need be scourged. But a modern Rome, the cosmopolis that New York was becoming in the third quarter of the nineteenth century, could only with difficulty organize its expanding and diverse population, its contended spaces, and its political and social tensions into an order. When Melville returned to New York from his years at Arrowhead, he found a city that had burst its older constraints, that resembled no previous American city. Its only analogues, indeed, were the old world cosmopolises; but in size, complexity, and diversity, New York seemed to have outstripped such ancient counterparts as Athens, Rome, Babylon, and Jerusalem. Nevertheless, New York shared with the ancient cities two essential elements: a stratified urban form and the power of the urban sublime. Although Melville chose not to represent New York itself in his writings after 1856, his thoughts did turn to ancient cities, and in particular Jerusalem, whose complex structure and power to awe might satisfy the worldly cosmopolite and otherworldly pilgrim alike. His pilgrimage there in 1857 suggests the grip of the ancient city's urban form on his imagination.

Melville was certainly not alone in recognizing the significance of New York's burst of development following the Panic of 1857: for many, New York became, in Philip Fisher's phrase, "a synecdoche for America."[7] Yet during the period when New York was beginning to assume its modern size and character, when its population began to approach one million, when it played a major national role in the Civil War, when its worsening social problems worked to produce the literature of reform and urban realism, when it created the first and most influential political machine in America, and when Melville himself was drawn back into its orbit and chose to live there and work in the Custom House – during this critical, ambiguous period Melville elected not to represent New York in his writings ("The House-Top" excepted), although he had often done so before. Instead, his thoughts seemed to turn, first to the West and a vision of the New Jerusalem, in *The Confidence-Man* (1857), written just before he left for the Holy Land, and then to the East and a vision of Old Jerusalem, in *Clarel* (1876). Although these works are separated not only by time but also by format (one being a novel, the other a long poem), as well as by manifold differences of theme and subject matter, they are rooted in the period of Melville's visit to Jerusalem and record his hopes for and disappointments at seeing that great world city, his first cosmopolis. A close look at *The Confidence-Man* and *Clarel* together reveals how in both works characters seem to be moving, as in a pilgrimage, toward a structural and social ideal, a City of God, even if they doubt they can find it.

The changing urban structure of New York in these years helps to explain why Jerusalem might seem an apt analogy for the modern city; turning to Jerusalem meant reencountering New York. In the journal of his travels to the Holy Land in 1857, Melville wrote, "There are *strata* of cities buried under the present surface of Jerusalem" (90). The ancient city, with its layers of history, resembles a labyrinth, though, unlike the labyrinth of the Five Points, Jerusalem's extends throughout the entire city on a number of levels. New York, too, was becoming more stratified. Whereas in the 1840s, the middle-class pedestrian might experience the city on two planes – that of the street and that of the plunge into an urban underworld (perhaps three, by climbing a church tower) – by the time of his writing *The Confidence-Man*, one might begin to move fluidly and swiftly through the city on a variety of levels. In 1846 the elevator was invented, by 1853 elevators used steam power, and in 1857 Elisha Graves Otis devised automatic brakes.[8] Although at first elevators proved most useful for lifting freight, they quickly spread into hotels and stores; by 1868 the Fifth Avenue Hotel boasted a "perpendicular railway intersecting each story."[9] Skyscrapers did not begin to appear until the 1880s, but the construction of the Crystal Palace in 1851 in London showed the possibilities of building with metal frames and glass walls.[10] Meanwhile, the development of manufacturing in Manhattan, both before and after the Civil War, created a demand for multistoried, multifunctional buildings to house not only the warehouses and shops but also the immigrants who could not afford to live anywhere but near or in their places of work.[11] In the fashionable shopping districts, the creation of large department stores and arcades, with private facilities for dining, recreation, and toilette, tremendously expanded the uses of a single building, as well as the possible range of women's mobility around the city.[12] When Alexander T. Stewart opened the first department store in 1846, he announced the beginning of a new era, not just in commerce, but in the uses and levels of public space:

> The main entrance opens into a rotunda of oblong shape, extending the whole width of the building, and lighted by a dome seventy feet in circumference. The ceilings and sidewalls are painted in fresco, each panel representing some emblem of commerce. Immediately opposite the main entrance . . . , commences a flight of stairs which lead to a gallery running around the rotunda. This gallery is for the ladies to promenade upon.[13]

As the construction of new useable space was making the city more stratified, new kinds of travel changed and defined the urban inhabitant's experience of that space. The world of the urban novel, Fisher suggests,

> is composed of images of motion of which the most profound are not the horizontal motions of train rides, carriage excursions, trips to Europe and walks on either Broadway or the Bowery, but instead the tragic and vertical movements of rising and falling: the motion of the rocking chair. The wealth of motion in the novel insists that the society itself is, by means of its new streetcars, railway systems, steamships, carriages, and endless places to walk, most itself when in motion. (155)

Melville might have known as early as 1846, beginning with John Randel, Jr.'s idea for an omnibus pulled by a rope over a raised track, of the proposals for an elevated railroad.[14] An early elevated railroad traveled up to 30th Street in 1871, and by 1875, new lines extended along Sixth and Ninth Avenues.[15] Melville may have taken the Third Avenue El to work in the Custom House.[16] Underground travel remained a fantasy until the twentieth century because of Manhattan's rocky base, but proposals for subways proliferated throughout the period. In imagination, and indeed in fact, Manhattan was beginning to exist on a number of levels previously unforeseen.

The new railroad, omnibus, and ferry lines were designed to make human travel around the city to the suburbs, stores, and businesses, and the shipment of goods to and from the interior and abroad, a good deal simpler. The new multilevel buildings for housing, commerce, and business were designed to create more space for people and enterprises within the city. It would seem that such developments would restore the intimacy and accessibility of the old Walking City. Suburbs would not be isolated, and classes would mingle freely and democratically, as indeed Walt Whitman rejoiced to find them doing on the Brooklyn ferry and the tramlines. But travel in this stratified terrain turned out to be much more complex than the simple uniplanar movements of the urban spectator. Instead of the grid existing in one dimension, it now extended into two; the grid became vertical.[17] In its physical topography, New York now included many new levels for pedestrians to travel on, and they might also find themselves in vehicles moving swiftly over the surface, seeing vistas and crowds from a perspective denied the man or woman in the street. With the rapid northward development and suburbanization of the town, areas that had once seemed wasted and open now became settled and, in the eyes of older city dwellers, newly unfamiliar and strange.

As the city's physical topography changed, becoming more stratified, multifunctional, and diversified, so too did its social geography,[18] and this affected the urban traveler's sense of his or her ability to travel easily through the landscape. With population growth, the city became denser, but also that population included immigrants from new sources, particularly Ireland and Germany, but by the end of the century increasingly Eastern Europe and Russia. Ethnic differences translated into class barriers that threatened to become impassable. The older literary forms of the urban detective story or newspaper sketch had called upon certain social skills in reading the markers of race, nation, and class, but in the face of this more challenging and diverse population, many older, entrenched urban dwellers simply drew the lines of class around them more firmly. The urban novels of Edith Wharton and Henry James show the perplexity of upper- and middle-class families as they define their status ever more strictly and narrowly, often in the end isolating themselves more than they had intended. Stephen Crane's and Theodore Dreiser's characters struggle with those class barriers from the other side. It need hardly be said that these novels, coming at the end of the century, reflect a whole generation's growing up in the conditions they describe. Although the Draft Riots revealed the city's complex social tensions and rivalries, it nevertheless took some time before writers like William Dean Howells and his circle brought their sensibilities to bear on the city's changing social structure. An extensive popular culture, however – growing out of the theaters of the Bowery and other working-class districts; the literature of urban guides, like Junius Browne's *The Great Metropolis* (1869) or Matthew Hale Smith's *Sunshine and Shadow in New York* (1869); popular journalism, which began to introduce new forms like the Sunday comics; and juvenile literature by authors like Horatio Alger, who gave new meaning to the idea of travels throughout the city in the streets of boys – all tested the waters of a new social tide.[19] These, along with the penny dreadfuls, crime novels, and Westerns, gave a more immediate sense of the city's social dynamism and potential violence than anything written by more genteel authors in the period.[20] It is all the more remarkable, then, that Melville drew so richly from some of these sources for *The Confidence-Man.*[21]

Travelers in the New York of the second half of the century found themselves in a changing physical and social geography that required new maps and new map-reading skills. As "The House-Top" suggests, older ways of reading the city as capital, labyrinth, or wasteland could not make adequate sense of the proud cosmopolis. But new fields of knowledge and travel accounts of previously neglected sites offered new ways of reading the modern city. The developing science and practice of archaeology was bringing to light forgotten cities whose structures informed Victorian readers of civilizations now lost.[22] The emerging disciplines of higher criticism, comparative religion, and sacred geography spurred efforts to find evidence of the religious past among the bones of old cities.[23] Along with the discovery of an urban aesthetic, the sublimity of the ancient or modern city, these new sciences gave to urban architecture and structure an awe-inspiring significance. One could begin to think of a great modern city in the grand terms that invested the ancient cosmopolis – as a City of God.

Of course, the modern traveler and urban archaeologist know that New York is not, as ancient Jerusalem was to its many pilgrims, a City of God. Jerusalem can provide only an ironic analogy to the New World metropolis. Jerusalem is the repository of the ages, a marker of "deep time," such as New York could never be.[24] And yet, as New York developed northward, upward, and outward, as new buildings moved in to replace the old at a bewildering rate, as streets changed their appearance seemingly overnight, a New Yorker might search as patiently as an archaeologist to find evidence of the old neighborhoods – especially if, like Melville, he had been away from the city for a while. New York might not *be* a City of God, except perhaps to a deluded immigrant, but it did resemble one in its stratified complexity.

In its relation to a questing modern traveler, New York, the American cosmopolis, might resemble the City of God in a spiritual sense as well. If the City of Man is a place where only Cain feels at home, where the good man Abel is but a sojourner, the City of God is the place where Abel comes to rest. To be at home in the city, if one is not a wicked Cain, is to see the city as a destination, the desired end of one's urban travels. In both *The Confidence-Man* and *Clarel,* Melville presents characters who find a home in the great city. Some are at home because they are cosmopolitans, citizens of the world. The cosmopolis is *their* city. Others feel at home because they are pilgrims who have reached the end of their quest. Because they travel through a stratified city, they must move along a vertical as well as a horizontal axis, in a structure that opens up new vistas of the city's public space and creates new challenges in reading it. Physical, social, and sacred geography combine to give the urban pilgrim a sense of home – not a home away from the city, as the sanctified domestic space was, but a home within the city, among its streets and stones. In his struggle to make his way through the city and in his decision to remain there, the pilgrim enacts a journey into a City of God.

Urban Topography and the Sublime

In *The Confidence-Man* and *Clarel,* Melville presents urban forms that, either implictly or explicitly, recall the multilayered, multifunctional space of an ancient city like Jerusalem. The problem of form in such a city is acute for the modern traveler hoping to make his or her way through the landscape or to find a home. Unlike the capital, the labyrinth, or even the City of Man, Jerusalem gives the urban traveler little freedom to move. As envisioned in *The Confidence-Man,* which presents the modern city as a New Jerusalem confined within the walls of a riverboat, the urban landscape is stratified and constricted; and the Jerusalem of *Clarel* is intricately structured, noisy, and difficult to comprehend. For each of these models of urban space, Melville stresses complexity and difficulty. But because the urban traveler in these works is in some sense a pilgrim rather than a tourist, he persists in his quest until, in some flash of revelation, he sees his way through the city's forms. The struggle against the city's topography, then, is resolved not by the traveler's physically overcoming its obstacles but by his discovering that they are no longer significant. When he arrives at that point, when he experiences the urban sublime, he has reached the end of his pilgrimage.

Pilgrimages typically end in cities: Canterbury, Mecca, Celestial. The wilderness of significant mountains and valleys through which the Pilgrim makes his linear, determined Progress gives way finally to the shining city of the pilgrim's hopes. Melville's pilgrims, the Confidence Man and Clarel, however, travel in urban landscapes, and so their travels do not progress or end in the conventional way. Since the pilgrims are already in the city, they do not have to arrive in the physical sense. Both narratives end indeterminately, with characters moving off into the urban crowd. But psychologically they do arrive at something, if no more than a pained decision to stay where they are. A city may be said to be a City of God when an urban pilgrim decides that he or she is at home there. In *The Confidence-Man* and *Clarel,* characters who have been traveling through the city indicate at the end of the narrative that their travels have finished, their restlessness ceased.

That moment of arrival and rest occurs when the characters experience urban topography and form as inviting rather than repelling them. In a shift that often resembles the poet's experience of the sublime in nature, the pilgrim discovers and comes to rest in the urban sublime. As Richard

Sennett argues, this moment comes when the traveler feels at home in the city: "Augustine's book [*The City of God*] would lay the theological foundation for a city whose architecture and urban forms would give the restless spirit a home" (Sennett, 7). The urban configurations of Melville's Fidèle and Jerusalem, in their complexity and stratification, give shape to his characters' pilgrimages so that they can arrive at meaning. As in the Walking City, the Labyrinth, and Cain's City, urban form channels urban movements, creating and limiting the possibilities for vision. But in all these previous configurations, the pilgrim moves between binary forms. He goes out to the wilderness and returns to the capital; he leaves the provinces and enters the labyrinth; or he lives in the city but is not of it. The pilgrim in Melville's City of God, however, changes *himself*, at first he is not at home in the city, and then he is.[25] In Bunyan's model, the pilgrim has to overcome the landscape in order to reach the City of God; transcendence of terrain leads him to the Celestial City. Melville's pilgrims, on the other, submit to their terrain. It leads them into the "heart of proudest town" (*C*, 496), and there they stay.

The urban forms of *The Confidence-Man* and *Clarel* are very different and act upon the urban pilgrimage in different ways. The city in *The Confidence-Man* does have a physical form, the riverboat, but it is obscured by the crowd that courses through it, and the boat itself is also in motion. The city, then, has a fluid form, whereas *Clarel*'s Jerusalem is fixed, visible, palpable, and oppressive in its structure. Both these forms influence urban travel in distinct ways.

Urban form in *The Confidence-Man* partakes of the fluid medium through which the riverboat moves. The Mississippi River, however, is not an innocent natural element but itself a part of a fluid urban environment. The *Fidèle* moves through a landscape as ideologically significant as Saddle Meadows in *Pierre,* a landscape that gives an urban meaning to what seems natural.[26] In the unpublished fragment "The River," widely believed to be a discarded introduction to *The Confidence-Man,* Melville suggests that he perceived complex social meanings in the Mississippi River's "cosmopolitan and confident tide" (*CM*, 9). Rather than signifying to him a spirit of unity – "the dashing and all-fusing spirit of the West, whose type is the Mississippi itself, which, uniting the streams of the most distant and opposite zones, pours them along" (9) – in the fragment, the river originally embodied dissension and social mixture. Melville, it appears, picked up this image of mixture from his source, Timothy Flint's *The History and Geography of the Mississippi Valley,* but added to it the implications of social and racial tensions that make "The River" a disturbing characterization – too disturbing, it would seem, for his novel.

Timothy Flint's description of the Mississippi remains strictly within the confines of natural history and travel narrative. Hence, though it is "invested with . . . interest and grandeur," seems "the [noblest] river in the

world," and produces "a feeling of sublimity," Flint does not claim for
the river any more than its natural beauty and impressiveness (515).[27]
That which culminates Melville's fragment, the confluence of the Missouri
River with the Mississippi, appears in the middle of Flint's account as part
of the general description:

> [The entrance of the Missouri] perceptibly alters its depth, its mass of
> waters, and, what is to be regretted, wholly changes its character. It is
> no longer the gentle, placid stream, with smooth shores and clean sand-
> bars; but has a furious and boiling current, a turbid and dangerous mass
> of *sweep*ing waters, *jagged* and dilapidated *shores*, and, wherever its waters
> have receded, deposites of mud. It remains a sublime object of contem-
> plation. The noble *forest* still rises along its banks. But its character of
> calm magnificence, that so delighted the eye above, is seen no more.
> [Northwestern–Newberry special brackets; italics are added to show
> which words Melville appropriated for "The River."] (516–7)

The language suggests no more than the observer's disappointment in
losing for the moment a spectacle of beauty and delight.

In Melville's fragment, however, the contrast between the Mississippi at
its source and from the point of the Missouri's tributary flow becomes
charged with conflicting meanings. Although he begins by describing the
river in idyllic terms – "Wood and wave wed, man is remote. The Unsung
Time, the Golden Age of the billow" (497) – at the critical juncture with
the Missouri, the river's "majestic amenity" gives way to turbulent elements:

> But at St: Louis the course of this dream is run. Down on it like a
> Pawnee from ambush foams the yellow-... painted Missouri. The calm-
> ness is gone, the grouped isles disappear, the shores are jagged and rent,
> the hue of the water is clayed, the before moderate current is rapid &
> vexed. The ... peace ... of the Upper River seems broken in the Lower,
> nor is it ever renewed.
>
> The Missouri would seem ... rather ... a hostile element than a filial
> flood.... Longer, stronger than the father of waters like Jupiter he de-
> thrones his sire & reigns in his stead. Under the benign name Mississippi
> it is ... the Missouri that now rolls to the Gulf, the Missouri that with
> the Timon ... snows from his solitudes freezes the warmth of the genial
> zones, the Missouri that by open assault or artful sap sweeps away forest
> & feild [*sic*] grave-yard & town, the Missouri that not a tributary but an
> ... invader enters the sea, long disdaining to yeild [*sic*] his white wave
> to the blue. (497–9)

At the very least, we have here an image of oedipal usurpation, racial
insurrection, and treacherous Timonism to sully the pure harmony of the

Mississippi's waters. As Karcher has noted, any reference to St. Louis would remind readers of Missouri's tarnished history as a slave state, beginning with the Missouri Compromise (1820), the Compromise of 1850, and by implication the 1854 Kansas-Nebraska Acts that tried to settle the issue of extension of slavery into the territories. The Missouri River's clayey hue, then, and its "long disdaining to yeild [*sic*] his white wave to the blue" raises the issue of color and suggests the stubbornness of Southern slaveowners in their unwillingness to submit to the harmonizing wave of Northern unity. As we shall see, the racial overtones of the passage raise issues of urban politics as well.

The urban implications arise from reading "The River" in conjunction with Melville's other known source, James Hall's *Sketches of History, Life, and Manners, in the West* (*CM*, 501–10). This selection adds a new meaning to the Mississippi's mixed tides; for Hall's account, the basis of Melville's story of Colonel John Moredock the Indian-hater, tells of civilization on the frontier. Not only does it present a graphic picture of the races in violent conflict, the white settlers seeking to destroy the Indians, but it also, as does Crèvecoeur's rather similar description of the frontiersman, accounts for the behavior of those who live outside of cities. These people, Hall states, represent one of the few racially pure and socially homogeneous groups left in America. Because they always move in advance of the great urban "tide of emigration" (Griscom's phrase as well as Hall's), they lack the urban tolerance for racial and social mixing:

> The pioneers, who thus dwelt ever upon the borders of the Indian hunting grounds, forming a barrier between savage and civilized men, have received but few accessions to their numbers by emigration. The great tide of emigration, as it rolls forward, beats upon them and rolls them onward, without either swallowing them up in its mass, or mingling its elements with theirs. (503)

As a result they know little of any social or racial Other. Moredock's fierce hatred of Indians may be explained as a kind of frontier provincialism that keeps him from being swallowed up in the tide of emigration.

Hall's human tide moves as forcefully as the river does across the continent. Melville conflates the two, the river and emigration, when he calls the Mississippi and its travelers "one cosmopolitan and confident tide" (9). At the back of the tide of emigration into the West stand powerful political forces emanating from and tending to the city. Melville, though making his river seem an innocent part of a sublime natural spectacle, subtly implies these political forces at work in urbanizing the landscape.

The first, already referred to, has to do with the spread of slavery into the West. To the passage of the Kansas-Nebraska Acts in 1854, Northern abolitionists like Henry Ward Beecher and Horace Greeley responded by promoting the Emigrant Aid Society, an effort to raise money to send emigrants into Kansas and resist the proslavery settlements there. This movement encountered and also produced desperate violence, culminating in John Brown's massacre of the settlers at Pottowatomie Creek in 1856. This context suggests what the *Fidèle*'s emigrant quarters were used for, and why, "owing to the present trip being a down-river one, [the emigrants' quarters] will doubtless be found comparatively tenantless" (72). Emigrants into Kansas would most likely have traveled south on the Mississippi until St. Louis, where they would follow the Missouri and Kansas Rivers to Kansas City. South of St. Louis they would travel through slave states, a fact that suggests why the Missouri imparts a "hostile element rather than a filial flood" to the Mississippi.

The second source of emigrants that Melville refers to is the population of urban dreamers and speculators seeking to exploit the West: the "men of business and men of pleasure; parlor men and backwoodsmen; farm-hunters and fame-hunters; heiress-hunters, gold-hunters, buffalo-hunters, bee-hunters, happiness-hunters, truth-hunters, and still keener hunters after all these hunters" (9). These do not differ markedly from the urban crowd of New York described by the lawyer in "Bartleby": "I remembered the bright silks and sparkling faces I had seen that day, in gala trim, swan-like sailing down the Mississippi of Broadway" (28). Whether they are "Northern speculators," "Eastern philosophers," or "Broadway bucks in cravats of cloth of gold" (*C-M*, 9), these emigrants bring the "Wall street spirit" (40) to all their enterprises, even philanthropy.

They are also looking for the great city of the West, as Melville satirically indicates in the conversation between the collegian and the agent for the Black Rapids Coal Company. This city, like the Eden of Dickens's *Martin Chuzzlewit*,[28] exists as an ephemeral ideal of urban form. It is important for any notion of Melville's City of God, for besides the ironic name of the New Jerusalem, the city has a progressive urban plan, which the agent ostentatiously produces. In many ways the map seems typical of any number of such urban schemes: "There – there, you see are the public buildings – here the landing – there the park – yonder the botanic gardens – and this, this little dot here, is a perpetual fountain, you understand. You observe there are twenty asterisks. Those are for the lyceums. They have lignum-vitae rostrums" (50).

The references to parks, gardens, and lyceums recall the plans for Central Park that tried to civilize an urban populace through cultural institutions in a garden setting. But also the plan resembles many of the quadrangular forms of Western cities that aimed to avoid the labyrinthine character or monotonous sprawl of Eastern cities by imposing a simple yet elegant design.[29] Melville refers to two other Eastern cities, neither of which seems a good model of urban form. One is Boston, which is so complex that, like the Liverpool that Redburn encountered, it requires a map; Melville uses Boston as an image of what a "studious youth" might find if he rejects novels as a guide: "it ought to fare with him something as with a stranger entering, map in hand, Boston town; the streets may be very crooked, he may often pause; but, thanks to his true map, he does not hopelessly lose his way" (71). The other appears a page later in his description of the three-tiered bunks in the emigrants' quarters: "As with the nests in the geometrical towns of the associate penguin and pelican, these bunks were disposed with Philadelphian regularity" (72). Boston crookedness is opposed to Philadelphian regularity as two polarities to be avoided in the new cities of the West. These cities will be modeled, not on the City of Man but on the City of God.

At the heart of Western urban planning is the image of the New Jerusalem in Revelations 21 and 22. John's vision makes it clear how God will use the city to undo the damage of Babylon and any other cities founded by mortals.[30] Melville refers ironically to human efforts at founding cities at two points: once, when the agent for the Black Rapids Coal Company recalls that "the first settlement was by two fugitives, who had swum over naked from the opposite shore" (50), and again, when Pitch challenges the Cosmopolitan. "Remorse drives man away from man? How came your fellow-creature, Cain, after the first murder, to go and build the first city? And why is it that the modern Cain dreads nothing so much as solitary confinement?" (137). Both passages point to the inadequate efforts of humans to create a New Jerusalem on earth.

The third force behind the tide of urban emigration is that of reformers acting in the interests of children. Pitch meets a representative of the Philosophical Intelligence Office who claims to be able to offer him a good "boy" who will work on his farm. Pitch has already had thirty-five boys sent to him by "the Commissioners of Emigration, all the way from New York, culled out carefully, in fine, at my particular request, from a standing army of eight hundred boys, the flowers of all nations, so they wrote me, temporarily in barracks on an East River island" (117–18). Charles Loring Brace, author of *The Dangerous Classes of New York* (1872), founded the Children's Aid Society in 1853 to help the needy children of New York. In a campaign to remove children from the vicious influences of New York life, and probably more immediately their parents, the CAS began "placing out" boys and girls with farm families nearby. By 1854 children had been placed as far west as Michigan, Illinois, and Iowa.[31] Presumably Pitch has been part of this benevolent effort to improve the lives of urban youth.

Melville's narration of this episode, however, reveals the dark side of urban child-emigration policies. For one thing, it suggests the horrors of that "standing army of eight hundred boys" living in barracks, hoping or dreading to be among those selected for emigration. "The flowers of all nations" are in reality poor and orphaned immigrants, a sad throng:

"American, Irish, English, German, African, Mulatto; not to speak of that China boy sent me by one who well knew my perplexities, from California; and that Lascar boy from Bombay" (117). This is not an Anacharsis Cloots Congress but a pitiful mass of neglected children. And rather than offering them the loving family environment and "humanizing domestic associations" that New York reformers fondly hoped the emigrants would find, the bachelor Pitch has exploited their labor and abused them. A "Chesterfieldian" lad who has lost his mother seeks in Pitch a loving substitute but receives only cold puzzlement: Pitch accuses him of, "In the strangest way, too, combining a filial affection with a menial respect. Took such warm, singular interest in my affairs. Wanted to be considered one of the family – sort of adopted son of mine, I suppose" (118). But Pitch cannot extend himself to these victims of urban hardship.

The Mississippi, then, is a cosmopolitan tide but one polluted by its associations with cities and their problems. The *Fidèle* travels along a tainted river and through a contaminated landscape. Karcher has fully explored the racist connotations of St. Louis, Missouri, and Alton, Illinois, scenes of race riots and lynchings (193). Melville further makes it clear that cities like St. Louis, where Black Guinea has to sleep on the pavement and Charlemont the gentleman-madman meets his ruin, or Cairo, home of "the old established firm of Fever & Ague" (129), make life wretched for their inhabitants. The fact that the Confidence Man appears to come from these cities – John Truman, for example, has his office in St. Louis, the Cosmopolitan comes aboard at Cairo – makes him by definition suspect. But the Western city has its roots in Eastern urban wickedness. In the story of the soldier of fortune made to languish in the Tombs because he had no friends, Melville exposes the miseries of New York. A reference to a desolate road at one of the landings, "which, from its narrowness, and its being walled up with story on story of dusk, matted foliage, presented the vista of some cavernous old gorge in a city, like haunted Cock Lane in London" (85) calls up images of the dense European city. When the Cosmopolitan speaks of "our Fair" (131), he implies that the whole world is one allegorical fallen City – surely a City of Man, not the City of God.

The *Fidèle*, too, is a city, like Melville's other city-ships. In another common urban metaphor, the man with the wooden leg refers to a "flock of fools, under this captain of fools, in this ship of fools" (15). But in the way the ship brings together its motley crowd, provides a structure in which frequent encounters may occur, and makes possible certain kinds of spectacle, exchange, and creation of meaning and fiction, the *Fidèle* is a cosmopolis, a metropolis of marvels, as Redburn saw London. Especially once the Cosmopolitan enters, the *Fidèle* becomes a sealed vessel and an extraordinary, mysterious environment. No more stops take place, the ship moves into night, the narrative includes more and more stories, myths, and dreams, and the city begins to take on a spectral character. People move freely back and forth, but the ship begins to limit their movements more, as it is cut off from the land. The reader becomes aware that the vessel has moved away from the earthly city and toward an unearthly place, a City of Fiction that resembles the City of God: "It is with fiction as with religion: it should present another world, and yet one to which we feel the tie" (183). The New Jerusalem of the *Fidèle* becomes that other world – the Town where the author goes to find original characters.

In its structure, the New Jerusalem of *The Confidence-Man* has little in common with what Clarel will find in the Old. The vessel seems not nearly as stratified as Jerusalem is, not as fully mapped or as complex. Yet Melville meticulously details the ship's structure and the opportunities it offers for urban encounters. Clearly the ship's topography helps to define the movements and open up the experiences of the travelers.

The *Fidèle* has a main deck where most activity takes place, a number of balconies from which passengers can look down on the deck or the shore, and a vaguely hinted-at lower level where the emigrants sleep. Obviously it most resembles a stage, the logical structure for a "Masquerade," as Mark Winsome reminds us by quoting Shakespeare's "All the world's a stage." As both a stage and a vessel, the ship is all public space (Jerusalem as tourist attraction will be mostly public too) and so also resembles the most public areas of the city: the plaza, shops, and markets. Like the large modern city, it has gender-based separate spheres: a ladies' cabin, where charitable women read their Bibles, and a gentlemen's cabin, where men smoke, drink, and play cards. There is also a strategic arrangement of such space. The barber, for example, with his exclusively male clientele, is placed "under a smoking-saloon, and over against a bar-room" (5). The captain's office, two doors down, receives crowds of passengers looking for tickets. Private encounters must take place where they can in this public space: in a "side balcony astern" (18) where the man with the weed approaches Mr. Roberts, in a corner (77) where the invalid seeks refuge, or "at the foot of the stairs leaning against the baluster" (106), where Pitch challenges the miser.

Other areas of the ship develop significance according to how the characters use them. The disabled characters, for example – Black Guinea, the man with the wooden leg, the soldier of fortune on crutches – seem to gravitate to the forward part of the vessel. The business-related meetings between the man with the weed and Mr. Roberts, the man with the weed and the collegian, and the collegian and the agent from the Black Rapids Coal Company take place in the after part of the ship. The herb-doctor does much of his work indoors, in the emigrants' quarters and in an antecabin, where male and female passengers mingle. The Cosmopolitan meets Charlie Noble in "the semicircular porch of a cabin, opening a recess from the deck, lit by a zoned lamp swung overhead, and sending its light vertically down, like the sun at noon" (139). They move from this somewhat unreal space to "a settee near by, on deck" (141), and then to a table outside of the bar, where the Cosmopolitan remains for much of the remainder of the novel. At the end he enters the barbershop and finally the gentleman's cabin, where he stays until the light goes out, when he leads the old man into the dark. Their destination, the man's stateroom, is the only semiprivate space mentioned, and even that is dangerously public, for the old man realizes he needs to lock the door.

Although the ship seems to have a simple, literally aboveboard structure, it is not easy to map. The space and uses of space are complex, not in the way that Jerusalem is, with many layers of space and time, but in the intricacy of the vessel and the movements of the crowd, which change the character of public space at any time. Melville makes this complexity clear from the beginning when he remarks that, although "the Fidèle . . . might at distance have been taken by strangers for some whitewashed fort on a floating isle" (8), that appearance of bare simplicity is an illusion. (Similarly, when Clarel approaches Jerusalem, he sees an austere exterior, "Like the ice-bastions round the Pole, / Thy blank, blank towers, Jerusalem!" (5) that belies its busy, lively interior.) Inside the ship the traveler finds a structure wondrously complicated: "Fine promenades, domed saloons, long galleries, sunny balconies, confidential passages, bridal chambers, state-rooms plenty as pigeon-holes, and out-of-the-way retreats like secret drawers in an escritoire, present like facilities for publicity or privacy" (8). This statement makes it clear that although the vessel provides the open space that a stage does, it also allows for the more intimate and devious activities found in a great city.

The most apt urban analogy, then, is not so much the stage as the arcade, that Parisian phenomenon that found its way from the Old World to New York.[32] Melville describes the ship's space "[a]s if the long, wide, covered deck, hereabouts built up on both sides with shop-like windowed spaces, were some Constantinople arcade or bazaar, where more than one trade is plied" (5). The Constantinople bazaar, of course, is an ancient market, the arcade, a modern technological achievement growing out of urban capitalism, but both offer the same dense, exciting, multifunctional structure in which the urban traveler may wander and never tire of its variety. When the Cosmopolitan calls this scene "our Fair" (131), he draws attention to the festival spirit of the market, as well as the more dour moral light in which Bunyan saw Vanity Fair. The arcade is a suitable structure for this holiday crowd.

The crowd itself, just as in Poe's and Baudelaire's urban poetics, plays an important part in making the ship a complicated structure. Although the Mississippi River seems to fuse the "pilgrim species" into a united stream, the human tide is diverse and strange: "though always full of strangers, she [the vessel] continually, in some degree, adds to, or replaces them with strangers still more strange" (8). Like the crowds of New York or Jerusalem, the crowds of the ferry contain many foreign faces, "[n]atives of all sorts, and foreigners" (9). Although Melville celebrates these "varieties of visage and garb" (9), particularly as they reach their apotheosis in the Cosmopolitan, he also shows the crowd, especially in the early appearances of the deaf-mute and Black Guinea, as suspicious and heartless. The crowd has an undeniable influence on individuals, and its movements sweep through the vessel, bending the steps of any passenger, except perhaps a pilgrim like the deaf-mute, "evenly pursuing the path of duty, lead it through solitudes or cities" (3).

Redburn, Pierre, Bartleby, even the narrator of "Temple Second," who finds himself drifting "amid those indescribable crowds" of London where "the unscrupulous human whirlpools eddied me aside at corners" (310), pay little sustained attention to urban crowds. In *The Confidence-Man*, Melville makes them part of a dense urban environment that can, as with Lydia Maria Child's visitor from New Zealand, "Shove me about" (129). It is not only urban topography that makes a traveler aware he is in a city, but the large, unpredictable, and potentially violent crowd. When it is there on the *Fidèle*'s decks, the space is public; when it recedes, the same space becomes private. The ship can serve a variety of functions, can provide the open yet covered and organized arcade where more than one trade is plied, but it is the crowd that determines how that space will be used and enjoyed.

As urban form, the *Fidèle* provides a stage where one can "take a part, assume a character" (133), a covered bazaar where one may choose among tempting offerings, a place for mingling and conviviality, business and pleasure. In some ways, however, it is the barest of sets. Pilgrims bring their meaning to it and, like the Protean easy chair, it is never the same: a "Rio Janeiro fountain, fed from the Corcovado mountains, which is ever overflowing with strange waters, but never with the same strange particles in every part" (8). It can be a City of Man, or, as we shall see when the Cosmopolitan becomes a pilgrim, it can suggest a City of God. Its structure adapts itself to a number of purposes, but these are defined and exploited by the crowd. The Jerusalem of *Clarel*, however, has a structure and meaning fixed by history, text, faith, and its own streets, walls, buildings, and stones. It partakes of the sublime and holds significant meaning for its pilgrims and cosmopolitans. But, like the vessel, it provides opportunity for urban acts and encounters of an astonishingly rich variety; and like the *Fidèle* it provides a shocking experience of the strange. It can be an earthly city and then, in a sudden shift, a City of God.

In this sense, Melville differs widely from his contemporary Charles Dickens, in whose fiction the City of Man exists as a realm distinct from a City of God, however nebulously defined.[33] The characters of *The*

Confidence-Man and *Clarel* travel in cities that contain multitudes, are City of Man and City of God at once. The pilgrim seeks the City of God *within* the City of Man; he does not hope to sojourn beyond it. In part Melville achieves this new sense of the city by importing to it the sublime. The pilgrim's journey into cosmopolis is not linear travel from the City of Man to the City of God, but a complete dislocation in experience, similar to what the Romantics meant by the Sublime in Nature. Jerusalem is not a cosmopolis by virtue of its size and diversity but because it has the power to awe, to produce this dislocation that makes room for an experience of the sublime.

Clarel brings to a head the Romantic discovery that the " 'natural' sublime"[34] could have no place in an urbanized world. Wordsworth might write, "This did I feel in London's vast Domain: / The Spirit of Nature was upon me there."[35] But in reality, during just the period when the Romantics were celebrating nature's sublime power, urban growth had already domesticated nature.[36] The problem was particularly acute in America, where a national identity based on wildness was threatened and confused by one based on rapid growth and urbanization.[37] In the first half of the century, however, many writers clung to their faith in the power of nature to produce an awe that could restore a sense of deity immanent in the world.

The breakdown of this faith in nature appears graphically in the transition from the sublime force of nature in *Moby-Dick* to its urban relocation in *Pierre*. *Moby-Dick* builds its tension on a confrontation between man and the natural sublime. The whale terrifies because it is at once remote and vast, like Shelley's Mont Blanc, yet noble and inspiring, like Wordsworth's countryside, and then daemonic and omnipotent, like Coleridge's ocean. The novel explores the whole range of human encounters with nature, and although, in the end, the investigation fails to find God in the tempest and the blast, and Melville claims to have written a blasphemous book, nevertheless we hear a still, small voice.[38] The coffin–life buoy emerges from the vortex, Ishmael sails on amid a peaceful universe – "The unharming sharks, they glided by as if with padlocks on their mouths; the savage sea-hawks sailed with sheathed beaks" (573) – and the maternal *Rachel* appears to rescue the storyteller. Most important of all, the sublime exists indubitably in nature. Ishmael must escape the city to find it, and nature satisfies his longing for the rehabilitative experience of radical dislocation.

In *Pierre*, however, two changes occur. First, as we have seen, the sublime shifts from nature to the city itself. Pierre's Berkshire mountains and Memnon stone elide into the stones of Broadway and the Tombs. Nature's terrors become replicated in the city's vastness, darkness, and roar, its confusion and unbearable contrasts, its suggestion of god or demon, father or Minotaur, at the center of the labyrinth. But second, that experience of sublimity brings no promise of transcendence. The deity is not there, the human spirit is deflated rather than expanded, and Pierre, rather than struggling to transcendent heights, crashes into an abyss.

Of course, the abyss itself is an image of the sublime,[39] and *Pierre* offers a graphic sense of how the sublime may be embodied in the city. By deliberately seeking infernal depth rather than celestial height, by moving from a higher world to an underworld, Pierre and other provincials find in the city an intensity of experience that nature, once wild and mythical as in *Moby-Dick*, can no longer provide. Although the physical context of the sublime has changed, its psychological elements – terror, alienation, loss of ego – have not, and given the domestication of nature, it may acquire a new emotional charge.

This urbanization of the sublime seems, indeed, a natural development from its intellectual roots. Thomas Weiskel traces the history of the sublime as "a history of anxiety" generated in the eighteenth century by Addison and Burke as "an antidote to . . . boredom":

> Burke began his treatise by laying down a premise that the passions are never engaged by the familiar. Boredom masks uneasiness, and intense boredom exhibits the signs of the most basic of modern anxieties, the anxiety of nothingness, or absence. In its more energetic renditions the sublime is a kind of homeopathic therapy, a cure of uneasiness by means of the stronger, more concentrated – but momentary – anxiety involved in astonishment and terror. (18)

The sublime, like modern horror films, is urban society's answer to urban anxiety, and it seems paradoxical at first that it would be located in nature. Yet nature is that which is least familiar to city dwellers – until, that is, the city acquires terrors of its own. *Pierre* and other urban novels, by presenting the city as seen by provincial eyes, exaggerate its terrors. The city so familiar to the urban spectator takes on a sublime aspect to the provincial that provides for urban readers a dislocation in sensibility – without their having to leave town.

In *The Confidence-Man*, however, there is no urban location for the sublime. Beneath the veneer of ordinary life, life as it is lived on the streets, in hotels and shops and coffeehouses, lurks the disorienting anxiety of urban life; and sometimes it erupts, especially when the Cosmopolitan puts his finger on a touchy spot in Pitch or Charlie, or when he tells a tale of violence or ruin. But the city contains its disturbances within a space that spreads them thinly over a horizontal plane. The sublime, if it does exist in *The Confidence-Man*, has become, not a concentrated, therapeutic experience of terror, but rather a diffused one that holds men and women in perpetual confusion and uncertainty.

It is from this generalized sense of the sublime, from this diffused and

therefore ineffectual terror, that *Clarel* attempts to extricate its urban characters. In turning to the ancient city, Melville suggests that some rehabil-
itation of the sublime, some new relation of humankind with terror and
mystery must exist in order for their pilgrimage through life to have any
meaning at all. Rather than locating his investigation in the modern city,
he moves to the ancient world, where for millennia people have pondered
the question of transcendence within the context of the city. Did Christ
walk the streets of Jerusalem or not? The answer lies in the city's very
topography, in its stones, which Melville shows both to resist and to contain meaning.

Stones themselves and stones as evidence of ancient fallen cities have
often appeared before in Melville's work. Bartleby gazes out over the
bricks and mortar of New York like Marius brooding over the ruins of
Carthage, and the lawyer compares him to "the last column of some ruined temple" (33). The Encantadas are a wilderness of stones and clinkers
that calls up images of Sodom, Gomorrah, Babylon, Rome, and London
as well. However, for Melville and his culture, the most compelling images
of the urban sublime cluster around the sublime monuments of Egypt.
Long before he visited Egypt himself, Melville's imagination turned to it
again and again. The Pyramids, like Jerusalem, seem to give sublime evidence of human contact with myth, if not deity, and of human attempts
to shape nature in that deity's image.

From his literary beginnings, Melville seems transfixed by images of
Egyptian stone. As early as *Typee*, the narrator encounters some "Remarkable Monumental Remains" hidden in the valley that remind him of "the
mighty base of the Pyramid of Cheops" (155). Tommo is particularly
impressed that the monument lacks a text, the hieroglyphs that might
offer an insight into its meaning: "There are no inscriptions, no sculpture,
no clue, by which to conjecture its history: nothing but the dumb stones"
(155). That very dumbness arrests the loquacious traveler in his tracks,
imposing a sublime silence.

Whereas Tommo's Pyramid of Cheops appears as a Romantic ruin overgrown with mystery and vines, the Egyptian monuments of *Redburn, Pierre,*
and *Israel Potter* seem less connected with natural or divine origins. In the
city, monuments exist as earthly monitory symbols, reminding urban
dwellers of a shameful and bloody past. Hence the Nelson monument in
Redburn's Liverpool suggests the slave trade that has contributed not to
the city's glory but to its disgrace. The Tombs where Pierre and Bartleby
die is a monument to human wickedness. Nevertheless, even urban monuments have a certain sublimity. We have seen in *Redburn* "the extent and
solidity . . . [of the docks which] seemed equal to what I had read of the
Old Pyramids of Egypt" (161) and in "Bartleby" the compelling "Egyptian character of the masonry" (44). Monuments provide visible remind-

ers of human aspirations toward the sublime, even when they have degenerated since their construction.

Stones, in nature or in the city, imply the ambiguous relation between man and his materials. In "I and My Chimney" the narrator declares that "the architect of the chimney must have had the pyramid of Cheops before him" (355), implying the architect's power to fashion dumb stones; yet the chimney has a power of its own that resists human efforts to alter it. The stones of the Encantadas suggest nature's stony grandeur, but also its sterility, which admits no human influence or power. Whether Melville describes stones as mysteries of nature, like the Memnon Stone or Mount Greylock; as cenotaphs like the monuments to Nelson, Wellington, or the patriots of Bunker Hill; as ruined columns like Bartleby or vast memorials like the Pyramids; as crude weapons like the cobblestone boulder with which Cain slew Abel, or the barren rubble of the Encantadas and Jerusalem, he continually plays upon the idea of stones as the junction of nature and art. At times, the sterility of the rocks implies that no art may shape or soften them. At others, he suggests that simply by piling a few stones on top of one another, as Vine does in *Clarel,* humans exhibit a primal drive to create the monuments, temples, tombs, streets, towers, and cities to which that simple act gives rise.

Melville's poem "The Great Pyramid" plays on this paradoxical coming together of nature and man, with or without the intervention of deity: "Your masonry – and is it man's? / More like some Cosmic artisan's," he begins (254–5). The Pyramids seem to be some supranatural creation that disdains all human and natural materials: "Shall lichen in your crevice fit? / Nay, sterile all and granite-knit." Built from nature's materials, they nevertheless majestically ignore the elements: "You – turn the cheek." But after asserting the Pyramids' supremacy over weather and time, Melville ends the poem by reasserting the godlike power of the men who built them.

> Craftsmen, in dateless quarries dim,
> Stones formless into form did trim,
> Usurped on Nature's self with Art,
> And bade this dumb I AM to start,
>   Imposing him.

The Pyramids appear to be monuments to some constructive force in humans that taps into a divine will. The artist has created something with nature's power to awe yet with an art that stands in opposition to nature. In much the same way, the human imposition of form on the ancient stones of Jerusalem suggests an intersection between human beings and "this dumb I AM" that produces sublime form.

Melville's preoccupation with the Pyramids and the ancient city did not occur in a cultural vacuum. The discovery, or rediscovery, of Egyptian and Holy Land ruins brought to nineteenth-century urban culture a heightened awareness of monuments. The obsession with Egypt brought the ancient sublime home to the modern city. A late-nineteenth-century book of illustrations of New York boasts of the Tombs Prison that "This building, which was finished in 1838, was probably the finest piece of Egyptian architecture in the country, and the finest specimen of Egyptian architecture outside Egypt."[40] The obelisks that Melville mentions in *Redburn* ("hermit obelisks of Luxor," 162) derived from Pompey's Pillar, Cleopatra's Needles, and other Egyptian monuments widely reproduced in popular engravings and in the Bunker Hill and Washington Monuments (begun in 1825 and 1848). E. D. Clarke's *Travels in Various Countries of Europe, Asia and Africa* (1818), Belzoni's *Travels in Egypt* (1820), and Champollion's work on the hieroglyphs in 1821 engendered an enthusiasm for Egyptian architecture that was reflected in English and American cityscapes.[41] Critics admired the "obelisks and pyramids of the factory chimneys" in England and promoted the vogue for vast, impressive architecture.[42] The Victorian concept of the urban sublime grew in part out of a longing for Egyptian impressiveness and an attempt to define contemporary culture in similarly vast and dignified terms. This longing created, as Nicholas Taylor has argued, a new urban aesthetic, with new associations for the sublime:

> [T]he Sublime was functionally the aesthetic of just those vast new purposes which upset the proportions of Beauty and the prettiness of Picturesque: warehouses, factories, viaducts, gas-works, lunatic asylums, country gaols, railway termini, dark tunnels. Furthermore, it became emotionally the aesthetic of those vast new passions which upset no less the nicely proportioned and the pretty: the haranguing of the Evangelical preacher; the ecstasy of the Anglo-Catholic Mass; the scientific wonder of panoramas and exhibition halls; the traveller's thrill in catching trains and climbing mountains; the capitalist's pride in the hum of mass production and the hubbub of the market.[43]

A culture changing so fast that it could scarcely recognize itself sought stability and reassurance in monuments and urban forms that suggested an ancient past, and, more importantly, one invested with divinity.

Egypt had not only its stone monuments to offer but also its texts, the hieroglyphs found on pyramid walls and on the Rosetta Stone that Napoleon brought back to Europe and Champollion deciphered.[44] The idea that stones might bear messages, that they might not be dumb but rather speaking stones, bringing sermons from the past, proved tremendously exciting. It suggested that even the ugly modern city might provide future they lie to this day" (90). But, in *Clarel*, Melville made the "Stony tropolis of stones" an image of the urban sublime. Jerusalem strikes young Clarel, on his first view of it, as a chilling sight, "like the ice-bastion round the Pole, / Thy blank, blank towers, Jerusalem!" (5). Melville's Lima in *Moby-Dick* suggests just such a sublime terror, in the whiteness that "spreads over her broken ramparts the rigid pallor of an apoplexy that fixes its own distortions" (193). Similarly, the Jerusalem of *Clarel* appears forbidding, a creation not quite of nature nor of the chisel, yet, like Lima, a fortress against human investigation.

From the beginning of *Clarel*, Melville stresses that Jerusalem, built from stones, retains the sublime elements of nature. In fact, as in the poem stones make their first appearance in the city, appearing only later in the desert, the same implications of barrenness, ruin, and monumental sublimity inhabit both the streets and the sands. The opening lines of the poem image urban stones as crushing masonry:

In chamber low and scored by time,
Masonry old, late washed with lime –
Much like a tomb new-cut in stone;
Elbow on knees, and brow sustained
All motionless on sidelong hand,
A student sits, and broods alone. (3)

Clarel begins in a contracted space like the Tombs where Pierre and Bartleby die, like the lime-washed cellar where Redburn witnesses death by starvation, like Israel Potter's chimney tomb. Yet Clarel never loses his sense of nature's living presence within or beneath the city's masonry: "The mountain-town, . . . / Saddles and turrets the ascent – / Tower which rides the elephant" (6). The city seems to grow almost organically out of the stony hills. Instead of the busy hubbub of human town life, Clarel sees from his rooftop the depth of nature's solitudes. The houses appear in organic unity with the mountains around them, "Base to stone structures seeming one / E'en with the steeps they stand upon" (7). Built with "walls of nature's sort" (7), the houses partake of nature's silence and solitude.

Stones contain even further meaning as they reveal themselves in the city's shapes and forms. The "*strata* of cities buried under the present surface of Jerusalem" give evidence of the abysses of time: "Forty feet deep lie fragments of columns &c" (*Journal*, 90). The city is a physical maze; but more than that it is a labyrinth of history, a place defined by strata of events and faiths, so that what was once a natural landscape of desert, woods, and hills becomes a complex structure and record of history. Nowhere is this urban development more clearly explained than in

travelers with mysterious clues, just as Belzoni, Layard, and Burkha:
found clues in the ancient cities. It suggested, by analogy, that stor
themselves spoke a kind of language, that the city's very structure a
architecture might speak volumes to an attentive rover-reader. Chester
recognized urban hieroglyphs as speaking a new poetry of the city:

> [F]or while nature is a chaos of unconscious forces, a city is a chaos c
> conscious ones. . . . But there is no stone in the street and no brick i
> the wall that is not actually a deliberate symbol – a message from som
> man, as much as if it were a telegram or a post card. The narrowe
> street possesses, in every crook and twist of its intention, the soul of th
> man who built it, perhaps long in his grave. Every brick has as huma
> a hieroglyph as if it were a graven brick of Babylon.

Chesterton saw the necessity for human intervention in nature in c
to make its "chaos of unconscious forces" conscious. The city could
body nature's sublimity in a new, technologically defined form. For
terton, as for the discoverers of the Holy Lands, "artifacts may now as
the value that was once supposed to inhere in the natural world a
and by finding beauty [or sublimity] in the constructions of mar
writer affirms a new kind of democratic humanism."[45]

Whether Melville shared this ideal of democratic humanism or n
pilgrims to Jerusalem, seeking to know the mysteries implied in the
stones, find a kind of democratic fraternity, both among themselve
with the past, that compensates them for the problems of decipheri
Clarel the city appears as a whole set of hieroglyphs for the modern st
to ponder and to find, in all likelihood, as inscrutable and subli
nature. Jerusalem, more than any other city in the world, provid
most – though also the most mysterious – monuments and texts f
traveler to read. Its very stones are hieroglyphs, physical embodime
the Judeo-Christian world of one great text. Reading this text and
ing through the city promises one of the few experiences of transcer
in the modern world.

The topography of Jerusalem, then, suggests the sublimity of
and the sublimity of divine texts. Yet it is built from stones that s
admit of little human or natural life. In his journal, Melville re
feeling depressed, rather than uplifted, by the sight of the "Stc
Judea": "Stony mountains & stony plains; stony torrents & stony
stony walls & stony feilds [sic], stony houses & stony tombs; stony
stony hearts" (90). It all looked to Melville too much like an urb
struction project gone wrong: "My theory is that long ago, some wh
King of the country took it into his head to pave all Judea, and
into contracts to that effect; but the contractor becoming bankru
way in his business, the stones were only dumped on the ground,

the canto "Via Crucis" at the end of the poem, when Clarel has his vision of cross-bearing humanity:

> Some leading thoroughfares of man
> In wood-path, track, or trail began;
> Though threading heart of proudest town,
> They follow in controlling grade
> A hint or dictate, nature's own,
> By man, as by the brute, obeyed.
>
>   Within Jerusalem a lane,
> Narrow, nor less an artery main
> (Though little knoweth it of din),
> In part suggests such origin.
> The restoration or repair,
> Successive through long ages there,
> Of city upon city tumbled,
> Might scarce divert that thoroughfare,
> Whose hill abideth yet unhumbled
> Above the valley-side it meets.
> Pronounce its name, this natural street's:
> The *Via Crucis* – even the way
> Tradition claims to be the one
> Trod on that Friday far away
> By Him our pure exemplar shown.
>
>   (496–7)

As at other important moments in the poem, Clarel viewing Jerusalem from a distance notices its connection with and growth from nature. The street begins, like the path leading from one of Hawthorne's forests, as a trail following the natural shape of the hill. Gradually the city forms around it, following nature's dictates even as city upon city tumbles on top of it. This perception of the city's powerful natural origins seems peculiarly characteristic of Melville. Few other nineteenth-century writers about the city, I think, would venture the oxymoron "natural street," – similar to that of "Nature's Roman" in "The House-Top" – or suggest the organic power of nature over man and brute within the "heart of proudest town." Yet this sense of an organic heart in the metropolis harks back to Melville's own Wordsworthian sense of nature residing in the very stones and ancient pathways of the city. This heart orients the labyrinth built around it, suggesting deep and natural roots beneath the strata of buildings and monuments.

The best example of labyrinthine structure overarching natural places is the Church of the Holy Sepulcher, where the ancient "caves and a crag" have given way over time to an enormous, gaudy temple:

To sum in comprehensive bounds
The Passion's drama with its grounds,
Immense the temple winds and strays
Finding each storied precinct out –
Absorbs the sites all roundabout –
Omnivorous, and a world of maze.

(12)

The temple has devoured nature, creating a new world to replace it, a "world of maze." Yet so long has the temple endured that it paradoxically seems natural. Tradition sanctions it, and although the pilgrim no longer sees the earth and sky, the temple's roof reminds him of the solemnity of the past. Over time the temple has become a sort of Holy Arcade:

And yet time was when all here stood
Separate, and from rood to rood,
Chapel to shrine, or tent to tent,
Unsheltered still the pilgrim went
Where now enroofed the whole coheres –
Where now thro' influence of years
And spells by many a legend lent,
A sort of nature reappears – .

(12)

The sense of a natural landscape within, behind, or beneath the temple gives it mystery, makes of the monument a place as hushed and sublime as the forest. In the monument, itself a structure and accretion of time and history, time seems to stand still and nature to regain its ascendancy over the soul.[46]

History and tradition keep the temple alive and renew nature within the urban labyrinth. For the monks and pilgrims, the monument serves to perpetuate Christ's story. History revives, rather than petrifying, the past:

... 'tis here
They scourged Him; soldiers yonder nailed
The Victim to the tree; in jeer
There stood the Jews; there Mary paled;
The vesture was divided here.
    A miracle-play of haunted stone –

(14)

That miracle play caught in stone still has the power to awe even the doubter. For not only the Christ story but also the succeeding centuries of pilgrim believers have sanctified the spot: "to think what numbers here, / Age after age, have worn the stones / In suppliance or judgment fear" (14). The generations of penitents have added their own histories to the monument, their tears and moans helping to build the temple's walls. "[S]uch ties, so deep,/ Endear the spot, or false or true / As an historic site" (14). Sacred history marks not simply the site of a miraculous event, as sacred geography does, but also the eons of devotion that have enriched the tradition, built a history labyrinth amid the temple labyrinth's stones.[47]

The sense of a historical structure rising from a natural one extends throughout the city at large, and Clarel is always aware that he is wandering through a labyrinth both of streets and of time. As he walks through the town, Clarel thinks of the river Kedron winding its way below the streets:

> Beneath the toppled ruins old
> In series from Moriah rolled
> Slips Kedron furtive? underground
> Peasants avouch they hear the sound
> . . . Far and deep
> What ducts and chambered wells and walls
> And many deep substructions be.
>
> (50)

The idea of "deep substructions," of cities beneath cities, suggests to the urban rover new possibilities for the detective mind; he may become an archaeological Vidocq, an explorer of urban depths not only psychological and social but also historical and structural.

> Under such scenes abysses be –
> Dark quarries where few care to pry,
> Whence came those many cities high –
> Great capitals successive reared,
> And which successive disappeared
> On this same site.
>
> (50-1)

Like Marius contemplating the ruins of Carthage, Clarel has a glimpse of the city's terrifying past. Only in the ancient city, he discovers and Chesterton was later to observe, can one read and traverse the past through the city's stones. Only there can the traveler connect himself both with nature and with history through the visible structures of the city.

As if aware of history tossing up structures all around them, *Clarel's* pilgrims spend considerable time ascending to heights and descending to abysses. Their movements through the city open up to them spaces, like those in New York, not hitherto known or seen. From Mount Olivet, Rolfe, Vine, Nehemiah, and Clarel gaze down over the city, viewing it in all its glory and misery as Christ might have observed it. " 'And here,' he [Rolfe] said, 'here did He sit – / In leafy covert, say – *Beheld / The city, and wept over it*' " (105). At this moment, to Rolfe, Jerusalem is a City of Man, a Tartarus of clinkers. Similarly, when Clarel visits the city's depths, he becomes aware of human evils he could not see from the safe middle ground of the tourist. The "By-Places" where Nehemiah takes Clarel may not resemble the Sodom-like dens that Redburn visited, but they have their own strangeness and mystery. The "Dismantled, torn, / Disastrous houses" seem quite abandoned, "and like plundered tombs appear" (70). The deserted streets hint of some lurking dread:

> – A waste
> Shut in by towers so hushed, so blind,
> So tenantless and left forlorn
> As seemed – an ill surmise was born
> Of something prowling there behind.
> (71)

The same towers that afford spectators like Vine, Rolfe, and Clarel a breathtaking view of urban life also oppress even the saintly Nehemiah with despair. At moments like these, Clarel enters the City of Man in Jerusalem.

But Jerusalem can also become, for the questing pilgrim, a City of God. Its physical structure, its heights and depths, its open spaces and dense mazes, its mountains and towers, temples and streets, tombs and rooms, high walls and low valleys, give Clarel an ample field for roving and intimations of transcendence at many times. Looking up toward Olivet on a hot night, Clarel sees it as sublimely distant and still: "Distinct, yet dreamy in repose, / As of Katahdin in hot noon, / Lonely, with all his pines in swoon" (11). The scene appears purely natural. Yet in an instant Clarel apprehends more:

> The nature and evangel clashed,
> Rather, a double mystery flashed.
> Olivet, Olivet do I see?
> The ideal upland, trod by *Thee?*
> (11)

At any moment, anywhere in the city, place becomes text, and the possibility of transcendent meaning gives that place a "double mystery." This suggestion of transcendence makes the city a City of God. And although many characters in the poem doubt that the transcendence exists, they still acknowledge and share this double vision, the constant sense that forms, at one moment dumb and material, at the next flash with a new meaning. Because the city so consistently provides this dislocating experience, it functions as the sublime in nature can; and because the experience is one of wonder aroused by the urban sublime rather than one of faith engendered by evidence of a divine presence, even those wavering in faith like Clarel and Rolfe may experience the therapeutic value of the sublime. The city replaces nature and God as the possible source of meaning, while yet drawing its sublime power from nature (through its stones) and from God (through texts and history). Paradoxically, the city that has separated humans from their natural and divine beginnings may take them back to them because its structure tells the story of where they came from. A pilgrimage through the city will reconnect them with these sources.

Cosmopolitans and Pilgrims

Urban form in the cosmopolis can change in an instant, so that what at one moment appears as the material, unyielding topography of the City of Man reveals, in a sudden moment of transcendence, its spiritual identity as a City of God. The urban traveler, too, can change, and in *The Confidence-Man* and *Clarel* does change. Both the Cosmopolitan and Clarel choose, at significant junctures, to turn away from the cosmopolitan point of view and assume the humbler position of the pilgrim among the urban throng. This choice, Melville implies, offers the city's truest satisfactions to the modern seeker.

Clarel, like the protagonist of "Poor Man's Pudding and Rich Man's Crumbs," has come to the city to roam and see. When the pilgrim Nehemiah asks him if he too is a pilgrim, Clarel replies, "I am a traveler – no more" (30). But although Clarel calls himself only a traveler – by which he means something like a spectator – he actually oscillates between two, not necessarily opposed, types of traveler – the pilgrim, who travels below and within the city, and the cosmopolitan, who remains above it, an aloof citizen of the world. Clarel has embarked on a pilgrimage, a search for faith in the Holy Land, and so considers himself a pilgrim. He is tempted, however, by cosmopolitanism, enough so that he can never, as Hawthorne said of Melville, "believe, nor be comfortable in his unbelief" (*Log*, 529). Cosmopolitanism is undeniably attractive as it appears in Rolfe, but in the end Clarel chooses the pilgrim path into the city.

The pilgrim is a new character type for Melville, called forth by the unique setting of Jerusalem. Perhaps only the deaf-mute traveler at the opening of *The Confidence-Man* gives a hint of his appearance in *Clarel*. But the cosmopolitan has appeared before, generally as an ambiguous figure, a butt of irony like the bachelor spectator, but also at times an admirable character in comparison with the provincials around him.[48] Unlike the spectator, a man of the city or a man-about-town, the cosmopolitan, who shares many of his characteristics, is nevertheless something more, a citizen of the world, unfettered by time, money, or place. As one who has traveled more widely and can see farther than his contemporaries, he has a certain moral and intellectual stature. But his lack of ties and commitments makes him seem at times lacking in faith or virtue. Thus Dr. Long Ghost in *Omoo* is a man of the world, and an amusing one, but because of his shallowness not to be taken seriously. Plotinum Plinlimmon in *Pierre* has acquired the cosmopolitan's knowledge of human nature and has lost the provincial's faith in arbitrary standards of morality, but he is also a cynic and a knave – above the world, apart, but also disembodied. Benjamin Franklin, whose interests and talents make him a little cosmopolis, both intrigues and repels Israel Potter. He has the cosmopolitan's ease and wit but also a certain coldness, a lack of domestic geniality. None of these cosmopolitans has nearly the fullness of Melville's later cosmopolitans: the Cosmopolitan of *The Confidence-Man*, Rolfe in *Clarel*, and Jack Gentian of the Burgundy Club sketches, whose appearance late in Melville's life indicates the tenacity of this character's hold on his imagination.

In *The Confidence-Man*, the Cosmopolitan has many of the qualities of Addison's spectator, Goldsmith's citizen of the world, the eighteenth-century man-about-town, and the nineteenth-century flaneur. With all of these, observation is consumption, and the Cosmopolitan loves both: "Served up à la Pole, or à la Moor, à la Ladrone, or à la Yankee, that good dish, man, still delights me; or rather is man a wine I never weary of comparing and sipping; wherefore am I a pledged cosmopolitan, . . . a taster of races" (133). Like the pickpocket, as Pitch notes, and like Cain, the Cosmopolitan loves crowds: "Say what you will, I for one must have my fellow-creatures round me" (137). But he also rises above the crowd to take the lofty view of the world, that of "a cosmopolitan, a catholic man; who, being such, ties himself to no narrow tailor or teacher, but federates, in heart as in costume, something of the various gallantries of men under various suns" (132). A tireless traveler, he "roams not over the gallant globe in vain" (132). But, unlike the relentless romantic Pierre, or the deaf-mute evangelist, he knows when to back up: "The best way, as I have heard, to get out of a labyrinth, is to retrace one's steps" (194). Seen on his first appearance through the skeptical eyes of Pitch, the Cosmopolitan seems a suspicious character, "[f]ine feathers on foul meat" (131), but his appetite for life, compared with the cold philosophies of Charlie Noble, Mark Winsome, and Egbert, makes him seem abundantly generous by comparison.

As a citizen of the world, the Cosmopolitan would appear to be worldly, and he certainly contrives to give that appearance. His multicultural costume, his unstinting use of wine and cigars, and his attitude of jolly tolerance proclaim, as White-Jacket said of the sailors, "the most liberal notions considering morality" (38):

> The stranger, now at rest, sideways and genially, on one hip, his right leg cavalierly crossed before the other, the toe of his vertical slipper pointed easily down on the deck, whiffed out a long, leisurely sort of indifferent and charitable puff, betokening himself more or less of the mature man of the world, a character which, like its opposite, the sincere Christian's, is not always swift to take offense. . . . (132)

By suggesting that the Cosmopolitan is the opposite of a sincere Christian, this passage presents his liberality, his indifference and leisure, his sweet smoke, and his cavalier body language as evidence of his immorality. But in fact the Cosmopolitan is not entirely what he says, nor is he the opposite of a sincere Christian. Although he claims to love that "racy creature, man" (133), he finds John Moredock, Mark Winsome, Egbert, and Orchis not to his taste. Rather than displaying an amoral acceptance of all mankind, he refuses to believe the story of John Moredock and finds the tale of China Aster "a story I can no way approve" (221). Although behaving sophisticatedly in some matters – for example, he seems to see through Charlie's attempts to intoxicate him, saying, "I find some little mysteries not very hard to clear up" (161) – he does not appear to have anticipated the challenges of Mark Winsome and Egbert. If his purpose is to win the confidence of others so that they will give him money, as the earlier incarnations of the confidence man have done, he fails, for he gives Egbert money after begging him endlessly for relief.

The Cosmopolitan proves himself to be, however, if not a sincere Christian then a sincere pilgrim. Like Clarel, he searches for faith in humankind, using the ingeniously simple method of asking people if they will place their confidence in him. His many rebuffs and disappointments do not appear to dampen his faith. In the gentlemen's cabin he asserts his belief in "a Committee of Safety, holding silent sessions over all, in an invisible patrol, most alert when we soundest sleep, and whose beat lies as much through forests as towns, along rivers as streets" (250), thus showing more faith than the Bible-reading old man with his money-belt, life preserver, and Counterfeit Detector. It is a remarkably urban image for Providence and suggests that the Cosmopolitan lives in a universe where he feels at home and protected. For him, the world is a City of God presided over by a benevolent patrol. Through this city he conducts his quest for charity, which concludes when, "in the darkness which ensued, the cosmopolitan kindly led the old man away" (251).

Melville has done everything he can to raise the reader's doubts about the Cosmopolitan, including hinting that he *is* the confidence man. In his chapter discussing the phrase "Quite an Original," however, he suggests how it may be possible to be both Cosmopolitan and pilgrim in an urban world, for the author is both: "Where does any novelist pick up any character? For the most part, in town, to be sure. Every great town is a kind of man-show, where the novelist goes for his stock, just as the agriculturist goes to the cattle-show for his. But in the one fair, new species of quadrupeds are hardly more rare, than in the other are new species of characters – that is, original ones" (238–9). Both the author and the Cosmopolitan love the town and feel at home in it. Both go there to find rare species of humans, "the very best brands of humanity" (133), as the Cosmopolitan puts it. Both, then, are pilgrims as well as Cosmopolitans: searching for perfection, with pilgrim seriousness and cosmopolitan pleasure.

The reward for the author is to create an original character, as "Hamlet is, or Don Quixote, or Milton's Satan" (238). All of these characters are questing pilgrims, truth-seekers, and at the same time cosmopolitans who rise above local prejudices, "raying away" from themselves like the "revolving Drummond light" (239). The Cosmopolitan's reward is more ambiguous. Perhaps when he leads the old man away at the end of the novel he performs an act of kindness in the pilgrim spirit, turning from his urbane masquerade and walking into the darkness. Or perhaps the confidence man has found another victim. But in either case, the pilgrimage ends in the heart of an urban ship, and the Cosmopolitan has engaged himself seriously in the issues of faith that come to plague future questers like Clarel, Rolfe, and Vine. He has exhibited the pilgrim side to cosmopolitanism and the cosmopolitan aspects of pilgrimage; in the end he appears to choose pilgrim obscurity over cosmopolitan brilliance.

Cosmopolitanism enters into *Clarel* partly by way of the cosmopolitan characters Clarel meets there, but also by the very nature of Jerusalem as a cosmopolis rather than a local capital like London or old New York. The earliest Christian traditions placed Jerusalem at the center of the world, and Clarel knows that, like Rome and Mecca, Jerusalem is a spiritual capital, perhaps the capital of all capitals.[49] It has little meaning as a political structure – in fact, Jerusalem was in a political shambles, ruled by Turks[50] – or as a national unity. Even less can it imply social organization, since the people who live there owe their allegiance not to each other but to their particular spiritual leaders. Besides, it is dubious that anyone really "lives" in Jerusalem. Either one comes to visit, as a tourist or cosmopolitan, or one stays indefinitely as a pilgrim, anticipating that death will remove him or her to another home. To the cosmopolitan, Jerusalem is the highest form of the earthly city; to pilgrims it is a City of God, but also a way station, perhaps for many the last. Its closeness to death and to another world gives it what Howard calls its "spectral, symbolical quality" (13).

The pilgrim, of course, tends to see Jerusalem more literally as a City of God than the cosmopolitan does. Among the earliest pilgrims, "the idea of the earthly Jerusalem became so confused with and transfused by that of the Heavenly Jerusalem that the Palestinian city seemed itself a miraculous realm, abounding both in spiritual and in material blessings."[51] Characters like Nehemiah, although he does not mistake the earthly city for the Celestial City of *Revelations,* come to Jerusalem to worship, taking the city as an image, more or less direct, of divine intention and presence. For the pilgrim, Jerusalem, more than any place on earth, represents a home, because no other home has significance. Even if he sees his time in Jerusalem as a journey toward death or the City of God, the pilgrim feels the city is an earthly endpoint. His sojourn there, then, has a purpose, whereas that of the Abel in Cain's City does not.

The first people Clarel encounters in Jerusalem are pilgrims. Abdon, a Black Jew or supposed descendant of the lost tribes of Israel, has spent his life traveling as a merchant sailor. Ever the sojourner, he seldom comes to rest, and even when he does he refuses to settle: the eternal nomad, "He pitched in Amsterdam his tent" (9). Age and loss, however, leave him, like Israel Potter, psychically homeless in a strange city: "loss came – loss, and I was led / To long for Judah – only her" (9). He comes to Jerusalem to run an inn for other pilgrims and leans his tombstone against the courtyard wall. Praying and meditating in his ancestors' home, he waits for death to come, at "No distant date . . . From Ind to Zion have I come, / But less to live, than end at home. / One other last remove!" (9).

Nathan, father of Clarel's sweetheart, Ruth, has also come to Jerusalem to worship and die. His pilgrimage begins in the American wilderness, where "Nature hath put such terror on" (57) that Nathan rejects his mother's Christian faith. The sublime in nature, rather than strengthening his reliance on God as it did for Wordsworth, turns him away. Yet his new faith – a deistic kind of pantheism – fails to satisfy him, and when he meets a Jewish woman, Agar, he energetically seizes upon hers. Taking up her ancestors' dream – "Next year in Jerusalem!" (62) – and the words embroidered on Agar's tablecloth – "IF I FORGET THEE, O JERUSALEM!" (85) – he moves his family to the Holy Land to help in Zion's restoration. As he did with the Indians in the American wilderness, however, Nathan alienates the desert Arabs, who murder him on his farm. Ruth and Agar remain immured in the city, constrained by mourning rites and by their enforced pilgrimage. They must tarry in Jerusalem, having now no other home to go to, and they too die before long.

Nathan as a religious convert represents a particularly fanatic breed of pilgrim, seeking in Jerusalem the home that he, a rough provincial and doubter, has never been able to find. Nehemiah disapproves of Nathan's harsh faith but in his own gentle way is no less fanatic. He of all the pilgrims comes closest to seeing Jerusalem as a real City of God. When

Clarel first meets him, Nehemiah offers the Bible as the best guide to Jerusalem, showing "The way to fields of Beulah dear / And New Jerusalem is here" (29). Just as the Bible guides Nehemiah around the city, Jerusalem appears to him a biblical text. Where Clarel sees a "rural well" (90), Nehemiah sees the pool where Christ washed blind men's eyes and made them see; he bends and scoops up the waters, too. Everywhere he goes he reads Jerusalem literally as a biblical inscription, hieroglyphs washed clean by Christ's touch so that anyone may read them.

Like the other pilgrims, Nehemiah sees Jerusalem as his true home. A carpenter from Connecticut, he lived as a hermit until, only once in his life making a friend, he was betrayed. He seeks in Jerusalem the comfort and solitude he could not find in his earlier rural life. Among the urban crowds, he travels safely and alone, like Melville's other taboo men:

> Latin, Armenian, Greek, and Jew
> Full well the harmless vagrant kenned . . .
> The Turk went further: let him wend;
> Him Allah cares for, holy one: . . .
>
> (29)

Although a pilgrim, then, Nehemiah has the cosmopolitan's knowledge of the many races of men. But he chooses the pilgrim way, living among the obscure "by-places," supported by Ruth's charity. Unlike the visitors Clarel, Rolfe, and Vine, he comes close to "living" in Jerusalem, melting into the mass of pilgrim humanity rather than ascending to philosophical heights above it.

Although Nehemiah does not die in Jerusalem, he does die in his dream of Jerusalem, a dream of the City of God. Dozing by the Dead Sea, he has a vision of the New Jerusalem that beckons him away; in his sleep he walks into the sea and drowns. To Mortmain, his death seems cruel and comfortless: "Thus Abel lay" (258). But for Nehemiah, death comes as it did for Abel, as a promise of the City of God opened up to the sinless sojourner in the City of Man. Nehemiah has found the end of his pilgrimage in the city.

Clarel admires Abdon's piety, Nathan's vigor, and Nehemiah's saintliness. He also admires and marvels at the stream of pilgrims flooding into Jerusalem's gates, "Like envoys from all Adam's race" (124). But for the greater part of the poem, he comes under the sway not of pilgrims but rather of cosmopolitans – men like Rolfe, Vine, and the Lyonese, who adopt a detached view of Jerusalem and pilgrim faith. For them Jerusalem is not a City of God but a complex version of the City of Man; not a home but a stopping place on their tour – though they pursue that tour with a certain pilgrim earnestness, especially Rolfe. They do not despise faith.

Rather, their doubts keep them in an eternal state of wandering, and their wanderings keep them in an eternal state of doubt.

In contrast with Clarel, provincial and pilgrim, the cosmopolitan characters have "worldly wit" (5). Whereas Clarel feels himself shallow and "local" (5), he realizes that the traveled and cosmopolitan mind abhors being "tied to one poor and casual form"(6). Rolfe seems to embody the noisy panoramic nature of the city itself:

> So to the novice streamed along
> Rolfe's filing thoughts, a wildering throng.
> Their sway he owned.
>
> (103)

Rolfe's very thoughts seem to Clarel as busy, various, and powerfully moving as urban crowds. And Rolfe himself appears to him an exceptional person, in the pilgrimage but not of it. Unlike the pilgrims, Rolfe consistently seeks a position above, not among, the world's competing sects and localities. His "daedal life in boats and tents" has given him the veneer of worldly experience while leaving him still "more bronzed in face than mind / Sensitive still and frankly kind – " (96). Intellectually he is "no scholastic partisan," yet he longs, in the Holy Land, to find some hidden verity, to "Slip quite behind the parrot-lore / Conventional" (96). Although Clarel wonders if Rolfe, with his elastic tolerance, might be no more than a "hollow, Manysidedness" (328), he recognizes that he is "sterling," one of the "exceptional natures" (97). Rolfe's earnestness marks him as a thought-traveler ever pressing on in the search for a faith he hopes but does not expect to find.

No other character in the poem quite has Rolfe's cosmopolitan openness, although most appear in relation to him more or less cosmopolitan, more or less pilgrim. Vine shares with him the lofty cosmopolitan heights from which they discourse on faith and doubt, looking down on Jerusalem from Mount Olivet. But whereas Rolfe seems genuinely interested in human nature and what he may find by scanning its various faces, Vine retreats from human contact. The true cosmopolitan maintains intellectual distance without intellectual aloofness. He travels over the world to "taste" man in all his varieties, not to view him, as Vine does, through a "leafy screen" (224). Vine has the Cosmopolitan's appreciation for intellectual issues and a far more refined sense of irony than Rolfe but little of his good heart. Derwent, a mock-pilgrim, seems to seek new truths in his travels but actually carries around his old beliefs as tiresome burdens. Although an urbane gentleman, he has none of the cosmopolitan's openness to new experience. Ungar and Mortmain are rebel-pilgrims, outcasts using the anodyne of travel to salve bitter wounds. But although they have traveled widely, their deep cynicism prevents them from being true cos-

mopolitans, who generally have the Melvillean geniality in great quantities. Clarel himself, beginning as a doubting pilgrim, gains broadly in
cosmopolitan wisdom without, however, ever achieving the cosmopolitan's
confident capacity for doubt. As each character is judged according to the
twin standards of pilgrim earnestness and cosmopolitan ease, none manages to combine these paradoxical virtues as comfortably as Rolfe, who
himself wavers among various beliefs.

Although deeply attracted to Rolfe's cosmopolitanism, however, Clarel
chooses in the end to join the pilgrim crowds of Jerusalem. At the end of
a journey into the wilderness, in a decision that combines the pilgrim's
humility with the cosmopolitan's longing for experience, he mingles
among the crowds wending their way up the Via Crucis, that "natural
street" along which Christ carried his cross. Alone, numb with grief for
Ruth, Clarel seeks solace among a stream of humanity who seem bur-
dened with sorrows like his own:

> As 'twere a frieze, behold the train!
> Bowed water-carriers; Jews with staves;
> Infirm gray monks; over-loaded slaves;
> Turk soldiers – young, with home-sick eyes;
> A Bey, bereaved through luxuries;
> Strangers and exiles; Moslem dames
> Long-veiled in monumental white,
> Dumb from the mounds which memory claims;
> A half-starved vagrant Edomite;
> Sore-footed Arab girls, which toil
> Depressed under heap of garden-spoil;
> The patient ass with paniered urn;
> Sour camels humped by heaven and man,
> Whose languid necks through habit turn
> With ease – for ease they hardly gain.
> In varied forms of fate they wend –
> Or man or animal, 'tis one:
> Cross-bearers all, alike they tend
> And follow, slowly follow on.

(497)

Like the stream of deathlike souls that Israel Potter encounters pouring
over the Thames River into London, this procession presents a cosmopolis
of suffering. Yet, unlike London's undifferentiated mass, the Jerusalem
crowd contains specimens of every gender, age, race, and creed, picked
out in striking detail against the solemn background of Easter and described with energetic particularity – Turk soldiers with homesick eyes,
sore-footed Arab girls. In this picture of the common, cross-bearing,

pilgrim spirit of humanity, existing in each particular diverse pilgrim, re-side the meaning and power of Jerusalem as a cosmopolis: not as the empty Dis-world of *Israel Potter*, nor as the noisy Vanity Fair of *The Confidence-Man*, but as the fully realized capital of the entire suffering world.

At this point in the poem, unable to acquire cosmopolitan distance, Clarel now finds the city opaque, no longer a labyrinth to explore but rather a dense surface:

> "They wire the world – far under sea
> They talk; but never comes to me
> A message from beneath the stone."
> (497–8)

The city's stones provide no tantalizing hieroglyphs for the scholar-pilgrim to read. Nevertheless, at our last glimpse of him, Clarel elects to leave the heights of superior contemplation and descend into Jerusalem's haunts.

> Dusked Olivet he leaves behind,
> And, taking now a slender wynd,
> Vanishes in the obscurer town.
> (498)

Clarel chooses to continue the pilgrimage in cosmopolis even without faith. For that decision he is awarded the wryly optimistic epilogue in which the narrator urges him to "Keep thy heart, though yet but ill re-signed . . . / Emerge thou mayst from the last whelming sea, / And prove that death but routs life into victory" (499). His pilgrimage has brought him deep into the City of Man, to the heart of the town, but it has not ended there. The cosmopolis offers continued prospects for the serious pilgrim; the coffin may prove life buoy at last.

In the end it seems that Jerusalem the world-city has come to represent a city-world. Life is a pilgrimage, not from the provinces to the urban centers or from the City of Man to the City of God, but from birth to death, pursued with pilgrim earnestness in a great cosmopolis. The city offers the possibility, if not the promise, of faith in a divine spirit, for that spirit resides, if anywhere, in the stones that people have erected to me-morialize it. The stones may appear as relics of a departed spirit, "But Faith . . . Inscribes even on her shards of broken urns" (498), and one may read faith's inscriptions there better, perhaps, than anywhere else. The sublime force that Ahab pursues so madly over an inhuman sea may, in the postnatural world, have taken up residence in the city. Clarel must look for it there.

Conclusion: Citified Man

———

The "obscurer town" into which Clarel vanishes at the end of his poem may well be the same town, the "man-show," where the author goes to get his characters in *The Confidence-Man*. Both narratives show that one does not need to make the pilgrimage to New Jerusalem or Old to find what the seeker needs. It is there in the town. One can get to the City of God by going to the town.

With *Clarel* one might say that the long trajectory of Melville's urban narratives ends; for *Clarel* is the last of Melville's urban travel writings. No longer does he write about the urban character's journey away from, through, or into the great city. The old patterns of urban movement – rambling, slumming, voyaging, sojourning, or making a pilgrimage – cease with the story of one man who decides to stay in the vast, diverse, stratified city he has chosen. And Melville, having made his decision to stay in New York and at the Customs House, having in *Clarel* ratified that decision, turns away from travel and toward, as the title of one of his collections of poems suggests, the "Fruit of Travel Long Ago." His late poems, sketches, and one story, *Billy Budd*, concern, not the urban outsiders – the spectator leaving the city behind, the provincial in a bewildering labyrinth, the sinless Abel sojourning in the wicked city, or the pilgrim journeying toward the urban center – but the quintessential insider: "citified man" himself.

In Melville's earlier works a culturally constructed urban form defines his protagonist's movements. The Walking City promises mobility and open-ended expansive space within a cultural capital. The Labyrinth provides a landscape of choice, where the Thesean character may find power or desire, darkness and truth, within its challenging confines. The City of Man is a city of public space, a flat, uninviting surface over which the sojourner drifts forlornly, though with an independence the comfortable citizens lack. And in the City of God, with its multidimensional space creating a social labyrinth and a labyrinth of time, the wanderer may find secular transcendence, an urban sublime. Urban form contains and makes possible certain kinds of space, certain public and private domains; but it is limited by an unjust ideology. Serving the interests of commerce and the masters of commerce rather than those of the common man or woman, this ideology offers to all the free use of urban space; yet in the cultural forms of capital, labyrinth, City of Man, or City of God, the modern city makes room only for those with the power to command it. Melville's characters test this ideology again and again. Drawn by desire or charity or curiosity or need into the city and into communion with their fellow beings, they find repeatedly that the city challenges their desires, prejudices, and hopes. And yet many of them create a space of their own within the city or find ways to travel through it. Urban form, as Lydia Maria Child discovered, is not all buildings, streets, and walls, but the structures of the mind that an active imagination can penetrate and refashion into more rich and forgiving forms. Redburn, Pierre, and Bartleby fail in this attempt at re-creation, but Ishmael, Israel Potter, the Confidence-Man, and Clarel in some measure succeed.

In the works of his last decades, however, Melville's characters, even if they live in cities, and many do not, make no travels through an urban form, nor does urban structure organize the literary space of narrative. Many of the poems return to the sea and to sailors – John Marr, Bridegroom Dick, Tom Deadlight – in an elegiac mood. "Weeds and Wildings," "Rip Van Winkle's Lilac," and "A Rose or Two" experiment with philosophical ideas, poetic conceits, and the flexible boundaries between poetry and prose, but they are the most purely pastoral of Melville's work. When he does write of cities, such as Corinth in *Timoleon* or Naples in "At the Hostelry," they provide a classical or historical backdrop for debates on moral and aesthetic questions. The city in a meaningful form seems to have disappeared from Melville's writing, or perhaps to have become so completely absorbed that it requires no particular attention.

The "Burgundy Club Sketches" suggest that the city requires no attention because it no longer stimulates Melville's interest or irony. The sketches of the Marquis de Grandvin and Jack Gentian, though ambiguous in their narration, seem to uphold the cosmopolitan virtues that Melville satirized in "The Paradise of Bachelors" and *The Confidence-Man*. It is true that Melville's narrator mocks Jack Gentian's outmoded patriotism, his Cincinnati badge, his decayed militarism, much in the way that Hawthorne mocked the same qualities in his officers of the Customs House. The Marquis certainly comes in for veiled jibes at his aristocratic sympathies and manners. And in the "House of the Tragic Poet," intended as a preface to the work, Melville satirizes the publisher who refuses to give his opinion of the manuscript until it has been published and approved by the public. But reading these sketches along with many of Melville's later poems, one finds much more tolerance of cosmopolitanism than in his early novels.[1]

With *Billy Budd*, however, Melville returns to narrative and plot, leaving behind the elegiac sketch, the gentlemanly portrait, the philosophical

poem, the love lyric, and the aesthetic debate. Except for casual references
to London and Bristol, Melville addresses the city directly at only one
point in the story, in an explanation of Billy's singular character, his innocence:

> And here be it submitted that apparently going to corroborate the
> doctrine of man's Fall, a doctrine now popularly ignored, it is observable
> that where certain virtues pristine and unadulterate peculiarly charac-
> terize anybody in the external uniform of civilization, they will upon
> scrutiny seem not to be derived from custom or convention, but rather
> to be out of keeping with these, as if indeed exceptionally transmitted
> from a period prior to Cain's city and citified man. The character
> marked by such qualities has to an unvitiated taste an untampered-with
> flavor like that of berries, while the man thoroughly civilized, even in a
> fair specimen of the breed, has to the same moral palate a questionable
> smack as of a compounded wine. To any stray inheritor of these primi-
> tive qualities found, like Caspar Hauser, wandering dazed in any Chris-
> tian capital of our time, the good-natured poet's famous invocation, near
> two thousand years ago, of the good rustic out of his latitude in the
> Rome of the Caesars, still appropriately holds:
>
> > Honest and poor, faithful in word and thought,
> > What hath thee, Fabian, to the city brought?
> >   (52–3)

The passage makes it clear that Billy Budd is that character from the
period prior to Cain's city, that therefore the whole fallen world is a City
of Man; fallen man is citified man, and citified man, even a fair specimen
like Captain Vere, is fallen man. Thus the old idea of a city, a physical,
political, social, and moral structure like Rome, has given way to a new
kind of City of Man, the city of the self or citified man. On the ship, Billy
is an Abel among citified men. Some, like Claggart, are emblems of Natural Depravity. Some, like Vere, seem wise and good but nevertheless give
a "questionable smack" to the palate.

Through the plastic medium of language, Melville involves urban form
throughout the story, in its labyrinthine plot, its citified characters, and
its urbane narrator, rather than reserving to it a particular site or space.
In fact, as in "The House-Top," he weaves in all the earlier urban forms
we have seen, though only by hints and implications. Hence, in the passage just quoted, Rome appears as a capital to which "any Christian capital
of our time" bears some resemblance. The honest Fabian is a provincial
drawn to the capital, and if Billy is that provincial, he quickly finds himself
pulled into a labyrinth – the labyrinth of the warship's martial structure
and of Claggart's evil. "[B]y indirection" (74) Melville's narrator describes Claggart's character as that of a labyrinth: "Well, for all that, I

think that to try and get into X—, enter his labyrinth and get out again, without a clue derived from some source other than what is known as 'knowledge of the world' – that were hardly possible, at least for me" (74). Billy Budd lacks this important clue and loses his way in the labyrinth of mysterious statements, temptations, and wiles that Claggart prepares for him. But Billy is also, as the earlier passage shows, an Abel sojourning in Cain's city; for although Melville's narrator compares Billy explicitly to Adam and Christ, he also ends up like Abel, slain by the Claggart-Cain on the altar of Vere's justice. In the end, however, Billy appears to escape the City of Man and ascend to a City of God, pictured as it was in *Mardi* in hints of a celestial world in the clouds.[2] All these reminders of urban form, however, which in Melville's other works seemed to point directly to contemporary cities, interweave themselves teasingly into the narration, so that if they had not appeared earlier in Melville's work, one might not recognize the urban references at all.

If the city in *Billy Budd* has been absorbed into citified man and an urbanized text, the most urbane voice in the story may well be that of the narrator. Through this ambiguous voice, Melville delivers himself of a final reflection on urban form: "The symmetry of form attainable in pure fiction cannot so readily be achieved in a narration essentially having less to do with fable than with fact. Truth uncompromisingly told will always have its ragged edges; hence the conclusion of such a narration is apt to be less finished than an architectural finial" (128). Melville's narrator suggests that he has been building an architectural form through narration, but that it is ragged, truthful. As proof of that ragged truthfulness, he offers three possible endings that give conflicting interpretations of what has happened in the story. This conclusion also suggests the artfulness of Ishmael's urban narration in the "Town-Ho Story." For Melville's triple ending implies three urban sites, as did Ishmael's multiple voices.

The first, the story of Vere's death in battle, brings to mind the imperial site of Lima in *Moby-Dick*. In the eyes of his country, Vere dies a tragic hero, having missed his opportunity to die like Nelson in "the fulness of fame" and murmuring Billy's name, "not in the accents of remorse" (129) but with the consciousness of his responsibility. This ending engenders pity for Vere, sympathy for the aristocratic hero who has fulfilled the demands of his empire at great cost to himself. This is the story as it will be understood by the cavaliers of London who value Vere's civilized execution of imperial law. At that site, "Forms, measured forms, are everything" (128), even when young sailors have to die to uphold them.

The second ending, the newspaper account that portrays Billy as a vicious criminal and Claggart as an upright officer, appears in a "naval chronicle" and is reminiscent of the "lasting record" of Ishmael's publication of the *Town-Ho* story in New York. But whereas Ishmael declares that the lasting record is true, Melville's narrator asserts that the published record is false: "The above, appearing in a publication now long ago superannuated and forgotten, is all that hitherto has stood in human record to attest what manner of men respectively were John Claggart and Billy Budd" (131). The publication is now not a "lasting record" but a "human record"; and although it once appeared in print as the truth, it is now "superannuated and forgotten," as most human records are. In the city where this account will be read, readers consume narrative only to throw it away.

The third ending, a sailor ballad claiming to re-create the voice of Billy himself as he faced death, is the last record of the story and, as it is circulated indefinitely among the sailors, is also a human record and the most lasting record of the three. Unlike Ishmael's story, preserved in publication and in a narrative form that trusts a literate urban audience, Billy's ballad is "rudely printed" (131), with none of the dignity of Ishmael's sophisticated narrative form. Yet in ending with the human record of Billy's death, Melville's narrator proves, as Ishmael does, his solidarity with the sailors. Even when the printed form has been lost, the song and Billy's story remain in the sailors' hearts. This final form implies a community of sailors, the Town that enacts its resistance to the City and citified man.

Billy Budd is written in the spirit of humane urbanity proclaimed by Ishmael. It uses form to enclose mystery and truth. Yet it mocks its own forms, especially the urban forms implied by its sites of narration and reception. And it proceeds with this mockery in passionate advocacy of those whom urban form excludes, oppresses, or crowds out.

Notes

Introduction: Proud City, Proudest Town

1. In fact, in the line that precedes this one, "weed follows weed through the Town"; see "The Swamp Angel," in Herman Melville, *Battle-Pieces*, ed. Hennig Cohen (New York: Thomas Yoseloff, 1963), 105.

2. See especially Elizabeth Blackmar, *Manhattan for Rent, 1785–1850* (Ithaca, N.Y.: Cornell UP, 1989); Paul Boyer, *Urban Masses and Moral Order in America, 1820–1920* (Cambridge, Mass.: Harvard UP, 1978); Amy Bridges, *A City in the Republic: Antebellum New York and the Origins of Machine Politics* (Ithaca, N.Y.: Cornell UP, 1984); John Hull Mollenkopf, *Power, Culture, and Place: Essays on New York City* (New York: Russell Sage Foundation, 1988); Edward K. Spann, *The New Metropolis: New York City, 1840–1857* (New York: Columbia UP, 1981); Christine Stansell, *City of Women: Sex and Class in New York, 1789–1860* (New York: Alfred A. Knopf, 1986); William R. Taylor, *In Pursuit of Gotham: Culture and Commerce in New York* (New York: Oxford UP, 1992); Sean Wilentz, *Chants Democratic: New York City and the Rise of the American Working Class, 1788–1850* (New York: Oxford UP, 1984).

3. *The Country and the City* (New York: Oxford UP, 1973), 1, 2.

4. *The Interpretation of Cultures: Selected Essays* (New York: Basic Books, 1973), 49.

5. *The City in History: Its Origins, Its Transformations, and Its Prospects* (New York: Harcourt Brace & World, 1961), 5.

6. Sigmund Freud, *Civilization and Its Discontents*, trans. and ed. James Strachey (New York: W. W. Norton, 1961), 17.

7. I have borrowed these terms from Yi-Fu Tuan, *Space and Place: The Perspective of Experience* (Minneapolis: U of Minnesota P, 1977).

8. *The Rites of Assent: Transformations in the Symbolic Construction of America* (New York and London: Routledge, 1993).

9. Charles N. Glaab and A. Theodore Brown, *A History of Urban America* (New York: Macmillan, 1967); John W. Reps, *The Making of Urban America: A History of City Planning in the United States* (Princeton, N.J.: Princeton UP, 1965); David Schuyler, *The New Urban Landscape: The Redefinition of City Form in Nineteenth-Century America* (Baltimore: Johns Hopkins UP, 1986).

10. Robert G. Albion, *The Rise of New York Port 1815–1860* (New York: Scribner, 1939; rpt. 1970); Isaac Newton Phelps Stokes, *The Iconography of Manhattan Island 1498–1909* (New York: Robert H. Dodd, 1915).

11. "In 1798, when they were digging in Broadway to lay the Manhattan pipes, by the south corner of Wall-street they dug up a large square post; from the gauge of my eye, I think it contained about ten solid feet. It was in a good state of preservation, and as the yellow fever was raging at the time, and very few pedestrians in the street, it was laid on the pavement for the inspection of the Board of Health, their deputies and officers, hearsemen and grave-diggers, with a few solitary mortals who found it inconvenient to leave the city. Many came to look at it, but none could conjecture what might have been its use. At last a very old man, who said he was born in 1695 in New-York, came to view it. He remembered seeing one of the city gate-posts stand there, and said, this was the bottom of the post. He added, that a stockade ten or twelve feet high ran from the East river up Wall-street and down to the North river, to keep out Indians." *Fifty Years; Reminiscences of New-York* (New York: Daniel Fanshaw, 1845), 215.

12. Peter G. Buckley, "Culture, Class and Place in Antebellum New York," in Mollenkopf, 25–52 (n. 2).

13. For reasons of convenience and efficiency, I have chosen from the vast literature on the nineteenth-century American city only those examples about and published in New York. Melville, and New York culture, would of course have encountered the urban literature of many other American and European cities.

14. Terry Eagleton, *The Function of Criticism: From* The Spectator *to Post-Structuralism* (London: Verso, 1984); Dana Brand, *The Spectator and the City in Nineteenth-Century American Literature* (New York: Cambridge UP, 1991); Brand does not include Melville in his very illuminating study.

15. Mikhail Bakhtin, *Rabelais and His World,* trans. Helene Iswolsky (Bloomington: Indiana UP, 1984), 161.

16. For many reasons, which will become clear in Chapter 2, the spectator differs from a closely related figure, the flaneur, as described by Walter Benjamin. Nevertheless, I have drawn repeatedly from Benjamin's work on the flaneur and from that of others who had treated it. See *Reflections: Essays, Aphorisms, Autobiographical Writing,* ed. Peter Demetz, trans. Edmund Jephcott (New York: Harcourt Brace Jovanovich, 1978); and *Charles Baudelaire: A Lyric Poet in the Era of High Capitalism,* trans. Harry Zohn (London: New Left Books, 1973).

17. See especially David S. Reynolds, *Beneath the American Renaissance: The Subversive Imagination in the Age of Emerson and Melville* (Cambridge, Mass.: Harvard UP, 1989).

18. On the pastoral tradition in American literature, see Leslie Fiedler, *Love and Death in the American Novel* (New York: Criterion Books, 1960); Leo Marx, *The Machine in the Garden: Technology and the Pastoral Ideal in America* (New York: Oxford UP, 1964); F. O. Matthiesson, *The American Renaissance: Art and Expression in the Age of Emerson and Whitman* (New York: Oxford UP, 1941); Henry Nash Smith, *Virgin Land: The American West as Symbol and Myth* (Cambridge, Mass.: Harvard UP, 1950).

19. *The City of Dickens* (Oxford: Clarendon Press, 1971).

20. Nina Baym, *Woman's Fiction: A Guide to Novels by and about Women in America, 1820–1870* (Ithaca, N.Y.: Cornell UP, 1978; rpt. Urbana: U of Illinois P, 1993); Nancy F. Cott, *The Bonds of Womanhood: "Woman's Sphere" in New England,*

1780–1835 (New Haven and London: Yale UP, 1977); Susan Harris, *19th-Century American Women's Novels: Interpretive Strategies* (Cambridge and New York: Cambridge UP, 1990); Mary Kelley, *Private Woman, Public Stage: Literary Domesticity in Nineteenth-Century America* (New York: Oxford UP, 1984); Mary P. Ryan, *The Empire of the Mother: American Writing about Domesticity 1830–1860* (Baltimore: Johns Hopkins UP, 1990); Stansell (n. 2); Jane Tompkins, *Sensational Designs: The Cultural Work of American Fiction, 1790–1860* (New York: Oxford UP, 1985).

21. Gillian Brown frames this question in terms of selfhood for male as well as female writers and readers. See her *Domestic Individualism: Imagining Self in Nineteenth-Century America* (Berkeley and Los Angeles: U of California P, 1990).

22. James Buzard, *The Beaten Track: European Tourism, Literature, and the Ways of Culture, 1800–1918* (Oxford: Clarendon Press, 1993); Franklin D. Walker, *Irreverent Pilgrims: Melville, Browne, and Twain in the Holy Land* (Seattle: U of Washington P, 1974).

23. For a recent essay on this subject, see Martha Banta, "The Three New Yorks: Topographical Narratives and Cultural Texts," *American Literary History* 7 (Spring 1995): 28–54.

24. One area where we see that making occur, an area I have had to exclude, partly for reasons of space and partly to emphasize the white middle-class culture Melville would have known best, is the literary culture of African American, Irish, German, Jewish, and other immigrant groups in New York. Not much is known about Melville's reading of any periodicals outside the white middle-class market. And although we know him to have traveled throughout the city observing working-class and ethnic neighborhoods, especially around the docks, to have entertained abolitionist views and sympathies, and to have informed himself about events of the city, I have not found evidence of his having read the more specialized periodicals of different ethnic or racial groups.

25. *Correspondence*, ed. Lynn Horth (Evanston and Chicago: Northwestern UP and the Newberry Library, 1993), 193.

26. Donald E. Pease, *Visionary Compacts: American Renaissance Writings in Cultural Context* (Madison: U of Wisconsin P, 1987).

27. On Melville and the canon wars, see Paul Lauter, "Herman Melville Climbs the Canon," *American Literature* 66 (March 1994): 1–24. For more general treatments of the subject, see Sacvan Bercovitch and Myra Jehlen, eds., *Ideology and Classic American Literature* (New York: Cambridge UP, 1986); Frederick Crews, *The Critics Bear It Away: American Fiction and the Academy* (New York: Random House, 1992); Paul Lauter, *Canons and Contexts* (New York: Oxford UP, 1991); Walter Benn Michaels and Donald Pease, eds., *The American Renaissance Reconsidered: Selected Papers from the English Institute, 1982–3* (Baltimore: Johns Hopkins UP, 1985); Russell J. Reising, *The Unusable Past: Theory and the Study of American Literature* (London: Methuen, 1986).

28. Morton and Lucia White, *The Intellectual versus the City* (Cambridge, Mass.: Harvard UP and MIT Press, 1962), 1, 2. See also their "The Intellectual versus the City: The Outlines of a Tradition," in Paul Kramer and Frederick L. Holborn, eds., *The City in American Life* (New York: G. P. Putnam's Sons, 1970), 246.

29. Newton Arvin, *Herman Melville* (New York: William Sloane, 1950), 89–90, 152, 105, 218.

30. Richard Chase, *Herman Melville: A Critical Study* (1949; rpt. New York: Haffner Publishing Company, 1971), 15.

31. Leon Howard, *Herman Melville* (Berkeley and Los Angeles: U of California P, 1967), 180.

32. Michael Rogin, *Subversive Genealogy: The Politics and Art of Herman Melville* (New York: Alfred A. Knopf, 1983). For other political readings, see Alan Heimert, "*Moby-Dick* and American Political Symbolism," *American Quarterly* 16 (April 1963); Helen Trimpi, *Melville's Confidence Men and American Politics in the 1850s* (Hamden, Conn.: Archon Books, 1987).

33. Wai-chee Dimock, *Empire for Liberty: Melville and the Poetics of Individualism* (Princeton, N.J.: Princeton UP, 1989).

34. Ann Douglas, *The Feminization of American Culture* (New York: Alfred A. Knopf, 1977); see Dennis Berthold, "Dürer 'At the Hostelry': Melville's Misogynist Iconography," *Melville Society Extracts* 95 (December 1993): 1–8; Elizabeth Renker, "Herman Melville, Wife Beating, and the Written Page," *American Literature* 66 (March 1994): 123–50; Robyn Wiegman, "Melville's Geography of Gender," *American Literary History* 1 (Winter 1989): 735–53.

35. Hershel Parker, "*Moby-Dick* and Domesticity," in *Critical Essays on Herman Melville's Moby-Dick*, ed. Brian Higgins and Hershel Parker (New York: G. K. Hall, 1992), 545–62; Laurie Robertson-Lorant, *Melville: A Biography* (New York: Clarkson N. Potter, Publishers, 1996); Charlene Avallone, "Calculations for Popularity: Melville's *Pierre* and *Holden's Dollar Magazine*," *Melville Society Extracts* 72 (February 1988): 6–9; Sheila Post-Lauria, " 'Philosophy in Whales . . . Poetry in Blubber': Mixed Form in *Moby-Dick*," *Nineteenth-Century Literature* 45 (December 1990): 300–16; and Wyn Kelley, " 'I'm Housewife Here': Melville and Domestic Economy," *Melville Society Extracts* 98 (September 1994): 7–10.

36. See Jonathan Katz, *Gay American History: Lesbians and Gay Men in the U.S.A.* (New York: Thomas Y. Crowell, 1976); Robert K. Martin, *Hero, Captain, and Stranger: Male Friendship, Social Critique, and Literary Form in the Sea Novels of Herman Melville* (Chapel Hill: U of North Carolina P, 1986); James Creech, *Closet Writing, Gay Reading: The Case of Melville's Pierre* (Chicago: U of Chicago P, 1993); Caleb Crain, "Lovers of Human Flesh: Homosexuality and Cannibalism in Melville's Novels," *American Literature* 66 (March 1994): 25–53.

37. Carolyn L. Karcher, *Shadow Over the Promised Land: Slavery, Race, and Violence in Melville's America* (Baton Rouge: Louisiana State UP, 1980). Henry Louis Gates, Jr., *The Signifying Monkey: A Theory of Afro-American Literary Criticism* (New York: Oxford UP, 1988); Toni Morrison, *Playing in the Dark: Whiteness and the Literary Imagination* (Cambridge, Mass.: Harvard UP, 1992); Sterling Stuckey, *Going Through the Storm: The Influence of African American Art in History* (New York: Oxford UP, 1994); Eric Sundquist, *To Wake the Nations: Race in the Making of American Literature* (Cambridge, Mass.: Harvard UP, 1993). See also Shelley Fisher Fishkin, *Was Huck Black? Mark Twain and African-American Voices* (New York: Oxford UP, 1993); Robert S. Levine, *Conspiracy and Romance: Studies in Brockden Brown, Cooper, Hawthorne, and Melville* (New York: Cambridge UP, 1989); Laurie Robertson-Lorant, "Herman Melville and Race: Themes and Imagery," Ph.D. diss., New York University, 1972.

38. Nicholas K. Bromell, *By the Sweat of the Brow: Literature and Labor in Antebellum America* (Chicago: U of Chicago P, 1993); Michael T. Gilmore, *American Romanticism and the Marketplace* (Chicago: U of Chicago P, 1985); Cindy Weinstein, *The Literature of Labor and the Labors of Literature: Allegory in Nineteenth-Century American Fiction* (New York: Cambridge UP, 1995).

39. Among the exceptions are Charlene Avallone, "Calculated for Popularity"; Perry Miller, *The Raven and the Whale: The War of Words and Wits in the Era of Poe and Melville* (New York: Harcourt, Brace, 1956); Sheila Post-Lauria, *Correspondent Colorings: Melville and Popular Literary Culture* (Amherst: U of Massachusetts P, 1996) – all of whom have helped supply the periodical context for Melville's work.

40. Hans Bergmann, *God in the Street: Urban Discourse and Herman Melville*, forthcoming from Temple UP; Shaun O'Connell, *Imagining New York* (Boston: Beacon Press, 1995).

41. General considerations of urban literature in America, including Melville's work, are: Michael H. Cowan, *City of the West: Emerson, America, and Urban Metaphor* (New Haven and London: Yale UP, 1967); George Arthur Dunlap, *The City in the American Novel, 1789–1900* (1934; rpt. New York: Russell and Russell, 1962); Blanche Houseman Gelfant, *The American City Novel* (Norman: U of Oklahoma P, 1954); Bernard Rosenthal, *City of Nature: Journeys to Nature in the Age of American Romanticism* (Newark: U of Delaware P, 1980); Adrienne Siegel, *The Image of the American City in Popular Literature, 1820–1870* (Port Washington, N.Y.: Kennikat Press, 1981); Janis Stout, *Sodoms in Eden: The City in American Fiction Before 1860* (Westport, Conn.: Greenwood Press, 1976).

42. John Henry Raleigh, "The Novel and the City: England and America in the Nineteenth Century," *Victorian Studies* 11 (1967/68): 320; Charles Moorman, "Melville's *Pierre* in the City," *American Literature* 27 (1956): 573–4; Alfred Kazin, "New York from Melville to Mailer," in Michael C. Jaye and Ann Chalmers Watts, eds., *Literature and the Urban Experience* (New Brunswick, N.J.: Rutgers UP, 1981), 84; Raleigh, 320; Stout, *Sodoms in Eden*, 134; James Polk, "Melville and the Idea of the City," *University of Toronto Quarterly* 41 (1972): 286.

43. See also Morris Dickstein, "The City as Text: New York and the American Writer," *TriQuarterly* 83 (Winter 1991–2): 183–204; Elizabeth Hardwick, "Bartleby in Manhattan," *Bartleby in Manhattan and Other Essays* (New York: Random House, 1983), 217–31; Harold T. McCarthy, "Melville's *Redburn* and the City," *The Midwest Quarterly* 12 (1971): 394–410; Paul McCarthy, "City and Town in Melville's Fiction," *Research Studies* 38 (1970): 214–29; Charles Moorman, "Melville's *Pierre* and the Fortunate Fall," *American Literature* 25 (1953): 13–30; Willard Thorp, "Redburn's Prosy Old Guidebook," *PMLA* 53 (1938): 1146–56; Nathalia Wright, "*Pierre*: Herman Melville's *Inferno*," *American Literature* 32 (1960): 167–81.

44. Leo Marx, "The Puzzle of Anti-Urbanism in Classic American Literature," in Jaye and Watts, *Literature and the Urban Experience*, 64.

45. *Correspondence*, 191. For the subversion argument, see especially: William Dillingham, *Melville's Short Fiction, 1853–1856* (Athens: U of Georgia P, 1977); Ann Douglas (n. 34); Marvin Fisher, *Going Under: Melville's Short Fiction and the*

American 1850s (Baton Rouge: Louisiana State UP, 1977); David S. Reynolds (n. 40).

46. A powerful argument against the idea of Melville as subversive appears in Sheila Post-Lauria's book (see n. 39 above). I have also benefited from conversations with her on the subject.

47. M. M. Bakhtin, *The Dialogic Imagination*, ed. Caryl Emerson and Michael Holquist (Austin: U of Texas P, 1981).

48. See Wyn Kelley, "Haunted Stone: Nature and City in *Clarel*," *Essays in Arts and Sciences* 15 (June 1986): 15–29.

49. *Herman Melville: Cycle and Epicycle* (Cambridge, Mass.: Harvard UP, 1953), 282.

1. Urban Space

1. Isaac Newton Phelps Stokes, *The Iconography of Manhattan Island 1498–1909* (New York: Robert H. Dodd, 1915), 1:407–8, 470–3; 3:477–82. Further references appear in the text. John W. Reps, *The Making of Urban America: A History of City Planning in the United States* (Princeton, N. J.: Princeton UP, 1965), 296–9.

2. Charles Rosenberg, *The Cholera Years* (Chicago: Chicago UP, 1962).

3. Roy Rosenzweig and Elizabeth Blackmar argue that in fact this area contained African American and Irish communities of "unusual stability." See their *The Park and The People: A History of Central Park* (Ithaca, N.Y.: Cornell UP, 1992), 67.

4. Elizabeth Blackmar, *Manhattan for Rent, 1785–1850* (Ithaca, N.Y.: Cornell UP, 1989), 6.

5. Stokes, I:472; 3:482; Reps, 297, 299. Louis Auchincloss, Joseph Veach Noble, and Jerry E. Patterson, *The City of New York: A History Illustrated from the Collections of the Museum of the City of New York* (New York: Harry N. Abrams, 1978), 91.

6. Stokes, I:399–402.

7. Edward K. Spann, *The New Metropolis: New York City, 1840–1857* (New York: Columbia UP, 1981), 430.

8. See Rosenzweig and Blackmar, chaps. 1 and 2.

9. Horace Greeley, *Glances at Europe: In a Series of Letters from Great Britain, France, Italy, Switzerland, &c.* (New York, 1851), 67; Andrew Jackson Downing, "The New York Park," *Horticulturalist* 6 (August 1851): 345, reprinted in Downing, *Rural Essays* (New York, 1853); Frederick Law Olmsted, "Description of Central Park," in *The Papers of Frederick Law Olmsted*, vol. 3: *Creating Central Park, 1857–1861*, eds. Charles E. Beveridge and David Schuyler (Baltimore: Johns Hopkins UP, 1983), quoted in David Schuyler, *The New Urban Landscape: The Redefinition of City Form in Nineteenth-Century America* (Baltimore: Johns Hopkins UP, 1986), 62–4, 77; Norval White, *New York: A Physical History* (New York: Atheneum, 1987), 93; Spann, 139–73. See also Rosenzweig and Blackmar (n. 3); Thomas Bender, *Toward an Urban Vision: Ideas and Institutions in Nineteenth-Century America* (Lexington: UP of Kentucky, 1975); and Frederick Law Olmsted, Sr., *Forty Years of Landscape Architecture: Central Park*, eds. Frederick Law Olmsted, Jr., and Theodora Kimball (1928; rpt. Cambridge, Mass.: MIT Press, 1973).

10. Rosenzweig and Blackmar, 50–8.

11. Vaux to Clarence C. Cook, June 6, 1865, Olmsted Papers; Olmsted to Henry W. Bellows, Oct. 30, 1860, Henry W. Bellows Papers, Massachusetts Historical Society, Boston, in Schuyler, *New Urban Landscape*, 81–2, 99, 94; Olmsted, *Forty Years*, 45–7; Rosenzweig and Blackmar, 95–149. Susanna S. Zetzel argues that Olmsted's aesthetic resisted the aristocratic, Anglocentric ideas of Andrew Jackson Downing; though embracing Thoreau's nonconformity and love of nature, he did not accept his anti-urbanism. Therefore, she is not as critical as Rosenzweig and Blackmar of the accommodations Olmsted had to make with the city's political structure, seeing the park as a synthesis rather than a compromise. See "The Garden in the Machine: The Construction of Nature in Olmsted's Central Park," in *Prospects: An Annual of American Cultural Studies*, ed. Jack Salzman (New York: Cambridge UP, 1989), 14:291–339.

12. Leo Marx, "The American Ideology of Space," Working Paper 8, Program in Science, Technology, and Society at the Massachusetts Institute of Technology, 1989. See also his *The Machine in the Garden: Technology and the Pastoral Ideal in America* (New York: Oxford UP, 1964).

13. Olmsted, 46.

14. Rosenzweig and Blackmar, 150–79.

15. For discussions of different class groups in New York during this period, see Thomas Bender, *New York Intellect: A History of Intellectual Life in New York City from 1750 to the Beginnings of Our Own Time* (New York: Alfred A. Knopf, 1987); Blackmar, *Manhattan for Rent* (n. 4); Stuart Blumin, *The Emergence of the Middle Class: Social Experience in the American City, 1760–1900* (New York: Cambridge UP, 1989); Douglas T. Miller, *Jacksonian Aristocracy: Class and Democracy in New York 1830–1860* (New York: Oxford UP, 1967); Edward Pessen, *Riches, Class, and Power before the Civil War* (Lexington, Mass.: D. C. Heath, 1973); Christine Stansell, *City of Women: Sex and Class in New York, 1789–1860* (New York: Alfred A. Knopf, 1986); Richard B. Stott, *Workers in the Metropolis: Class, Ethnicity, and Youth in Antebellum New York City* (Ithaca, N.Y.: Cornell UP, 1990); Sean Wilentz, *Chants Democratic: New York City and the Rise of the American Working Class, 1788–1850* (New York: Oxford UP, 1984). For the Melville family biography, see: Leon Howard, *Herman Melville* (Berkeley and Los Angeles: U of California P, 1967); Jay Leyda, *The Melville Log* (New York: Gordian Press, 1951), hereafter referred to in the text as *Log*; Laurie Robertson-Lorant, *Melville: A Biography* (New York: Clarkson N. Potter Publishers, 1996).

16. Allan Melvill to Thomas Melvill, May 2, 1816, Melville Family Papers in the New York Public Library; quoted in Michael Paul Rogin, *Subversive Genealogy: The Politics and Art of Herman Melville* (New York: Alfred A. Knopf, 1983), 23–4.

17. Allan Melvill diary, collection of Melville Family Papers, Houghton Library, Harvard University, Cambridge, Mass.

18. See Robert G. Albion, *The Rise of New York Port* (New York: Scribner, 1939; rpt. 1970); Blackmar (n. 4); Stokes (n. 1).

19. Rogin, *Subversive Genealogy*, 29–30. See also T. Walter Herbert, *Moby-Dick and Calvinism: A World Dismantled* (New Brunswick, N.J.: Rutgers UP, 1977), 47–53. Wai-chee Dimock argues that Melville achieves a similar kind of invisible control over narrative in *The Confidence-Man*: "And so, the spirit of Adam Smith presides not only over the marketplace. It presides here as well. In the freedom

and unaccountability of the Invisible Hand, Melville has finally found a model of freedom that suits him, a model after which he can fashion his own authorial hand." *Empire for Liberty: Melville and the Poetics of Individualism* (Princeton, N.J.: Princeton UP, 1989), 206.

20. Although most biographies insist that Allan Melvill died insane, a more recent consideration suggests that he suffered from delirium following fever. See Susan Weiner and William J. Weiner, "Allan Melvill's Death: A Misdiagnosis," *Melville Society Extracts* 67 (September 1986), 9–11.

21. For an excellent discussion of a shorter period within this development, see Hans Bergmann, "Panoramas of New York, 1845–1860," in *Prospects: An Annual of American Cultural Studies*, ed. Jack Salzman (New York: Columbia UP, 1985), 10:119–37.

22. John A. Kouwenhoven, *The Columbia Historical Portrait of New York: An Essay in Graphic History* (New York: Harper & Row, 1972), 44–5, 52–5.

23. Ibid., 131. Kenneth C. Lindsay, *The Works of John Vanderlyn, from Tammany to the Capital: A Loan Exhibition October 11 to November 9, 1970* (Binghamton, N.Y.: University Art Gallery, 1970). On the connections between Melville and John Vanderlyn, see Wyn Kelley, "Melville and John Vanderlyn: Ruin and Historical Fate from 'Bartleby' to *Israel Potter*," in *Savage Eye: Melville and the Visual Arts*, ed. Christopher Sten (Kent, Ohio: Kent State UP, 1991).

24. Kouwenhoven, 190–95. E. Porter Belden, "New-York – As It Is," in *New-York: Past, Present, and Future* (New York: G. P. Putnam, 1849), 2–13. On later versions of the urban panorama, and the role of photography in giving the genre new aesthetic and ideological dimensions, see William R. Taylor, "New York and the Origin of the Skyline: The Visual City as Text," in *Prospects: An Annual of American Cultural Studies*, ed. Jack Salzman (New York: Cambridge UP, 1988), 13:225–48; and "New York and the Origin of the Skyline: The Commercial City as Visual Text," in *In Pursuit of Gotham: Culture and Commerce in New York* (New York: Oxford UP, 1992), 23–33.

25. Spann, *The New Metropolis*, 242–80; Charles Dickens, *American Notes and Pictures from Italy* (1842: rpt. London and New York: Macmillan, 1893); Seymour J. Mandelbaum, *Boss Tweed's New York* (New York: John Wiley, 1965); see also Carroll Smith-Rosenberg, *Religion and the Rise of the American City: The New York City Mission Movement, 1812–1870* (Ithaca, N.Y.: Cornell UP, 1971); Stansell (n. 15).

26. Kouwenhoven, 22, 263.

27. "New-York Daguerreotyped," *Putnam's Monthly Magazine* I (February/ April/ June 1853); 2 (July/September 1853); 3 (January/February/March 1854). Citations appear in April 1853, 356–8, 368, and February 1853, 127; see Kouwenhoven, 150, 153.

28. Matthew Hale Smith, *Sunshine and Shadow in New York* (Hartford, Conn.: J. B. Burr and Company, 1869); Lydia Maria Child, *Letters from New York* (New York: C. S. Francis & Co., 1844), 2. David S. Reynolds, *Beneath the American Renaissance: The Subversive Imagination in the Age of Emerson and Melville* (Cambridge, Mass.: Harvard UP, 1989) discusses the mystery-and-misery fiction but does not pursue the theme in the graphic arts or describe it as a way of representing urban space.

29. Kouwenhoven, 200, 270, 301.

30. Margaret Fuller labeled Lydia Maria Child the "New-York Spectator." See Carolyn Karcher, *The First Woman in the Republic: A Cultural Biography of Lydia Maria Child* (Durham and London: Duke UP, 1994), 317. Karcher's chapter, "*Letters from New York:* The Invention of a New Literary Genre" (295–319), emphasizes Child's innovations in, rather than indebtedness to, popular urban genres.

31. Elizabeth Wilson, *The Sphinx in the City: Urban Life, the Control of Disorder, and Women* (Berkeley and Los Angeles: U of California P, 1991), 25.

2. Spectator in the Capital

1. See chapter 7, "The Use of Urban Space," in Edward K. Spann, *The New Metropolis: New York City, 1840–1857* (New York: Columbia UP, 1981), 139–73.

2. "Town and Country," *The Knickerbocker* 8 (November 1836): 537–9, in Bayrd Still, *Urban America: A History with Documents* (Boston: Little, Brown, 1974), 195.

3. See Max Byrd, *London Transformed: Images of the City in the Eighteenth Century* (New Haven and London: Yale UP, 1978); Jacques Ellul, *The Meaning of the City*, trans. Dennis Pardee (Grand Rapids, Mich.: William B. Eerdmans, 1970); Blanche Gelfant, *The American City Novel* (Norman: U of Oklahoma P, 1954); Lewis Mumford, *The City in History: Its Origins, Its Transformations, and Its Prospects* (New York: Harcourt, Brace and World, 1961); Burton Pike, *The Image of the City in Modern Literature* (Princeton, N.J.: Princeton UP, 1981); Adrienne Siegel, *The Image of the American City in Popular Literature, 1820–1870* (Port Washington, N.Y.: Kennikat Press, 1981); Janis Stout, *Sodoms in Eden: The City in American Fiction before 1860* (Westport, Conn.: Greenwood Press, 1976); David Weimer, *The City as Metaphor* (New York: Random House, 1966).

4. Yi-Fu Tuan, *Space and Place: The Perspective of Experience* (Minneapolis: U of Minnesota P, 1977).

5. *The Poetics of Space*, trans. Maria Jolas (New York: Orion Press, 1964).

6. Perry Miller, *The Raven and the Whale: The War of Words and Wits in the Era of Poe and Melville* (New York: Harcourt, Brace and Company, 1956).

7. For the fullest discussion of the Marquesas as culturally contested ground, see T. Walter Herbert, *Marquesan Encounters: Melville and the Meaning of Civilization* (Cambridge, Mass.: Harvard UP, 1980).

8. Percy G. Adams, *Travel Literature and the Evolution of the Novel* (Lexington: UP of Kentucky, 1983); Thomas M. Curley, *Samuel Johnson and the Age of Travel* (Athens: U of Georgia P, 1976).

9. See Joseph Addison and Richard Steele, *The Spectator*, ed. Donald Bond (Oxford: Clarendon Press, 1965); Dana Brand, *The Spectator and the City in Nineteenth-Century American Literature* (Cambridge: Cambridge UP, 1991); William Frank Bryan and Ronald S. Crane, *The English Familiar Essay: Representative Texts* (Boston: Ginn, 1916); Curley (n. 8); Terry Eagleton, *The Function of Criticism: From "The Spectator" to Post-Structuralism* (London: Verso, 1984); Peter Gay, "The Spectator as Actor: Addison in Perspective," *Encounter* 29, no. 6 (1967): 27–32; Melvin R. Watson, "The *Spectator* Tradition and the Development of the Familiar Essay," *ELH* 13 (1946): 189–215.

10. Addison and Steele, *The Spectator*, I:3–4. Further references appear in the text in parentheses.

11. See Ian Watt, *The Rise of the Novel: Studies in Defoe, Richardson, and Fielding* (Berkeley and Los Angeles: U of California P, 1957).

12. Merton M. Sealts, Jr., *Melville's Reading* (Columbia: U of South Carolina P, 1988). Jay Fliegelman shows the importance of Chesterfield, Gregory, and Fenelon for American readers and for the cultivation in America of a moral and aesthetic sensibility like that of London, in his *Prodigals and Pilgrims: The American Revolution Against Patriarchy, 1750–1800* (Cambridge: Cambridge UP, 1982).

13. On the importance of Hugh Blair for Melville's early work, see Bryan C. Short, *Cast by Means of Figures: Herman Melville's Rhetorical Development* (Amherst: U of Massachusetts P, 1992).

14. Lindley Murray, *The English Reader: or Pieces in Prose and Poetry, Selected from the Best Writers* (Rutland, Vt.: Fay and Burt, 1819), iii. See also William Gilman, *Melville's Early Life and Redburn* (New York: New York UP, 1951), 55; and Sealts, *Melville's Reading*, 201.

15. Donald Davie, *The Purity of Diction in English Verse* (New York: Schocken Books, 1967), 26–7.

16. As Melville was to proclaim in "Hawthorne and His Mosses," "we want no American Goldsmiths" (*PT*, 248); he urged the need for American Shakespeares. Marvin Fisher points out this passage in his unpublished essay, "The Burden of Literary History in *Redburn*."

17. *English Lands, Letters, and Kings: From Elizabeth to Anne* (New York: Charles Scribner's Sons, 1907), 277.

18. Miller, *The Raven and the Whale*, 16. For further readings of Irving as spectator, traveler, and sojourner, see Philip McFarland, *Sojourners* (New York: Atheneum, 1979); and Jeffrey Rubin-Dorsky, *Adrift in the Old World: The Psychological Pilgrimage of Washington Irving* (Chicago: U of Chicago P, 1988).

19. Miller, 30, 31. Miller gives the full history of the Knickerbocker writers and their relationship to Melville. But he does not discuss the urbanity of *Typee* and Melville's other early writings, nor does he mention the spectator prototype.

20. Short makes a similar argument in his chapter, " 'Dumb and deaf': Melville's Youth," *Cast by Means of Figures*, 12–22.

21. See Robert G. Albion, *The Rise of New York Port 1815–1860* (New York: Scribner, 1939; rpt. 1970); E. Porter Belden, *New-York: Past, Present, and Future* (New York: George Putnam, 1849); Elizabeth Blackmar, *Manhattan for Rent, 1785–1850* (Ithaca, N.Y.: Cornell UP, 1989); John A. Kouwenhoven, *The Columbia Historical Portrait of New York: An Essay in Graphic History* (New York: Harper & Row, 1972); Spann (n. 1); Isaac Newton Phelps Stokes, *Iconography of Manhattan Island, 1498–1909* (New York: R. H. Dodd, 1915).

22. Like Dana Brand, I will, for convenience's sake, treat "flaneur" as an English word (*The Spectator and the City*, 198–9).

23. I will also accept the convention that the flaneur is male, although Lydia Maria Child's *Letters from New York* and some of Margaret Fuller's journalism give evidence of a female flaneur sensibility. Christine Stansell's and Elizabeth Blackmar's works make it clear that although working-class and poor women had the freedom of the streets in antebellum New York, middle-class

women felt increasingly threatened by urban street life. They were consumers, not producers, of spectator culture. Elizabeth Wilson's discussion of the female flaneur – as prostitute, lesbian, or journalist – exposes the gender politics of spectatorship and indicates the problem of trying to identify the female flaneur at all; see *The Sphinx in the City: Urban Life, the Control of Disorder, and Women* (Berkeley and Los Angeles: U of California P, 1991), 1–11.

24. See Mikhail Bakhtin, *Rabelais and His World*, trans. Helene Iswolsky (Bloomington: Indiana UP, 1984); Charles Baudelaire, *The Painter of Modern Life and Other Essays*, trans. and ed. Jonathan Mayne (London: Phaidon Publishers, 1964); Walter Benjamin, "Paris, Capital of the Nineteenth Century," in *Reflections*, ed. Peter Demetz, trans. Edmund Jephcott (New York: Harcourt Brace Jovanovich, 1978); and *Charles Baudelaire: A Lyric Poet in the Era of High Capitalism* (London: New Left Books, 1973); Marshall Berman, *All That Is Solid Melts into Air: The Experience of Modernity* (New York: Simon and Schuster, 1981); Brand (n. 9); Susan Buck-Morss, *The Dialectics of Seeing: Walter Benjamin and the Arcades Project* (Cambridge, Mass.: MIT Press, 1989); Robert H. Byer, "Mysteries of the City: A Reading of Poe's 'The Man of the Crowd,' " in Sacvan Bercovitch and Myra Jehlen, eds., *Ideology and Classic American Literature* (New York: Cambridge UP, 1986); Mary Ann Caws, ed., *City Images: Perspectives from Literature, Philosophy, and Film* (New York: Gordon and Breach, 1991); Eagleton (n. 9); Donald Fanger, *Dostoyevsky and Romantic Realism* (Cambridge, Mass.: Harvard UP, 1965); Philip Fisher, "City Matters: City Minds," in J. H. Buckley, ed., *The Worlds of Victorian Fiction* (Cambridge, Mass.: Harvard UP, 1975); Peter Jukes, *A Shout in the Street: An Excursion into the Modern City* (New York: Farrar, Straus, and Giroux, 1990); Miller (n. 6); David S. Reynolds, *Beneath the American Renaissance: The Subversive Imagination in the Age of Emerson and Melville* (Cambridge, Mass.: Harvard UP, 1989); Richard Sennett, *The Fall of Public Man* (New York: Alfred A. Knopf, 1977); Susan Sontag, *On Photography* (New York: Farrar, Straus, and Giroux, 1977); Raymond Williams, *The Country and the City* (New York: Oxford UP, 1973); Rosalind Williams, *Notes on the Underground: An Essay on Technology, Science, and the Imagination* (Cambridge, Mass.: MIT Press, 1990); and Wilson (n. 23) on the meaning of the flaneur, the spectator, and the modern city.

25. "The Man of the Crowd," in *Collected Works of Edgar Allan Poe*, ed. Thomas Ollive Mabbott (Cambridge, Mass.: Belknap Press of Harvard UP, 1978), 2: 515.

26. Hugh W. Hetherington, *Melville's Reviewers: British and American, 1846–1891* (Chapel Hill: U of North Carolina P, 1961), 24; Jay Leyda, *The Melville Log: A Documentary Life of Herman Melville, 1819–1891* (New York: Gordian Press, 1969), 206, 205, 228, 210. See also reviews in *The Nottingham Review*, quoted in Richard E. Winslow, "New Reviews Trace Melville's Reputation," *Melville Society Extracts* 89 (June 1992): 8. Sheila Post-Lauria discusses the class issues in the reception of Melville's early novels. See her chapters 1 and 2, "*Typee*: (Re)Making the Best Seller" and "Engaging Readers in *Omoo* and *Mardi*" in *Correspondent Colorings: Melville and Popular Literary Culture* (Amherst: U of Massachusetts P, 1996).

27. Leyda, 211, 216, 210.

28. Charles Robert Anderson, *Melville in the South Seas* (New York: Columbia UP, 1939), gives a full description of Melville's sources in travel literature and sailors' reminiscences.

29. Post-Lauria argues, however, in chapter 2, "Engaging Readers in *Omoo* and *Mardi*," that Melville adopts the "plain style" of the Nautical Reminiscence in order to expand his readership.

30. Sealts, *Melville's Reading*, 163.

31. Michael Paul Rogin, *Subversive Genealogy: The Politics and Art of Herman Melville* (New York: Alfred A. Knopf, 1983), and Edwin Havilland Miller, *Melville* (New York: George Braziller, 1975), respectively make much of his political and his psychological influence. Short does describe Gansevoort's education in relation to Melville's (12–16) and argues that Gansevoort's death in 1846 freed Herman to find his own voice and rhetorical authority (181–2). For a glimpse of Gansevoort's diplomatic writings, see Janet Gallignani Casey, "New Letters of Gansevoort Melville: 1845–1846," in *Studies in the American Renaissance 1991*, ed. Joel Myerson, 141–50.

32. Gilman, *Melville's Early Life*, 72–3 (n. 14).

33. Quoted in Burton R. Pollin, "Melville in Richmond, *Figaro!* and Elsewhere," *Melville Society Extracts* 89 (June 1992): 16.

34. This definition of taboo suggests that, like cannibalism, the taboo may encode and protect homosexuality. Caleb Crain discusses this use of cannibalism, though not taboo, in "Lovers of Human Flesh: Homosexuality and Cannibalism in Melville's Novels," *American Literature* 66 (March 1994): 25–53.

35. Hetherington, *Melville's Reviewers*, 67, 72 (n. 26).

36. Ibid., 79; see also Lynn Horth, "Two Albany *Argus* Reviews of *Omoo*," *Melville Society Extracts* 89 (June 1992): 13.

37. Lawrence, *Studies in Classic American Literature* (New York: Albert and Charles Boni, 1930), quoted in *Omoo*, "Historical Note," 341; Newton Arvin, *Herman Melville* (New York: William Sloan, 1950), 85, 86, 87.

38. Post-Lauria argues in chapter 2, "Engaging Readers in *Omoo* and *Mardi*," that this realistic portrayal of the working-class sailors is a convention of the Nautical Reminiscence that Melville would have employed consciously.

39. Gail Coffler, *Melville's Classical Allusions* (Westport, Conn.: Greenwood Press, 1985).

40. Wai-chee Dimock, *Empire for Liberty: Melville and the Poetics of Individualism* (Princeton, N.J.: Princeton UP, 1989), 71.

41. See Wyn Kelley, "Melville's Cain," *American Literature* 55 (March 1983): 24–40.

42. Lewis Mumford, *The City in History* (New York: Harcourt, Brace and World, 1961), 65.

43. On anthropocentrism and the relationship between humans and chimpanzees, see Dale Peterson and Jane Goodall, *Visions of Caliban: On Chimpanzees and People* (Boston: Houghton Mifflin, 1993).

44. Bernard Rosenthal, *City of Nature: Journeys to Nature in the Age of American Romanticism* (Newark: U of Delaware P, 1980) discusses the myth of Cain, nature, city, and *Mardi*, but not with the reading I have given the book.

3. Provincial in a Labyrinth

1. Walter Whitman, *Franklin Evans, or The Inebriate: A Tale of the Times*, in *The Early Poems and Fiction* of *The Collected Writings of Walt Whitman*, ed. Thomas L. Brasher (New York: New York UP, 1963), 148.
2. *The Country and the City* (New York: Oxford UP, 1973), 165.
3. See especially Elizabeth Blackmar, *Manhattan for Rent, 1785–1850* (Ithaca, N.Y.: Cornell UP, 1989); Carroll Smith-Rosenberg, *Religion and the Rise of the American City: The New York City Mission Movement, 1812–1870* (Ithaca, N.Y.: Cornell UP, 1971); and Edward K. Spann, *The New Metropolis: New York City, 1840–1857* (New York: Columbia UP, 1981).
4. Penelope Reed Doob, *The Idea of the Labyrinth from Classical Antiquity through the Middle Ages* (Ithaca, N.Y.: Cornell UP, 1990). Further references appear in parentheses in text.
5. *The Confessions of an English Opium-Eater*, in *The Collected Writings of Thomas DeQuincey*, ed. David Masson (London: A. & C. Black, 1897), 375.
6. *The Life and Adventures of Martin Chuzzlewit* (London and New York: Oxford UP, 1966), 127.
7. For discussion of the literature of mystery and misery, see Benedict Giamo, *On the Bowery: Confronting Homelessness in American Society* (Iowa City: U of Iowa Press, 1989); David S. Reynolds, *Beneath the American Renaissance: The Subversive Imagination in the Age of Emerson and Melville* (Cambridge, Mass.: Harvard UP, 1989); Adrienne Siegel, *The Image of the American City in Popular Literature: 1820–1870* (Port Washington, N.Y.: Kennikat Press, 1981); and Janis Stout, *Sodoms in Eden: The City in American Fiction before 1860* (Westport, Conn.: Greenwood Press, 1976).
8. "Reification and American Literature," in *Ideology and Classic American Literature*, eds. Sacvan Bercovitch and Myra Jehlen (New York: Cambridge UP, 1986), 188–9. See also Carolyn Porter, *Seeing and Being: The Plight of the Participant Observer in Emerson, James, Adams, and Faulkner* (Middletown, Conn.: Wesleyan UP, 1981); Georg Lukács, *History and Class Consciousness: Studies in Marxist Dialectics* (Cambridge, Mass.: MIT Press, 1971); Ira Katznelson, *Marxism and the City* (Oxford: Clarendon Press, 1992).
9. Giamo, *On the Bowery*, 31.
10. *The Physiology of New York Boarding-Houses* (New York: Mason Brothers, 1857), 12. Further references appear in parentheses in text.
11. See Peter G. Buckley, "Culture, Class, and Place in Antebellum New York," in John Hull Mollenkopf, *Power, Culture, and Place: Essays on New York City* (New York: Russell Sage Foundation, 1988), for a detailed mapping of the city.
12. Clarence Cook, "New York Daguerreotyped," *Putnam's Monthly Magazine* 1 (February 1853): 124. Further references appear in parentheses in text.
13. Joel Ross, *What I Saw in New York; or A Bird's Eye View of City Life* (Auburn, N.Y.: Derby & Miller, 1851), 14. Further references appear in parentheses in text.
14. Graham Russell Hodges, *New York City Cartmen, 1667–1850* (New York: New York UP, 1986).
15. *A Glance at New York* (New York: A. Greene, 1837), 178. Further references appear in parentheses in text.

16. Smith-Rosenberg, *Religion and the Rise of the American City*, 169–70; Spann, *New Metropolis*, chap. 3.

17. *The City That Was*, ed. John Duffy (Metuchen, N.J.: Scarecrow Reprint Corporation, 1973), 66–7. See also John Duffy, *The History of Public Health in New York City, 1625–1866* (New York: Russell Sage Foundation, 1968).

18. George Foster, *New York by Gas-Light*, ed. Stuart M. Blumin (Berkeley and Los Angeles: U of California P, 1990), 100. Further references appear in parentheses in text.

19. *Glimpses of New York City* (Charleston: J. J. McCarter, 1852), 14. Further references appear in parentheses in text.

20. *Hot Corn: Life Scenes in New York Illustrated* (New York: DeWitt and Davenport, 1854), 22–3. Further references appear in parentheses in text.

21. See E. Porter Belden, *New York: Past, Present, and Future* (New York: George Putnam, 1849), 36. Further references appear in parentheses in text. See also Pamela Jones, *Under the City Streets* (New York: Holt Rinehart and Winston, 1978); John Kouwenhoven, *The Columbia Historical Portrait of New York: An Essay in Graphic History* (New York: Doubleday, 1972); Spann, *The New Metropolis*; Isaac Newton Phelps Stokes, *The Iconography of Manhattan Island, 1498–1909* (New York: R. H. Dodd, 1915).

22. See Foster, *New York by Gas-Light*; Jones, *Under the City Streets*; Wolfgang Schivelbusch, *Disenchanted Night: The Industrialization of Light in the Nineteenth Century*, trans. Angela Davies (Berkeley and Los Angeles: U of California P, 1988).

23. *American Notes and Pictures from Italy* (London: Macmillan, 1893), 76. Further references appear in parentheses in text.

24. *New York: Its Upper Ten and Lower Million* (1853; rpt. Upper Saddle River, N.J.: Literature House/ Gregg Press, 1970), 116. Further references appear in parentheses in text.

25. For information on Pease, see Smith-Rosenberg, *Religion and the Rise of the American City*, 224–44, and Spann, *The New Metropolis*, 275.

26. *Life in New York* (New York: Robert Carter, 1847), 173. Further references appear in parentheses in text.

27. See also Buckley, in Mollenkopf, *Power, Culture, and Place*, 28–34.

28. Benedict Giamo (n. 7) describes the conventions and aesthetics of the "police lantern tour" in books and journals. "As trope, the police lantern was at once the vehicle for perception as well as its vanishing embodiment. This procedure of lighting and shading the scenes of poverty, disclosing and dissolving, incarnated an attitude of mystification which became a paradigm for followers of the sensationalistic genre. Together, as motif and trope, the police lantern provided a practical means of entry into the labyrinth of subculture along with an effortless way out by virtue of its interpretive legerdemain" (*On the Bowery*, 49).

29. *The Mysteries and Miseries of New York* (New York: Berford & Co., 1848), 89. Further references appear in parentheses in text.

30. Carolyn L. Karcher, *Shadow Over the Promised Land: Slavery, Race, and Violence in Melville's America* (Baton Rouge: Louisiana State UP, 1980), covers the racial issues in Melville's work thoroughly but has not included the particular context of New York.

31. I have been influenced, in my ideas on taxonomy and its social implications,

by two very different works: Michel Foucault, *The Order of Things: An Archaeology of the Human Sciences* (New York: Pantheon Books, 1970); and Harriet Ritvo, *The Animal Estate: The English and Other Creatures in the Victorian Age* (Cambridge, Mass.: Harvard UP, 1987). Dana Brand, *The Spectator and the City in Nineteenth-Century American Literature* (New York: Cambridge UP, 1991), discusses the "Theophrastian character book" as an early form of urban taxonomy and describes it as, in Foucault's and Benjamin's terms, "a form of social control" (24).

32. Asa Greene, *A Glance at New York* (New York: Asa Greene, 1837), 79–80.

33. "The Man of the Crowd," in *Collected Works of Edgar Allan Poe*, ed. Thomas Ollive Mabbott (Cambridge, Mass.: Harvard UP, 1978), 506–10. Further references appear in parentheses in text.

34. *New York Naked* (New York: Robert M. DeWitt, 1854), 17.

35. *Sunshine and Shadow in New York* (Hartford: J. B. Burr & Co., 1869).

36. Madame Resimer is based on a woman named Madame Restell who inhabits the pages of Ellington's *The Women of New York* and Sutton's *The New York Tombs*. See Siegel, *Image of the American City*, 40.

37. The female rush to ruin is an established convention of the seduction novel, beginning with such examples as Hannah Webster Foster's *The Coquette* and Susannah Rowson's *Charlotte Temple*. See Cathy N. Davidson, *Revolution and the Word: The Rise of the Novel in America* (New York: Oxford UP, 1986).

38. Harrison Gray Buchanan, *Asmodeus: or, Legends of New York* (New York: John D. Munson, 1848), 31.

39. *The Empire City: Or New York by Night and Day. Its Aristocracy and Its Dollars* (Freeport, N.Y.: Books for Libraries Press, 1969), 28. Further references appear in parentheses in text.

40. See David S. Reynolds, *George Lippard* (Boston: Twayne Publishers, 1982).

41. *Sensational Designs: The Cultural Work of American Fiction, 1790–1860* (New York: Oxford UP, 1985).

42. For discussions of *Redburn* and the city, see William Gilman, *Melville's Early Life and Redburn* (New York: New York UP, 1951); Harold T. McCarthy, "Melville's *Redburn* and the City," *The Midwest Quarterly* 12 (July 1971): 394–410; James Polk, "Melville and the Idea of the City," *University of Toronto Quarterly* 41 (1972): 277–92; Reynolds (n. 7); Stout (n. 7); Willard Thorp, "Redburn's Prosy Old Guidebook," *PMLA* 53 (December 1938): 1146–56.

43. Sheila Post-Lauria shows that Redburn in fact grows in maturity and cognitive depth. See her chapter 3, "Writer and Community in *Redburn* and *White-Jacket*," in *Correspondent Colorings: Melville and Popular Literary Culture* (Amherst: U of Massachusetts P, 1996).

44. Marvin Fisher argues that the book directly attacks this literary culture, especially the works of Cotton Mather, Benjamin Franklin, Timothy Dwight, Washington Irving, and Oliver Goldsmith. He also suggests that Redburn is a mock-spectator: "When he tried to speak Addisonian English to his hosts in the English countryside, Redburn became more than a curiosity. Here he was a representative of a brash New World democracy trying to sound like a ridiculous relic of Augustan England"; in "The Burden of Literary History in *Redburn*," unpublished manuscript.

45. Reynolds, *Beneath the American Renaissance*, 146.

46. See Nicholas K. Bromell, "The Erotics of Labor in Melville's *Redburn*," in *By the Sweat of the Brow: Literature and Labor in Antebellum America* (Chicago: U of Chicago P, 1993), 61–79.

47. David Reynolds argues, on the contrary, that Redburn's breaking of the pledge carries with it "dark consequences" and deep guilt (*Beneath the American Renaissance*, 145).

48. In some ways my reading of race in *Redburn* borrows from Carolyn Karcher's reading of Ishmael's relationship with Queequeg. See *Shadow Over the Promised Land: Slavery, Race, and Violence in Melville's America* (Baton Rouge: Louisiana State UP, 1980).

49. See M. Wynn Thomas, "Whitman's Tale of Two Cities," *American Literary History* 6 (Winter 1994): 633–57.

50. On Melville's connection with Mike Walsh, see Reynolds, *Beneath the American Renaissance*, 81, 458, and 464, where he identifies him as "the prototypical bhoy politician."

51. On the b'hoys, see Reynolds, *Beneath the American Renaissance*, 285, 463–6, 508–16, and 543–4; and Sean Wilentz, *Chants Democratic: New York City and the Rise of the American Working Class, 1788–1850* (New York: Oxford UP, 1984), 263.

52. In, for example, Gilman (n. 42), Reynolds (n. 7), and Stout (n. 7).

53. *Letters from New York* (New York: C. S. Francis, 1844), 27. Henry P. Tappan had this to say about the Tombs:

> Where the Tombs . . . now stand, there was once a little lake which connected with the Hudson, by a little outlet through Canal Street. Near the lake was a hill with a natural and abundant fountain. Had the shores of that lake and fountain been preserved and embellished, had the outlet been left open and spanned with tasteful bridges, how charming that portion of the city would have been! Now there are the Tombs and mean shops and dwellings; the hill with its fountains is sunk to fill up the lake, and the running stream is changed into a covered sewer. (Quoted in Spann, *The New Metropolis*, 115)

54. See Charles Rosenberg, *The Cholera Years: The United States in 1832, 1849, and 1866* (Chicago: Chicago UP, 1962).

55. Among the writers who have discussed the urban implications of the *Neversink* are: Newton Arvin, *Herman Melville* (New York: William Sloane Associates, 1950); F. O. Matthiesson, *The American Renaissance: Art and Expression in the Age of Emerson and Whitman* (1941; rpt. New York: Oxford UP, 1977); Polk (n. 42); Reynolds (n. 7); Stout (n. 7); and Howard P. Vincent, *The Tailoring of Melville's White-Jacket* (Evanston, Ill.: Northwestern UP, 1970).

56. Post-Lauria shows that in *White-Jacket* Melville makes his protagonist's quest for community a positive choice, analogous to his own efforts to enter the literary culture. See her "Writer and Community in *Redburn* and *White-Jacket*" (n. 43).

57. Here Melville challenges the romantic view of boardinghouses, found in Jules Janin's remark: "[The peculiar organization of the city may offer] something more curious than the pyramids of Egypt, the Kremlin, or the glaciers of Switzerland, something more astonishing than all the marvels that one goes to see at such cost in money and fatigue – a great Parisian building, in a crowded quarter, tenanted from the basement right up to the roof." Quoted in Donald

Fanger, *Dostoyevsky and Romantic Realism* (Cambridge, Mass.: Harvard UP, 1965), 23.

58. *Memoirs of Vidocq* (London, 1828; rpt. New York: Arno Press, 1976); see also J. P. Stead, *Vidocq: A Biography* (New York: Roy Publishers, 1954). Neither Merton M. Sealts, Jr., *Melville's Reading* (Columbia: U of South Carolina P, 1988), nor Mary K. Bercaw, *Melville's Sources* (Evanston, Ill.: Northwestern UP, 1987) cites Vidocq's memoirs. Melville's two references here, however, suggest that he knew the legend well. In *Moby-Dick* he mentions Vidocq's early life: "some have surmised that the man who first thus entitled [gave the name of schoolmaster to] this sort of Ottoman whale, must have read the memoirs of Vidocq, and informed himself what sort of a country-schoolmaster that famous Frenchman was in his younger days, and what was the nature of those occult lessons he inculcated in some of his pupils" (393).

59. On the iconography of subterranean environments, see Rosalind Williams, *Notes on the Underground: An Essay on Technology, Society, and the Imagination* (Cambridge, Mass.: MIT Press, 1990).

60. For a political reading of the country in *Pierre*, however, see Samuel Otter, "The Eden of Saddle Meadows: Landscape and Ideology in *Pierre*," *American Literature* 66 (March 1994): 55–81.

61. Sheila Post-Lauria shows, however, what the novel owes to the sensational French romances of Sue, Balzac, Hugo, and others. See "Genre and Ideology: The French Sensational Romance and Melville's *Pierre*," *Journal of American Culture* 15 (Fall 1992): 1–8.

62. For readings of *Pierre* and the city, see Charles Moorman, "Melville's *Pierre* in the City," *American Literature* 27 (1956): 571–77; Polk (n. 42); John Henry Raleigh, "The Novel and the City: England and America in the Nineteenth Century," *Victorian Studies* 11 (1967/8): 291–328; Reynolds (n. 7); Stout (n. 7); Nathalia Wright, "*Pierre*: Herman Melville's *Inferno*," *American Literature* 32 (1960): 167–81.

63. Richard Brodhead suggests that Melville himself becomes trapped in the fictional labyrinth of the novel: "As Melville comes to see himself as trapped within the debased fictional means by which he had initially hoped to open up new dimensions of psychic experience, his 'book of sacred truth' becomes increasingly conscious of itself as a lie." *Hawthorne, Melville, and the Novel* (Chicago: U of Chicago P, 1976), 186.

64. Eric Sundquist suggests that "to descend into the heart of a man like Pierre" is to enter a genealogical labyrinth: "Genealogical source and ethical motive become lost in an inexplicable tangle of obscurity and ambiguity opening out over an abyss, a sarcophagus without a body." *Home as Found: Authority and Genealogy in Nineteenth-Century American Literature* (Baltimore: Johns Hopkins UP, 1979), 161–2.

65. The Cretan labyrinth is somewhat different from the many Christian constructions of the labyrinth, where choice ends once one has entered the labyrinth. See Doob (n. 4) and my "*Pierre* in a Labyrinth: The Mysteries and Miseries of New York," in Robert Milder, ed., *The Evermoving Dawn: Essays in Celebration of the Melville Centennial* (Kent, Ohio: Kent State UP, 1996).

66. A number of critics have located that site of crime and passion in Pierre's and Melville's own sexuality, or his father's sexuality. See Amy Puett Emmers, "Mel-

ville's Closet Skeleton: A New Letter About the Illegitimacy Incident in *Pierre*,"
Studies in the American Renaissance (1977): 339–43; and "New Crosslights on
the Illegitimate Daughter in *Pierre*," in Brian Higgins and Hershel Parker, eds.,
Critical Essays on Herman Melville's "Pierre: Or the Ambiguities" (Boston: G. K. Hall,
1983), 237–40; Philip Young, *The Private Melville* (University Park, Pa.: Penn-
sylvania State UP, 1993); James Creech, *Closet Writing/Gay Reading: The Case of
Melville's "Pierre"* (Chicago: U of Chicago P, 1993).

67. Reynolds argues: "The second half of the novel is not only about the kind of
dark city mysteries and philosophical ambiguities that typified popular sensa-
tionalism; it is simultaneously about the contemplation of such mysteries and
ambiguities by the reflective American novelist," *Beneath the American Renaissance*, 294.

68. In chapter 3 of *Moby-Dick*, "The Spouter-Inn," Ishmael examines a dubious
portrait of a whale hunt by the "unequal cross-lights" of the dark entry of the
inn: "it was only by diligent study and a series of systematic visits to it, and
careful inquiry of the neighbors, that you could any way arrive at an understanding of its purpose" (*MD*, 12).

69. Michael Rogin suggests that the urban plot itself is a reversal of the typical
American plot, which he sees as a journey into the wilderness: "In sending
Pierre from the country to the city and reversing the direction typical of clas-
sical American literature, Melville was imitating the French pattern." *Subversive
Genealogy: The Politics and Art of Herman Melville* (New York: Alfred A. Knopf,
1983), 176.

70. Brodhead puts the problem another way: "The search for final truth has been
defeated too many times, the mind has discovered the fictiveness of its representations of the real too often" (*Hawthorne, Melville, and the Novel*, 193).

4. Town Ho

1. "Whose American Renaissance?" in *The Critics Bear It Away: American Fiction
and the Academy* (New York: Random House, 1992), 16–46. See Sacvan Bercovitch, "The Problem of Ideology in a Time of Dissensus," in *The Rites of
Assent: Transformations in the Symbolic Construction of America* (New York:
Routledge, 1993), 353–76.

2. *The City Assembled: The Elements of Urban Form Through History* (Boston: Little,
Brown, 1992), 305. See also Kostof's companion volume, *The City Shaped: Urban
Patterns and Meanings Through History* (Boston: Little, Brown, 1991).

3. See Elizabeth Blackmar, *Manhattan for Rent, 1785–1850* (Ithaca, N.Y.: Cornell
UP, 1989).

4. See especially Leo Marx, *The Machine in the Garden: Technology and the Pastoral
Ideal in America* (New York: Oxford UP, 1964); Sheila Post-Lauria, *Correspondent
Colorings: Melville and Popular Literary Culture* (Amherst: U of Massachusetts P,
1996); Michael Rogin, *Subversive Genealogy: The Politics and Art of Herman Melville*
(New York: Alfred A. Knopf, 1983).

5. See Kostof (n. 2); John Mock, "We Have Always Lived Under the Castle:
Historical Symbols and the Maintenance of Meaning," in Robert Rotenberg
and Gary McDonogh, eds., *The Cultural Meanings of Urban Space* (Westport,
Conn.: Bergin & Garvey, 1993); Lewis Mumford, *The City in History: Its Origins,*

Its Transformations, and Its Prospects (New York: Harcourt, Brace, 1961); John W. Reps, *The Making of Urban America: The History of City Planning in the United States* (Princeton, N.J.: Princeton UP, 1965).

6. *The Culture of Cities* (New York: Harcourt, Brace, 1938), 44. Further references appear in parentheses in text.

7. Hawthorne, in the last scene of *The Scarlet Letter,* similarly unites sailors, Native Americans, and the town dwellers within one urban form, the frontier town; but he presents the different social groups in a stylized, carefully composed picture that places them in separate and distinct areas. I am indebted to Laurie Robertson-Lorant for pointing out this connection.

8. "The city of the dead antedates the city of the living" (Mumford, *City in History,* 7); cities first existed, claims Mumford, to give homes for the dead. Even when the living wandered about following their sources of food, they returned to their ancestors' graves in seasonal rituals of remembrance.

9. For a discussion of the politics of sailor fraternity, see Robert K. Martin, *Hero, Captain, and Stranger: Male Friendship, Social Critique, and Literary Form in the Sea Novels of Herman Melville* (Chapel Hill: U of North Carolina P, 1986). See also Wilson Carey McWilliams, *The Idea of Fraternity in America* (Berkeley and Los Angeles: U of California P, 1973).

10. See especially Marx, *The Machine in the Garden;* F. O. Matthiesson, *The American Renaissance: Art and Expression in the Age of Emerson and Whitman* (New York: Oxford UP, 1941). Nicholas K. Bromell argues, in contrast, that *Moby-Dick* does not provide a satisfying picture of labor: "The difficulty of representing manual work as it is felt and understood and valued by manual workers is equally plain in *Moby-Dick,* that novel which at first glance seems to consist largely of workers performing work, but which on closer inspection turns out to render seamen and their labors practically invisible." See his *By the Sweat of the Brow: Literature and Labor in Antebellum America* (Chicago: U of Chicago P, 1993), 36.

11. This is the definition that appears in the *Oxford English Dictionary,* quoting the *Collections of the Massachusetts Historical Society* (1810), 3:154.

12. On the social and racial implications of the *Town-Ho* mutiny, see Robert S. Levine, *Conspiracy and Romance: Studies in Brockden Brown, Cooper, Hawthorne, and Melville* (New York: Cambridge UP, 1989), 192–5.

13. Ishmael makes this point especially clear when he associates Steelkilt with the French Revolution, portraying him and the mutineers as battling oppression from behind their Parisian barricades.

14. See Setha M. Low, "Cultural Meaning of the Plaza: The History of the Spanish-American Gridplan–Plaza Urban Design," in Rotenberg and McDonogh, *Cultural Meanings of Urban Space,* 75–93.

15. The plaza appears also in "Benito Cereno," but as a site of open cultural conflict rather than cultural exchange. Babo's head, "that hive of subtlety, fixed on a pole in the Plaza, met, unabashed, the gaze of the whites" (*PT,* 116).

16. Post-Lauria details the methods by which Melville designed the novel to reach an urban audience. See her chapter 4, "Designing Methods: Originality in *Moby-Dick,*" in *Correspondent Colorings;* and " 'Philosophy in Whales . . . Poetry in Blubber': Mixed Form in *Moby-Dick,*" *Nineteenth-Century Literature* (1990): 300–16.

17. On American Protestant constructions of Catholicism, see Jenny Franchot, *Roads to Rome: The Antebellum Protestant Encounter with Catholicism* (Berkeley and Los Angeles: U of California P, 1994).

18. Most recently, Thomas Farel Heffernan, "Eonism on the *Town-Ho:* or What *Did* Steelkilt Say?" *Melville Society Extracts* 83 (November 1990): 10–12.

5. Sojourner in the City of Man

1. Catharine Beecher, *A Treatise on Domestic Economy* (Boston: T. H. Webb, 1842).

2. Melville's personal feelings about home, recorded in the 1849 *Journal,* suggest that repose is essential to his notion of home: "Would that One I know were here. Would that the Little One too were here. – I am in a very painful state of uncertainty. I am all eagerness to get home – I ought to be home – my absence occasions uneasiness in a quarter where I must beseech heaven to grant repose" (41). For a full theoretical treatment of the aesthetics of repose, see John Bryant, *Melville & Repose: The Rhetoric of Humor in the American Renaissance* (New York: Oxford UP, 1993).

3. On Melville's domestic life, see Laurie Robertson-Lorant, *Melville: A Biography* (New York: Clarkson N. Potter Publishers, 1996); Hershel Parker, *"Moby-Dick* and Domesticity," in *Critical Essays on Herman Melville's "Moby-Dick",* ed. Brian Higgins and Hershel Parker (New York: G. K. Hall, 1992), 545–62.

4. Carol Colatrella, however, argues that the interactions between husband and wife show the dynamism and flexibility of their relationship. See her "Home Improvement: Melville's Narratives and Domestic Culture," unpublished manuscript.

5. See Nina Baym, *Woman's Fiction: A Guide to Novels by and about Women in America* (Ithaca, N.Y.: Cornell UP, 1978; rpt. Urbana: U of Illinois P, 1993); Nicholas K. Bromell, *By the Sweat of the Brow: Literature and Labor in Antebellum America* (Chicago: U of Chicago P, 1993); Gillian Brown, *Domestic Individualism: Imagining Self in Nineteenth-Century America* (Berkeley and Los Angeles: U of California P, 1990); Barbara Leslie Epstein, *The Politics of Domesticity: Women, Evangelism, and Temperance in Nineteenth-Century America* (Middletown, Conn.: Wesleyan UP, 1981); Susan K. Harris, *19th-Century American Women's Novels: Interpretive Strategies* (Cambridge and New York: Cambridge UP, 1990); Mary Kelley, *Private Woman, Public Stage: Literary Domesticity in Nineteenth-Century America* (New York: Oxford UP, 1984); Sheila Post-Lauria, *Correspondent Colorings: Melville and Popular Literary Culture* (Amherst: U of Massachusetts P, 1996); Mary P. Ryan, *The Empire of the Mother: American Writing about Domesticity 1830–1860* (New York: The Haworth Press, 1982), and *Women in Public: Between Banners and Ballots, 1825–1880* (Baltimore: Johns Hopkins UP, 1990); Christine Stansell, *City of Women: Sex and Class in New York, 1789–1860* (New York: Alfred A. Knopf, 1986); and Jane Tompkins, *Sensational Designs: The Cultural Work of American Fiction, 1790–1860* (New York: Oxford UP, 1985).

6. Gillian Brown clearly states this, calling Melville a misogynist (*Domestic Individualism,* 160). Lora Romero argues, however, for a less oppositional relationship between Melville and the domestic novel: "the need to manufacture the difference that would separate canonical from noncanonical, one could argue, dictates that Herman Melville's *Pierre* (1852) be generally regarded as a *parody*

of the domestic novel rather than an *instance* of it" (112); see her "Domesticity and Fiction," in *The Columbia History of the American Novel*, ed. Emory Elliott (New York: Columbia UP, 1991), 110–29.

7. Elizabeth Blackmar, *Manhattan for Rent, 1785–1850* (Ithaca, N.Y.: Cornell UP, 1989), 169–70. See also Paul S. Boyer, *Urban Masses and Moral Order in America, 1820–1920* (Cambridge, Mass.: Harvard UP, 1978); Carroll Smith-Rosenberg, *Religion and the Rise of the American City: The New York City Mission Movement, 1812–1870* (Ithaca, N.Y.: Cornell UP, 1971).

8. Quoted in Alexander Welsh, *The City of Dickens* (Oxford: Clarendon Press, 1971), 55. See also Augustine, *The City of God*, trans. Gerald G. Walsh and Grace Monahan (Washington, D.C.: Catholic U of America P, 1952); Michael H. Cowan, *City of the West: Emerson, America, and Urban Metaphor* (New Haven and London: Yale UP, 1967); Jacques Ellul, *The Meaning of the City*, trans. Dennis Pardee (Grand Rapids, Mich.: William B. Eerdmans, 1970); Bernard Rosenthal, *City of Nature: Journeys to Nature in the Age of American Romanticism* (Newark: U of Delaware P, 1980).

9. See Wyn Kelley, "Melville's Cain," *American Literature* 55 (March 1983): 24–40.

10. Melville goes on, in this letter, to imply a pun on Cornelius Mathews's nickname, Big Abel (after his novel, *Big Abel and Little Manhattan*): "Do you and Mathews pitch paving-stones, & play ball that way in the cool of the evening, opposite the Astor-House?" In notes scribbled on a back page of his Shakespeare, Melville indicated that he was contemplating writing a comic story about devils and wrote a scrap of dialogue on Cain: " 'Yes, Madam, Cain was a godless froward boy, & Reuben (Gen: 49) & Absalom' Many pious men have impious children"; quoted in "Historical Note" to *Moby-Dick*, 969. Both references, remarkably humorous, are quite different from the dire tone in which Melville refers to Cain in his fiction.

11. Gary McDonogh demonstrates that emptiness, as a category in urban space, signifies conflict rather than openness and freedom: "In this essay, I have argued that we must recognize and explore empty places as culturally created and socially meaningful zones rich in interest for our analysis of the city. As these cases have suggested, such spaces do not define a vacuum, an absence of urbanness, so much as they mark zones of intense competition: the interstices of the city. This intensification may mean points of trace and conflict in history, across social divisions, in planning, although both extremes betray impositions of urban power." See "The Geography of Emptiness," in Robert Rotenberg and Gary McDonogh, eds., *The Cultural Meaning of Urban Space* (Westport, Conn.: Bergin & Garvey, 1993), 13.

12. *The Poor Rich Man and the Rich Poor Man* (New York: Harper & Brothers, 1836), 113.

13. John Griscom, *The Sanitary Condition of the Laboring Population of New York* (New York, 1845), 9; quoted in Anthony Jackson, *A Place Called Home: A History of Low-Cost Housing in Manhattan* (Cambridge, Mass.: MIT Press, 1976), 5.

14. Blackmar (n. 7); Rosenberg (n. 7); Edward K. Spann, *The New Metropolis: New York City, 1840–1857* (New York: Columbia UP, 1981); Stansell (n. 5); Sean Wilentz, *Chants Democratic: New York City and the Rise of the American Working Class, 1788–1850* (New York: Oxford UP, 1984).

15. The European bildungsroman includes a few dispossessed aristocrats – Balzac's Rastignac comes to mind – but few fall from as eminent a height as Pierre does.

16. See Nancy Fredericks, *Melville's Art of Democracy* (Athens & London: U of Georgia P, 1995), 98–111; and Samuel Otter, "The Eden of Saddle Meadows: Landscape and Ideology in *Pierre*," *American Literature* 66 (March 1994), 55–81.

17. Blackmar, *Manhattan for Rent*, 76, 156.

18. Spann, *The New Metropolis*, 151–2.

19. Astor's greed for land was insatiable: "Could I begin life again . . . knowing what I now know, and had money to invest, I would buy every foot of land on the Island of Manhattan"; quoted in Spann, 208.

20. Blackmar, 104.

21. See Blackmar, 213–49, on the modes of resistance tenants used to limit the power of landlords. It is curious that Melville does not represent life in the tenements as completely miserable but shows instead a lively tenement subculture, albeit in a kind of Fourieristic parody.

22. See Fredericks on tenancy melodramas, 106.

23. Michael Paul Rogin, *Subversive Genealogy: The Politics and Art of Herman Melville* (New York: Alfred A. Knopf, 1983), 196. Herbert F. Smith, "Melville's Master in Chancery and His Recalcitrant Clerk," *American Quarterly* 17 (Winter 1965): 734–41, is especially useful in clarifying the significance of the lawyer's appointment as Master in Chancery.

24. See especially Blackmar, chaps. 1 and 2.

25. See also David Leverenz, *Manhood and the American Renaissance* (Ithaca, N.Y.: Cornell UP, 1989), 88–9.

26. Spann, 36.

27. See Rogin, 52.

28. See Spann, 228–33, on Trinity Church as landholder. Mike Walsh saw Astor and Trinity Church as partners in crime (233).

29. Walter H. Eitner, "The Lawyer's Rockaway Trips in 'Bartleby, the Scrivener,'" *Melville Society Extracts* 78 (September 1989): 14–16, argues for a more purposeful journey, that the lawyer visits the sites of Astor's residences "as on a pilgrimage, to places where he might find comforting confirmations of the success of the Astor ethic and of lawyers' roles in it" (15).

30. The fact that "Jimmy Rose" appeared in *Harper's* magazine, which favored sentimental treatments of social issues, helps to explain the story's differences from "Bartleby," written for *Putnam's*, which promoted more direct, confrontational efforts at reform. See Sheila Post-Lauria's chap. 7, "Editorial Policies and Politics in the Magazine Fiction," in *Correspondent Colorings: Melville and Popular Literary Culture* (Amherst: U of Massachusetts P, 1996).

31. Beecher (n. 1); Andrew Jackson Downing, *The Architecture of Country Houses* (New York: Appleton, 1861).

32. See Brown (n. 5); Ann Douglas, *The Feminization of American Culture* (New York: Alfred A. Knopf, 1977); Rogin (n. 23); Tompkins (n. 5). On Melville and the feminine, see *Melville Society Extracts* 65 (February 1986), a special issue on "Women in Melville's Art"; and Laurie Robertson-Lorant, "Melville's Embrace of the Invisible Woman," *Melville Society Extracts* 80 (February 1990): 3.

33. See Eric Sundquist, *Home as Found: Authority and Genealogy in Nineteenth-*

Century American Literature (Baltimore: Johns Hopkins UP, 1979), 146: "But everything we would wish to say about Melville's book indicates how much the act of founding a home is at its very heart, though with a consistent ironic inversion."

34. Richard Sennett, *The Fall of Public Man* (New York: Random House, 1977).

35. A recipe for negus appears in the cookbook Melville purchased for his wife in 1854 and reads as follows: "Upon three ounces of pearl barley pour a couple of quarts of boiling water, a quarter of a pound of pounded loaf sugar, and a lemon sliced. Strain it when it is cold, and add a pint of port or sherry wine and one glass of pale brandy." See Matilda Marian Pullan, *The Modern Housewife's Receipt Book: A Guide to All Matters Connected with Household Economy* (London: Aird and Hutton, 1854), 149.

36. Fanny Fern, *Ruth Hall and Other Writings*, ed. Joyce W. Warren (New Brunswick, N.J.: Rutgers UP, 1986).

37. Stansell, 64–75. These visits also supported the goals of feminists. See Smith-Rosenberg, 118–24.

38. Stansell, *City of Women*, 202. See also Ronald Zboray, *A Fictive People: Antebellum Economic Development and the American Reading Public* (New York: Oxford UP, 1993), on the connections between domestic morality, reading habits, and the home.

39. Stansell, 48, 70–4, 196.

40. Quoted in ibid., 74.

41. Ibid., 203.

42. See especially Douglas (n. 32), Rogin (n. 23), and Robyn Wiegman, "Melville's Geography of Gender," *American Literary History* 1 (1989): 735–53.

43. Wai-Chee Dimock has argued most persuasively against totalizing "readings" of class in literary texts and in Melville's story. See her "Class, Gender, and a History of Metonymy," in *Rethinking Class: Literary Studies and Social Formations*, eds. Wai-Chee Dimock and Michael T. Gilmore (New York: Columbia UP, 1994).

44. See Cowan (n. 7), Ellul (n. 8), Rosenthal (n. 8), Welsh (n. 8); and John Henry Raleigh, "The Novel and the City: England and America in the Nineteenth Century," *Victorian Studies* 11 (1967): 291–328.

45. Dimock, however, does not address the matter of Bartleby's imperial self in *Empire for Liberty: Melville and the Poetics of Individualism* (Princeton N.J.: Princeton UP, 1989).

46. Richard Chase, *Herman Melville: A Critical Study* (New York: Hafner, 1971), 184; Harry Levin, *The Power of Blackness: Hawthorne, Poe, and Melville* (New York: Alfred A. Knopf, 1958), 191; John T. Frederick, "Symbol and Theme in Melville's *Israel Potter*," *Modern Fiction Studies* 8 (1962): 270, 272; Frederick W. Turner III, "Melville and Thomas Berger: The Novelist as Cultural Anthropologist," *The Centennial Review* 13 (1969): 112; Janis Stout, *Sodoms in Eden: The City in American Fiction before 1860* (Westport, Conn.: Greenwood Press, 1976), 134–5.

47. Michael Rogin, however, argues that "Israel is buried alive, not merely in the London pyramid but also in the sepulcher of his own Revolution" (228).

6. Pilgrim in the City of God

1. On the Melville biography for this period, see: Hennig Cohen and Donald Yannella, *Herman Melville's Malcolm Letter: "Man's Final Lore"* (New York: Fordham University Press and the New York Public Library, 1992); Stanton Garner, *The Civil War World of Herman Melville* (Lawrence: UP of Kansas, 1993); Leon Howard, *Herman Melville* (Berkeley and Los Angeles: U of California P, 1967); Laurie Robertson-Lorant, *Melville: A Biography* (New York: Clarkson N. Potter, Publishers, 1996).

2. The best source on Melville and the Civil War is Stanton Garner, *The Civil War World of Herman Melville*. For other information on the Draft Riots, see Iver Bernstein, *The New York City Draft Riots: Their Significance for American Society and Politics in the Age of the Civil War* (New York: Oxford UP, 1990), and Adrian Cook, *The Armies of the Streets: The New York City Draft Riots of 1863* (Lexington: UP of Kentucky, 1974). For a contemporary history by a Know-Nothing Whig observer, see Joel Tyler Headley, *The Great Riots of New York, 1712–1873*, eds. Thomas Rose and James Rodgers (New York: Bobbs-Merrill, 1970), first published 1873. For material on New York politics of the period, see Amy Bridges, *A City in the Republic: Antebellum New York and the Origins of Machine Politics* (Ithaca, N.Y.: Cornell UP, 1987); Alexander B. Callow, Jr., *The Tweed Ring* (New York: Oxford UP, 1966); and Seymour J. Mandelbaum, *Boss Tweed's New York* (New York: John Wiley, 1965).

3. This is the view of Bernstein, *New York City Draft Riots*, 71–2.

4. Garner shows that the speaker is a "Union Leaguer" who "expresses the aristocrats' view of the rabble on the streets" – a view, however, which is contrary to Melville's own (*Civil War World of Herman Melville*, 256). The Union League Club included in its membership the Melville family minister, Henry Whitney Bellows; several signers of the Astor Place riots petitions, which Melville endorsed; as well as William Cullen Bryant, George William Curtis, Pierre Irving, Frederick Law Olmsted, and Henry A. Smythe, through whose friendship Melville got his job in the Customs House (see also Bernstein, 148–61, 272–6). I am also indebted to Laurie Robertson-Lorant for discussions of the significance of the Union League Club.

5. Although Jenny Franchot does not specifically address this poem, her treatment of Rome in the American culture provides a rich gloss on this line. See her *Roads to Rome: The Antebellum Protestant Encounter with Catholicism* (Berkeley and Los Angeles: U of California P, 1994).

6. Robert S. Levine, *Conspiracy and Romance: Studies in Brockden Brown, Cooper, Hawthorne, and Melville* (Cambridge: Cambridge UP, 1989), 216, 210.

7. Fisher is describing Dreiser's Chicago with this phrase, but the idea certainly applies to New York in the 1850s through the 1870s. See *Hard Facts: Setting and Form in the American Novel* (New York: Oxford UP, 1985), 129.

8. Richard Sennett, *The Conscience of the Eye: The Design and Social Life of Cities* (New York: Alfred A. Knopf, 1990), 58.

9. Callow, *The Tweed Ring*, 50.

10. Sennett, 59.

11. Emanuel Tobier, "Manhattan's Business District in the Industrial Age," in

John Hull Mollenkopf, *Power, Culture, and Place: Essays on New York City* (New York: Russell Sage Foundation, 1988), 81–5.

12. On arcades, I have been most influenced, of course, by Walter Benjamin's *Charles Baudelaire: A Lyric Poet in the Era of High Capitalism*, trans. and ed. Jonathan Mayne (London: Phaidon Publishers, 1964), and *Reflections*, trans. Edmund Jephcott (New York: Harcourt Brace Jovanovich, 1978); also Susan Buck-Morss, *The Dialectics of Seeing: Walter Benjamin and the Arcades Project* (Cambridge, Mass.: MIT Press, 1989). On women and department stores, see Elizabeth Wilson, *The Sphinx in the City: Urban Life, the Control of Disorder, and Women* (Berkeley and Los Angeles: U of California Press, 1991), 58–60.

13. Quoted in Edward K. Spann, *The New Metropolis: New York City, 1840–1857* (New York: Columbia UP, 1981), 97.

14. Ibid., 288.

15. Mandelbaum, *Boss Tweed's New York*, 65, 123.

16. Stanton Garner, "Surviving the Gilded Age: Herman Melville in the Customs Service," *Essays in Arts and Science* 15 (June 1986): 9.

17. Sennett, *Conscience of the Eye*, 46–62, describes this process.

18. I have borrowed this term from sociology, but not all the technical methods. See Emrys Jones and John Eyles, *An Introduction to Social Geography* (London: Oxford UP, 1977).

19. See William R. Taylor, "The Launching of a Commercial Culture: New York City, 1860–1930), in Mollenkopf, *Power, Culture, and Place*, 107–33. See also Taylor, *In Pursuit of Gotham: Culture and Commerce in New York* (New York: Oxford UP, 1992).

20. See Michael Denning, *Mechanic Accents: Dime Novels and Working-Class Culture in America* (New York: Verso, 1987).

21. David S. Reynolds discusses popular sources for *The Confidence-Man* in *Beneath the American Renaissance: The Subversive Imagination in the Age of Emerson and Melville* (Cambridge, Mass.: Harvard UP, 1989). See also Tom Quirk, *Melville's Confidence Man: From Knave to Knight* (Columbia: U of Missouri P, 1982).

22. Rosalind Williams, *Notes on the Underground: An Essay on Technology, Society, and the Imagination* (Cambridge, Mass.: MIT Press, 1990), has an excellent chapter on the cultural implications of archaeology ("Excavations I: Digging Down to the Truth," 22–50).

23. Dorothee Metlitsky Finkelstein, *Melville's Orienda* (New Haven and London: Yale UP, 1961), is still the fullest discussion of Melville and sacred geography. See also Walter Bezanson, "Herman Melville's *Clarel*," Ph.D. diss., Yale U, 1943; and Franklin Walker, *Irreverent Pilgrims: Melville, Browne, and Twain in the Holy Land* (Seattle: U of Washington Press, 1974).

24. Williams, *Notes on the Underground*, 23.

25. Although the literary culture abounds with narratives of women journeying toward a City of God – Stowe's *Uncle Tom's Cabin* and Susan Warner's *The Wide, Wide World* come most obviously to mind – all of Melville's pilgrims are male. I leave the deconstruction of this phenomenon to others.

26. See Carolyn Karcher, *Shadow Over the Promised Land: Slavery, Race, and Violence in Melville's America* (Baton Rouge: Louisiana State UP, 1980), especially 193–4, 237, and 252–3, on the implications of the Southern landscape; and Mi-

chael Paul Rogin, *Subversive Genealogy: The Politics and Art of Herman Melville* (New York: Alfred A. Knopf, 1983), 221-4, 236-56, on the politics of *The Confidence-Man*.

27. "Melville's 'River' Source" and "The River" appear in the "Editorial Appendix" to the Northwestern–Newberry edition of *The Confidence-Man*, 490–9, 511–15.

28. See Bruce Franklin's edition of *The Confidence-Man* (New York: Bobbs-Merrill, 1967) for a discussion of *Martin Chuzzlewit* in relation to Cairo, Illinois (179).

29. See Michael H. Cowan, *City of the West: Emerson, America, and Urban Metaphor* (New Haven and London: Yale UP, 1967); John W. Reps, *The Making of Urban America: A History of City Planning in the United States* (Princeton, N.J.: Princeton UP, 1965).

30. In his 1857 *Journal*, Melville visited the island of Patmos and wrote, "Could no more realize that St: John had ever had revelations here, than when off Juan Fernandez, could beleive [*sic*] in Robinson Crusoe according to DeFoe" (97).

31. Christine Stansell, *City of Women: Sex and Class in New York, 1789–1850* (New York: Alfred A. Knopf, 1986), 196, 210.

32. Melville visited the Burlington Arcade in London in 1849: "Walked about a little & bought a cigar case for Allan in Burlington Arcade. Saw many pretty things for presents – but could not afford to buy" (*Journal*, 40). *Cruchley's Picture of London* describes it thus: "Burlington Arcade, Piccadilly, is a covered avenue, upwards of 200 yards in length, with elegant shops on each side, fitted up with great taste. . . . It is lighted by gas; and in an evening presents a brilliant appearance"; quoted in notes to the *Journal*, 359. On the arcade, see Walter Benjamin, "Paris, Capital of the Nineteenth Century," in *Reflections*, ed. Peter Demetz, trans. Edmund Jephcott (New York: Simon and Schuster, 1981); Susan Buck-Morss, *The Dialectics of Seeing: Walter Benjamin and the Arcades Project* (Cambridge, Mass.: MIT Press, 1989).

33. Cowan, *City of the West*, 73–179; Bernard Rosenthal, *City of Nature: Journeys to Nature in the Age of American Romanticism* (Newark: U of Delaware P, 1980); Alexander Welsh, *City of Dickens* (Oxford: Clarendon Press, 1971), 55–60.

34. Thomas Weiskel, *The Romantic Sublime: Studies in the Structure and Psychology of Transcendence* (Baltimore: Johns Hopkins UP, 1976), 11.

35. William Wordsworth, *The Prelude*, in *The Fourteen-Book Prelude*, ed. W. J. B. Owen, in *The Cornell Wordsworth* (Ithaca, N.Y.: Cornell UP, 1985), 11:158. See *City Images: Perspectives from Literature, Philosophy, and Film*, ed. Mary Ann Caws (New York: Gordon and Breach, 1991), 15–21 and 213–17, for a discussion of the urban iconography of the *The Prelude*.

36. Raymond Williams, *The Country and the City* (New York: Oxford UP, 1973).

37. John F. Kasson, *Civilizing the Machine: Technology and Republican Values in America, 1776–1900* (New York: Grossman, 1976); Barbara Novak, *Nature and Culture: American Landscape and Painting 1835–1875* (New York: Oxford UP, 1980); Leo Marx, *The Machine in the Garden* (New York: Oxford UP, 1964); Perry Miller, *The Raven and the Whale: The War of Words and Wits in the Era of Poe and Melville* (New York: Harcourt, Brace, 1956). See also Cowan (n. 29) and Rosenthal (n. 33).

38. Novak identifies the idea of the "still, small voice" as one aspect of the sublime (28–33).

39. Ibid., 34–7.

40. *Pictures of Old New York: The New Metropolis* ([New York]: n.p., n.d.), 1:56.

41. Finkelstein, *Melville's Orienda*, 121–44.

42. Nicholas Taylor, "The Awful Sublimity of the Victorian City: Its aesthetic and architectural origins," in *The Victorian City: Images and Realities*, ed. H. J. Dyos and Michael Wolff (London and Boston: Routledge and Kegan Paul, 1973), 2:434.

43. Ibid., 434. Although Taylor is describing an English city, this aesthetic appeared in America too. See Kasson, who at points echoes Francis D. Klingender, quoted in E. D. Johnson, "Victorian Artists and the Urban Milieu," in Dyos and Wolff, 2:450: "Still surrounded by romantic scenery, the great ironworks, with their smouldering lime kilns and coke ovens, blazing furnaces and noisy forges, had a special attraction." Even Nathaniel Hawthorne felt the romantic attractions of lime kilns ("Ethan Brand," 1851), though Rebecca Harding Davis did not find the iron mills sublime ("Life in the Iron Mills," 1864).

44. See John T. Irwin, *American Hieroglyphics: The Symbol of the Egyptian Hieroglyphic in the American Renaissance* (New Haven and London: Yale UP, 1980). Sir Thomas Overbury suggested that urban characters presented a similar kind of text. A "Character," he wrote, is "an Aegyptian hieroglyphicke, for an impresse, or short embleme; in little comprehending much"; quoted in Dana Brand, *The Spectator and the City in Nineteenth-Century American Literature* (New York: Cambridge UP, 1991), 22. Brand's first two chapters treat in some detail the implications of legibility in urban literature.

45. Quoted in G. Robert Stange, "The Frightened Poets," in Dyos and Wolff, 2:489, 490.

46. See Wyn Kelley, "Haunted Stone: Nature and City in *Clarel*," *Essays in Arts and Sciences* 15 (June 1986): 15–29.

47. On sacred geography, see Walter Bezanson, introduction to "Herman Melville's *Clarel*"; Finkelstein (n. 23); E. S. Shaffer, *"Kubla Khan" and the Fall of Jerusalem: The Mythological School in Biblical Criticism and Secular Literature, 1770–1880* (Cambridge: Cambridge UP, 1975); and Arthur Penrhyn Stanley, "Sacred Geography," *London Quarterly Review* 94 (1854).

48. The fullest discussion of the Cosmopolitan and cosmopolitanism appears in John Bryant, *Melville & Repose: The Rhetoric of Humor in the American Renaissance* (New York: Oxford UP, 1993).

49. Donald R. Howard, *Writers and Pilgrims: Medieval Pilgrimage Narratives and Their Posterity* (Berkeley and Los Angeles: U of California Press, 1980), 12.

50. See *Jerusalem in History*, ed. K. J. Asali (New York: Olive Branch Press, 1990), and Walker's *Irreverent Pilgrims*. Bayard Taylor, in his poem "Jerusalem," in *Poems of the Orient* (Boston: Ticknor & Fields, 1856), 150–3, stresses Jerusalem's lack of a political center:

> Thy strength, Jerusalem, is o'er,
> And broken are thy walls. . . .
> Who shall rebuild Jerusalem? –
> Her scattered children bring
>   From Earth's far ends, and gather them
> Beneath her sheltering wing?

51. Norman Cohen, *The Pursuit of the Millennium* (New York: Harper, 1961), quoted in Howard, *Writers and Pilgrims*, 13.

Conclusion: Citified Man

1. I have used the Raymond Weaver editions of Melville's poems and sketches, though not for *Billy Budd:* See his *Billy Budd and Other Prose Pieces* (London: Constable, 1924); and *Poems* (London: Constable, 1924). The "House of the Tragic Poet" appears in Robert A. Sandberg, " 'House of the Tragic Poet'; Melville's Draft of a Preface to His Unfinished Burgundy Club Book," *Melville Society Extracts* 79 (November 1989): 1, 4–7. See also Merton M. Sealts, Jr., "Melville's Burgundy Club Sketches," in *Pursuing Melville, 1940–1980* (Madison: U of Wisconsin P, 1982), 78–90; and "The Melvilles, the Gansevoorts, and the Cincinnati Badge," *Melville Society Extracts* 70 (September 1987): 1–4.
2. See Wyn Kelley, "Melville's Cain," *American Literature* 55 (March 1984): 25–40.

Index